Christian Sacred Music
in the Americas

Christian Sacred Music in the Americas

Edited by Andrew Shenton
and Joanna Smolko

ROWMAN & LITTLEFIELD
Lanham • Boulder • New York • London

Published by Rowman & Littlefield
An imprint of The Rowman & Littlefield Publishing Group, Inc.
4501 Forbes Boulevard, Suite 200, Lanham, Maryland 20706
www.rowman.com

6 Tinworth Street, London SE11 5AL, United Kingdom

Copyright © 2021 by The Rowman & Littlefield Publishing Group, Inc.

All rights reserved. No part of this book may be reproduced in any form or by any electronic or mechanical means, including information storage and retrieval systems, without written permission from the publisher, except by a reviewer who may quote passages in a review.

British Library Cataloguing in Publication Information Available

Library of Congress Control Number: 2020948894
ISBN 9781538183564 (paperback)
ISBN 9781538148747 (electronic)

For Robert (Bob) Judd

Contents

Acknowledgments	ix
Introduction: Exploring Christian Sacred Music in the Americas *Andrew Shenton and Joanna Smolko*	xi

I	**LITURGICAL MUSIC**	1
1	Liberation Theology: Affirmation and Homage in Three Brazilian Masses *Cathy Ann Elias*	3
2	The Guatemalan Choirbooks: Facilitating Preservation, Performance, and Study of the Colonial Repertoire *Martha E. Thomae*	23

II	**HYMNOLOGY**	59
3	Sweet Harmonies of Praise: Reviving Shape-Note Singing in Rural Arkansas *S. Andrew Granade*	61
4	Shape-Note Hymn Traditions in Athens, Georgia *Joanna Smolko*	81
5	The Hymn Tunes of Thomas Hastings *David W. Music*	107

III CONTEMPORARY WORSHIP — 131

6. "Além do *gospel*": A History of Brazil's Alternative Christian Music Scene — 133
   Marcell Silva Steuernagel

7. Ethics, Justice, and Politics in Contemporary Worship Music — 155
   Jeff R. Warren

IV PARALITURGICAL MUSIC — 175

8. "Resignation" and Virgil Thomson's *Hymns from the Old South* — 177
   Zen Kuriyama

9. Rock of Ages: Jesus in American Popular Songs, 1969–2019 — 197
   Delvyn Case

V DIASPORIC MUSIC — 219

10. The Folk Scholarship Roots and Geopolitical Boundaries of Sacred Harp's Global Twenty-First Century — 221
    Jesse P. Karlsberg

11. Anglican Church Music in the United States: Tracing the Diaspora of English Traditions from the Eighteenth to the Twenty-First Century — 241
    Matthew Hoch

VI INDIGENOUS AND AFRICAN AMERICAN MUSIC — 263

12. "God with Me Speaking": Envisioning the Study of Indigenous Christian Song in Brazil — 265
    Andrew Janzen and Meiry Yakawa

13. "Lift Every Voice and Sing": Embodying Black Theology in Song — 289
    Stephen Michael Newby and Chelle Stearns

14. From the Sun to the Son: How Choctaw Spiritual Practices Expressed Through Music Changed in Response to Christian and Anglo-American Contact — 307
    Emma Wimberg

Epilogue: Singing Worlds in the Americas — 329
   Michael O'Connor

Index — 339

About the Contributors — 345

Acknowledgments

The editors wish to thank the Society for Christian Scholarship in Music (SCSM) for their support of this publication. In particular, we are grateful for the support of the Publications Committee of the SCSM and for the unflagging support of the current president, Mark Peters. We acknowledge with gratitude the contributions of each of the authors of this collection and their hard work crafting such thoughtful and engaging essays.

We wish to personally thank Janice Archer, Karen Westerfield Tucker, and Tim Smolko for their support of our work. We also thank Rowman & Littlefield for taking on this project, our editor Michael Tan for his thoughtful advice, and our production team for their care in getting this collection into print.

We dedicate this volume with gratitude and affection to Bob Judd (1956–2019), who was one of the founding members of the Society and one of its most loyal supporters. In a tribute to Bob's service, former SCSM president Johann Buis noted that "every past president (and board members) of the SCSM can vouch for the significance of Bob's contribution to the society. He was the '(in)visible hand' behind the vision, the logistics, and the inspiration that we all depended on as the SCSM leadership."

Andrew Shenton & Joanna Smolko
September 2020

Exploring Christian Sacred Music in the Americas

Andrew Shenton and Joanna Smolko

This essay collection, devoted to exploring the richness of Christian musical traditions in the Americas, reflects the distinctive critical perspectives of the Society for Christian Scholarship in Music (SCSM), an association of scholars dedicated to exploring the intersections of Christian faith and musical scholarship. As we move to our twentieth anniversary in 2022, we seek to celebrate our work in the world and bring it to a larger audience by offering a cross-section of the most outstanding scholarship from an international array of writers. The present collection follows a first volume published to celebrate the fifteenth anniversary of the Society (*Exploring Christian Song*, edited by M. Jennifer Bloxam and Andrew Shenton [Lexington Books, 2017]). The first volume focused on Christian song in a variety of different contexts. This collection surveys a broad geographical area and demonstrates the enormous diversity of music-making and scholarship within that area. While there are some studies that focus on a single country or region and its sacred music (see the literature survey), this will be the first collection to present a representative cross-section of the range of sacred music in the Americas and the approaches to studying them in context.

The essays include several by distinguished senior scholars in the field (including David W. Music, Baylor University, and Jeff R. Warren, Quest University, Canada). Several essays are by noted specialists in the field (including Jesse P. Karlsberg, Emory University, and Cathy Ann Elias, DePaul University), and some are by emerging scholars (including Zen Kuriyama, Brandeis University, and Emma Wimberg, University of North Texas). SCSM is particularly keen to promote the work of students. The work of these rising stars thus appears alongside the work of veteran scholars working in the area of Christian sacred music, ensuring a stimulating mix of subjects, viewpoints, and methodologies.

There has been a steady increase in studies of music in the Christian tradition in recent years. Introductions to Christian musical practices include Patrick Kavanaugh, *The Music of Angels: A Listener's Guide to Sacred Music from Chant to Christian Rock* (Loyola 1999), Wilfrid Mellers, *Celestial Music? Some Masterpieces of European Religious Music* (Boydell 2002), and Tim Dowley, *Christian Music: A Global History* (Augsburg Fortress, 2011), while recent histories and cultural analyses of Christian music include Stephen Marini, *Sacred Song in America* (UI Press, 2003), David W. Stowe, *How Sweet the Sound: Music in the Spiritual Lives of Americans* (Harvard University Pres, 2004), and Jonathan Arnold, *Sacred Music in Secular Society* (Ashgate, 2014). Other than *Exploring Christian Song*, there is only one collection of essays that brings a variety of perspectives to bear on the study of Christian music and religion; however, it is focused exclusively on the experience in the United States, including but not entirely dedicated to the Christian tradition (*Music in American Religious Experience*, edited by Philip V. Bohlman, Edith L. Blumhofer, and Maria M. Chow [Oxford 2006]). Other notable texts include the *Oxford Handbook of Music and World Christianities*, edited by Jonathan Dueck and Suzel Ana Reily (Oxford, 2016), as well as volumes by prominent author Paul Westermeyer and recent historical surveys such as John Ogasapian's *Church Music in America, 1620–2000* (Mercer University Press, 2007). Our collection of essays is thus unique in presenting a broad range of topics focused entirely on the rich diversity of Christian musical traditions.

We hope this collection will make a significant addition to the general scholarship on sacred music in the Americas and contribute to discussions about Christian music in different contexts and in broad consideration. The essays expand discussions of spirituality in music and, in particular, to the unifying aspects of Christian sacred music across time, space, and faith traditions. They utilize and develop interdisciplinary methodologies including media studies, cultural studies, theological studies, and different analytical and ethnographical approaches to music. They will begin to fill in gaps in English language literature on South and Central American sacred traditions and demonstrate ways in which sacred music in the Americas intersects with other traditions (classical, popular, folk music). The essays utilize appropriate techniques, including oral history as an analytical tool, and the use of digital technologies in archival research. All translations are by the respective authors unless otherwise noted. The original language for quotations has been omitted unless the source is unpublished or the meaning obscure and subject to more than the usual degree of interpretation. For practical reasons, images in this text are reproduced in black and white; however, access to high-quality color images is available in the eBook format. We have also endeavored to give links to other images where available.

Exploring Christian Sacred Music in the Americas xiii

The collection will appeal to theologians and cultural historians interested in ritual and liturgical studies (especially those who deal with the intersection of faith and music); musicologists and ethnomusicologists (especially those concerned with sacred music, choral music, and source studies); music theorists (especially those who analyze text/music relationships); performers (especially choral directors, singers, organists, and others involved in liturgical and nonliturgical music); people interested in recording technology and in the intersections of music and media; people interested in performance practice, including both general scholar/performers and those who perform in sacred spaces; as well as people interested in the sociology of music, especially those interested in oral traditions. We hope that this collection also moves dialogue forward on several important and topical issues: indigeneity, immigration, colonialism, settler culture, globalization, the role of technology and media, and diaspora studies.

The collection is divided into six related parts. The first part discusses two different aspects of the study of liturgical music. First, in her essay "Liberation Theology: Affirmation and Homage in Three Brazilian Masses," Cathy Ann Elias addresses issues of liberation theology, African and Amerindian religious traditions, and the use of their language and music of the mass in their historical, cultural, and theological contexts. Two of the masses, *Missa da Terra Sem Males* and *Missa dos Quilombos*, are apologetic. Dom Pedro Casaldáliga, a liberation theologian, and Pedro Tierra composed the texts for these masses. The *Missa da Terra Sem Males* uses traditional South American melodies arranged by Martin Coplas. The *Missa dos Quilombos* has original music by Milton Nascimento. The third mass, *2 IHU Kewere: Rezar* by Marlui Miranda is a celebration of Amerindians and incorporates Amerindian chants sung in Tupi. Besides their musical qualities, these masses are also important as necessary artifacts in the healing process of injustices done to the Brazilian Indians and to the descendants of African slaves. Their texts, the history of their creation, and the rhetorical processes used (both in the text and in the music) are embedded in a complex network of historical, social, political, and theological motivations, influences, and struggles that extend from early colonial times to the end of the Brazilian military dictatorship in 1985. The reception of these works by the public, by the Vatican, and by the military governing Brazil provides an unusual insight into the interactions among religion, music, and a long-lasting struggle for individual and racial freedom.

The second essay in the liturgical music part explores the process of digitization in creating access to and contextualizing six large choirbooks held in the Cathedral of Guatemala in Guatemala City that were in use from around 1600 to around 1800. The manuscripts contain sixteenth-century polyphonic music by Spanish composers such as Victoria, Morales, and

Guerrero, as well as a few pieces by Lassus and Palestrina. They also contain music by composers who worked as choirmasters at the Cathedral of Guatemala. Martha E. Thomae's essay "The Guatemalan Choirbooks: Facilitating Preservation, Performance, and Study of the Colonial Repertoire" seeks to increase access to the music of this collection in order to understand the role of music in the liturgy of colonial Guatemala. To achieve this, she utilizes cutting-edge digitization and music-encoding technologies, including optical music recognition and automatic transcription. Thomae takes as her focus the book of masses GuatC 1, describing the digitization and encoding processes carried out. She illustrates the advantages of encoded music for accessibility through modern transcriptions and audio playback and for musicological analysis through the automatic comparison of concordant sources.

The second part of this volume concentrates on hymnology with two essays that discuss different aspects of shape-note singing and one that evaluates ten of Thomas Hastings's hymn tunes in the context of the reform philosophy of church music he espoused. S. Andrew Granade's essay "Sweet Harmonies of Praise: Reviving Shape-Note Singing in Rural Arkansas" uses the theoretical frameworks of musical revival to explore the work of shape-note enthusiast Orene Pittman as she reestablished a seven-note shape-note singing tradition in Arkansas in the United States. In 1969, Pittman established a singing school through her Sweet Home Church in Alpine, Arkansas. She did so to restore the "sweet harmonies of praise" that reverberated from her childhood, harmonies that resulted from the shape-note singing system employed by those who gathered to sing in her Primitive Baptist community. Using fieldwork conducted by the author with Pittman and her Sweet Home Group, this essay documents the growth of shape-note singing in southern Arkansas, focusing on the development of singing schools and the publication of seven-note shape-note songbooks in Thornton, Arkansas. Granade's essay proposes that the study of those who revive from within their heritage has two immediate benefits: first, it allows for an alteration in the word "revival" to include the transforming of traditions rather than only the revival of them, and second, it answers the question so often skimmed over or ignored in revivalist scholarship, that of why a particular group resurrected a genre. Identifying which traditions are revived within their original cultures and which are allowed to languish in disuse indexes those elements of a musical culture that hold value for the group that created them. Using the Sweet Home Church as a case study, this essay then discovers that these transformative revivals are often caused by faith rather than the need to construct community in a fragmented world and a need to bolster a geographical and spiritual community seen as slowly vanishing.

Joanna Smolko's essay "Shape-Note Hymn Traditions in Athens, Georgia" explores the town as a nexus both for traditional shape-note singing practices and for scholarly research into and publication of shape-note hymnals. The collaboration between researchers and singers created a feedback loop that strengthened and renewed the local practice of shape-note traditions. This study uses archival research and oral histories of local singers to explore the distinctive nature of the Athens area singings, focusing on key historical moments, individuals, and venues.

During the nineteenth century, Athens hosted local singings and participated in nearby conventions. Classified sections of local newspapers featured ads from booksellers eager to sell the newest shape-note books as well as ads for local and regional singings. Local practice of the tradition diminished in the opening decades of the twentieth century but revived in the early 1970s with John Garst's research on the *Social Harp*, which led to its republication and the establishment of an Athens-based annual local singing convention. This blossomed into multiple singings that continue to the present. The Athens tradition is characterized by the use of multiple hymnals in local singings and the role of local area singers in the editing, publication, and republication of hymnals such as *The Sacred Harp*, *The Social Harp*, *The Christian Harmony*, and *The Georgian Harmony*. Athens models ways in which university and other community resources can reinvigorate local practices through mutual collaboration, dialogue, and shared resources.

The last essay in this part turns to nineteenth-century hymnology. Thomas Hastings (1784–1872) is best known today as a reformer, philosopher, and compiler of church music. Much of his life's work, however, was devoted to writing music, particularly hymn tunes. Together with his contemporary Lowell Mason, Hastings developed a hymn tune idiom that featured an active melody, a plain harmonization, and an overall simplicity of style that became the standard form for hymnody in the United States well into the twentieth century.

Despite his prolific composition of hymns and the important role he played in developing an "American" tune style, Hastings is today little known and largely ignored as a composer. In his essay "The Hymn Tunes of Thomas Hastings," David W. Music notes that while Hastings was not a "great" composer, his music also does not deserve the near-total neglect it has received at the hands of scholars. Music's essay gives a brief biography of Hastings, describes his role in the church music reforms of the nineteenth century, and discusses his chief publications. It then analyzes the musical elements of ten of Hastings's tunes that he himself printed most often (including his best-known tunes, "Ortonville," "Retreat," "Rock of Ages," and "Zion"), which he presumably considered to be among his most successful pieces. The works are also evaluated in their relationships to the texts they set. The declining use of Hastings's tunes in recent American hymnals is noted and reasons are suggested for this situation.

The third part of the collection contains two essays that explore different aspects of contemporary worship. Marcell Silva Steuernagel uses oral history interviews and participant observation to explore "indie" music and musicians who work outside the mainstream of Brazil's distinctive gospel music tradition in his essay "'*Além do gospel*': A History of Brazil's Alternative Christian Music Scene." Steuernagel notes that the rise of gospel music in Brazil has been documented by several scholars. Nevertheless, he believes that this narrative glosses over an alternative scene composed of artists who, although historically connected to the nascent *Música Cristã Brasileira* scene in the 1970s and 1980s, developed an "indie" circuit instead of associating themselves with the industry's major labels. Steuernagel's investigation contributes to the study of church music from a global perspective, offering scholars interested in Latin American Christian music traditions a glimpse into the development of national religious music industries that, while connected to North American developments in Christian popular music, have found ways to ground themselves in local cultural expressions and indigenous modes of performance, distribution, and mediatization.

While contemporary worship music (CWM) makes claims that it is about spirituality and therefore beyond politics, the essay "Ethics, Justice, and Politics in Contemporary Worship Music" by Jeff R. Warren argues that CWM participates in ethics, justice, and politics and is therefore implicated in questions of race, class, gender, and citizenship. Millions of people across the Americas sing contemporary worship music every week. CWM is dominant within evangelical churches, and its influence includes albums topping the *Billboard 200* charts with claims from one CWM organization that fifty million people a week sing their songs in church. Warren contends that individual musical experiences of CWM are mediated by musical institutions, churches, and wider political structures. For example, white evangelicals compose most CWM, and in the 2016 US general election over 80 percent of white evangelicals voted Republican. Warren questions how the purportedly nonpolitical practice of singing praise to God relates to strong political affinities within white evangelicals, yet how at the same time CWM retains the ability to be sung by evangelicals with diverse political leanings. Because white evangelicals are, however, increasingly a smaller percentage of evangelicals, the essay concludes by asking if CWM might also be a future site for evangelical resistance.

Because music in the Christian tradition is not exclusively for liturgical use, the next part of the collection has two contrasting essays that discuss types of paraliturgical music. Zen Kuriyama's essay "'Resignation' and

Virgil Thomson's *Hymns from the Old South*" explores Thomson's distinctive tonal treatment of the shape-note hymn "Resignation" in the context of his and other composers' arrangements of the hymn. Thomson's shape-note hymnody seed planting began in 1937, when the composer was commissioned to write music for *The River*, a documentary film on the Mississippi River and threats to its environment. In *The River*, listeners hear the "Resignation" hymn tune several times, which Thomson came across in an 1854 edition of William Walker's *Southern Harmony* and which served as the genesis for *Hymns from the Old South* over a decade later. Kuriyama's analysis of this tune is in three parts: inspiration, synthesis, and reception/performance notes for concert or liturgical service. This holistic deconstruction of Thomson's anthem "My Shepherd Will Supply My Need" traces not only the history of "Resignation" but also the great hymn and singing tradition of nineteenth-century Protestantism. Kuriyama argues that Thomson's treatment of the "Resignation" tune (his synthesis) is distinct from other composers, most notably in his use of harmony and contrapuntal texture. A thorough analysis of the anthem is provided, offering not only traditional musicological dissection but also an exploration in affect and in declamation. A brief overview of the critical reception of *Four Southern Folk Hymns* is also provided, in addition to comments on its "performativity" and place within Christian worship by prominent American church musicians, situating this work within the aesthetic tastes of twentieth-century American sacred and secular music.

Delvyn Case's essay "Rock of Ages: Jesus in American Popular Songs, 1969–2019" uses an extensive survey as well as close analysis of case studies to demonstrate how secular pop songs have functioned as an influential source of popular Christology over the past fifty years.

Jesus has appeared as a character in hundreds of secular pop songs, written by artists representing all genres. Working outside of the church or the Christian music industry, yet profoundly influenced by the ideas and conceptions about Jesus woven through American society, these artists have depicted him in ways that range from the orthodox to the profane. Taken as a whole, these songs provide an extraordinary record of the ways contemporary society has grappled with the importance and meaning of Jesus during a time of rapid secularization. This essay looks at almost 450 of these songs and identifies various trends and patterns in the ways Jesus has been depicted, understood, and reimagined by popular musicians. It begins by focusing on the subset of songs in which Jesus is compared to figures in contemporary society, identifying trends in those depictions and then discussing the kinds of insight they provide. It then considers the entire collection of songs in order to describe the fundamental conceptions of Jesus that undergird them. In so doing, it describes the ways these songs reflect the uniquely secular nature of religion in the contemporary world and also suggests ways that these songs can contribute to the spiritual lives of Christians who are negotiating the meanings of their faith today.

In the fifth part of the collection we have two essays on diasporic music. Jesse P. Karlsberg addresses the transcultural appeal of Sacred Harp music and its practice across over two dozen countries in the twenty-first century in his essay "The Folk Scholarship Roots and Geopolitical Boundaries of Sacred Harp's Global Twenty-First Century." In the past few decades, Sacred Harp, a once-regional practice of sacred community singing from the 1844 southern shape-note tunebook *The Sacred Harp*, has spread to two dozen countries on four continents. This essay, which compliments the two Sacred Harp essays in the second part of this volume, analyzes the music cultural features, folklore scholarship roots, and geopolitical contours channeling the spread of this sacred "subcultural sound." Though vastly expanded in geography, Sacred Harp is still a "micromusic," convening small groups of people with strong community bonds often beneath the level of broad cultural attention. Despite its increasing reach, the new span of Sacred Harp singing refracts certain aspects of its history and practices: first, the style's reception reacts to a history of political, economic, and cultural relationships and has spread only to developed countries where US popular culture and media have a large imprint and garner a comparatively favorable reception. Second, participation carries longstanding associations with deep roots in the "revival" of Sacred Harp in the United States, which privileges emulating practices associated with folk cultures of the southern United States. Third, aspects of Sacred Harp's music and associated cultural practice, such as its spirituality, participatory orientation, and full voiced exuberance, have transcultural appeal. Karlsberg's essay documents the present scope of Sacred Harp singing outside the United States, examines the eighty-five-year-old folklore genealogies that factor into the style's recent spread, and briefly addresses the musical practices that support Sacred Harp's adoption and the transnational political and cultural histories affecting the form of participation.

Matthew Hoch examines the gradual Americanization of English church music over the course of the past 240 years within the Episcopal Church while discussing distinctive new genres and liturgies that have been established alongside traditional ones in his essay "Anglican Church Music in the United States: Tracing the Diaspora of English Traditions from the Eighteenth to the Twenty-First Century." At the time of its founding in 1789 as the Protestant Episcopal Church in America, there was little distinction between the music of the Episcopal Church and the Anglican music heard in English cathedrals and parishes. For over two centuries, many of these traditions endured, and

Anglican repertoire can still be heard in many Episcopal churches throughout the United States, particularly in historic churches in the urban Northeast. Over time, however, newer traditions have also emerged, offering a distinctly American Anglicanism that merges the traditional liturgies of the Book of Common Prayer with the fresh sounds of the New World. This essay profiles select parishes that offer distinctly modern musical services while remaining true to Anglican liturgies: the jazz masses of Canterbury House at the University of Michigan, the all-Taizé services of All Saints' Episcopal Church in Beverly Hills, the all-Spanish liturgies heard at the School of Theology at the University of the South, and the "paperless" music that emerged from St. Gregory of Nyssa Episcopal Church in San Francisco are several examples. The evolution of Episcopal hymnody over the past century is also examined; becoming increasingly less influenced by its nineteenth-century English parent hymnals, an authentically American body of Episcopal hymns has now been established.

The final part includes three essays that deal with Indigenous and African American music. First, Andrew Janzen and Meiry Yakawa collaborate to analyze Yakawa's song "God with Me Speaking" as an expression of Indigenous Brazilian culture, particularly in its use of Indigenous hymn traditions and theology. Their essay "'God with Me Speaking': Envisioning the Study of Indigenous Christian Song in Brazil" takes as its starting point a song received by Meiry Yakawa, a Bakairi Christian in west-central Brazil, during a difficult period in her life. Though her song provides encouragement in her life and teaching, Yakawa has struggled in the past against fear and shame in sharing her song and explaining its importance to others. Using this song as a lens through which to examine Indigenous Christian music in Brazil, this essay explores two related questions: What are the disciplinary barriers impeding adequate representation of Indigenous Christian music, and how can the significance of one Indigenous song be measured? The essay draws insights from the anthropology of Christianity where scholars now acknowledge that newly Christian populations have long been considered inappropriate subjects of study or simply "inauthentic." Perhaps, as a result, there is an absence of studies documenting Indigenous Christian musicking, even though a quarter to a half of all Brazilian Indigenous people identify as Christian. Against this broader social and scholarly setting, this essay employs collaborative methodology to develop an argument for the significance of Yakawa's song that privileges Indigenous ways of knowing by highlighting Yakawa's perspective of the spiritual, emotional, and culturally symbolic effects of her song. To this end, Yakawa's experiences are compared with ethnomusicological accounts of Kiowa and Crow Christianity in North America, specifically the narrative of the Crow singer Georgine Falls Down, which aids to underscore the worth of "just one song."

Stephen Michael Newby and Chelle Stearns analyze the Black National Anthem "Lift Every Voice and Sing" using the tools of Black Liberation Theology and musical analysis. In their essay "'Lift Every Voice and Sing': Embodying Black Theology in Song," Newby and Stearns explore how and why the spirituals created and sung by enslaved persons are an embodied theology, bearing witness in song to how God has been present with the Black community throughout American history. This hymn is connected to a rich history of performance and composition, which can help to elucidate the often-overlooked theological work of the Black community in America. It engages many of the enduring themes of Black Liberation Theology, encouraging those in the congregation to "sing a song full of faith that the dark past has taught us, / sing a song full of the hope that the present has brought us." Black music thus expresses some of the deepest resources about God's interaction and presence with humanity.

To help adumbrate the theological resonance of this tradition of song, the authors look to the work of theologians James Cone, Cheryl Kirk-Duggan, and M. Shawn Copeland. Each theologian, in their own way, turns to the spirituals as a deep theological tradition through which to unpack and rearticulate Black American theology. These theologians recover the musical theological work of those denied a voice in formal Western theology, believing that God is revealed where the community of the oppressed bears witness to movement of the Spirit.

Finally, Emma Wimberg's essay "From the Sun to the Son: How Choctaw Spiritual Practices Expressed Through Music Changed in Response to Christian and Anglo-American Contact" assesses the ways Christianity was adopted and adapted by the Choctaw through a review of their 1850 hymnal. At the turn of the twentieth century there was some academic interest in Choctaw culture, but this research faded in the 1930s and left many Choctaw spiritual practices unidentified by outside researchers. The 1850 Choctaw Hymnal, and its later versions, are important documents that indicate the state of Christian practices in this tribe, which Wimberg supplements with firsthand oral reports from senior members of the tribe. The hymnal contains original tunes by Choctaw members, Choctaw texts sung to Anglican tunes, and translated Anglican hymns. Through this essay Wimberg begins to explore the hymns written by and for the Choctaw people. As a member of the Choctaw tribe, Wimberg grew up with the stories and culture of the Choctaw people. This inherited insider position has given her foundational knowledge that has broadened through extensive research, including communication with tribal historic preservation offices. Most of what we know about Choctaw culture comes from post-Christian practices passed down by oral tradition. This essay seeks to understand sacred music practices before and after Christianity came to the tribe, with special attention to post-Christian assimilation of spiritual practices. Because there was no written language, the Choctaw worked with Anglo-American missionaries to translate the Christian message into Choctaw, which created new hymns, a number of which were composed and sung on the Trail of Tears and are treasured by Choctaw communities today. While Choctaw history is consciously inconsistent concerning tribal origins, the sun was a known prominent religious figure. A common phrase about finding "the light path" was adapted to fit new Christian beliefs and is featured in a frequently sung Choctaw hymn. What we witness through the study of these practices is the move from Choctaw worship of the Sun, finding the light path, to following the Son as an adapted Christian belief. This is part of Wimberg's ongoing work to preserve the history and practices of the Choctaw people, explain them to society, and keep the traditions alive.

As an epilogue to the collection, Michael O'Connor has written a short concluding essay drawing together themes from the collection and placing them in the context of ongoing scholarship. O'Connor explores the essential concepts of "the Americas" and of "sacred music" as he examines and contextualizes the people who inhabit this region. In particular, he evaluates the notion of musical world-building that is described in several essays in the collection that refer to Indigenous, African American, and settler communities. O'Connor also names what is at the heart of this collection: although the essays are framed along certain geographical and topical lines, what is the essence of them (and of the work of the SCSM) is the notion that music is central to the Christian faith. As O'Connor notes, "Engaging whole-heartedly in music-making, as composer, performer, listener, or all three, does not leave us unchanged. . . . When we make music, music makes us. It helps build our sense of the world and of ourselves in it."

In this book's tapestry, the geography of two continents and multiple countries form a weft against which is woven many genres of sacred music. The tapestry becomes even more complex when viewed through the multiple disciplines that are represented within this volume. The intricate pattern that emerges shows the ways in which sacred music shaped traditional Christian institutions and media but also shaped music outside of traditional sacred spaces, including the history, culture, and politics within many countries. As a small fragment of current scholarship on Christian sacred music in the Americas, this volume serves as a microcosm of methodology and musical styles. It celebrates both the diversity of musical traditions and the way that music serves to unite all Christians.

I
LITURGICAL MUSIC

Chapter One

Liberation Theology

*Affirmation and Homage
in Three Brazilian Masses*

Cathy Ann Elias

I will discuss three masses by Brazilian composers that respond to the history of oppression and injustice in the history of colonization of the Americas with strong political messages about injustice and oppression. The first, the *Missa dos Quilombos*, by Milton Nascimento, with text by Dom Pedro Casaldáliga and Pedro Tierra, is a protest and an apology for the injustices committed against Blacks throughout Brazilian history. The second, the *Missa da Terra Sem Males*, was composed in 1978 for the year of the Martyrs of Missões.[1] This text is also by Dom Pedro Casaldáliga and Pedro Tierra; the music is arranged by Martin Coplas. The message of this mass is about the injustices against the Amerindians by colonizers and by the Church. The last mass, by Marlui Miranda, *2 IHU Kewere: Rezar*, was composed for the fourth centenary of the death of Padre José de Anchieta, the Apostle of Brazil. Miranda uses melodies from various Brazilian Indian Nations and presents the text often in Tupí mixed with parts of the Roman Rite.

Before discussing these masses and their sociopolitical environment, it is important to briefly review the historical and intellectual background. One of the things I will discuss in these modern masses is the addition of tropes to the liturgy, a practice that was banned by the Council of Trent (1545–1563) because it obfuscates the meaning of the canonical texts. The rigid format of the Tridentine Mass was only eased up by the Second Vatican Council (1962–1965), which sought, among other things, to make it more relevant to the people by, for example, having the priest face the audience and the celebration of the mass in the vernacular.

It is important to situate these masses within the Brazilian politics of the second half of the twentieth century. Fearing that the country would become a Fidel Castro–like communist regime, the Brazilian military seized power in 1964.[2] In a few years, the regime became very oppressive, suppressing free press, jailing opponents, and using torture and extrajudicial killings to maintain power. Many intellectuals, artists, and composers became exiles. Eventually, the military allowed a very slow movement toward restoring democracy. A general amnesty was granted both to the torturers and to the opponents of the military, the exiles returned, and by the late 1970s censorship, while still very much present, was no longer absolute. Democracy was restored in 1985.

The Catholic Church was present in Brazil from the time of its discovery. Some priests, like Padre José de Anchieta, S.J. (1534–1597), discussed later, or the Jesuits who founded the Missions in Southern Brazil, sought to protect the native Amerindians, and some pointed out the evils of slavery. Still, the Church was complicit with slavery, and by the second half of the twentieth century large segments of the hierarchy were sustaining the elite of a very unequal society.

Liberation Theology, inspired by Vatican II and by subsequent papal encyclicals, opened up an important space for the oppressed. Latin American bishops and priests developed a theology that aimed to bring not only salvation in the afterlife but also social justice on earth to the poor of Latin America.[3] This theology, and the Base Ecclesial Communities (grassroots organizations of self-help and Bible study sponsored by the Church in response to the scarcity of priests) were viewed by the military as part of the communist opposition to their rule.

Racial democracy affirms that Brazilian identity reflects its coexisting European, African, and Amerindian roots. The ideology of Liberation Theology, while criticizing some of the rosy views of racial coexistence in Brazil, engages the Church in the fight for a just society, with economic and political structures that affirm the personhood of all, including the poor and minorities. This is an effort to realize racial democracy as part of the ideal we strive for rather than believing it is a contemporary Brazilian reality.

The three musical compositions I discuss exalt the importance of Brazil's Amerindian, African, and Portuguese heritage within unorthodox musical settings of the Catholic mass: *Missa da Terra Sem Males*, the *Missa dos Quilombos*, and *2 IHU Kewere: Rezar*.[4]

There are liturgical questions associated with these masses that will be explored within the essay. The first two masses employ an extensive use of tropes within the formal liturgy. Their emphasis is on social and race questions that, as far as the Vatican was concerned, distracted from the celebration of the Eucharist. As we shall see, the Vatican strongly objected to these works being called and used as masses, as opposed to nonliturgical oratorios. The third mass uses the Tupi language, that required special approval, as it was not a vernacular in São Paulo.

MISSA DA TERRA SEM MALES (THE LAND WITHOUT EVIL)

Dom Pedro Casaldáliga and Pedro Tierra wrote the text for the *Missa da Terra Sem Males*. The music is by Martin Coplas, and the tunes were borrowed from many different regions of South America. The first performance was at Catedral da Sé in São Paulo on April 22, 1979. The mass was composed for the 1978 Year of the Martyrs declared by the Church and apologizes for the injustices against the Amerindians.

Manuel da Nóbrega (1517–1570), the first Jesuit Provincial of Brazil, complained that the Tupí-Guarani peoples of Brazil ate human flesh, married more than one woman, went to war at will, did not wear clothing, and believed in sorcerers.[5] His companion, Padre José de Anchieta, while advocating that the way to preach was with the sword and spear, showed true concern for the well-being of the Indians because the colonists were often trying to enslave them.[6] Over time, the missionaries tried to work with the Indians through inculturation, renaming things and explaining them from within their culture. For example, Tupã, the Tupí supernatural entity responsible for thunder, lightning, and rain who lived in the sky, became their God. The evil spirits living in the forest and Yurupari became the devil.[7]

An aspect of their culture that the missionaries dismissed and saw as a problem was that they did not stay in one place but rather kept migrating, searching for a type of utopia, "the land without evil." Naturally, another reason why they migrated was to avoid repression and enslavement by the colonialists. This notion of a paradise on earth was at odds with the teachings of the missionaries regarding heaven and hell, so they did not use it as part of the inculturation process. While it is difficult to reconstitute the exact Tupí notion of what "the land without evil" was supposed to be, cultural anthropologists, based on surviving documents and surviving Amerindians, believe that it was supposed to be almost like a heaven on earth that living people struggle to find. It was a place without pain, with plenty of food growing everywhere, a place where they sing and dance, and where no one dies. Many thought it was where the land and sky came together. In essence, the people the Jesuits thought to have no spirituality were making pilgrimages to a "holy land." These beliefs parallel Liberation Theology's stance that one should strive for the Kingdom of God, even if not fully realized, here and now on earth.[8]

Dom Pedro Casaldáliga has devoted his life to helping Amerindians. He and his flock were threatened, one of his priests and many natives were murdered, yet he persisted trying to protect the people. This mass was a tribute to all marginalized people living with institutional organized violence. In the booklet that accompanied the original recording, Dom Pedro writes a poetic motivation for the mass that I paraphrase and translate, adding my own explanations:

> Here in Brazil, 1978 was the year of the martyrs. This was to honor three Jesuits [Padres Roque Gonzales, Afonso Rodrigues, and João de Castilho] who were killed while trying to catechize Indians in Rio Grande do Sul, 350 years ago. The Brazilian Indian Missionary Council of the church decided that one should commemorate not only them but also the death of the thousands of Indians, sacrificed by the Christian Empires of Spain and Portugal. They were all martyrs for the Indian cause. They all share the cross amongst all of them: the missionaries, dying for Christ, and the Indians massacred in name of Christ and Emperor.[9]

Specifically, the mass honors the Indian victims of the Battle of Caiboaté (February 7, 1756) when about 1,500 people were massacred by a joint Spanish and Portuguese expedition. The victims were assembled by the local "Corregidor" Sepe Tiarju to resist the evacuation of Guarani Indians from the Mission of São Miguel, one of the Missions established in the area by the Jesuits who followed the path of the martyrs.

The text of the mass has extensive use of tropes with the Church apologizing for the cruelties and declaring itself in solidarity with oppressed and massacred native communities in all of Latin America. Bishop Casaldáliga gives a long justification for the penitential attitude and text:

> I believe in the mission that was Christ's vocation, which is, according to Vatican II, the essence of the Church. And I feel the heir to yesterday's missionaries—heir to both their sins and to their virtues. The "we" of the "Penitential Memory" of the Mass is an ecclesiastic "we," a collective "we." What kind of Christian can deny, and not assume responsibility for the mistakes committed by the Church of Jesus yesterday and today—even if they were committed with the best of intentions? How can we assume responsibility, if we do not try to repair the mistakes? Men err, and Christians are still human.[10]

Casaldáliga also defends the work, against the Vatican that tried to suppress it, as a genuine and authentic mass, the kind of mass that should be celebrated today, not in spite of the strong nonliturgical content but exactly because of it. I am paraphrasing again from his preface:

> I believe that the *Missa da Terra Sem Males* is orthodox. The almost forty bishops that participated in its first celebration, in the Sé Cathedral (of the city of São Paulo), on April 22, 1979, did not object, much to the contrary, they participated in the ceremony. The mass respects the liturgical scheme. It should not be viewed as an oratorio, much less a "show." It is a musical and recited text that translates and transports into a Native Indian inspiration the real Celebration of the Eucharist.

Yes, it does so passionately. Because we are who we are, and, in the words of the French evangelist theologian Georges Casalis, a theological or liturgical or pastoral writing that is devoid of passion would no longer reflect the practice, death, and life of Jesus of Nazareth.[11]

Although this work assumes the basic outline of the Catholic mass (Introductory Rites, Liturgy of the Word, Liturgy of the Eucharist, and Concluding Rites and Final Blessing), it does not use the traditional texts or prayers associated with a mass. Instead it aims to convey the mass's spirit and meaning, but in a very specific manner, embracing the spirit and the devotion of the Amerindians. The correspondence between the Missa da Terra Sem Males and the standard one is illustrated below.

The Mass	**The Roman Rite**
Abertura (Opening)	Introductory Rites
Memória Penitencial (Penitential Memory)	—Penitential Act
Aleluia (Alleluia)	Liturgy of the Word
Ofertório (Offertory)	Liturgy of the Eucharist
Rito da Paz (Rite of Peace)	—Mystery of the Faith
Comunhão (Communion)	
Compromisso Final (Final Commitment)	Concluding Rites / Final Blessing

One could consider the text *Abertura* (Introductory Rites) an example of both troping of the original text, albeit in a very loose fashion keeping the spirit the same (see discussion shortly) and inculturation (for example, *Maíra de tudo, excelso Tupã*). In a traditional mass we would expect the following:

Priest: In the name of the Father, and of the Son, and of the Holy Spirit.

People: Amen.

Priest: Grace to you and peace from God our Father and the Lord Jesus Christ.

As illustrated in the *Abertura* (Introductory Rites), the basic message is similar but the text is greatly expanded:

Em nome do Pai de todos os Povos, Maíra de tudo, excelso Tupã.	In the name of the Father of all peoples, Maíra of all, exalted Tupã.
Em nome do Filho, que a todos os homens nos faz ser irmãos.	In the name of the Son, that makes all of us men brothers.

No sangue mesclado com todos os sangues.	In the blood mixed with all the bloods.
Em nome da Aliança da Libertação.	In the name of the Alliance of Liberation.
Em nome da Luz de toda Cultura.	In the name of the Light of all Culture
Em nome do Amor que está em todo amor.	In the name of Love that is in all love.
Em nome da Terra-sem-males, perdida no lucro, ganhada na dor, em nome da Morte vencida, em nome da Vida, cantamos, Senhor!	In the name of the Land-without-evil, lost in profit, won in pain, in the name of triumph over Death in the name of Life we sing, O Lord!

The same can be applied to the second part of the Introductory Rites, the Penitential Act.

What one would expect from a traditional mass at the beginning is the following:

Priest: Brothers and Sisters, let us acknowledge our sins that we may prepare ourselves to celebrate the sacred mysteries.

Priest: Have mercy on us, O Lord.

People: For we have sinned against you.

Priest: Show us, O Lord, your mercy.

People: And grant us your salvation.

Priest: May almighty God have mercy on us and lead us, with our sins forgiven, to eternal life.

People: Amen.

The spirit ("Brothers and Sisters let us acknowledges our sins. . . . For we have sinned against you") is the theme of the selected lines I present here, but this time it is the Church who "has sinned against you" (the Amerindians). In fact, it becomes a dialogue between the missionaries (Church) and the Amerindians. It details the horrors the Amerindians were subjected to, acknowledges the sins the Church was complicit with, and reaffirms the faith on God's mercy through Resurrection in the *Memória Penitencial* (Penitential Memory):[12]

Herdeiros de um Império de extermínio, filhos da secular dominação, queremos reparar nosso pecado, viemos celebrar a nova opção:	Heirs of an Empire of extermination, children of secular domination we want repair our sin, we came to celebrate the new option:

Ressurreição.
Na Ceia da Morte e da Vida,
a antiga memória perdida;
a morte dos Povos do passado
na Festa do Povo esperado:
Ressurreição;
a História da América inteira,
nesta Memória de Libertação;
na Páscoa do Ressuscitado,
a Páscoa Ameríndia
ainda sem ressurreição
. . .
Queremos reparar
a História desta Terra,
. . .
Eu tinha uma cultura de milênios,
antiga como o sol,
. . .
Eu plantava os filhos e as palavras.
Eu plantava o milho e a mandioca.
Eu cantava com a língua das flautas.
Eu dançava, vestido de luar,
enfeitado de passaros e palmas.
Eu era a Cultura em harmonia com a
Mãe Natureza.
E nós a destruímos,
cheios de prepotência,
negando a identidade
dos Povos diferentes,
todos Família Humana.

Eu era a Paz comigo
e com a Terra ...
E nós te violamos
ao fio das espadas,
no fogo do arcabuz
queimamos teu sossego.

E nós te missionamos,
infiéis ao Evangelho,
cravando em tua vida
a espada de uma Cruz.
Sinos de Boa-nova,
num dobre de finados!
Infiéis ao Evangelho,

Resurrection.
In the Supper of Death and Life,
the old lost memory;
the death of Peoples of the past
in the Feast of the People awaited:
Resurrection;
the entire History of America,
in this Memory of Liberation;
in the Easter of the Resurrected,
the Amerindian Easter
still without resurrection
. . .
We want to repair
the History of this Earth,
. . .
I had a culture of millennia,
old as the sun,
. . .
I planted the children and the words.
I planted corn and cassava.
I sang with the language of flutes.
I danced, dressed in moonlight,
adorned with birds and palms.
I was a Culture in harmony with
Mother Nature.
And we destroyed it,
full of arrogance,
denying the identity
of different People,
all Human Family.

I was at Peace with me
and with the Earth . . .
And we violated you
with the edge of the sword,
with the fire of musket
we burned thy peace.

And we missionized you,
unfaithful to the Gospel,
digging into your life
the sword of a Cross
Bells of the Good News,
in a death knell!
Unfaithful to the Gospel,

do Verbo Encarnado,	to the Incarnate Word
te demos por mensagem,	gave you as a message,
cultura forasteira.	an outsider culture.
...	...
O amor do Pai de todos	The love of the Father of all
me batizou com água da Vida	baptized me with the water of Life
e da Consciência	and of Consciousness
e semeou em mim a Graça do	and sowed in me the Grace of
seu Verbo,	His Word,
Semente universal de Salvação.	Universal seed of Salvation.
Quando nós te ferramos	When we branded you
com um Batismo imposto,	with an imposed Baptism,
marca de humano gado,	a tag of human livestock,
blasfêmia do Batismo,	a blasphemy of Baptism,
violação da Graça	violation of Grace
e negação do Cristo.	and denial of Christ.
Eu era um Povo de milhões de vivos,	I was one of millions of people alive,
de milhões e milhões de Gente Humana,	millions and millions of Human People,
milhões de imagens vivas do Deus Vivo.	millions of living images of the Living God.
E nós te dizimamos,	And we decimated you,
portadores da Morte	carriers of Death
missionários do Nada.	missionaries of Nothing.
Eu vos dei a beleza do Mar	I gave you the beauty of the Sea
e suas praias,	and its beaches,
eu vos dei minha Terra e seus segredos,	I have given you my Earth and its secrets
os pássaros, os peixes, os animais amigos.	birds, fish, animal friends.
...	...

Casaldáliga links together the concept of *Land without Evil* to the Catholic faith and to Liberation Theology. To paraphrase his eloquent plea from the booklet of the recording:[13]

The Land without evil—that the Guarani mysticism has sought for centuries in an emotionally moving exodus—is attainable here, on Earth. Bringing about such a *Land without Evil* is the fundamental duty that humans have been charged with through history: it is the tense joy of our hope in Jesus Christ, the

Risen Lord. It is the New Heaven and New Land that God the Father swore to give to His children.

In summary, the *Missa da Terra Sem Males* follows the format of the Roman Catholic mass, focusing on the Penitential Rite. The new text dramatizes the struggles between the Amerindians and colonizers and missionaries. This work echoes the Easter tradition of the Passion (their suffering) to their hopeful Resurrection (their freedom from oppression). The music is composed of short solos and choruses set to simple folk tunes from various places in South America, a gesture that emphasizes that the penitence is for all Amerindians, not only the ones massacred in Brazil. The stark dark text finds its redemption through the communal singing.

MISSA DOS QUILOMBOS

Milton Nascimento is a prominent Brazilian singer, composer, and guitarist. When his mother, a Black maid, died, the people who employed her, Josino Brito Campos, a bank employee and mathematics teacher, and his wife Lilia, a housewife, were glad to raise Milton as their own alongside their daughter and two other adopted children. The family moved from Rio to Tres Pontas, a small town in the state of Minas Gerais, when Milton was a baby. In 1963, Milton moved to Belo Horizonte, where his career eventually took off with his album *Clube da Esquina* (*Corner Club*) in 1972. He became a highly acclaimed composer with songs such as "Maria, Maria" and "Coração de Estudante" ("Student's Heart"). He was referred to by many as the Portuguese Troubadour because of his lyrical voice and eclectic mastery of musical sounds. He combined many styles—dance tunes from bars, slave hymns, Gregorian chants brought by the Jesuits, and Brazilian folk songs—packaging them in jazz-, rock-, and pop-inspired idioms. Caetano Veloso described Milton with the pun "mil tons," "a thousand tones" in Portuguese.[14] Chris McGowan points out that "his work is informed in a profound way by his having grown up in a small town in Minas Gerais, where he absorbed the music of the churches, religious processions, and the local folk traditions, as well as the mysticism, hopes, and suffering of the local people."[15] He blends masterfully a plethora of styles that embrace many genres, from religious to ethnic to jazz and foreign pop. His performance is immediately identifiable by his unusually large vocal range and its unique timbre. It was this blend of styles—unique ones to Minas—that cut across many genres, from religions to ethnic to foreign pop, combined with his unusual voice that made him unique. As McGowan notes,

Minas has its own specialities and traditions, and is rich with rhythms and musical styles like *jongo*, *calango*, *caxambu* and *toada*. It has street festivals related to the Roman Catholic liturgical calendar that acquired Afro-Brazilian elements such as *reisado*, performed by the *folia de reis* groups.[16]

During the period of military dictatorship in Brazil, Nascimento suffered from military censorship that forced him to release many of his songs without lyrics. His political stance was clear: he stood for freedom. His song "Coração de Estudante" seems like a simple celebration of youth but is actually a requiem for the student Edson Luís (1950–1968), who was killed by police during an antigovernment protest in Rio. In the waning days of the dictatorship, it became the anthem of the pro-democracy movement, much like the way "We shall overcome" acquired a special meaning in the sixties in the United States.

In 1979 Milton Nascimento heard a performance of the *Missa da Terra Sem Males*. Dom Hélder Câmera, Archbishop of Recife, wanted to have a "Negro Mass" to complete, with the *Missa da Terra Sem Males*, a liturgical project for the excluded.[17] As in the mass for the Indians, Dom Pedro Casaldáliga and Pedro Tierra collaboratively wrote the text for the *Missa dos Quilombos*. Milton took almost two years to finish the musical composition, as he had many concurrent projects.

Missa dos Quilombos celebrates the death and resurrection of the Afro-Brazilian people in the death and resurrection of Christ. Quilombos were settlements established by runaway slaves and by freeborn natives during the Portuguese colonial period. The largest and most famous quilombo was Palmares, which lasted for most of the seventeenth century as a large self-sustaining political entity. The last chief of Palmares, Zumbi, was killed after the main city was conquered by a large Portuguese-Brazilian force. His head was cut off, preserved, and brought to Recife, where the governor had it exhibited in the Paço do Carmo (the square in front of the local Cathedral) to dispel the rumor that he was immortal or was still alive.[18]

The mass was first performed on November 20, 1981, in the city of União dos Palmares, as part of the first Brazilian National Symposium about Quilombo.[19] Two days later, it was celebrated by Dom José Maria Pires, Archbishop of Paraíba and, at the time, one of the relatively few black Brazilian Catholic priests, at the Paço do Carmo. The location was chosen by Don Hélder Câmera, as yet another symbolic gesture of atonement by the Church.

The relationship of the Church to Blacks and to slavery in Brazil has been ambiguous and too complicated to be discussed in detail here. From the earliest colonial days, the Church tolerated slavery as part of the social structure. At the same time, many priests clamored against oppression and cruelty. Padre Anchieta raised his voice to protect the Indians, and the greatest

Portuguese-Brazilian writer of the seventeenth century, the Jesuit Padre Antonio Vieira, spoke eloquently in support of Black people. It is worthwhile to quote two excerpts from his sermons:

> Are these men not sons of the same Adam and the same Eve? Were these souls not redeemed by the blood of the same Christ? These bodies, are they not born and do they not die like our bodies? Do they not breathe the same air? Are they not under the same sky? Are they not warmed by the same sun?[20]
>
> . . . but what theology is there or could there be that would justify the lack of humanity and the gruesomeness of the exorbitant punishments with which these very slaves are treated? "Treated" I said, but the word is too short for the meaning that it contains, or that it hides. Tyrannized, I should have said, or martyred, for they hurt the miserable ones, marked, sealed, cut to pieces, with salt rubbed onto them, and subject to bigger excesses that I will not speak of, but that deserve the name of martyrdom rather than punishment.[21]

Few abolitionists have written more eloquently. Yet Vieira did not go as far as to fight slavery: it is an ongoing debate exactly why. Vieira tried to protect slaves against cruelty, and attempted to console them by equating their plight with that of Christ, saying that their suffering was a true imitation of Christ and would earn them salvation in the afterlife.

It is within this tradition of the Church, the church of the sermons of Vieira, that two centuries later Milton Nascimento, Dom Pedro Casaldáliga, and Dom Pedro Tierra spoke. In the lyrics of their mass they were more demanding than Vieira: they were not content with promises for the afterlife, but demanded equality in the present and an apology for the crimes of the past.

At the time of the creation of Milton's mass, the dictatorship had eased somewhat. Censorship was still active and elections were manipulated, but there was a ferment of voices of the opposition. Throughout the dictatorship the figure of Zumbi and the movement of Palmares were viewed as symbols not only of the fight against slavery but also as universal symbols of the struggle for freedom and, in particular, also freedom from the military dictatorship. Thus, Milton's work proclaimed a message of resistance to oppression and belief in the final victory of the human spirit. The *Missa dos Quilombos* is an affirmation of the worth of the Blacks and a demand of an apology from the Church, all within the context of an Easter mass, a mass that is a statement of suffering and resurrection and therefore of forgiveness and faith in the future. Its message was strongly supported by progressive members of the clergy.

Milton combined the (maculelê) African-style percussion of Candomblé with liturgical items from the traditional Latin mass. The combination of elements intertwined from African traditions and Catholic rituals, Orishás

(Yoruba Gods) conflated with Catholic saints were strongly opposed by the Catholic Church.

As it turns out, the Vatican did not allow both the *Missa da Terra Sem Males* and the *Missa dos Quilombos* to be celebrated as masses. We have some of the details about the fate of the *Missa dos Quilombos*. As we saw, its celebration was encouraged and endorsed by Dom Hélder Câmera, an important Brazilian archbishop. He even wrote the words to "Invocação a Mariama," a prayer to Holy Mary that concludes the mass. We also saw earlier the strong defense of the *Missa da Terra Sem Males* as a mass by Dom Pedro Casaldáliga. Yet the Curia was not convinced. Here is an excerpt from a letter by Dom Giuseppe Casoria, prefect of the Congregation for Divine Worship and the Discipline of the Sacraments, to Dom Ivo Lorscheiter, then president of the Brazilian Bishop's Congregation:

> Allow me, excellency, to say that the answer received, while well meditated, seems to not have noted exactly the true signification of our allusion to the *Missa da Terra Sem Males* [previously banned]: neither does it express the desired response ("che si sarebbe gradito"), ensuring that in the future the celebration of the Eucharist will be, as it should be, and as it is, only a memorial of the death and resurrection of our Lord, and not the demands of any human or racial group.[22]

It is perhaps worth noting that the prohibition was less severe than it could be. It was not universal but addressed to a particular clergy, the Brazilian bishops. Nascimento recorded the work, under somewhat challenging conditions: they decided to do it at a famous Brazilian baroque monument in Minas Gerais, the Caraça Seminary. As related by Minamini, after taking the bulky recording equipment, musicians, and chorus to the church, they discovered that it had pretty horrible acoustics.[23] They spent the night preparing for the recording by wrapping percussion instruments with pillows and bedsheets borrowed from the seminary. They put the chorus to one side and Milton, singing by himself on the other, but even so, they were not totally satisfied with the acoustic quality of the final product.

The prohibition certainly did not extend to performance (as opposed to liturgical celebration) of the *Missa dos Quilombos*. It was performed many times, even in Santiago de Compostela, in front of the cathedral. The ban was eventually lifted, as there was a relatively recent performance of the work as a celebration of the mass on November 15, 1995, at the Cathedral of Aparecida. It was celebrated by Dom Ronival dos Reis, the local priest, with the participation of over eighty performers in front of twenty thousand people. The ceremony started with Milton carrying an image of Our Lady of Aparecida to the main altar before the start of the performance of the mass.[24]

Unlike the *Missa da Terra Sem Males*, we see more of the traditional liturgy mixed with the new text. In fact, parts such as the Kyrie resemble the type of troping of the liturgy that one finds in masses before the Council of Trent forbade the practice. Also, the parts of the Liturgy of the Word and the Liturgy of the Eucharist are not presented in order: the Alleluia, for example, is out of place.

A De Ó (Estamos Chegando)	Introit (Proper): *We are arriving*
Em Nome Do Deus	*In the name of God*
Rito Penitencial	Troped Kyrie (Ordinary)
Ofertório	Offertory
Ladainha	Litany
Aleluia	Alleluia
Rito Da Paz	Rite of Peace
Comunhão	Communion
Senhor É Santo	Sanctus
Louvação À Mariama	Praise to Mary
Marcha Final	Ite, missa est
—*De Banzo e de Esperança*	—From Longing to Hope
—*Invocação À Mariama*	—Invocation to Mary

"A De Ó" ("Estamos Chegando") and "Em Nome Do Deus" from the Introductory Rites might in fact present a problem when the text reflects the possibility of multiple Gods. Naturally one can read it as one God with many names.

We are arriving . . .
In the name of God . . .
In the name of the *God of all names*
Yahweh, Obatalá, Olorum, Oió[25]
In the name of God who made all men
Of tenderness and of dust
In the name of the Father who made all flesh
The black one and the white one
Red in their blood . . .
. . . in the name of the People who await,
Within the grace of Faith
Hear the voice of Xangô
The Quilombo-Easter that will make it free.[26]

The Kyrie text in the *Missa dos Quilombos* represents a standard way of troping the liturgy before the Council of Trent as we see at the beginning of the Kyrie:

Text: Roman Rite	Added Tropes
Kyrie eleison	
Christe eleison	
Kyrie eleison	
	The soul is not white
	mourning is not black
	black is not folk
Kyrie eleison	
	Lord of Bonfim[27]
	of the good beginnings
	let the happiness
	not be that of a single day
	let not the merrymaking
	be restricted to having a procession
	on your avenue.
	Let it be, finally
	your liberation from slavery
	and let the street belong to us
	Lord of Bonfim
Kyrie eleison	
Christe eleison	
Kyrie eleison	

While masses for extraordinary occasions were common before the Council of Trent, with abundant troping connecting the mass to the event commemorated, contemporary Catholic doctrine considers that one should not use the *Missa dos Quilombos* for the celebration of the Eucharist, as the message distracts from the liturgical context. It is, however, a powerful musical work, with a message of equality and freedom that still needs to be proclaimed.

IHU 2 KEWERE: REZAR

Marlui Miranda was invited by Padre Cesar Augusto dos Santos, director of Brazilian Program of the Vatican Radio, to compose a mass in honor of the anniversary of the death of Padre José de Anchieta (1534–1597), a Canarian Jesuit who dedicated his life to teaching, and protecting and learning from, the Amerindians.

Marlui Miranda (b. 1949 in Fortaleza) moved to Rio de Janeiro in the early 1970s to begin her career as a singer, performer, and composer of Brazilian popular music, working with established musicians such as Milton Nascimento. During this period she began researching the music of the Amerindians of northern Brazil. She became well known with her recording

IHU Todos Os Sons (1995).[28] *IHU*, from Kamayurá, means "all sound that reaches the ear, including the sound of the spirits and the magical entities of the forest."[29] For the recording, Marlui collected music from many Indian Nations and arranged the songs keeping (as much as possible) their original melodic and rhythmic structure yet repackaging them in a modern idiom as "art" songs. For example, the eleventh track of the CD, "Hirigo," is part of a festival song of the Tupari Indians giving thanks to those who worked in the fields. Most of these songs are all spiritual in nature, expressing the faith of various Amerindian Nations.

2 *IHU Kewere: Rezar* (1997), the sequel to *IHU Todos Os Sons*, is a mass written for the celebration of Padre José de Anchieta, who spent a big part of his life (often in danger) trying to stop the colonists from enslaving the Amerindians. As part of his missionary work, he oversaw the education and conversion of the Indian children. He became fascinated with the Tupí culture, and quickly learned Tupí-Guarani, writing the first Grammar Book for the Tupí language: *The Art of the Grammar of the Language Most Used on the Brazilian Coast* (*Arte de gramática da língua mais usada na costa do Brasil*). On the cover is the seal of the Jesuits, and around it is written *Turris fortissima nomen Domini ad ipsum currit iustus et exaltabitur* (The name of the Lord is a strong tower: the righteous run to it, and are safe), a quotation from Proverbs 18:10.

In the title of the mass, Marlui combines several languages to reflect the different ethnic groups of Brazil coming together as one nation. Marlui points out that *Kewere* from Tupí has several meanings. For example, it can mean to release one from a spell, to pray for one who is sick, and a spirit healing of the soul.[30] *Ihu* is from Kamayurá describing all sounds, and *Rezar* is from the Portuguese, meaning to pray. Marlui blends Indigenous chants of Amazonian tribes and the Tupí language (both sixteenth-century versions by Anchieta and contemporary) within the frame of the Catholic mass. As illustrated below, this mass follows a more traditional form of the Roman Rite.

Introit = *Canto de entrada*	Introductory Rites
Kyrie	
Glória	
Aleluia = Alleluia	Liturgy of the Word
Credo	
Ofertório = Offertory	Liturgy of the Eucharist
Pai nosso = Paster Noster	
Agnus Dei	
Comunhão = Communion	
Ação de Graças	
Canto final = Ite, missa est	Closing Rites

Marlui explains (in Portuguese) what she is trying to achieve by the confluence of faiths, religions, and sounds:

> The central idea in Kewere is the contraposition of faiths: on one hand, the songs of the shamans and on the other hand the Christian verses of Padre José de Anchieta and the liturgical texts, accommodated in the same compositional framework. The Indigenous songs I have selected have a solemn, lyrical nature, and therefore they dignify the mass and they are appropriate to be interpreted by a symphonic orchestra and chorus. Thus, the choice of such an ensemble seems pertinent to the idea of catechism, the conversion of the Indians to a European religion. The ancestral Tupí language unifies the composition into a single whole.
>
> At the same time that the mass separates us from Indian origins, we become nearer to them, because part of the vocal interpretation is done in an ethnic manner, evoking the Indian people, and their forgotten voices in the past of catechism. . . .
>
> Kewere is a composition with a delicate equilibrium, in which I tried to make adequate the poetic sense of Indian languages (the Aruá, of the Tupari of the Urubu-Kaapor). These songs are as light and as fragile as the spirits that brought them through the world of dreams. It is on this fragile structure that the poems of Padre José de Anchieta rest.[31]

Marlui struggled with the realization of this work. For example, when imagining Kewere she asked herself what would a specifically Indian Kyrie, Gloria, and the other parts of the Roman Catholic mass sound like?

> When imagining Kewere I asked myself: what could sound like an Indian Kyrie? A Gloria? An Agnus Dei? An Introit? An Alleluia? I thought of the difficult situation facing sixteenth century Jesuits needing to translate Christian concepts to the field of sacred indigenous [concepts.] I thought of myself, however, as doing an inverse musical catechesis, forcing myself to find where a Kyrie, a Gloria, an Introit, and so on could find shelter in the selected indigenous repertory.[32]

I will discuss several parts of the mass to illustrate Marlui's compositional process of combining diverse material—music, language, and faith-based fragments—in a coherent manner. For our first example, the traditional text for the Kyrie is translated into Tupí for the mass:

> Tupã oré r-ausubar-iepé / Senhor, tende piedade de nós / Lord have mercy on us
> Christo oré r-ausubar-iepé / Cristo, tende piedade de nós / Christ have mercy on us

Marlui explains how she uses the traditional liturgical text, now in Tupí:

In the Kyrie, the Indian woman sings on her way, mixing two faiths: "Kyrie Eleyson . . . *Tupã oré . . . oré r-ausubar-iepé* . . . *Tupã* Eleyson . . ." while, in parallel, a "Gregorian" chant and a chant of "nomination" are used, and the latter explained as a kind of "baptism," inspired in Indian traditions is sung.[33]

The Credo is orthodox, by beginning with the text "I believe in one God" (*Arobiar Tupã tuba!*) also illustrating an example of inculturation by using *Tupã* for the word *God*. The rendering of the Lord's Prayer, *Ore rub*, into Tupí was taken from a Catechism published in the seventeenth century. According to the preface of the 1952 facsimile reprinting of the *Catecismo na lingoa brasilica*, written by Father A. Lemos Barbosa, it is very likely that much of this work is based on a sixteenth-century work by Anchieta.[34]

In the Agnus Dei, instead of simply translating the text into Tupí, Marlui layers several elements together. The Agnus Dei text is sung in the background while two tropes are sung with it. The first trope is an Aruá Indian tune in Tupí. The translated text is "I am going to the house of my brother to ask for light and help." The second trope, which is a melody by Marlui and poetry in Tupí by Padre Anchieta, follows. The text is: "We want to love you very much and we give you offerings. So that you give us your son Jesus. To honor your house, I come to dance in it. Wash my soul to take away the blemishes of evil."

All of these melodies are set within the context of a symphony orchestra using both traditional and Indigenous instruments. The different languages create a polylingual dialogue of faiths within a rich musical soundscape—distinctively Brazilian and Catholic in spirit—that is an embodiment of the ideal of equality across religions and races.

2 IHU Kewere: Rezar was performed as a mass at the São Paulo Cathedral, an ideal venue, as Anchieta was one of the founders of São Paulo, and the cathedral is very near the location of the first structure built by the Jesuits. The celebration took place on June 8, 1997, as the highlight of the four-hundredth anniversary celebrations in honor of Anchieta's death. In attendance were representatives of the city, state, federal government, and clergy. Cardinal Arns, Archbishop of Sao Paulo, gave specific permission to have the mass sung mostly in Tupí.

The role of music in the liturgy and the style of music performed in church have a long and controversial history: Saint Augustine's concern that the beauty of music will distract from devotion, the edicts of the Council of Trent with their prohibition of troping the liturgy and frowning upon polyphonic settings that obscure the text, the concerns of Brazilian clergy about the "contamination" of the rite and of the faith by Afro-Brazilian "pagan superstitions," and the requirements of Vatican II to conduct the Mass in understandable, native languages but with limitations. Casaldáliga, Milton, and Marlui in their masses include many such controversial features, but their message required them. They remind us that Catholic, as defined in the Oxford English Dictionary, is having "sympathies with, or embracing all" and that Amerindians and Black slaves are an integral part of what makes Brazil a unique and culturally rich nation today.

These three masses are important cultural artifacts, representing a troubled yet important part of Brazilian history and of the role of the church in it. They also were an important step in recognizing, acknowledging, and asking forgiveness for past wrongs committed by or with the help of the Church, "even if they were committed with the best of intentions."[35] They are part of a process of healing and of building a better future, an affirmation of hope, faith, and belief that is welcome and necessary, not only in Brazil but in the world.

NOTES

1. Padres Roque Gonzales, Afonso Rodrigues, and João de Castilho were killed while trying to set up *Missões*, religious communities for Guarany Indians.

2. See "Democratic Governance and Developmentalism, 1946–1964" and "The Generals in Power and the Fight for Democracy, 1964–1985" in *The Brazil Reader: History, Culture, Politics*, second edition, revised and updated, edited by James N. Green, Victoria Langland, and Lilia Moritz Schwarcz (Durham: Duke University Press, 2018); Thomas E. Skidmore, *The Politics of Military Rule in Brazil, 1964–85* (New York: Oxford University Press, 1988).

3. The essence of the argument, as explained in Christian Smith, *The Emergence of Liberation Theology: Radical Religion and Social Movement Theory* (Chicago: University of Chicago Press, 1991), 37. Jesus proclaimed "a kingdom of justice and liberation, to be established in favor of the poor, the oppressed, and the marginalized of history. . . . The only Justice is the definitive justice that builds, starting right now, in our conflict-filled history, a kingdom in which God's love will be present and exploitation abolished." The quote is from Gustavo Guitíerrez, *The Power of the Poor in History* (Maryknoll, NY: Orbis Books, 1983), 14.

4. I am unaware of any previous syncretized Brazilian masses.

5. Judith Shapiro, "From Tupã to the Land without Evil: The Christianization of the Tupí-Guarani Cosmology," *American Ethnologist* 14 (1987): 28.

6. Ibid.

7. Ibid., 26.

8. "In accordance with the general tenets of liberation theology, whereby working to realize the Kingdom of God requires engagement in the actual political struggles of the day, the missionary acts out his vocation in the arena of land claims cases and confrontations with state-supported multinational corporations." Shapiro, "From Tupã to the Land without Evil," 133.

9. For the full text in Portuguese, see http://www.servicioskoinonia.org/Casaldaliga/poesia/terra.htm, accessed June 25, 2020.

10. Ibid.; all translations are my own unless otherwise noted.
11. Ibid.
12. Ibid.
13. Ibid.
14. Claus Schreiner, *Música Brasileira: A History of Popular Music and the People of Brazil* (New York: Marion Boyars, 1993), 231.
15. Chris McGowan, *The Brazilian Music Book: Brazil's Singers, Songwriters and Musicians Tell the Story of Bossa Nova, MPB, and Brazilian Jazz and Pop* (Santa Monica: Culture Planet, 2012), Loc 5544, Kindle.
16. Ibid., Loc 5554, Kindle.
17. Edison Minami, "Milton Nascimento e o diálogo interreligioso na Missa dos Quilombos," *Conhecimento & Diversidade* 1 (2009): 116.
18. From a letter of March 14, 1696, from Caetano de Melo de Castro, governor of Pernambuco, to the King of Portugal: "Determinei que pusessem sua cabeça em um poste no lugar mais público desta praça, para satisfazer os ofendidos e justamente queixosos e atemorizar os negros que supersticiosamente julgavam Zumbi um imortal, para que entendessem que esta empresa acabava de todo com os Palmares." "Zumbi dos Palmares," Wikipedia, accessed June 25, 2020, http://pt.wikipedia.org/wiki/Zumbi_dos_Palmares.
19. Martiniano J. Silva, "O Cristo Negro e a proibição da Missa dos Quilombos," *O Popular*, August 31, 1984, accessed June 25, 2020, http://www.miltonnascimento.com.br/assets/pdf/1980N-01_6.pdf.
20. Padre Antonio Vieira, "Sermão Vigesimo Sexto," in *Sermões do Padre Antonio Vieira*, IX (Lisboa: J. M. C. Seabra and T. Q. Antunes, 1856), 353. All Vieira translations are mine.
21. Padre Antonio Vieira, "Sermão Vigesimo Setimo," in *Sermões do Padre Antonio Vieira*, XV (Lisboa: J. M. C. Seabra and T. Q. Antunes, n.d.), 384.
22. Parts of this letter are cited by Silva, "O Cristo Negro." It is freely translated from Portuguese.
23. Minami, "Milton Nascimento e o diálogo interreligioso na Missa dos Quilombos," 117.
24. "*Missa dos Quilombos* Reúne 20 mil em Aparecida," in *Folha de São Paulo*, November 16, 1995, accessed June 25, 2020, http://www1.folha.uol.com.br/fsp/1995/11/16/cotidiano/21.html.
25. These are names of Yoruba Gods.
26. All lyrics from the mass are my translations from the liner notes. Xangô is a powerful Yoruba God.
27. Our Lord of Bonfim is a church in Salvador, Bahia, with a famous yearly Afro-American procession. There is also a pun here: *Bonfim* is "bom fim," meaning "good ending."
28. Marlui Miranda, *IHU Todos Os Sons*, Pau Brazil, 1995, compact disc, liner notes.
29. "Ihu or the Music of the Amazon Indians," Music and Folklore Mari-Brazil, accessed June 25, 2020, http://www.maria-brazil.org/ihu.htm.

30. From a conversation with Marlui Miranda, December 2014, in São Paulo, Brazil.
31. Miranda, *IHU 2*, liner notes.
32. Ibid.
33. Ibid.
34. Father A. Lemos Barbosa, "Apresentação," in Padre Antônio de Araújo, *Catecismo na Língua Brasílica*, edição facsimilar da primeira edição, IX–XVII, Biblioteca de Língua Tupi, Vol. 1, 1618 (Rio de Janeiro: Pontifícia Universidade Católica), accessed June 25, 2020, http://biblio.etnolinguistica.org/barbosa-1952-catecismo.
35. Pedro Casaldáliga, http://www.servicioskoinonia.org/Casaldaliga/poesia/terra.htm. I would like to thank Thomas Schmidt for his editing and helpful suggestions.

FURTHER READING

Dominian, Helen G. *Apostle of Brazil: The Biography of Padre José De Anchieta, S.J., 1534–1597.* First edition. New York: Exposition Press, 1958.
Gutiérrez, Gustavo, and Robert R. Barr. *The Power of the Poor in History.* Maryknoll, NY: Orbis Books, 1992.
McGowan, Chris, and Ricardo Pessanha. *The Brazilian Sound: Samba, Bossa Nova, and the Popular Music of Brazil.* Revised and expanded edition. Philadelphia: Temple University Press, 2009.
Murphy, John P. (John Patrick). *Music in Brazil: Experiencing Music, Expressing Culture.* New York: Oxford University Press, 2006.
Smith, Christian. *The Emergence of Liberation Theology: Radical Religion and Social Movement Theory.* Chicago: University of Chicago Press, 1991.
Vásquez, Manuel A. *The Brazilian Popular Church and the Crisis of Modernity.* Cambridge; New York: Cambridge University Press, 1998.
Vatican Council (2nd: 1962–1965: Basilica di San Pietro in Vaticano), and Walter M. Abbot. *The Documents of Vatican II: In a New and Definitive Translation with Commentaries and Notes by Catholic, Protestant and Orthodox Authorities.* New York: Herder and Herder, 1966.
Voeks, Robert A., and American Council of Learned Societies. *Sacred Leaves of Candomblé: African Magic, Medicine, and Religion in Brazil.* Third paperback printing. Austin: University of Texas Press, 2003.

Chapter Two

The Guatemalan Choirbooks

Facilitating Preservation, Performance, and Study of the Colonial Repertoire

Martha E. Thomae

Six large choirbooks were in use in the cathedral of Guatemala's main city between c. 1600 and c. 1800.[1] They were mostly copied in the seventeenth century (see table 2.1).[2] Currently, they are held in the music vault of the Archdiocesan Historical Archive of Guatemala (AHAG).[3] The choirbooks contain essentially sixteenth-century polyphonic music by Spanish composers (for example, Victoria, Morales, and Guerrero), as well as a few pieces by Lassus and Palestrina. They also contain music by composers who worked as choirmasters at the cathedral. Although the first four choirbooks have been inventoried and a general overview of the repertoire and history of the whole collection has been provided, access to the musical contents of these sources (with the notable exception of the transcribed fourth choirbook) is difficult.[4] There are poor digital images of some of the books made from microfilm, but they are almost unusable because many pages are cropped. Access to the books on site requires special permission. Furthermore, the use of mensural notation restricts performance of the music to experts. Local musicologists Dieter Lehnhoff and Omar Morales Abril have made efforts to preserve and disseminate these colonial sources by transcribing them into modern notation and performing their music, but these efforts cover only a small fraction of the music found in the choirbooks.[5]

It is my goal to increase access to the music of this collection in order to understand the role of music in the liturgy of colonial Guatemala. To achieve this, I use digitization and music-encoding technologies, including optical music recognition and automatic transcription. In this essay, I will focus on the book of masses GuatC 1, describing the digitization and encoding processes carried out. I will also illustrate the advantages of encoded music for accessibility purposes, through modern transcriptions and audio playback, and musicological analysis. I will compare the Kyrie of Palestrina's *Missa sine nomine* as it appears in GuatC 1 with a concordant European source already encoded in a symbolic format (**kern), showing how future scholars will use these tools to evaluate the transmission of music from Europe to Latin America and identify local traditions of counterpoint and performance.[6]

BACKGROUND

The Guatemalan Cathedral Choirbooks

The collection of choirbooks from Guatemala's cathedral (GuatC) consists of five large bound books and a sixth small unbound one. In choirbook format, each voice is presented as a self-contained block occupying its own space on the page or opening. These blocks are synchronized either by fitting an entire section on an opening or by coordinating the page breaks in all voices. For four-part texture, as is the case for most pieces in GuatC 1, each voice occupies one of the four quadrants of the opening (figure 2.1). The actual distribution of the voices in these quadrants depends on the source.[7]

Figure 2.1. Example of choirbook format for a four-voice section in GuatC 1.

Three of the six GuatC choirbooks have been known for a few decades. GuatC 1–3 were inventoried by Pujol, Stevenson, and Snow.[8] GuatC 4, discovered after the 1976 earthquake, was studied and transcribed in its entirety by Snow.[9] The last two choirbooks were discovered in 2010 in the AHAG. The fifth book was found by Omar Morales Abril and Javier Marín López in July 2010.[10] In October of the same year, Morales Abril found, among unclassified music sheets, what he considered to be a small unbound choirbook.[11] This sixth book consists of a few pages attached together with three pieces of thread. Despite its small dimensions (21.5 cm × 30 cm) and number of folios (nineteen folios), the parts are written in choirbook format.

GuatC 1 is a book of masses, GuatC 2 is a book of hymns and Magnificats, GuatC 3 and 5 are books with miscellaneous contents, GuatC 4 is a book for Holy Week and Salve services, and GuatC 6 presents an Office for the Dead. Table 2.1 provides general information about each of the six books in the collection.

The choirbooks contain pieces from composers active in different regions (see figure 2.2), maintaining a balance between the number of Hispanic composers active and not active in the Americas. Of the twenty-seven composers present in the GuatC corpus, ten of them visited and worked in the territory of the Viceroyalty of New Spain (nine in Guatemala and one in Mexico). There are also ten Iberian-Peninsular composers who never set foot in the Americas, together with four other non-Hispanic composers and three composers whose origin remains to be uncovered. Non-Hispanic composers include names such as Palestrina and Lassus, while Peninsular composers include the great triumvirate of Spanish polyphonists Tomás Luis de Victoria, Cristóbal de Morales, and Francisco Guerrero, among others. The most prolific local composers include Hernando Franco, Pedro Bermúdez, and Gaspar Fernández, who were choirmasters at the Metropolitan Cathedral of Guatemala from 1569 to 1574, 1601 to 1603, and 1603 to 1606 respectively.[12] These three are among the most frequently found composers in various archives from the Mesoamerican region.[13] Gaspar Fernández was also the scribe of choirbooks 2 and 4 and of a *Libro de Kyries* on which choirbook 1 was based. Out of the ten composers active in the Viceroyalty of New Spain, five of them were born or trained in the Americas: Gaspar Fernández, Juan José Guerrero, Manuel José de Quirós, and Fray Francisco de Quirós in Guatemala, and Juan Matías de Rivera in Mexico.[14]

Table 2.1. General information for each of the choirbooks GuatC 1–6

Choirbook Number		Type	General Information and Copyists
1		Book of Masses	Copied from Gaspar Fernández's book (*Libro de Kyries* 1602) by Manuel José de Quiroz c. 1760–1765
2	A	Hymns	Copied by Gaspar Fernández and obtained by the cathedral in 1606
	B	Magnificats (and Benedicamus settings)	
3		Many motets and varied content (hymns, sequences, litanies, and masses)	Intervention in the eighteenth century: new folios were pasted over old ones either to hide a piece or to substitute it with another one. The binding was not restored and, eventually, it became infested by silverfish. This caused both the old and new folios to be detached, resulting in the disorganized/incomplete aspect of the book. Nicolás Márquez Tamariz (1627–93), choirmaster from November 1669 to October 1693, copied most of the music of the original folios. Juan Fernández de Leon (1671–1731), originally from Oaxaca (México), was active in Guatemala beginning in 1696 and served as choirmaster between 1717–31. He added two pieces to the last folio. Manuel José de Quirós (fl. 1694–1765), choirmaster and Guatemalan composer, copied the music of the new folios during the mid-eighteenth century.
4		Holy Week and Salve services	Gaspar Fernández (in 1605)

5	Diverse content	Copied by different scribes during the mid-seventeenth to mid-eighteenth centuries: Juan José Guerrero, who was active as a composer in the Metropolitan Cathedral of Guatemala since 1644 and served as choirmaster from July 1658 to October 1669. He copied and composed a set of polychoral psalms for Vespers. Nicolás Márquez Tamariz, who was Guerrero's successor. He copied two motets, an invitatory, and a psalm for Vespers. The Oaxacan musician Juan Fernández de León copied two responsories. An unknown scribe copied another invitatory. Manuel José de Quirós copied the last ten pieces, which consist of a Benedicamus Domino, a Christmas invitatory, and various sections of the Mass Ordinary.
6	Office of the Dead	Probably copied during the first half of the seventeenth century. Maybe by Diego de Galvez Prado (fl. 1597–1648), choirmaster between 1636 and 1648.

Omar Morales Abril, "Música local y música foránea en los libros de polifonía de las Catedrales de Guatemala y México," *Jahrbuch für Renaissancemusik* 14 (2015): 96–103.

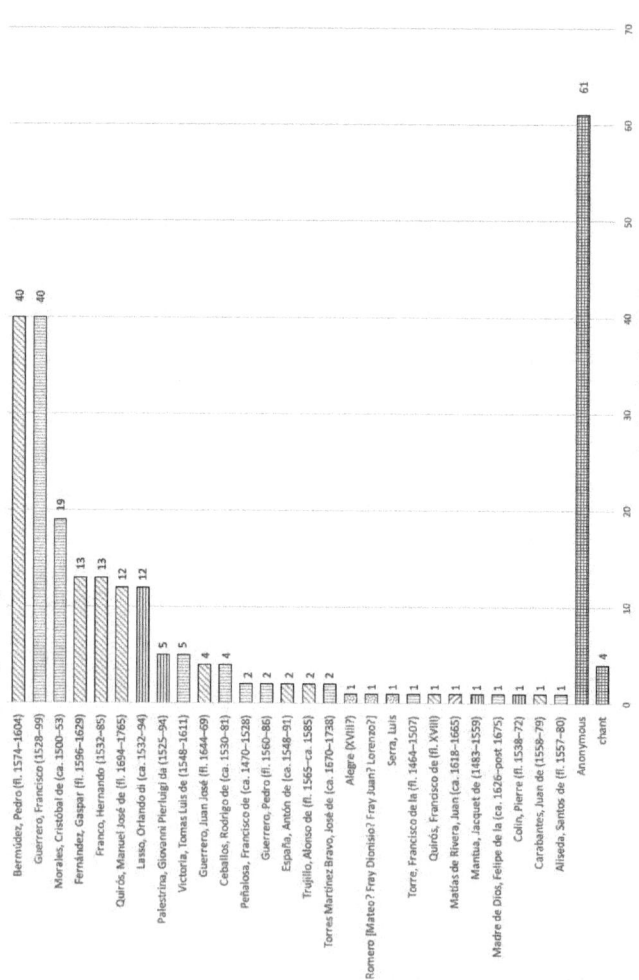

Figure 2.2. Composers present in the GuatC choirbooks and number of pieces written by each of them.
Key: upward diagonal stripes for local composers (i.e., composers active in Guatemala), downward diagonal stripes for composers active in other parts of the Viceroyalty of New Spain (here only Juan Matías de Rivera, in Oaxaca), vertical stripes for Iberian Peninsular composers, dots for Iberoamerican composers whose actual region of activity is undetermined, horizontal stripes for composers from other parts of Europe, and grid for Anonymous and chant.

Morales Abril, "Musica local," 119–21

The GuatC 1 Choirbook

In this project, I created high-quality digital images (digitized) and encoded the music of the GuatC 1 choirbook. According to the conservation report requested to the Centro de Rescate, Estudios y Análisis Científico para el Arte (CREA), the GuatC 1 choirbook is one of the best preserved of the whole collection.[15] From the set of choirbooks suitable for digitization (based again on the conservation report), GuatC 1 was the only one with triple-meter sections, which are of special interest given the context-dependent nature of the duration of mensural notes in triple meter. This is why I chose this volume to be the first for digitization and encoding. The inventory of the GuatC 1 contents is provided in table 2.2.[16]

All of the masses from the original *Libro de Kyries* except one, Pedro Bermúdez's *Missa de Bomba*, were brought from Europe. Snow mentions concordant sources for Morales, Palestrina, Colin, and one of Ceballos's masses (his popular *Missa tertii toni*).[17] The *Missa de 8° Tono* by Ceballos is his *Missa Simile est regnum caelorum*, a parody mass based on a motet by Morales. The *Missa de Bomba* by Pedro Bermúdez, Guatemalan choirmaster between 1601 and 1603, is a parody mass based on the ensalada *La Bomba* by Mateo Flecha (el Viejo). According to Snow, from the group of six masses added in the eighteenth century, only the ones by Torres, Serra, Alegre, and Rivera appear to be unique to this manuscript.[18]

METHODOLOGY

The goal of this project is to increase access to the music of the GuatC 1–6 choirbook collection, which will be achieved through digitization and music-encoding technologies. There are three barriers to accessibility in this corpus: (1) the lack of high-quality digital images, (2) the notation style, and (3) its layout. While digital images obtained from microfilms from 1984 can be found online, the set of microfilms is incomplete. It only includes the books 1–3, it is missing a few pages at the beginning of the GuatC 1, and some of the folios seem cropped.[19] Therefore, access to the complete collection has been limited to people visiting the AHAG. Second, the use of mensural notation restricts performance of the music to experts because in triple sections the duration of the notes depends on the context and there are no barlines. Last, the choirbook layout separates the parts on different areas of the opening instead of aligning them vertically as in a modern score format. Together the context-dependent nature of the notation and the separate-parts layout hinder the appreciation of the polyphonic texture of the music. It is only when musicians acquainted with the notation sing the various parts together or

Table 2.2. Inventory of the GuatC 1 choirbook

No.	Folios	Piece	Composer	Genre	Voices	Information
1	1v–4r	Asperges me	[¿Pedro Bermúdez?]	antiphon	4	
2	4v–7r	Asperges me	Anonymous	antiphon	5	
3	7v–11r	Vidi aquam	Pedro Bermúdez	antiphon	4	
4	11v–14r	Vidi aquam	[Hernando Franco]	antiphon	4	
5	14v–17r	Asperges me	[Alonso de Trujillo]	antiphon	4	
6	17v–31r	Missa sobre las vozes	Cristóbal de Morales	mass	4	From the 1602 book. This is Morales's hexachord mass.
7	31v–43r	Missa sine nomine	Giovanni Pierluigi da Palestrina	mass	4	From the 1602 book.
8	43v–54r	Missa Pere de nous	Pierre Colin	mass	4	From the 1602 book.
9	54v–71r	Missa de 3° tono	Rodrigo de Ceballos	mass	4	From the 1602 book.
10	71v–85r	Missa sine nomine	José de Torres y Martínez Bravo	mass	4	Added in the eighteenth century.
11	85v–95r	Missa O quam gloriosum	Tomás Luis de Victoria	mass	4	Added in the eighteenth century.
12	95v–109r	Missa Ave maris stella	Tomás Luis de Victoria	mass	4	Added in the eighteenth century.
13	109v–119r	Missa de 5° tono	Luis Serra	mass	4	Added in the eighteenth century.
14	119v–133r	Missa de 4° tono	Alegre	mass	4	Added in the eighteenth century.
15	133v–152r	Missa de 8° tono	Rodrigo de Ceballos	mass	4, Agnus a 5	From the 1602 book. Ceballos's *Missa Simile est regnum cælorum*, parody mass based on a motet by Morales.

16	152v–169r	Missa de Bomba	Pedro Bermúdez	mass	4	From the 1602 book. Parody mass based on Mateo Flecha's (el Viejo) ensalada la Bomba.
17	169v–180r	Missa sine nomine	Juan Matías de Rivera	mass	4	Added in the eighteenth century.
18	180v–181r	Christus natus est	Pedro Bermúdez	invitatory	4	
19	181v–183r	Christus natus est	Pedro Bermúdez	invitatory	8	
20	183v–184r	Christus natus est	Anonymous	invitatory	5	
21	184v–186r	Surrexit Dominus vere	Anonymous	invitatory	5	
22	186v–187r	Lumen ad revelationem	Hernando Franco	antiphon	5	
23	187v–188r	Lumen ad revelationem	Pedro Bermúdez	antiphon	5	
24	188v–189r	Lumen ad revelationem	Pedro Bermúdez	antiphon	4	
25	189v–190r	Surrexit Dominus vere	Anonymous	invitatory	4	
26	190v–192r	Victimæ Paschali laudes	Francisco Guerrero	sequence	4, 2a Pars a 5	
27	192v–193r	Tantum ergo	[Pedro Bermúdez]	hymn	4	

when an expert transcribes the music into a modern score that these textures can be really perceived and enjoyed. The layout of the original music deters its study even for experts because it is hard to visualize the vertical relationships between notes sung simultaneously in two different voices, something that only becomes clear when the music is presented in score format.

To unravel these barriers, I followed a three-stage methodology:

1. *Digitization* to obtain full-color high-resolution digital images of each of the pages of the choirbook, allowing high-quality access to the original sources of the music.
2. *Optical music recognition* (OMR) to obtain symbolic files encoding the music content as it appears in the source.
3. *Automatic scoring up* to transform the encoded music of the piece from a separate-parts layout into a score by interpreting the duration of the notes according to the context and combining them in score.

This three-stage methodology transforms the physical object into symbolic scores (that is, machine-readable scores that encode the music content of each piece) and performable modern scores. While the first stage will handle the digitization barrier, the third stage will handle the context-dependent nature of the notation and the layout barriers. The OMR process is the link between the two technologies, transforming a digital (pixel) domain into a symbolic (machine-readable) domain. The process will result in the digitization and encoding of the repertoire as musical scores in Music Encoding Initiative (MEI) format, one of the few formats that provide support for mensural notation.[20] More details about each of these steps follow.

Digitization Process

The digitization process was authorized by the chancellor of the Ecclesiastical Curia of Santiago de Guatemala and director of the AHAG, father Eddy René Calvillo, on October 31, 2018. The process was conducted at the AHAG to avoid the transportation of the books outside of their current location. There are some characteristics of the GuatC collection that influenced the choice of imaging systems to use, namely that the volumes are old manuscripts, bound, and oversize items. According to the Federal Agencies Digital Guidelines Initiative specifications, for bound volumes of rare or special collections, the recommended imaging technology is a manually operated planetary book scanner (or similar setups that digitize the pages from the top using digital cameras and book cradles) without glass or plastic platens.[21] Because no book scanner of the appropriate dimensions was available in Guatemala, I made my own and created high-quality color images of the manuscript. All the parts of the book scanner were either built or borrowed.[22]

The digitization process of GuatC 1 took place in the AHAG between January 7 and 15, 2019. Because the AHAG does not have conservation and digitization departments, these tasks had to be outsourced. The conservators from CREA were in charge of the assessment of the material for digitization, and its preparation for it. Unfortunately, I was not able to find a digitization technician with training on special collections.

By the end of November 2018, I received the conservation report (written by CREA) evaluating the conservation conditions of the choirbooks and whether they were suitable for digitization. On January 7, GuatC 1 received basic conservation treatment to prepare it for digitization. The equipment was set up and tested the next day (Daniel Hernandez Salazar, a Guatemalan professional photographer, set up the camera parameters). Imaging started on January 9 and continued for the next four business days. I handled the manuscript during digitization.

The successful digitization of GuatC 1 would not have been possible without the advice of staff at the Digital Image Archive of Medieval Music (DIAMM), the Bibliothèque et Archives Nationales du Québec (BAnQ), and the Digitization Lab at McGill University Library.[23] These institutions have experience in the digitization of special collections. DIAMM has experience with digitizing medieval music manuscripts and has some guidelines about this topic.[24] DIAMM's project manager Julia Craig-McFeely and main photographer Lynda Sayce provided specific advice for this project through email. BAnQ has its own conservation and digitization departments. These departments offered a great number of useful recommendations for the project, including handling of the material, general conservation treatments for paper, evaluation of parts of the equipment (for example, light choices), and possible configurations of the equipment (cradle, lights, and camera).[25] The McGill Library, in addition to pointing to an online resource for DIY book scanners, provided advice on where to get archival materials (for example, book serpents) and possibilities for improving the design of the book scanner in the future.[26]

Optical Music Recognition

Optical music recognition (OMR) is the process of converting the digital image of a music document into a machine-readable file encoding the music content of that image. This process is similar to optical character recognition (OCR), which is used to make digital text documents readable by the computer. Well-established OMR applications already exist for common Western music notation (CWMN).[27] There are, however, not many early music notation OMR systems. The only OMR system developed explicitly for mensural notation is Aruspix, a music scanning software for early music prints.[28] Some machine learning-based OMR models can be trained on a particular notation system by presenting them with examples of the different "characters" (that is, music symbols) of that notation until they learn enough to recognize them. A few examples of these systems include:

- The Gamera recognition framework, which has already been used for building recognition systems for lute and neumatic notation.[29]
- A holistic staff-level recognition method. This is a method that recognizes the sequence of symbols in a staff as a whole, provided that there is only one voice per staff. It has been used for CMN and mensural notation.[30] The latter, the holistic mensural model, is the one used in this essay.[31]
- A page-level recognition method that was used for mensural notation.[32]

All of these machine learning (ML) models need to first learn the different classes of symbols present in the corpus; this process is known as training. Once the ML model has been trained, it can be used to classify (identify) the music symbols of the complete manuscript; this process is referred to as classification. To train an ML model, one needs to present it with labeled examples from which it can learn. These examples normally consist of pages where each symbol of the page has been manually labeled as belonging to a particular class of music symbol (for example, minim note, breve rest, custos, and G clef). This set of labeled examples used to train the model to learn the different classes of symbols present in a corpus is known as training data or a training set. The preparation of the training data can be a very time-consuming task. To minimize the training data preparation time, I used the holistic staff-level OMR model developed by Calvo-Zaragoza, Toselli, and Vidal (2019) because it has already been trained in Spanish mensural notation, very similar in appearance to the mensural notation in the GuatC collection.[33]

OMR also requires the preprocessing of the data to make it a suitable input for the model and the correction of the results of the model (figure 2.3). Because the model used works at the staff level, the data (that is, the image of a digitized manuscript page) has to be annotated to show the staff regions (figure 2.4). This staff annotation step constitutes the preprocessing stage for the symbol recognition task.

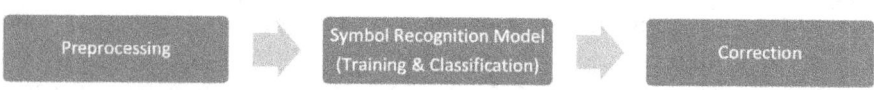

Figure 2.3. Stages of symbol recognition within OMR.

I used the Music Recognition Encoding and Transcription (MuRET) framework to facilitate the preprocessing, symbol recognition, and correction of the results during the OMR. MuRET is an online framework for OMR.[34] With MuRET, I selected the staff regions of the page for preprocessing using its so-called "Document Analysis" interface (figure 2.4). The pretrained symbol recognition model was uploaded into MuRET, which facilitated visualizing the results of the OMR (the symbols recognized by the model), as well as correcting them.

Figure 2.4. Document Analysis interface in MuRET. This is a preprocessing interface that allows the user to draw bounding boxes to select the different regions in the image (for example, staff, lyrics, and text). Here, only the staff regions are shown.

The visualization and correction of the results are done within the "Agnostic" interface of MuRET (figure 2.5). In the Agnostic interface, the user can select any of the staff regions created in the Document Analysis interface, as well as the classification model to be used to classify the symbols in that staff. The selected staff is shown as a region of the image, and the recognized symbols are shown in the transcription below. If any of the recognized symbols is wrong, the user can correct them by clicking on the symbol and changing either the category of the symbol (by using the lower panel) or its pitch (by using the arrows to the left).

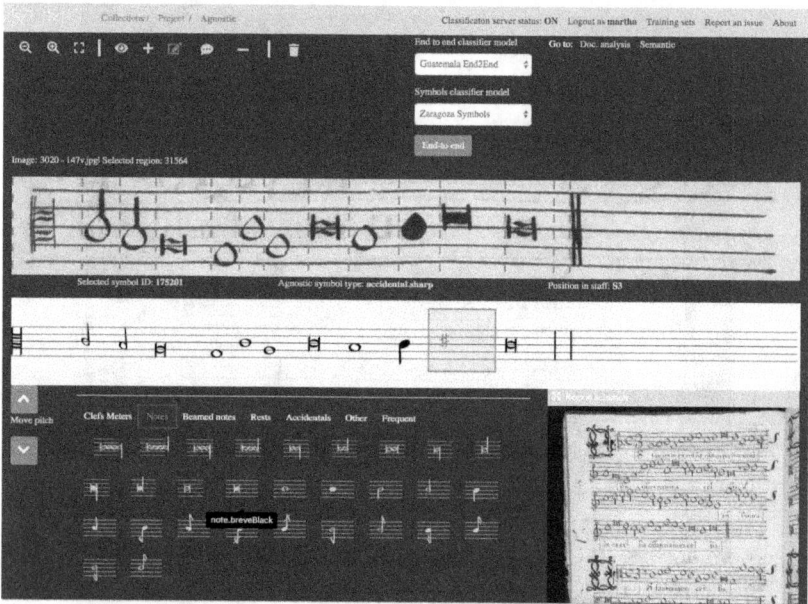

Figure 2.5. MuRET's Agnostic interface. This is a classification and correction interface. The user selects a region and the OMR model to be used to classify the symbols in the region. Correction options, the lower panel and arrows, are activated when clicking over a symbol (see highlighted accidental).

Scoring Up, Transcription into Modern Values, and Playback

The scoring up (combining the voices in mensural notation into a score) was done with MuRET. In the case of sections in duple meter, the score can be generated immediately after the correction of the symbol recognition results. In the case of triple meter sections, one can use the "Semantic" interface of MuRET (figure 2.6) to include details regarding the *perfect*, *imperfect*, and *altered* quality of the notes, as well as the *addition* or *division* function of the dots.[35] These details are needed to convey the correct duration of the notes in order to score up the voices correctly. MuRET will soon incorporate the Mensural Scoring-Up Tool as a plug-in to automatically interpret the note duration in triple meter movements.[36] MuRET's Semantic interface provides a table indexing the symbols recognized in a particular staff (figure 2.6). The user can edit this table to provide semantic information about the symbols (this is, the perfect / imperfect / altered quality of the notes and the addition / division functionality of the dots) provided that the user is familiar with the **smens encoding shown in the table, a variation of the **mens encoding.[37]

The mensural scores obtained from MuRET are encoded into Mensural MEI files. MEI was chosen as the encoding format because it provides support for mensural notation. The translation of these mensural scores into

Figure 2.6. MuRET's Semantic interface. Here the user can provide information regarding the semantics of the symbols rather than just the graphical information provided by the symbol recognition model.

modern values was performed with the Mensural MEI Score to CMN MEI Score Translation Tool.³⁸ The modern transcriptions are encoded on another flavor of MEI for encoding common Western music notation, the CMN MEI. The music encoded in both MEI files (the one encoding the mensural score and the one encoding the modern transcription) can be displayed and played back through the Verovio MEI Viewer.³⁹ The next section shows examples of the mensural and modern scores generated in this project as rendered by Verovio, together with a discussion of the advantages of music encoding.

BENEFITS OF DIGITIZATION AND OMR

Digitization of the choirbook resulted in full-color high-resolution images that provide high-quality access to the music of this manuscript. In appendix A, one can find four images corresponding to the 31v–33r folios of GuatC 1, which contain the Kyrie movement of the *Missa sine nomine* by Palestrina (concordant with that of the 1567 *Missarum liber secundus*, RISM A/I P 660); these are examples of the images produced during digitization. Examples of the symbolic scores obtained at the end of the OMR and Scoring-up processes are shown in figure 2.7 (in mensural values) and figure 2.8 (in modern values) as rendered by Verovio. These scores show only the second Kyrie, corresponding to the folios 32v–33r. For the complete Kyrie movement, see appendix B.

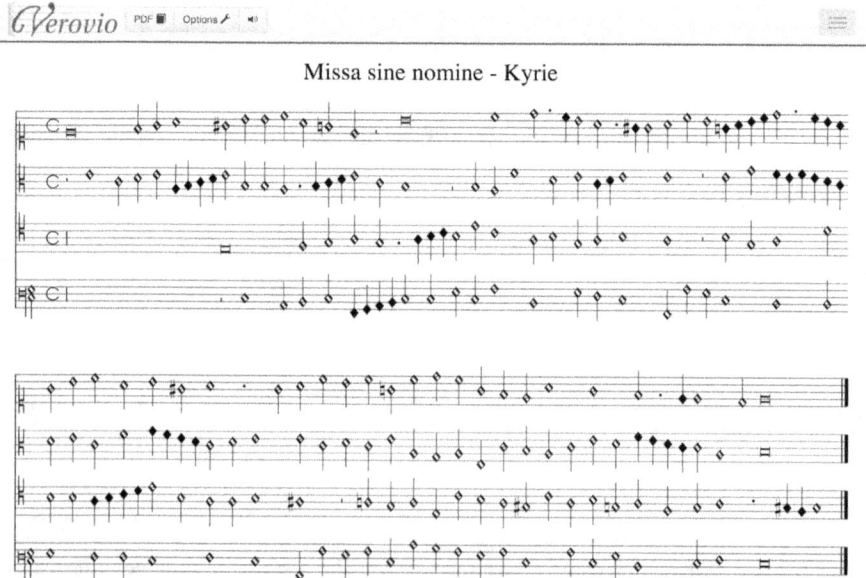

Figure 2.7. Verovio rendering of the Mensural MEI file encoding the second Kyrie of Palestrina's *Missa sine nomine* Kyrie movement as appears in GuatC 1 folios 32v–33r (images can be found in appendix A).

The Guatemalan Choirbooks

Figure 2.8. Verovio rendering of the CMN MEI file encoding the modern transcription of the second Kyrie of Palestrina's *Missa sine nomine* Kyrie movement as it appears in GuatC 1 folios 32v–33r (images can be found in appendix A). This file was obtained from the Mensural MEI score (figure 2.7) encoding the same passage, with the Mensural MEI Score to CMN MEI Score Translator.

The clear advantage of both the mensural and the modern score is the visualization of vertical sonorities, which are not available in the choirbook layout of the original source, and the possibility of playback, which makes the music accessible to a broader audience. The Verovio MEI Viewer includes a speaker button to play the encoded music in both Mensural and CMN MEI files (see figure 2.7 and figure 2.8, top left corner), together with a button for exporting the score into a PDF.

The main benefit of a modern transcription, though, is that it allows modern musicians to perform the music (figure 2.8). On the other hand, mensural scores have their own benefits as well (figure 2.7). While a mensural score shows the vertical alignment of the voices, it does so without any loss of information due to translation of the music into modern values, providing a better source for musicological studies than a modern transcription.[40]

Symbolic files encoding the scores offer other advantages over mere digital images. Because these files are machine readable, the computer can extract a wide variety of information from them useful for music analysis. There are many tools developed for empirical symbolic music research (for example, music21, Humdrum, jSymbolic, and the VIS Framework).[41]

Feature-extraction software, such as jSymbolic, can extract quantitative information associated with a wide range of musical characteristics (including pitch statistics, melodic intervals, vertical intervals, rhythm, instrumentation, texture, and dynamics). The extracted features can be used to train the computer to classify music into different categories (for example, classify music by composer, genre, style, or region).[42] Symbolic files have been used for counterpoint studies as well, with the help of the Vertical Interval Successions (VIS) Music Analysis Framework. In these studies, the VIS Framework is used to extract successions of vertical intervals (called n-grams) and use them to analyze different contrapuntal aspects.[43] In the present study, the VIS Framework was used to facilitate the detection of counterpoint errors in the recognized pieces (see rounded boxes in figure 2.8).[44] An additional error was found in the Christe section of the Kyrie, as will be seen shortly.

Another benefit of symbolic music is that it facilitates the comparison of variant readings in versions of a piece found in different sources. The Palestrina *Missa sine nomine* in GuatC 1 is concordant with the third mass of the 1567 *Missarum liber secundus* (RISM A/I P 660).[45] The movements of the *Missa sine nomine* in RISM A/I P 660 have been encoded into **kern files, which can be found in the ELVIS Database.[46] These **kern files are easily convertible into CMN MEI files. Current technologies for comparing two sources in MEI require lots of cleaning up to remove "noisy" information in the coding. Still, they do show where the differences between the two files are, which significantly reduces the amount of work because one can go right to those sections rather than going through each note of the movement. Future work will make these comparison techniques more efficient and automate the cleanup of the MEI files before comparison.

Examples of this comparison process for the Kyrie movement of the *Missa sine nomine*, between GuatC 1 and the RISM A/I P 660 sources, are shown in figure 2.9. The first Kyrie is nearly identical in both sources, except for two accidentals shown in figure 2.9a. The actual difference between the movements starts at the end of the Christe section, where GuatC 1 has extra notes (see figure 2.9b and figure 2.10). Using the VIS Framework, we can detect that there is a mistake in measure 32 of GuatC 1 Christe because the F in the bass is dissonant against the E and G in the soprano and alto respectively. It is possible that the penultimate measure in the bass should have been C F (rather than F C). This way, the chord formed at the beginning of measure 32 in GuatC 1 would be the same as the one shown in measure 32 of RISM A/I P 660 (see figure 2.10). In addition to these variant readings in the first two sections, Kyrie 2 is entirely different in both sources. The second Kyrie in RISM A/I P 660 is a repetition of the first one, while the second Kyrie in GuatC 1 is completely new. Both Kyrie sections can be seen in figure 2.16

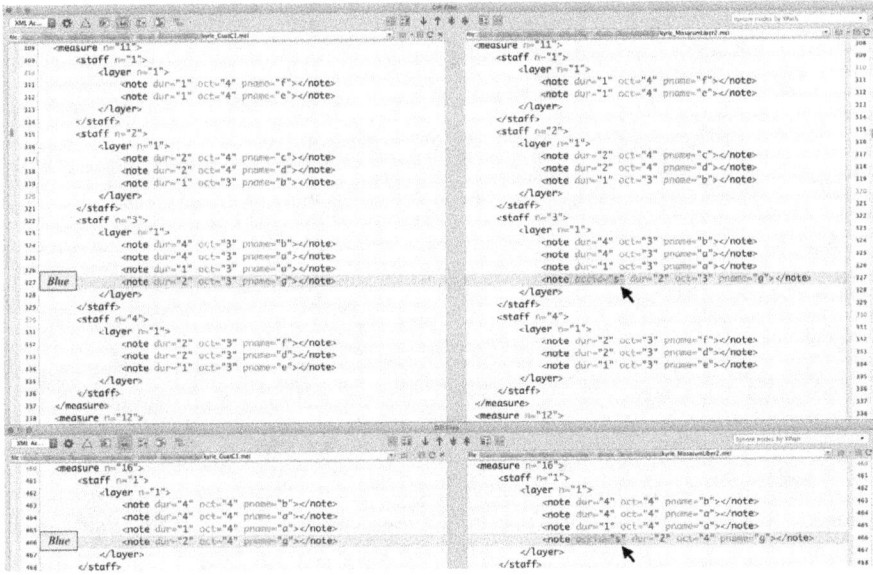

Figure 2.9a.

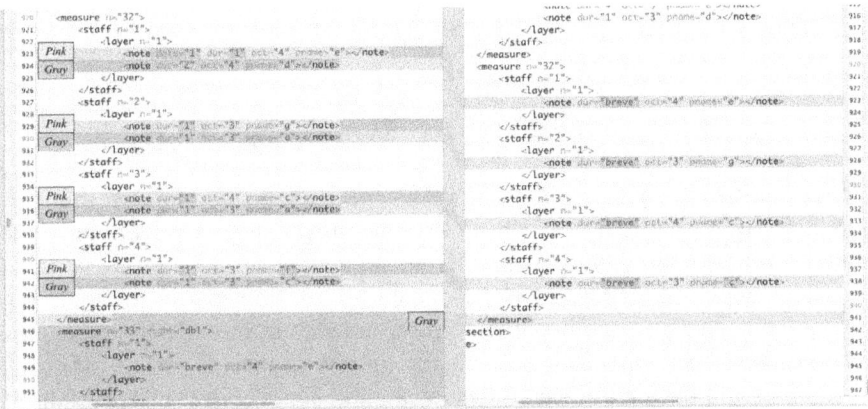

Figure 2.9b.
Comparison of the CMN MEI files obtained from the OMR of GuatC 1 (left) and the ELVIS Database **kern file encoding the *Missa sine nomine* from the *Missarum liber* 2 (*right*). The comparison was made using the "Diff files" application from Oxygen. Diff uses blue to indicate an addition on the right side, gray to indicate an addition on the left side, and pink to identify modifications on either side. (a) Extra accidental in the *Missarum liber* 2 at measure 11 and 16 (see highlighted accid="s"). (b) Ending of the Christe section. Measure 32 has similar notes but with different durations, and measure 33 only exists for GuatC 1. These differences can be visualized in figure 2.10, where the music at the end of the Christe section is displayed.

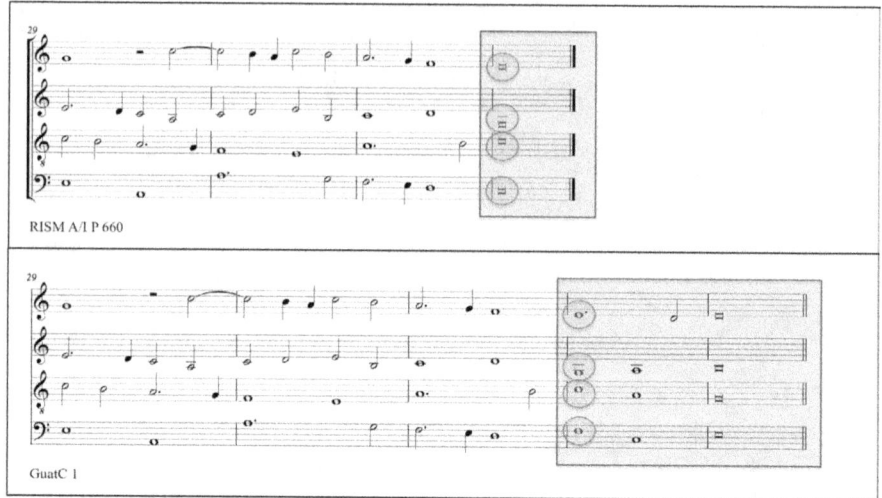

Figure 2.10. Ending of the Christe section of the Kyrie movement in Palestrina's *Missa sine nomine*.

(appendix B). Kyrie 1, the same in both sources, is shown in measures 1–17, and the new Kyrie 2 is in measures 34–51.

CONCLUDING REMARKS

Online digitization platforms are opening the music collections of archives and libraries to a global audience. Digital images are, however, only the start of true accessibility because the music content of these images cannot be searched by a computer. Optical music recognition makes the most out of these images by encoding their music content into a machine-readable representation. This makes it possible to search and analyze images of music documents online, dramatically increasing the accessibility and usefulness of digital collections. Moreover, software for automatic transcription of early music into modern values facilitates the publishing of modern editions, increasing access to early music. The advantages of these music-encoding technologies have been shown in this essay using one of the Guatemalan choirbooks.

The set of six choirbooks from the Guatemala cathedral documents a continuous performance tradition of sacred polyphonic music from the Renaissance until the end of the eighteenth century. I digitized and encoded the contents of the first choirbook (GuatC 1) to guarantee the preservation of the manuscript and increase access to its contents. The images obtained in this project offer high-quality access to the manuscript source, and the symbolic files (obtained through optical music recognition and automatic scoring up of the individual parts) increase access to the music itself by allowing for playback, modern transcriptions of the pieces, and performance. The symbolic files also allow for computational analysis of the repertoire, facilitating the comparison of variant readings and the study of counterpoint. Therefore, in addition to preservation and increasing access to the music, the encoding of the Guatemalan choirbooks can contribute to study the transmission of music from Europe to Latin America.

I plan to use the lessons learned in this pilot project to improve my procedures and technologies and to apply them to the complete choirbook collection. All the tools I used are open access (see the "Further Reading" section) for use by other scholars and musicians who want to rescue and preserve other forgotten repertories.[47]

MANUSCRIPT AND PRINTED SOURCES

GuatC 1

- [Census Catalogue of Music] Guatemala. Guatemala City. Catedral, Archivo Capitular. *MS 1.*
- [Signature, current location] Guatemala. Guatemala City. Archivo Histórico Arquidiocesano de Guatemala (AHAG). *Archivo de la catedral de Santiago de Guatemala. Sección litúrgica, libro de misas 1602–1760.*
- Other sigla: GCA-Gc 1

RISM A/I P 660

Palestrina, Giovanni Pierluigi da. Missarum liber secundus. Rome: Dorico, Valerio, eredi and Luigi Dorico, eredi. 1567. Print.

APPENDIX A: EXAMPLES OF THE IMAGES OBTAINED FROM GUATC 1

Kyrie movement of Palestrina's *Missa sine nomine a 4* as appearing in GuatC 1, folios 31v–33r.

Figure 2.11.

Figure 2.12.

Figure 2.13.

Figure 2.14.

APPENDIX B: EXAMPLES OF THE SYMBOLIC FILES OBTAINED

Figure 2.15. Mensural score of the complete Kyrie movement (folios 31v–33r) of Palestrina's *Missa sine nomine* as appearing in GuatC 1, as encoded in the Mensural MEI file obtained from the OMR and Scoring-up processes. Each system shows each of the three sections of the Kyrie: the first Kyrie, the Christe, and the second Kyrie.

Figure 2.16. Modern transcription of the complete Kyrie movement of Palestrina's *Missa sine nomine* in GuatC 1, as encoded in the CMN MEI file obtained from the Mensural MEI score (figure 2.15). The first Kyrie is mm. 1–17, the Christe is mm. 18–33, and the second Kyrie is mm. 34–51.

Figure 2.16. *(Continued)*

Figure 2.16. *(Continued)*

NOTES

1. The main city changed place in 1776. The city moved from Santiago de los Caballeros de Guatemala (now Antigua Guatemala) to the Nueva Guatemala de la Asunción (now Guatemala city, its current location).
2. Only choirbooks 1, 3, and 5 have pieces added in the eighteenth century. Half of the masses of GuatC 1 (copied in 1760–1765) come from a *Libro de Kyries* from 1602. GuatC 2 was copied in 1606. GuatC 3 and 5 were copied by different scribes during the mid-seventeenth to the mid-eighteenth centuries. GuatC 4 was copied in 1605. And GuatC 6 was probably copied during the first half of the seventeenth century.
3. Archivo Histórico Arquidiocesano de Guatemala, "Francisco de Paula García Peláez," located within the Palacio Arzobispal (7ª avenida 6-21 zona 1) next to the Metropolitan Cathedral.
4. Inventories: David Pujol, "Polifonía española desconocida conservada en el Archivo Capitular de la Catedral de Guatemala y de la Iglesia parroquial de Santa Eulalia de Jacaltenango," *Anuario Musical* 20 (1965): 3–10; Robert Stevenson, *Renaissance and Baroque Musical Sources in the Americas* (Washington, DC: General Secretariat, Organization of American States, 1970), 65–71; Robert Snow, "A New-World Collection of Polyphony for Holy Week and the Salve Service: Guatemala City, Cathedral Archive, Music MS 4," in *Monuments of Renaissance Music 9* (Chicago: University of Chicago Press, 1996), 25–26. Overview: Omar Morales Abril, "Música local y música foránea en los libros de polifonía de las Catedrales de Guatemala y México," *Jahrbuch für Renaissancemusik* 14 (2015): 95–124.
5. Transcriptions include Dieter Lehnhoff, *Música de la época colonial en Guatemala: primera antología* (Antigua Guatemala: Centro de Investigaciones Regionales Mesoamericanas, 1984); Dieter Lehnhoff, *Las misas de Pedro Bermúdez* (Guatemala City: Universidad Rafael Landívar, 2001); Dieter Lehnhoff, *Choral Music from Guatemala: For SATB Choir* (Niedernhausen: Edition Kemel, 2008); Omar Morales, Jorge Pellecer, Igor de Gandarias, and Arturo Duarte, *Missa de bomba a 4: Guatemala, siglo XVI* (2001); Omar Morales Abril, "'Jesu nostra redemptio,' himno de vísperas para la Ascensión, de Pedro Bermúdez," *Heterofonía: revista de investigación musical*, no. 129 (2003): 109–27. Recordings include Dieter Lehnhoff, conductor, Ensemble Millennium, and Schola Cantorum, compact disc "Coros de Catedral," in *Música Histórica de Guatemala*, Vol. 2 (Guatemala: Fundación para la Cultura y el Desarrollo, 1995), HGG20394CD.
6. **kern is an encoding format that provides support for common Western music notation.
7. Thomas Christian Schmidt, Christian Thomas Leitmeir, and J. P. Gumbert, *The Production and Reading of Music Sources: Mise-En-Page in Manuscripts and Printed Books Containing Polyphonic Music, 1480–1530* (Turnhout: Brepols, 2018), 32–34.
8. Pujol, "Polifonía," 3–10; Stevenson, *Renaissance*, 65–71; and Snow, "A New-World," 25–26.
9. Snow, "A New-World," ix.

10. Morales Abril, "Música local," 97.
11. Ibid.
12. See the "Further Reading" section.
13. Alfred Lemmon, "Toward an International Inventory of Colonial Spanish American Cathedral Music Archives," *Revista de Musicología* 16, no. 1 (1993): 92–98.
14. Morales Abril, "Música local," 115. While it was previously believed that Fernández was born in Évora (Portugal), in "Gaspar Fernández: su vida y obras como testimonio de la cultura musical novohispana a principios del siglo XVII" (see the "Further Reading" section), Morales Abril has provided evidence that Guatemala's chapelmaster and Évora's Gaspar Fernandes are two different people. The de Quirós brothers, identified as such in the header of the GuatC 3 *Sancta Maria Succurre* piece, were both born in Guatemala as well (see the "Further Reading" entries for Lemmon and Stevenson). Finally, Juan José Guerrero and Juan Matías de Rivera are identified as "criollo" and "indigeneous" respectively in their corresponding entries on the Books of Hispanic Polyphony website (see the "Further Reading" section).
15. Centro de Rescate, Estudios y Análisis Científico del Arte (CREA, Center for Restoration, Study, and Scientific Analysis of the Art Work), https://fundacionrozasbotran.org/cultura-y-arte/crea/, a nonprofit organization focused on the conservation and restoration of Guatemalan religious heritage.
16. The information in table 2.2 comes from the index page of GuatC 1 (which separates the twelve masses into two groups, the ones copied from the *Libro de Kyries* and the newly added ones) and the inventories by Pujol, "Polifonía," 4; Stevenson, *Renaissance*, 65–71; Snow, "A New-World," 25–26; and Morales Abril (unpublished). Most information regarding genre was obtained from Pujol, although he divides piece 21 into two invitatories (*Surrexit Dominus vere* and *Alleluia, alleluia, alleluia*) and identifies piece 26 as the motet *Agnus redemit*. The latter has been corrected by Snow to *Dic nobis Maria* from *Victimae paschali laudes*, which is a sequence. The composer attribution comes from Morales Abril. Information regarding the folios and number of voices has been doubled checked against the manuscript.
17. Snow, "A New-World," 19.
18. Ibid.
19. The microfilms are held at the archive of the Centro de Investigaciones Regionales de Mesoamérica (CIRMA) in Antigua Guatemala, Guatemala. CIRMA made them in 1984 with the authorization of the chancellor of the Ecclesiastical Curia, Monsignor Efraín Hernández (Thelma Porres, director of CIRMA's historical archive, email communication, March 2020). Guatemalan musicologist Dieter Lehnhoff conducted the microfilming process, starting in June 1984, with staff and equipment provided by William Swezey, current director of CIRMA. This is according to Dieter Lehnhoff, *Rafael Antonio Castellanos: vida y obra de un músico guatemalteco* (Guatemala: Universidad Rafael Landívar, 1994), 3–4. According to the Música Colonial Archive (http://www3.cpdl.org/wiki/index.php/Música_Colonial_Archive), the microfilms were borrowed from CIRMA and brought momentarily to the Miami University Libraries in 2002. Here the microfilms were digitized into TIFF files in 2003, and they were then converted into DjVu files in 2004 to be shared online. These DjVu files can be consulted at http://conan.lib.miamioh.edu/musica/data/. The files belong-

ing to the ninth reel (starting with the number "9") are the ones corresponding to the GuatC choirbooks. Selected items from the microfilms have been transcribed into modern scores and are available in the Choral Public Domain Library "Música colonial scores" site (http://www0.cpdl.org/wiki/index.php/Category:Música_colonial_scores). Unsurprisingly, because the GuatC 1 choirbook is well preserved, many of its pieces have been transcribed. Ten out of its twelve masses can be found in the CPDL Música colonial scores website (missing only 7 and 12 from table 2.2), together with four out of its fifteen short pieces (corresponding to numbers 18, 20, 22, and 25 from table 2.2).

20. Perry Roland, Andrew Hankinson, and Laurent Pugin, "Early Music and the Music Encoding Initiative," *Early Music* 42, no. 4 (2014): 605–11.

21. Federal Agencies Digital Guidelines Initiative, "Technical Guidelines for Digitizing Cultural Heritage Materials: Creation of Raster Image Files," 2016, http://www.digitizationguidelines.gov/guidelines/FADGI%20Federal%20%20Agencies%20Digital%20Guidelines%20Initiative-2016%20Final_rev1.pdf.

22. The book cradle was built by German Thomae (my father) in Guatemala, the camera was borrowed from the Marvin Duchow Music Library at McGill University, and the lights were borrowed from the Distributed Digital Music Archives and Libraries (DDMAL) Lab, also at McGill University. The camera allowed for an image resolution of 300ppi, an adequate archival resolution value (consistent with a three-star FADGI project). For more details on DIY book scanners, see the "Further Reading" section.

23. DIAMM, https://www.diamm.ac.uk; BANQ, http://www.banq.qc.ca/accueil/; McGill Library's Digitization Lab, https://www.mcgill.ca/library/services/research/digitization.

24. "Technical Overview," DIAMM, accessed February 25, 2019, https://www.diamm.ac.uk/about/technical-overview/.

25. Special thanks to Jessica Régimbald (conservator at the direction du dépôt légal et de la conservation des collections patrimoniales), Marie-Chantal Anctil (coordinator of the section de la reproduction et des ateliers audiovisuels and direction de la numérisation), and Michel Legendre (photographer of the direction de la numérisation and section de la reproduction).

26. Special thanks to Gregory Houston (New Media and Digitization Administrator of the Digital Initiatives Department, McGill Library).

27. Finale and Sibelius include their own OMR software.

28. The tool, developed by Laurent Pugin, can be accessed at http://www.aruspix.net. See the "Further Reading" section.

29. See the "Further Reading" section.

30. For the CMN model, see the "Further Reading" section.

31. Jorge Calvo-Zaragoza, Alejandro H. Toselli, and Enrique Vidal, "Handwritten Music Recognition for Mensural Notation with Convolutional Recurrent Neural Networks," *Pattern Recognition Letters* 128 (2019): 115–21.

32. See the "Further Reading" section.

33. The page-level model has also been used with Spanish mensural notation. Still, I decided on using the staff-level model instead because, although a model that works

at the page level makes the classification process more efficient, it is more susceptible to errors, prolonging the time invested in correcting the results.

34. MuRET was introduced in David Rizo, Jorge Calvo-Zaragoza, and José M. Iñesta, "MuRET: A Music Recognition, Encoding, and Transcription Tool," in *Proceedings of the 5th International Conference on Digital Libraries for Musicology* (Paris: ACM, 2018), 52–56. The tool can be accessed at https://muret.dlsi.ua.es/muret/#/. Currently, it requires log-in credentials that can be provided by its developer, David Rizo.

35. The *punctus additionis* (dot of addition) and *punctus divisionis* (dot of division) have different functions in mensural notation. A dot of addition behaves like a common dotted note; it adds half the value to the original length of a note. A dot of division is used in triple meter to divide the notes into perfect groupings; this division changes the interpretation of some notes.

36. This tool is introduced in Martha E. Thomae, Julie E. Cumming, and Ichiro Fujinaga, "The Mensural Scoring-Up Tool," in *Proceedings of the 6th International Workshop on Digital Libraries for Musicology* (The Hague: ACM, 2019), 9–19. The source code is available at https://github.com/ELVIS-Project/scoring-up.

37. The **mens encoding was introduced in David Rizo, Nieves Pascual León, and Craig Stuart Sapp, "White Mensural Manual Encoding: From Humdrum to MEI," *Cuadernos de Investigación Musical*, no. 6 (2018): 373–93. The specifications of this format can be found at http://doc.verovio.humdrum.org/humdrum/mens/.

38. Source code available at https://github.com/DDMAL/Mensural_MEI_Score_to_CMN_MEI_Score.

39. The Verovio MEI Viewer can be found at https://www.verovio.org/mei-viewer.xhtml. Verovio is a music notation engraving library developed by Laurent Pugin.

40. Examples of information that can be lost in a modern transcription are the use of dots of division and the difference between an imperfect note and an altered note of the next smaller degree.

41. Music21, https://web.mit.edu/music21/; Humdrum, https://www.humdrum.org; jSymbolic, http://jmir.sourceforge.net/jSymbolic.html; VIS Framework, https://vis-framework.readthedocs.io/en/v3.0.5/.

42. jSymbolic, along with machine learning, has been used for studying composer attribution, exploring the stylistic origins of genres, and distinguishing between regional styles (such as Iberian and Franco-Flemish). For more information, see the "Further Reading" section.

43. Including stylistic change between the Ockeghem, Josquin, and Palestrina generations in the Renaissance, contrapuntal repetition on Lassus duos, and consistency between theory and practice. For more information, see the "Further Reading" section.

44. The VIS Framework can index the piece according to different events. Indexing the piece by the melodic and vertical intervals (or by 2-grams) can aid with the identification of counterpoint errors.

45. Original source at https://imslp.org/wiki/Missarum%2C_Liber_2_(Palestrina%2C_Giovanni_Pierluigi_da).

46. https://database.elvisproject.ca/piece/2309/.

47. This research has been supported by Fonds de Recherche du Québec—Société et Culture (FRQSC), Bourse au doctorat en recherche (13D - Musique) 2019-B2Z-261749. Special thanks to Professor Julie Cumming for the help in editing this essay, and to Professor Ichiro Fujinaga for his revision of the "Optical Music Recognition" section.

FURTHER READING

Computational Music Analysis

Antila, Christopher, and Julie Cumming. "The VIS Framework: Analyzing Counterpoint in Large Datasets." In *Proceedings of the 15th International Society for Music Information Retrieval Conference (ISMIR)*, Taipei, Taiwan, 2014, 71–76.

Cumming, Julie, and Cory McKay. "Revisiting the Origins of the Italian Madrigal." Paper presented at the Medieval and Renaissance Music Conference (MedRen), Maynooth University, Maynooth, Ireland, July 2018. http://jmir.sourceforge.net/publications/cumming18revisiting.pdf.

McKay, Cory. "Performing Statistical Musicological Research Using JSymbolic and Machine Learning." Paper presented at the International Conference on the Anatomy of Polyphonic Music around 1500, Cascais, Portugal, June 2018.

McKay, Cory, Julie Cumming, and Ichiro Fujinaga. "Characterizing Composers Using JSymbolic2 Features." In *Extended Abstracts for the Late-Breaking Demo Session of the 18th International Society for Music Information Retrieval Conference*, Suzhou, China, 2017. http://jmir.sourceforge.net/publications/mckay17characterizing.pdf.

McKay, Cory, Tristano Tenaglia, Julie Cumming, and Ichiro Fujinaga. "Using Statistical Feature Extraction to Distinguish the Styles of Different Composers." In *Abstracts of the Annual International Medieval and Renaissance Music Conference (MedRen)*, Prague, Czech Republic, 2017. http://jmir.sourceforge.net/publications/mckay17using.pdf.

Morgan, Alexander. "Renaissance Interval-Succession Theory: Treatises and Analysis." PhD Diss., McGill University, 2017.

Schubert, Peter, and Julie Cumming. "Another Lesson from Lassus: Using Computers to Analyse Counterpoint." *Early Music* 43, no. 4 (2015): 577–86.

Musicology

Gembero Ustárroz, María. "El compositor español Hernando Franco (1532–85) antes de su llegada a México: Trayectoria profesional en Portugal, Santo Domingo, Cuba y Guatemala." *Latin American Music Review* 26, no. 2 (2005): 273–317.

Lemmon, Alfred E. "Las obras musicales de dos compositores guatemaltecos del siglo XVIII: Rafael Antonio Castellanos y Manuel José de Quiroz." *Mesoamérica* 5, no. 8 (1984): 389–401.

Morales Abril, Omar. "Características de estilo en la obra de Pedro Bermúdez (fl. 1574–1604)." *Revista de Musicología* 30, no. 2 (2007): 343–91. https://doi.org/10.2307/20797891.

Morales Abril, Omar. "Gaspar Fernández: su vida y obras como testimonio de la cultura musical novohispana a principios del siglo XVII." In *Enseñanza y ejercicio de la música en México*, edited by Arturo Camacho Becerra, 71–125. México, DF: CIESAS, El Colegio de Jalisco y Universidad de Guadalajara, 2013.

Stevenson, Robert. "Guatemala Cathedral to 1803." *Inter-American Music Review* 2, no. 2 (1980): 27–71.

Optical Music Recognition

Calvo-Zaragoza, Jorge, and David Rizo. "End-to-End Neural Optical Music Recognition of Monophonic Scores." *Applied Sciences* 8, no. 4 (2018): 606.

Dalitz, Christophe, and Thomas Karsten. "Using the Gamera Framework for Building a Lute Tablature Recognition System." In *Proceedings of the 6th International Conference on Music Information Retrieval (ISMIR)*, London, UK, 2005, 478–81.

Droettboom, Michael, Karl MacMillan, and Ichiro Fujinaga. "The Gamera Framework for Building Custom Recognition Systems." In *Symposium on Document Image Understanding Technologies*, 2003, 275–86.

Hankinson, Andrew. "Optical Music Recognition Infrastructure for Large-Scale Music Document Analysis." PhD Diss., McGill University, 2014.

Pacha, Alexander, and Jorge Calvo-Zaragoza. "Optical Music Recognition in Mensural Notation with Region-Based Convolutional Neural Networks." In *Proceedings of the 19th International Society for Music Information Retrieval Conference (ISMIR)*, Paris, France, 2018, 23–27.

Pugin, Laurent, and Tim Crawford. "Evaluating OMR on the Early Music Online Collection." In *Proceedings of the 14th International Society for Music Information Retrieval Conference (ISMIR)*, Curitiba, Brazil, 2013, 439–44.

Online Resources

Marín-López, Javier. "Guerrero, Juan José." In Books of Hispanic Polyphony, edited by E. Ros-Fábregas, accessed December 4, 2019, https://hispanicpolyphony.eu/person/24640.

Marín-López, Javier. "Mathías Ribera, Juan." In Books of Hispanic Polyphony, edited by E. Ros-Fábregas, accessed December 10, 2019, https://hispanicpolyphony.eu/person/24266.

DIY Book Scanner. "Book Scanner Rigs." https://www.diybookscanner.org/en/index.html.

Tools Used

MuRET (Music Recognition Encoding and Transcription) Online Framework, https://muret.dlsi.ua.es/muret/#/.

Mensural Scoring-up Tool, https://github.com/ELVIS-Project/scoring-up.

Mensural MEI Score to CMN MEI Score Translation Tool, https://github.com/DDMAL/Mensural_MEI_Score_to_CMN_MEI_Score.

VIS (Vertical Interval Successions) Music Analysis Framework, https://vis-framework.readthedocs.io/en/v3.0.5/#.

Verovio MEI Viewer, https://www.verovio.org/mei-viewer.xhtml.

II
HYMNOLOGY

Chapter Three

Sweet Harmonies of Praise

Reviving Shape-Note Singing in Rural Arkansas

S. Andrew Granade

It was a dark, muggy, muddy Tuesday evening. An early spring shower had reduced the dirt road leading to Sweet Home Primitive Baptist Church to a dark smear that soaked up headlights. The stream of cars arriving that night had no recourse but to rely on the taillights in front of them for direction. As they pulled onto the church grounds, members of both the community and the Pittman family parked haphazardly on concrete, rock, or grass. They climbed from their vehicles, taking care not to lose their footing on the slick ground. The stream of cars turned into a stream of people, and the small church was soon filled with the sound of neighbors and relatives greeting one another and visitors from nearby Mount Ida and Arkadelphia. They exchanged stories and proudly displayed pictures while the group swelled to near fifty and the people worked their way to a seat in one of the wooden pews.

My invitation to the Sweet Home Group came from Orene Pittman, and I slid into a pew next to Orene and her family in the warm and inviting church. Every inch of the space was covered in wood from ceiling fans buzzing overhead to the rich oak paneling on the walls and oak pews lining the narrow space. Except for red songbooks stacked at the end of each pew and a wooden cross hanging at the front, no decoration of any kind, no fabric dampened or soaked up the sound of voices laughing and talking. A few minutes after 7:00 p.m., Mt. Ida Primitive Baptist Church pastor Tim Montgomery stood and walked to the front of the one-room church. He smiled at a few of the people seated in the front pews, particularly at the Pittman patriarch Orene, called out a hymn number, and began to sing, "do, do, do - mi - sol - mi - do." Across the room, various people began to sing with him on the tonic arpeggio but in different octaves. Satisfied that the key was firmly established, Pastor Tim launched into "Once More We Come Before Our God." After a few beats, the entire congregation was singing along in four-part harmony with a boisterous, uninhibited sound.

At the song's end, after a scattering of "Amens" from those gathered, Pastor Tim began: "I'm so thankful that, on behalf of the Alpine Sweet Home Church, I appreciate your presence here tonight. I'm so thankful for this opportunity to meet together and sing praises unto our Lord and Savior. It's good to see everyone, it's good to fellowship . . . but most of all it's good to sing sweet harmonies of praise."[1]

Those "sweet harmonies of praise" resulted from the shape-note singing system employed by those gathered that evening. This seven-note system is directly descended from the four-note version that began in colonial New England often called "fasola," "Sacred Harp," or simply "shape-note singing." These names have often been used interchangeably in the literature about shape-notes for the four- and seven-note systems, and as a result many believe them to be one and the same.[2] The systems, however, are distinctive in harmony, pedagogy, and performance aesthetics.

Most available literature on revivals of shape-note singing focuses on singings from and singers of the *Sacred Harp*.[3] They ably demonstrate how Sacred Harp singing has moved out of the rural South into the Midwest and New England (primarily in urban settings), how it has moved beyond its Christian origins to become a pluralistic community brought together solely by the music, and how it has acquired the patina of a fundamentally American music. This focus on Sacred Harp singing has obscured the continued relevance and surprising tenacity of the seven-note system that arose after the *Sacred Harp*'s four-note one. And while both systems have been revived in recent years, inherent differences have determined who has revived them and for what reasons.

This essay uses Orene Pittman's Sweet Home Group in Alpine, Arkansas, described in the earlier vignette, as a case study to investigate the reasons singers across the country still gravitate toward singing shape-notes. After a discussion of shape-note singing's history and origins in Arkansas, it outlines the Sweet Home Group's history beginning with its origins in a 1969 singing school at the Sweet Home Church and the men and women involved in its continuation. Then, using Tamara Livingston's model of music revivals, it examines Sweet Home Group activities to determine if their experiences qualify as a revival, and if so, what type, and how their practices could inform how scholars view and discuss that musical phenomenon, particularly in relation to shape-note revivals.[4] Throughout, the discussion is grounded in my personal experience and interviews with the Sweet Home Group and other shape-note and Sacred Harp groups in Arkansas.

I want to begin with an overview of the seven-note shape-note system used by the Sweet Home Group. Most musicians and scholars today are familiar with the four-note shape-note system found in the *Sacred Harp*, but that system began falling out of favor in the mid-nineteenth century as music teachers began to create new systems.[5] For instance, Philadelphia music teacher Jesse B. Aikin decided that if the solfège system was going to be used in shape-note singing, it would be easier to sight-read if shapes were not repeated. In his *Christian Minstrel*, he employed triangle, half-circle, diamond, flag, oval, square, and wedge, corresponding to the full system of solfège syllables: Doe Ray Mee Faw Sole Law See (see figure 3.1). Although initially unpopular in the South, Aikin's system spread to that region as singing school teachers realized this new system's utility.[6] Within twenty years, six other compilers created songbooks using different shapes, but Aikin's proved the most popular. By 1880, almost forty years after their development, his shapes had become the standard and remain so to this day.

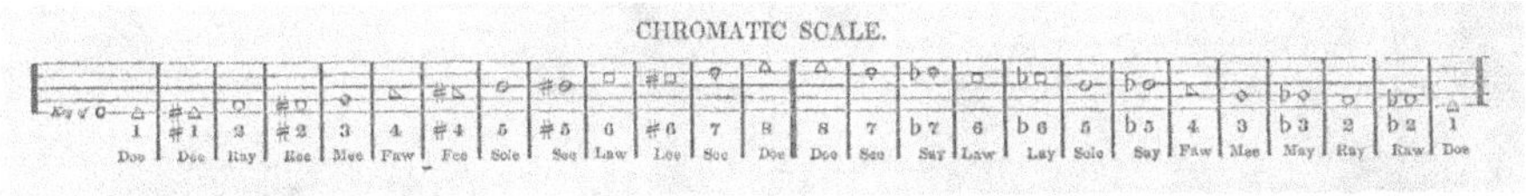

Figure 3.1. Jesse B. Aikin's seven-note system from his hymn book *Christian Minstrel*, page 27.

While the shapes and syllables sung changed, the repertoire of those seven-note hymnals remained basically the same as that found in four-note ones; the music's typeset simply altered to accommodate seven notes. Similarly, seven-note hymnals were used in the same settings as *Sacred Harp* hymnals: camp meetings, Sunday morning church services, revivals, and singing schools. Their ability to be grafted onto, then replace an existing system is what allowed the seven shapes to supplant the four quickly in the years following the Civil War.

Aikin's system of shape-notes took firm hold throughout the South, particularly among Primitive Baptists in Arkansas, Texas, and Louisiana. The use of the seven-note system by Primitive Baptists might be surprising, particularly because of the literature detailing the Original Alabama Primitive Baptist Association of Crawfordite Primitive Baptists that still meets in Hoboken, Georgia, to sing. Members of the Lee family from that association have, over the past twenty-five years, become some of the most sought-after teachers of the *Sacred Harp* style, praised for their authenticity and endlessly studied.[7] But in the western portions of the South, the seven-note system rooted deeply thanks to Elder Claudius Hopkins Cayce and his company Cayce Publishing in Thornton, Arkansas. Cayce incorporated his publishing company in 1886, and for over a century it has been the source for Primitive Baptist Church publications in the area, particularly through its hymnal, *The Good Old Songs*. First published in 1913, *The Good Old Songs* was Elder Cayce's response to the "jigs and operatic tunes" he heard sung in local churches (see figure 3.2) Keeping "tunes of the modern sort" out of his hymnal, Cayce focused instead on tunes found in the *Sacred Harp* and similar publications and on music instruction, opening his hymnal with singing school material and putting the melody in the soprano voice instead of its traditional placement in the tenor.[8]

Figure 3.2. Cover and page 75 of *The Good Old Songs*, compiled by Elder C. H. Cayce (Thornton, AR: Cayce Pub. Co., 1914).

Cayce's hymnal was so influential in the ArkLaTex region that Orene Pittman, architect of the Alpine Sweet Home Group, learned to sing from it as a small girl growing up in rural Texas in the 1920s. Although the practice basically died out in the north and west, singing schools still occurred in the southern United States sporadically through the twentieth century's early decades. The difference between these schools and their predecessors lay in the instructors. Widespread use of the seven-note system led to abandonment of the itinerant teacher model. Instead of teachers visiting a town only every three or four years, local musicians began teaching every year in a county or two.[9] Pittman grew up in the northeastern corner of Texas and was fortunate enough to live in a town that hosted a singing school every summer of her childhood. Over a three-week period, she learned the fundamentals of music theory through intervallic training, the proper style of singing and vocal production, and most importantly, the correlation between shapes printed in the hymnal and syllables often sung before a hymn during Sunday morning services. These schools had a more utilitarian focus than nineteenth-century ones, which attempted to impart a general music education. The method of teaching Orene Pittman experienced was directed toward promoting four-part harmony within the framework of congregational singing.[10]

By her teenage years, the singing school no longer took place every summer. The dissolution of the singing school of Pittman's youth was part of a trend in the late 1930s and early 1940s.[11] As the Great Depression lingered and then as the country plunged into World War II, singing schools became an unsustainable luxury. Many churches continued to use shape-note hymnals, but children were no longer instructed in the practice. By the 1950s, when the newly married Pittman followed her husband to southern Arkansas, round notes had replaced shaped ones in most branches of the Presbyterian, Methodist, and Baptist churches. Only the most rural of churches continued the shape-note practice, but even there the notes were printed on a staff complete with key signature in a paperback gospel-style hymnal.[12]

Orene Pittman and her husband settled in Alpine, a small community about five miles outside Amity, toward the county seat in Arkadelphia, Arkansas. They purchased a dogtrot-style home on a small dirt road and began an upholstery business in a converted shed in the backyard. By the mid-1960s, their business venture had grown, as had their family, with five children added in a decade and a half. They established themselves in the community at large and especially in the congregation of the local Sweet Home Primitive Baptist Church, which was just up the road and across the highway to Amity from their home.

Despite the stability that came from these establishments, Pittman felt something was lacking from her daily life. By the late 1960s, she had realized that the songs and ways of singing from her youth were what she had been missing. She began talking with community and church members about reviving the practice of shape-note singing. She discovered that most community members had grown up in singing schools and were receptive to her ideas, although they had no knowledge of how to teach the system.

Her enthusiasm undiminished, Pittman began asking friends and relatives outside of Arkansas if they knew of any singing schools still being held. She finally found the answer to her problem of reviving this tradition in J. J. Huckabee, a preacher and musician from Oklahoma whose introduction to the practice also occurred in Texas. The two of them reached an arrangement with her Sweet Home Church to host an event, and in early June of 1969, the first singing school in Alpine was held.

In conversation, Pittman was characteristically reticent about discussing her past; with a quick laugh and twinkle in her eye, she often deflected questions with a flourish, saying, "I've just fed the people to keep 'em coming; talk to them about the singing." Her flippant attitude belied the fact that she was the driving force behind shape-note singing in southern Arkansas.

Before exploring the details of how Orene Pittman revived the seven-note system in Alpine, Arkansas, I want to construct a framework through which to approach this revival. When Pittman and her daughter Elaine first related this story to me, I questioned whether or not they had created a revival because their actions do not neatly fit into the definitions of "revival" found in most of the scholarly literature. Livingston defines revivals as social movements that attempt to restore, for the benefit of contemporary society, a musical system that is believed to be disappearing.[13] These restoration attempts largely occur in urban middle-class cultures that look to a tradition outside of the one in which they were reared.[14] Those traditions are often of rural and lower-class heritage, and therefore revivals often take on a liberal veneer of educating the masses in a musical form that has been neglected through ignorance.[15] Revivals of this nature also usually have an overt political and cultural agenda of opposition to the mainstream society in which the participants operate.[16]

Examining the Sweet Home Group, I believe this standard definition roughly fits Orene Pittman's revival. Pittman started the group to restore shape-note singing to her life as an act of continuity with her childhood, where she was "making visible that which has been hidden."[17] But as she told me, "I wanted to get back to singing shape-notes for my kids; I wanted them to have what I had." In other words, the most important reason for reviving the styles was so her children would be reared not only in that singing system but also with the values she associated with it. She revived shape-note singing for the benefit of the next generation rather than contemporary society.

There is also a sense of opposition to societal norms in the Sweet Home Group's activities. They recognize that the majority of US Christians do not use shape-notes, although the extent of their knowledge of the system's history is unclear. They pride themselves on the fact that they use shape-notes and actually look down upon those who do not. They believe that singing shape-note hymns produces a sound more desirable than any other, evidenced by some of the first words Tim Montgomery spoke to me: "It may be my bias, but to me nothing is sweeter than unaccompanied four-part harmony." They view themselves as different, but this stance is not part of an agenda to create a culture opposite to and in conflict with the popular American one. Their opposition focuses only on the music because, with the exception of the way in which they sing, group members embrace the trappings of modern American consumerist society.

Once we move past these surface details, we get to the reasons I questioned if Pittman's actions were a revival and to the shortcomings in the standard definition of "revival." After studying the Sweet Home Group, I am convinced that we need to continue the work begun by recent scholarship on expanding the definition of revival by designating the activities of Pittman and her group a "renewal."[18] Although I outlined the literature's most salient features of revivals earlier, Tamara Livingston helpfully created a list of a music revival's basic ingredients that serves well in delineating what is missing from the term's current usage. Her list includes:

1. a group of core revivalists
2. the use of original sources
3. the construction of a revivalist ideology
4. the creation of a revivalist community bound together by the music
5. the organization of revivalist activities such as conventions and festivals
6. a commercial and/or nonprofit enterprise that creates a revivalist marketing group.[19]

Weigh this list against the Sweet Home singers: Pittman and Huckabee constitute a group of core revivalists. They use original sources (their hymnal).[20] The singing schools are taught in the same manner as when Pittman was growing up, and they work to achieve a sound influenced by "the way it's always been sung." A community has definitely been established around this group and the church, one bound together by music and a shared faith, and they hold revivalist activities in the singing schools and monthly sings outside of worship services.

Similarly, Bithell and Hill note that "revivals are often set in motion by individuals or clearly defined groups who are partial outsiders to the chosen tradition rather than core culture-bearers."[21] They identify four "motivational categories" for revival activity: dissatisfaction with elements of modern society; strengthening the identity of a group people, especially in opposition to other groups; political activism; and as a result to natural disasters or tragedies that have ripped away musical practices.[22] Adding these categories to Livingston's ingredients provides a fairly comprehensive overview of what features scholars point to as necessarily in labeling a movement a "revival."

Most of those revivalist features are present in the Sweet Home Group, but there is a disconnect in the larger implications of current revival definitions. The Sweet Home Group is firmly middle class and Pittman made a definite decision with her choice of shape-note singing, but opposition to the mainstream and, even beyond that, exoticization inherent in the appropriation of cultures in most revivals are not evident.²³ Separation from the tradition one is attempting to revive is also not evident in the Sweet Home Group. The complete opposite is actually the case. Instead of searching for a musical culture that was unknown yet attractive, Pittman yearned to return to the system in which she had been reared and to provide those same experiences for her children. In reviving shape-note singing, Pittman was looking to her own cultural heritage.

I would argue that examining this form of music revival, what I'm calling a renewal of a music from within a musical culture, brings two immediate benefits. The first is a more complete understanding of the meanings of revivals to participants. Once we examine which traditions are renewed within their original cultures, and how, we will better see which elements of a musical culture hold value for the group that created them.

The second benefit is an alteration in use of the word "revival" itself. By examining renewals of a music in its original culture and focusing our attention on what remains instead of what changes, music revivals traditionally studied are seen as transformations of tradition rather than revivals of them.²⁴ Indeed, acknowledging that music traditions are not static, these revivals can best be described as a transformative reenergizing of a remembered tradition. This semantic shift allows for transformative revivals to be considered traditions unto themselves. Alterations made to the original tradition through this process then become normative steps instead of destruction of the musical culture's purity. Likewise, notions of authenticity become notions of authenticity to the transformed musical culture rather than to ideas of purity projected upon the original one.

It is therefore useful to examine how the Sweet Home Group revived their musical heritage as an example of a renewal of a music from within its culture. The key to any discussion of Orene Pittman's motivations for revival is her religious faith, so we begin there.

Pittman and her husband are members of the Primitive Baptist Church, a denomination that formed in 1826 and continues to thrive in Southern and rural communities.²⁵ As Primitive Baptists do not practice evangelism, new converts are rare, and the church subsists primarily by family replenishment of the congregation—creating a closed community. Because they do not believe in an educated clergy, no educational institutions have been created to serve its members, and the denomination's name is little known outside of the areas in which it operates.

In one of the few studies of the Primitive Baptist faith, Brett Sutton explicates hymn singing's central role in Primitive Baptist life.²⁶ Always distrustful of change, the church long sang out of the hymnals first created when the denomination was founded. These hymnals contained no music, only text. On

Sunday mornings, congregants sang familiar melodies slowly and in union without any musical accompaniment, and even though most of the tunes were taken from the four-part hymns used in shape-note songbooks of the period, use of shape-notes was sporadic. Primitive Baptists sang to focus on the words, and every aspect of their singing reflected this motivation. Not until the early twentieth century, around the time a young Orene Pittman began attending, did the singing school institution slowly begin making its way into the lives of Primitive Baptists. Soon the old hymnals gave way to shape-note songbooks and publishing companies like Cayce Publishing emerged to meet the demand. Still tied tightly to their tradition, communicants sang the songs in four-part harmony without musical accompaniment. These songs became part of Primitive Baptist life in and outside the church, as followers sang them while at work, at impromptu gatherings in members' homes, and even to the sick as they lay dying.[27]

In this dynamic context, Orene Pittman learned to sing. The songs and faith upon which they were based pervaded every aspect of her life. When she moved to Arkansas, she naturally continued her involvement in the denomination through the Sweet Home Church. It was also natural for her to feel something amiss when she discovered that, although the church used a shape-note hymnal, they sang in unaccompanied unison rather than four-part harmony, a throwback to the denomination's earliest years. The dissolution of singing schools over the previous decades had produced a dearth of musical literacy and the congregation could not sing in four parts even had they so desired.

In the context of this history, Pittman, along with J. J. Huckabee as teacher, renewed the practice of shape-note singing in Alpine, Arkansas. In structuring the school, Pittman drew from her own experiences in singing school forty years earlier, her knowledge of children based on rearing her own, her understanding of the community in which the school would take place, and Huckabee's recommendations. The format has proven so successful that, over forty years later, the school is still held every summer during the first week in June.

To begin with, Pittman reduced the school's length from the three-week norm of the first part of the twentieth century to five days.[28] All involved felt that three weeks would prove too large a time commitment and might discourage potential participants. The five days were then given over completely to the singing school instead of it taking place primarily in the evenings as in the past.

The school's schedule remains the same today as in those early years. Mornings begin with breakfast taken at the home, then a three-hour class lasting until lunchtime. Following lunch, classes reconvene for another three-hour session, ending at supper. After an evening meal, often taken together and often at Pittman's home, the church hosts a general sing. During the final night of the school, the teacher asks each class to come down to the front of the church and demonstrate what they have learned. Younger children sing simple songs on solfège syllables in two-part harmony. Older children and teenagers lead a few congregational hymns and demonstrate their new abilities by singing more complex fuging tunes, first on the syllables and then with the words, always in four-part harmony.

Classes are divided not by experience but by age. Elaine Funderburk recalled that this was a conscious choice to break with the traditional method of creating classes based on previous knowledge. In the past, entire families attended so children's attendance was compulsory. Now all involved believed that with modern transportation and distraction, older children and teenagers who had never attended before would be less likely to attend if they were forced into a class with younger kids while their friends and peers were laughing in an adjacent room.

The youngest class is the most rudimentary. Children primarily learn the shapes through games and puzzles designed to help them connect the shape with the syllable assigned to it. For example, the children learn the system's seven shapes by cutting out the shapes from construction paper and then crafting a "Mr. Do," a man built entirely from those seven shapes. This knowledge is then applied to the singing of simple, largely pentatonic, hymns.

Classes for older children and adults stress the importance of independent singing, sight-reading, music theory, and the ability to lead the group. Students practice commonly used songs first by singing the syllables. Only after each part has been perfected in that manner do they add words. Frequently, students receive music sheets for songs they have never encountered, with instructions to sing each twice, once on the syllables and once with the words. As Montgomery explained to me, "I like to pick a new song they've never seen before to test if they are really singing by shapes." During these sessions, he also teaches the basic conducting pattern, which consists of a basic "down-up" pattern that involves the entire arm. All time signatures are divided into a grouping of two: 4/4 is grouped 1-2 and 3-4, 2/4 is grouped 1 and 2, 6/8 and 6/4 are both grouped as 1-2-3 and 4-5-6, and 3/4 is grouped into 1-2, each on half of the down swing, and 3 on the up. The sharp, strong, almost jerky movements displayed while conducting emphasize both the song's rhythm and the physicality expected by all who participate in the singing.

This method of teaching, while similar to the one Pittman experienced in the 1920s, employs modern pedagogical tools and theories such as Jerome Bruner's theory of scaffolding. It builds upon the student's previous knowledge but is basic enough in content to be picked up by a first-time attendee.

Their simplicity does not mean that classes become stale after years of attending. Teachers are conscious of this danger and constantly bring in new songs and push regular attendees to lead songs so that the experience does not become routine. They recognize that for shape-note singing to flourish in the community, participants must know how to read and use shape-notes, and they do not want a return to mid-century unison singing. Their efforts have been successful. Average attendance for the singing school is forty to fifty, roughly the size of their congregation, but in many years the number has been as large as one hundred.

Although singing school elements have been modified to appeal to younger generations, its overall thrust has remained the same. Pittman wanted to resuscitate her experiences and was obviously successful. She was willing to change the learning process where she thought it necessary, but in the substance—the style of singing—the opposite was true. The Sweet Home Group sings in the same manner as their ancestors.

In the Primitive Baptist Church, singing has always occupied an important place at both worship services and social gatherings. The Sweet Home Group continues that custom through weekly Sunday morning services and sings—monthly assemblies where interested shape-note singers from the community, surrounding towns, and other Primitive Baptist churches meet to sing from their songbook *The Good Old Songs*. Although these sings are not the spontaneous get-togethers that characterized the early history of shape-note singing in the church, which more often centered on food, with singing desirable but of secondary importance to the fellowship, they do serve an important function similar to those of yesteryear. Both were times for the creation and perpetuation of community through singing.

Sings generally begin in the evening, around 7:00 p.m., after a supper that Pittman often hosts for out-of-town guests and her family. The church's interior is plain, almost completely of wood, and the seating is arranged with twelve pews on either side of a center aisle and three more pews at the front in a semi-circle facing back toward the entrance. This arrangement is designed to make all members of the church feel equal. Therefore participants in the sing arrive and are able to sit wherever they wish. Generally, older members move toward the front, and younger members, especially those with small children, remain in the rear. Within this stratification, clusters of people on a pew are usually defined by family. The age range of the participants is vast, from eighty years old to babies in their mothers' laps.

I use the word *participants* purposefully. One shape-note singing ideal is its participatory nature. The atmosphere is relaxed, the people inclusive, and everyone is encouraged to sing. Indeed, no one in the church on those evenings, regardless of age, sits idly and listens. All sing, all are involved. In conversations before and after the sing with participants, most mentioned the fact that shape-note music is singer's music. To truly hear and appreciate the music and its sound, one has to sing it.

Everyone sings, and all are involved in choosing songs as well. Sings open with the leader, often a singing school teacher or local pastor, shouting out the number of a hymn. He then pitches the song, singing the tonic note "do" several times and often outlining the tonic triad of "do, mi, sol, mi, do." Participants slowly begin singing "do" with the leader and then move to find their opening pitch in relation to that tonic. Once the leader is satisfied that everyone firmly has their pitch, he throws his arm down for the first downbeat and begins singing the song's first line. Participants quickly stagger in, and by the end of the first line of text, they are all singing their parts. At the end of this first song, the leader offers a few words of welcome, voices an opening prayer, and, looking out over the faces upturned toward him, asks for the next number.

This pattern continues throughout the night, with the leader asking for the numbers of favorite songs, pitching the selection, and then starting the song with voice and gesture. The event's participatory nature is heightened by its revolving leadership role. After leading three or four songs, the original leader steps aside and allows another to come forward and lead. At some point during the evening, children lounging in the back pew will be asked to lead a few songs. They usually do so, but only with the support of their peers at the front as well. Four or five children amble down and quietly begin a song. As at the singing school, participants in the sing are always enthusiastic about and responsive to the children's efforts, recognizing that the group's future rests with its young.

Woman rarely act as leaders at sings or Sunday morning services. They can and often do suggest songs to sing but will not rise to the front to voice the pitch or conduct the song. Primitive Baptist doctrine does not preclude women from leading the singing as it does women from preaching. Instead habit and decorum keep women from attempting to lead.[29] Everyone with whom I spoke remarked that it would be strange to see a woman leading a song at any service.

As shape-note singing is a participatory genre that encourages everyone, no matter the level of experience, amount of vocal training, or personal belief in ability to sing, the sound produced by a group is often startling and striking to those outside the tradition. The most immediate impression of the Sweet Home Group's sound is its power. The singing is loud and uninhibited with little dynamic variation. Participants sing with abandon, and the church quite literally vibrates for several moments after a song ends with the overtones produced by their four-part harmony. Members of the group view this aspect as one of the ways shape-note singing is superior to round-note. Elaine Funderburk remarked that "I don't like round notes with instruments because too often the people follow the piano. The other week I went to church in Camden at a church that uses the round notes and the people just didn't sing out; they tried to hide in the sound of the organ and most just sang the melody. They are too dependent on the piano and if the pianist doesn't show up, they're up a creek."

Connected with the power of the singing is the type of vocal production. Participants sing with very little vibrato, instead employing a straight tone. Their tone is forced out through a tightened, squeezed throat to the point of rasp on the edges of the sound. They sing with a false nasality, a pinched sound that seems to come from the nose that was characteristic of many older country singers. This nasal twang produces high overtones and a brightness in the voice that help explain the group's piercingly loud sound.

There are musical as well as physical explanations of shape-note singing's sound. Hymnals in the seven-note system were first compiled later than those in the four-note system, and they borrowed the majority of their songs from that earlier system, altered to fit the seven-note one. Early colonial American hymns found in those four-note books often break the rules of Western common practice voice leading. Chords are voiced in open rather than closed positions, parallel movement of fifths and octaves is allowable, and nonharmonic tones are often left unresolved. The resultant sound in performance is more open and the harmonic movement puzzling to ears conditioned to European tonality. Also, as four-note shape-note singing highly values the independence of all four parts, the texture often subsumes the melodic line, leaving listeners with little to follow during first encounters with the music.[30]

The shape-note syllables' role in sings and Sunday morning worship is different from its role in singing schools. In schools, teachers are trying to make sure that students know the notes and are singing based on their recognition of shapes rather than the placement of those shapes on the staff. Participants at a sing assume that all in attendance already know the shapes well enough to sing most of the hymns. The only time they sing syllables, a practice referred to as "singing the notes," is when a new piece is introduced or a fuging tune is sung. At these points, the leader will instruct participants to sing the notes through once and then to proceed straight into singing the words. The relatively sparse use of the syllables appears to be consistent with practice in the Primitive Baptist Church in the first part of the twentieth century and marks a sharp difference with Sacred Harp singing.

All of these practices and traditions, from Mr. Do to *The Good Old Songs* to the vocal production, are elements Orene Pittman remembered from her growing up and then revived for her children and extended family. Now that we have those elements listed, it is time to see what we can learn from them. I argued earlier that by exploring what practices were retained by revivalists from within a musical tradition and that they transformed, we are able to develop new insights into the meaning of that tradition to its original culture. Why then did Orene Pittman revive this music of her youth, and what has been its larger meaning with the group that now perpetuates it? The one aspect of shape-note singing that every participant stressed, to which every book on the subject returns, and that remained unaltered is its participatory and community-building nature. When I interviewed Tim Montgomery, the first subject we discussed was why he felt shape-note singing was important. I expected this singing school teacher and pastor to value the music's sound, its ability to teach scriptural truths, or its heritage and connection to the denomination. Instead he responded that "the reason to sing shape-note music is for worship and sweet fellowship. You know, churches die without good fellowship, so singing keeps them alive."

Montgomery's notion is one that is endlessly repeated in the literature on shape-note singing, whether on the four- or seven-note system. Janet Herman discovered in her analysis of participants in Sacred Harp singing in California that the singers valued the music for the sense of community it offered in what they saw as an isolating world. Even though the majority were not Christians, they enjoyed singing hymns because in the lyrical imagery they found a source and sense of union with other people.[31] Similarly, Kiri Miller, in arguing against the common division between Northern singers (who are viewed as liberal folk revivalists) and Southern singers (who are understood to be fundamentalist traditional singers), declared that those who participate in modern Sacred Harp conventions are part of a diaspora, drawn together in community by the music they embody.[32] Laura Clawson cited decades of sociological research to support her view that singing created social solidarity in communities that used the *Sacred Harp*; music was less about imparting specific biblical doctrines than developing a communal spirituality.[33] Finally, Brooks Blevins argues that where singing schools were revived within their original culture, they acted as "an expression of regional, spiritual, historical distinctiveness" to unite people marginalized by contemporary American Christian society.[34] The scholars' observations ring true for the Sweet Home Group. Primitive Baptists have long used singing to knit their communities together. Shape-note hymns were sung at weddings and funerals, during apple peelings and harvest, on long trips, and after communal meals. Certain songs were identified with members of the community so that even after they passed away, their names would be invoked when the hymn was sung, providing a feeling of permanence and history to the community that might otherwise go unexpressed.[35] As Christopher Small so rightly observed, "the act of musicking [involving oneself with music] establishes in the place where it is happening a set of relationships, and it is in those relationships that the meaning of the act lies."[36]

But only looking at the communal aspect of the Sweet Home revival misses the larger, and in many ways more important, picture. Exploring which traditions are renewed within their original cultures and which are allowed to languish in disuse, as we have done here, indexes those elements of a musical culture that hold value for the group that created them. For the Sweet Home Group, it allows us to acknowledge that the participants seek something other than human connection—and perhaps something other than human agency is at work. In her revealing memoir, historian of American religion Lauren F. Winner cogently noted that

> there would be some truth in all those theories. But this is why historians would be wrong, why all those scholars who try to explain away the Great Awakening are wrong, why my senior thesis is wrong. They recognize that conversion is complicated, that it is about family, and geography, and politics, and psychology, and economics. They just forget that it is also about God.[37]

In *After Heaven*, Robert Wuthnow speaks of three modes of spirituality: dwelling, seeking, and practice.[38] Most Primitive Baptist Churches, built upon blood lines and lacking the evangelistic fervor of many of their Baptist cousins, operate in the dwelling mode—their religion comes from family ties to specific churches. But Orene Pittman has moved her church into a new mode of spirituality, that of practice, where "people engage intentionally in activities that deepen their relationship to the sacred."[39] As a result, when we explore the why of Orene Pittman's renewal of shape-note practices, we quickly discover that it was caused by nothing more or less mysterious than faith, the desire to instill a belief in God, and the work of the Holy Spirit, rather than, as so many ethnomusicologists, historians, and anthropologists have noted, only the need to construct community in a fragmented world.

Jeff Todd Titon, through his work with Old Regular Baptists in Kentucky, has documented a similar situation. Although the Old Regular Baptists do not use the same hymnals as the Primitive Baptists, nor ascribe to the same theology, their singing serves a similar function. In their services, hymns are lined out, a practice in which a leader sings one line of text that is then sung back to him by the congregation, so there is no music leader as in Primitive Baptist Churches. Their hymn singing also does not contain the strong, marked rhythm that characterizes shape-note singing. Yet even singing unpulsed music without a conductor, the Old Regular Baptists always breathe, move note by note through the melody, and end phrases together. Puzzled by how this was accomplished, Titon examined statements about the singing from congregation members and compared sung phrases through transcriptions and precise measurements of their length. He discovered that it was not merely through repetition that they were able to sing together but also through shared religious beliefs and experiences.[40] In other words, this group's belief in God and a call to worship knit them together. The sense of community this belief created was then made manifest and reaffirmed through the music as they sang and acted in unison. It was through the music that their belief and community were revealed.

Perhaps the clearest metaphor for the type of community Orene Pittman created is the modest house she bought when she and her husband first moved to Alpine, Arkansas. Just large enough for the two of them and a few children, it served the growing family well for a number of years. As the children matured, married, and began having children of their own, Pittman wanted a home where her entire family could gather. As spouses and grandchildren were added, rooms were added to the house as well. Building materials were salvaged from older structures in the community being destroyed, resulting in one room boasting the flooring from the local gymnasium and another bricks from the fire station. The house today is a sprawling complex with a large kitchen and dining area that will seat all four generations of the Pittman family and guests when they gather to eat before an evening sing. It is truly one of the two focal points of Orene Pittman's life.

The revival, or renewal of spiritual practices, that continues to be formed in Alpine, Arkansas, occupies the other focal point of Pittman's life. It is a renewal of practices from within her own musical heritage brought about to serve both her extended and church families in bonding together as a community. Like her house, which has grown in tandem with the shape-note singing community, the revival wastes nothing. The old has been made new again, reborn from its original position in the community to fulfill a new use. Out of the necessity created by a different time and place, changes have been made to the original materials, but in their new form, echoes of the original still ring, evident and cherished.

NOTES

1. The sing described here occurred on March 16, 2003, and information about the group in Alpine, Arkansas is based on interviews with Orene Pittman (the founder of the Sweet Home Group), her daughter Elaine Funderburk, and Pastor Tim Montgomery, as well as attendance at events from 2003 to 2005 and 2008 to 2010. All quotations in this essay are taken from those interviews, conducted in Alpine, Arkansas, at the home of Orene Pittman.

2. David Stanley, "The Gospel-Singing Convention in South Georgia," *Journal of American Folklore* 95 (1982): 3–5. In order to avoid confusion, throughout this essay, I will use the term "Sacred Harp" for the four-note system and "shape-note" for the seven-note one.

3. This focus on *The Sacred Harp* perhaps comes from George Pullen Jackson's pioneering text *White Spirituals in the Southern Uplands* (Chapel Hill: University of North Carolina Press, 1933), where he first postulated singers of that text as preserving a unique Southern musical and cultural tradition. It continued through Buell E. Cobb Jr.'s *The Sacred Harp: A Tradition and Its Music* (Athens: University of Georgia Press, 2004) and into more recent studies such as Joe Dan Boyd's *Judge Jackson and the Colored Sacred Harp* (Tuscaloosa: University of Alabama Press, 2005), Stephen Marini's *Sacred Song in American: Religion, Music, and Public Culture* (Urbana: University of Illinois Press, 2010), Kiri Miller's *Traveling Home: Sacred Harp Singing and American Pluralism* (Urbana: University of Illinois Press, 2010), and David Warren Steel with Richard H. Hulan's *The Makers of the Sacred Harp* (Urbana: University of Illinois Press, 2010). These books and numerous other monographs and articles demonstrate the wide reach of *The Sacred Harp*'s aesthetic contours beyond the American South, but they consider neither the distinctive brand of singing contained in the seven-note system nor its continued presence or revival in Southern communities.

4. Livingston's model is taken from her article "Music Revivals: Towards a General Theory," *Ethnomusicology* 43 (1999): 66–85.

5. William Lynwood Montell, *Singing the Glory Down: Amateur Gospel Music in South Central Kentucky 1900–1990* (Lexington: University of Kentucky Press, 1991), 13.

6. Aiken argued for the system's use, writing in his preface, "Nothing is more easily demonstrable than the superiority of this to the four-syllable system. For if anything at all is gained by giving names to the different sounds in the octave—and of this there can be no question—it is easy to perceive that the nomenclature which appropriates to each sound in the octave a distinct name, must have the decided advantage over that which requires the same name to be applied to different sounds." Jesse Aiken, *The Christian Minstrel* (Philadelphia: T. K. and P. G. Collins, 1847), 9.

7. See, for example, John G. Crowley, "The Sacred Harp Controversy in the Original Alabama Primitive Baptist Association," *Baptist Studies Bulletin* 3, no. 7 (July 2004), accessed December 18, 2019, http://www.centerforbaptiststudies.org/bulletin/2004/july.htm, and Laurie Kay Sommers, "Hoboken Style: Meaning and Change in Okefenokee Sacred Harp Singing," *Southern Spaces*, August 17, 2012, accessed December 18, 2019, http://www.southernspaces.org/2010/hoboken-style-meaning-and-change-okefenokee-sacred-harp-singing.

8. David W. Music and Paul Akers Richardson, *"I Will Sing the Wondrous Story": A History of Baptist Hymnody in North America* (Macon, GA: Mercer University Press, 2008), 450.

9. Montell, *Singing the Glory Down*, 18–19. He relates how these local teachers became so prized and admired that each county in which they worked would claim them as a native son and argue viciously with others who disputed the claim.

10. Ibid., 199.

11. John Bealle, *Public Worship, Private Faith: Sacred Harp and American Folksong* (Athens: University of Georgia Press, 1997), 76.

12. Montell, *Singing the Glory Down*, 27–28. Brooks Blevins notes that Montell was writing at the end of the singing school tradition, but that in the thirty years since that publication, there has been a revival in singing schools, much like the one documented here. "Where Everything New Is Old Again: Southern Gospel Singing Schools," *Southern Cultures* 22, no. 4 (Winter 2016): 144.

13. Livingston, "Music Revivals," 68.

14. David King Dunaway argues for three revivals in US history: the first in the early twentieth century as collectors like Carl Sandburg and John and Alan Lomax published their recorded songs in collections and released field recordings; the second in the late 1950s as young singer-songwriters from Greenwich Village to San Francisco recorded the music from the first revival and created new music themselves; and the third, and final, began in the 1990s as the internet gave young musicians access to folk music the world over and they combined it, creating what *Rolling Stone* called the "YouTube Folk Revival." *Singing Out: An Oral History of America's Folk Music Revivals* (Oxford: Oxford University Press, 2010), 2–4. In each case, members of the American middle class adopt music from rural areas and bring them into more urban settings.

15. Kiri Miller argues that shape-note revivalism is a form of "nostalgia at the margins," where individuals join the singings as outsiders but quickly take the aesthetic as their own and form an obligation to remember and value it as a disappearing, and truly American, art form. The result of this obligation is usually some form of activism. *Traveling Home*, 204–6.

16. In her groundbreaking study of the English Folk Revival, Georgina Boyes rightly argues that "a revival is inherently both revolutionary and conservative. It simultaneously comprehends a demand for change in an existing situation and a requirement of reversion to an older form." *The Imagined Village: Culture, Ideology, and the English Folk Revival* (Manchester: Manchester University Press, 1993), 3.

17. Caroline Bithell and Juniper Hill, "An Introduction to Music Revival as Concept, Cultural Process, and Medium of Change," in *The Oxford Handbook of Music Revival*, ed. Caroline Bithell and Juniper Hill (Oxford: Oxford University Press, 2014), 5.

18. For examples of some of this work, see Hill and Bithell, Ronström, and Livingston's contributions to *The Oxford Handbook of Music Revival*, ed. Caroline Bithell and Juniper Hill (Oxford: Oxford University Press, 2014), 3–72.

19. Ibid., 69.

20. They use the thirty-ninth edition of *The Good Old Songs*, originally compiled by Elder C. H. Cayce and published in Thornton, Arkansas, the site of an important group of Sacred Harp singers in the state. To see this hymnal, visit https://dl.mospace.umsystem.edu/mu/islandora/object/mu%3A89339.

21. Bithell and Hill, "An Introduction to Music Revival as Concept, Cultural Process, and Medium of Change," 15.

22. Ibid., 10–12.

23. Bealle, *Public Worship, Private Faith*, 189. Bealle uses the term "cultural intervention" in his discussion of this phenomenon, but also points out that this reenergizing is a unique aspect of Sacred Harp revival among other revivals of the 1980s. This "spiritual maintenance," as several singers called it, is the focus of his examination of that revival.

24. I draw this idea largely from Burt Feintuch, "Musical Revival as Musical Transformation," in *Transforming Tradition: Folk Music Revivals Examined*, ed. Neil V. Rosenberg (Urbana: University of Illinois Press, 1993) and from the helpful discussion in Owe Ronström, "Traditional Music, Heritage Music," in *The Oxford Handbook of Music Revival*, 45, where he describes revivals as *"shifts* between different historic, geographic, social, and cultural contexts, between the individual and collective, private and public, informal and formal, and between different mythical geographies."

25. Primitive Baptists coalesced from several different strains in the early part of the nineteenth century as part of a broad controversy over mission work among Baptists. Baptists in the United States have traditionally been Arminian, disavowing any belief in the predestination of people to heaven or hell. That belief requires missionary work to convert people to Christianity, as the state of their souls is not yet determined, and the opportunity exists to save them from eternal torment. Calvinism made great inroads among Baptists in the late eighteenth and early nineteenth centuries, bringing with it the belief that because grace is irresistible to God's elect, mission work is futile, a waste of time and money. The flashpoint between those beliefs came in 1826 in North Carolina, when the Kehuckee Association declared itself against evangelistic missions. The line drawn, congregations began to align themselves with the Kehuckee Association and birthed the Primitive Baptist Church, which counts as part of its doctrine acceptance of a Calvinist stance for predestination, autonomy of the local church, and the practice of closed communion. For more information, see Sydney E. Ahlstrom, *A Religious History of the American People* (New Haven: Yale University Press, 1972), 721–23, and for a more thorough account of the rise of Primitive Baptists, see H. Leon McBeth, *The Baptist Heritage* (Nashville: Broadman Press, 1987), 717–22.

26. Brett Sutton, "In the Good Old Way: Primitive Baptist Traditions," *Southern Exposure* 5 (Summer/Fall 1977): 100–104. Singing is so critical to Primitive Baptist faith that Sutton devotes fully half of his article to the subject.

27. Ibid., 103. Sutton remarks that the songs' ability to permeate the complete lives of Primitive Baptists is the best explanation for the denomination's and songs' survival and expressive power.

28. Information concerning the singing school's structure is drawn from interviews with Pittman, her daughter Elaine Funderburk, and the most recent singing school teacher, Tim Montgomery between 2003 and 2005 and 2008 and 2010.

29. Pastor Tim Montgomery related to me that in some instances, in some groups he has led, women have been the most qualified and able to lead at a sing. In those cases, a woman would lead the singing, but instead of standing at the front, would sit in one of the front pews and lead from there, relying on her voice to keep a steady beat rather than her physical presence.

30. Janet Herman, "Sacred Harp Singing in California: Genre, Performance, Feeling" (PhD diss., University of Los Angeles, 1997), 75–76.

31. Herman, "Sacred Harp Singing in California," 200–202.

32. Miller, *Traveling Home*, 28–35.

33. Laura Clawson, "'Blessed Be the Tie that Binds': Community and Spirituality Among Sacred Harp Singers," *Poetics* 32 (2004): 311.

34. Blevins, "Where Everything New Is Old Again," 147.

35. Sutton, "In the Good Old Way," 104.

36. Christopher Small, *Musicking: The Meanings of Performing and Listening* (Hanover: University Press of New England for Wesleyan University Press, 1998), 13.

37. Lauren F. Winner, *Girl Meets God: On the Path to a Spiritual Life* (Chapel Hill: Algonquin Books, 2002), 64.

38. Robert Wuthnow, *After Heaven* (Berkeley: University of California Press, 1998), 3–4.

39. Ibid., 169.

40. Jeff Todd Titon, "Tuned Up with the Grace of God: Music and Experience among Old Regular Baptists," in *Music in American Religious Experience*, ed. Philip V. Bohlman, Edith L. Blumhofer, and Maria M. Chow (New York: Oxford University Press, 2006), 311–34.

FURTHER READING

Campbell, Gavin James. "'Old Can Be Used Instead of New': Shape-Note Singing and the Crisis of Modernity in the New South, 1880–1920." *The Journal of American Folklore* 110, no. 436 (Spring 1997): 169–88.

Dueck, Jonathan. "Binding and Loosing in Song: Conflict, Identity, and Canadian Mennonite Music." *Ethnomusicology* 55, no. 2 (Spring/Summer 2001): 229–54.

Guthman, Joshua. *Strangers Below: Primitive Baptists and American Culture*. Chapel Hill: University of North Carolina Press, 2015.

Hammond, Paul. "Jesse B. Aikin and *The Christian Minstrel*." *American Music* 3, no. 4 (Winter 1985): 442–51.

Miller, Kiri. "'Like Cords Around My Heart': Sacred Harp Memorial Lessons and the Transmission of Tradition." *Oral Tradition* 25, no. 2 (2010), doi:10.1353/ort.2010.0020.

Patterson, Beverly Bush. *The Sound of the Dove: Singing in Appalachian Primitive Baptist Churches*. Urbana: University of Illinois Press, 2001.

Chapter Four

Shape-Note Hymn Traditions in Athens, Georgia

Joanna Smolko

Franklin County was established in 1784 and in the subsequent year, the University of Georgia was chartered; the town of Athens was founded in 1806, in the area rechristened as Jackson County.[1] In addition to being a university town in the nineteenth century, Athens was known for its agricultural work, its work in manufacturing, and as an early railroad terminal (1833), connecting the town with other regional centers, such as Marthasville (present-day Atlanta).[2] Athens also became a hub for hymnody found in four-shape and later seven-shape hymnals. In this essay I explore several phases of hymn traditions in the Athens Clarke-County area and its surrounding counties. Much of my research on the hymnbooks in the nineteenth century was done through the Georgia Historic Newspapers database, while the post-1973 revival research relied on oral histories sponsored by the Athens Music Project and participant observation.[3] This essay uses a generally chronological approach to explore key publications, institutions, and events in the broader Athens area. My research speaks to Athens's distinctive history as a rural Southern town that also houses the resources of a university but could also serve as a model for understanding the dissemination and practice of shape-note hymns in other similar towns.

In the mid-nineteenth century local booksellers advertised hymnbooks, and local singings would be featured in the society columns and other pages. Newspapers featured songbooks compiled by Georgian song compilers, such as *The Social Harp* (1855) by John G. McCurry from nearby Hart County, as well as hymnals from farther afield. As the twentieth century opened, the four-shape hymnals and their surrounding traditions were both absorbed by and supplanted by revivalist gospel songs, though there is evidence that traditional practices continued. The relative ease of printing and publication during this time led to a plethora of hymnals published throughout Georgia, including Athens. Local singer and hymn author J. B. Vaughan (1862–1918) compiled and published hymnbooks in Athens and organized social events, such as the statewide singings hosted in Athens in 1914 and 1915. His hymnal *Resurrected Songs* (1904) shows the preservation and reinterpretation of earlier traditions.[4]

By the 1930s the role of shape-note singing and gospel singing as social events in Athens appears to have died down; rather than community events, hymn-singing appears to primarily have taken place within churches. While other groups, such as the Chattahoochee Singing Convention in west Georgia, continued to host singings from shape-note hymnals, especially *The Sacred Harp*, singers from the Athens area would have had to travel widely to participate in these.

Shape-note singing was revived in the Athens area through the work of John Garst and John Hollingsworth, who moved to Athens in the 1960s. Along with coeditor Daniel Patterson, John Garst republished an edition of *The Social Harp* (1973).[5] This led to the founding of an annual Athenian "Old Harp" singing that continues to this day. John Hollingsworth, a lifelong singer from Mississippi, moved to work at the University of Georgia. His family sang from the seven-shape hymnal *The Christian Harmony* (1866) for generations. His and his son Bill worked on an editorial team with others such as Mike Spencer of nearby Bishop, Georgia, which generated a new edition of *The Christian Harmony* (2010) as well as publication of songs by Raymond Hamrick (1915–2014), a watchmaker and hymn writer from Macon, Georgia. In the past few decades a warm relationship has developed between Athens-area singers and other local area singings, especially Atlanta-area singings. Singers from Athens participate in the Sacred Harp diaspora as defined by Kiri Miller, a "dispersed network of singing communities" in the United States and around the world who gather together in singing conventions and other events, and within online communities.[6] Shannon Primm, for example, host of the current shape-note singing group, has traveled around the world to singings and hosts singers from around the world who come to Georgia as part of a pilgrimage trip to the American South. In the following section I will look at the nineteenth-century advertisements, with excursions into the life and music of John G. McCurry and J. B. Vaughan. This will be followed by a discussion of the renewal of the tradition in 1973 and the unfolding of the hymn traditions since that time.

There were several hymnals in usage in Athens in the nineteenth century advertised in local newspapers. Though the data generally correspond with publication dates, hymnbooks were widely advertised soon after publication, there are ongoing trends that suggest how the hymnals may have been disseminated and used in the local area. One of the most jarring elements of this research is the ways in which advertisements for hymnals exist side by side with the advertisement of the sale of enslaved African Americans.

Figure 4.1. *Southern Watchman* (Athens, Georgia), December 30, 1858, p. 3. Advertisements for books and enslaved people.

The very mundanity of these advertisements points to the callousness of this commodification.

Albon Chase (1808–1867), a bookseller and businessman in Athens, frequently advertised new hymnals; because he also edited and published the *Southern Banner*, many of these advertisements would appear in this newspaper, though they also appeared in the rival *Southern Whig*.[7] Most frequently the ads for hymnbooks stood alone; this suggests that their popularity would make it profitable to invest funds into a prominent ad. When included in a list, the hymnbooks would lead the list or be set in a larger font.

The first hymnbook advertised by A. Chase is William Walker's *The Southern Harmony* (1835), which ran from 1841 to 1845. The initial advertisements in 1841 indicated that they had a supply of three hundred copies of the book, by 1842 the advertised numbers were two hundred copies, and in subsequent years the numbers were not included (presumably because they were so small). In December 1844, the ad noted that they were carrying the "latest edition" of the book, perhaps the "edited, corrected and revised" edition of 1844. Though *The Southern Harmony* continued to be released in new editions through 1854, the newer revisions were not advertised after 1845. As booksellers frequently advertised hymnbooks until the 1870s, this suggests that *The Southern Harmony* may have been supplanted by newer, and perhaps more popular, hymnals.

The Hesperian Harp (1848) compiled by Dr. William Houser in nearby Jefferson, Georgia, was advertised a handful of times in the late 1840s.[8] The first advertisement is significant for what it suggests about the process of disseminating hymnals.[9] Agents were requested "immediately" in order to "canvas every place in the land," with discounts offered for bulk orders. It claimed that "the Hesperian Harp is the largest and cheapest Music Book ever offered to the American public." It foregrounds the eclectic nature of the hymnal, preserving past hymns and introducing new tunes, and highlights the hymns' social functions, including temperance. The ad reads:

> [This work will contain] a larger number of the Church Tunes used by the religious denominations South and West, than have ever been embraced in one volume; Odes, Anthems, Sunday School, Infant, Missionary, and Temperance Pieces. Many of these tunes are entirely new, while many of those fine old airs that have long been used at prayer, camp, and other meetings, and in the social circles, but have never been before collected and harmonized, with numerous Scotch, Irish, German, and other fine tunes, will be found in the HESPERIAN HARP.

Subsequent ads by A. Chase in 1847, 1849, and 1850 echo this effusive prose.

The Sacred Harp was widely advertised in Athens-area newspapers from 1847 to 1866. The first ad by A. Chase in 1847 featured the hymnbook within a longer list of featured titles, but its 1849 ads were standalone and stated that the bookseller had one hundred copies of the work. In 1866, McAllister and Johnston took out a series of standalone advertisements for *The Sacred Harp*, stating that they had in stock "50 Copies. Sacred Harp New Improved and much Enlarged Edition."[10] Often *The Sacred Harp* and *The Social Harp*, discussed later, were paired together in advertisements.

In terms of sheer numbers of advertisements, *The Christian Harmony* widely outstripped all other hymnbooks, with at least thirty-five individual ads between 1872 and 1875 and was the only nineteenth-century hymnbook to be advertised in local newspapers after 1867. Predating these ads was an editorial article in the *Southern Banner* on Christmas Day 1867, in which the editor(s) were presented with a copy of *The Christian Harmony* "just issued from the press." The editorial takes a nostalgic tone and addresses itself to "readers, who like ourselves, are becoming *advanced young men* who [encountered?] the pleasure, in their youth, of attending country singing schools."[11] This statement strongly suggests that the singing school tradition had become less frequent locally.

The ads for *The Christian Harmony* were primarily from TA Burke, Burke and Hodgson, and Burke's bookstore. There were also a couple of advertisements by the publisher's house itself, which points to the kinds of social functions the book was expected to fulfill.[12] "Designed for CHOIRS, SINGING SCHOOLS and MUSICAL SOCIETIES," special discounts were given to music teachers. Though this was not the first book to use a seven-note system, the book was advertised as using a "NEW, NATURAL and EASY system" that would quarter the time it would take one to read music.

I found no advertisements for the sale of oblong hymnals in the Athens-area newspapers after 1875, even though editions of hymnals like *The Sacred Harp* and *The Christian Harmony* continued to be released. All-day singings and conventions in other towns were frequently advertised in the early 1900s, but the ads often do not specify the hymnbooks to be used, so it is unclear whether these singings used oblong shape-note hymnals or if they used newer gospel-style hymnbooks.

Occasionally, other articles and ads suggest that Athens-area singers continued to have ties to the tradition. An advertisement for a Sacred Harp singing at the West End Baptist Church in 1909 suggests that these hymnals continued to be in use and in circulation in the area.[13] By the 1910s, ads for all-day singings of *The Sacred Harp* in nearby towns showed up periodically within Athens-area newspapers. A 1917 article affectionately praises a local singer, "Big Foot" Ben Collier, who traveled to all of the all-day singings within a forty-mile radius.[14]

By the 1910s, the repertoire had gained a romanticized aura, a historicization as an older way of singing that should not be neglected. This is perhaps best exemplified in the 1913 poem by "D. G. B." simply titled "The Old-Time Songs," found in *The [Athens] Banner*, August 17, 1913.[15] The first verse lauds the use of shaped-notes, favoring them over round-notes:

I ain't much on music no way, on the style it should be done,
An' these round notes sorter bother—mind, I'm not a-makin' fun—

The poem continues with a reference to specific hymnals, *The Christian Harmony* takes up the remaining of the first verse, and the second, then singers are asked to pick up *The Sacred Harp*, and finally they are told to take out *The Temple Star*, a seven-note hymnal compiled by Aldine Kieffer (1877). The chorus following each verse is drawn from a hymn chorus referenced in the verse "'Tis the old time religion," "Will the waters be chilly?," "I have brothers over yonder," and finally "I'm going home to die no more" as the closing song. Specific elements within the singing tradition are referenced: "tribbles" ("trebles" who sing the lead melody), "git the pitch," (pitching the song) "s-ol . . . f-a, m-e, r-a" (singing on the syllables), and suggesting that the songs should be sung loudly, "make believers shout," and "sing in mighty hearty, mighty fine." The specific reference to performance practice elements also strongly suggests that this was a living and active tradition within the area during the time, even if newspaper references are rarer.

Because of its proximity to the Athens area and the hymnal's use in later revivals, we will turn back to survey *The Social Harp* and the life of its compiler John G. McCurry in closer detail. George Pullen Jackson, a seminal researcher on these traditions, sketched out McCurry's biography, on which John Garst and Daniel Patterson expanded in their republication of *The Social Harp*.[16]

John G. McCurry was born in Hart County in 1821 to a farming family, and he continued to work as a farmer for much of his life. He was active within his community holding a variety of civic positions and volunteering with (and sometimes leading) community organizations, such as the local agricultural club, the democratic club, and a committee to bring the railroad through Hart County. In 1855 he had his hymnal *The Social Harp* published, printed in Philadelphia by "T. K. Collins, Jr." There were other editions during his lifetime, though little is known about them.

Though noting that his means were "modest," within his community he was well known and at least during periods of his life was wealthy. Patterson and Garst note that

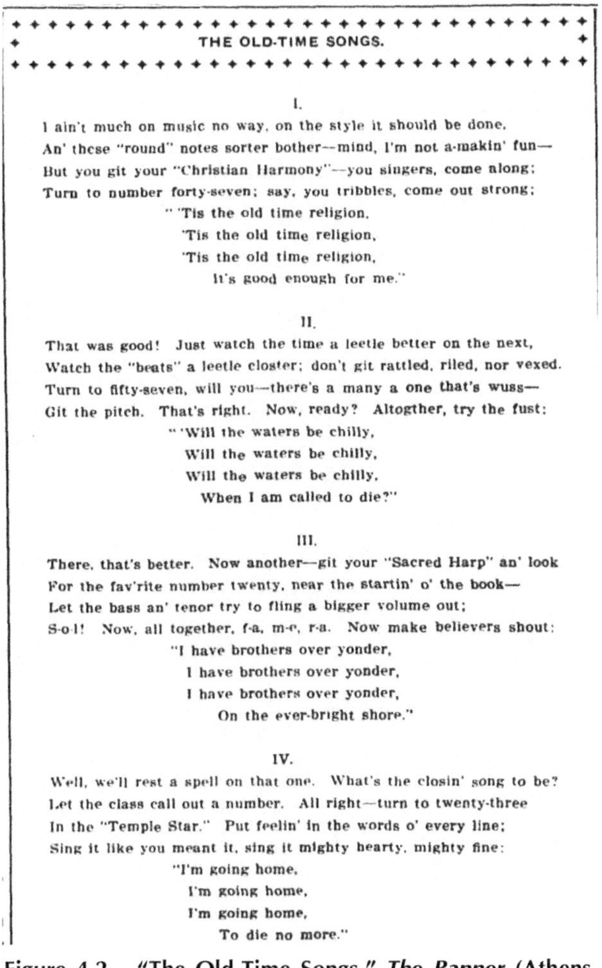

> ```
> + + + + + + + + + + + + + + + + + + + + + + + + + + + + + + + +
> +              THE OLD-TIME SONGS.                             +
> + + + + + + + + + + + + + + + + + + + + + + + + + + + + + + + +
> ```
>
> I.
>
> I ain't much on music no way, on the style it should be done,
> An' these "round" notes sorter bother—mind, I'm not a-makin' fun—
> But you git your "Christian Harmony"—you singers, come along;
> Turn to number forty-seven; say, you tribbles, come out strong;
> > "'Tis the old time religion,
> > 'Tis the old time religion,
> > 'Tis the old time religion,
> > It's good enough for me."
>
> II.
>
> That was good! Just watch the time a leetle better on the next,
> Watch the "beats" a leetle closter; don't git rattled, riled, nor vexed.
> Turn to fifty-seven, will you—there's a many a one that's wuss—
> Git the pitch. That's right. Now, ready? Altogther, try the fust:
> > "'Will the waters be chilly,
> > Will the waters be chilly,
> > Will the waters be chilly,
> > When I am called to die?"
>
> III.
>
> There, that's better. Now another—git your "Sacred Harp" an' look
> For the fav'rite number twenty, near the startin' o' the book—
> Let the bass an' tenor try to fling a bigger volume out;
> S-o-l! Now, all together, f-a, m-e, r-a. Now make believers shout:
> > "I have brothers over yonder,
> > I have brothers over yonder,
> > I have brothers over yonder,
> > On the ever-bright shore."
>
> IV.
>
> Well, we'll rest a spell on that one. What's the closin' song to be?
> Let the class call out a number. All right—turn to twenty-three
> In the "Temple Star." Put feelin' in the words o' every line;
> Sing it like you meant it, sing it mighty hearty, mighty fine:
> > "I'm going home,
> > I'm going home,
> > I'm going home,
> > To die no more."

Figure 4.2. "The Old-Time Songs," *The Banner* (Athens, Georgia), August 17, 1913.

his total worth in 1860 was eighty-four hundred dollars. But even so he was among the more substantial men in the county. He had eight slaves—seven of them children—a farm of several hundred acres, proprietorship of a songbook, and perhaps by this time his saw mill and cotton gin.[17]

A survey of newspaper advertisements sheds further light on his activities, including his work for many years within the local sheriff's office. Here, he participated in selling enslaved people that were "repossessed," including children.[18]

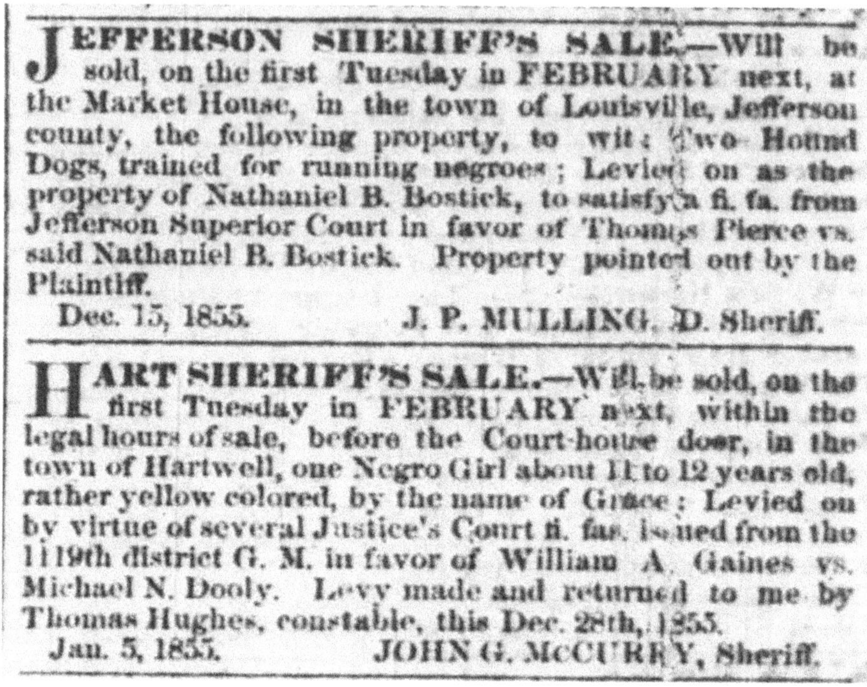

> JEFFERSON SHERIFF'S SALE.—Will be sold, on the first Tuesday in FEBRUARY next, at the Market House, in the town of Louisville, Jefferson county, the following property, to wit: Two Hound Dogs, trained for running negroes; Levied on as the property of Nathaniel B. Bostick, to satisfy a fi. fa. from Jefferson Superior Court in favor of Thomas Pierce vs. said Nathaniel B. Bostick. Property pointed out by the Plaintiff.
> Dec. 15, 1855.   J. P. MULLING, D. Sheriff.
>
> HART SHERIFF'S SALE.—Will be sold, on the first Tuesday in FEBRUARY next, within the legal hours of sale, before the Court-house door, in the town of Hartwell, one Negro Girl about 11 to 12 years old, rather yellow colored, by the name of Grace; Levied on by virtue of several Justice's Court fi. fas. issued from the 1119th district G. M. in favor of William A. Gaines vs. Michael N. Dooly. Levy made and returned to me by Thomas Hughes, constable, this Dec. 28th, 1855.
> Jan. 5, 1855.   JOHN G. McCURRY, Sheriff.

Figure 4.3. *Daily Chronicle and Sentinel* (Hart, Georgia), January 5, 1855. Sale of enslaved people by John G. McCurry at the Hart Sheriff's Office.

Thomas D. Russell notes that slave trafficking via local sheriff offices has often been overlooked, writing, "Historians have largely failed to notice the slave sales that courts ordered or supervised . . . half of all slave sales were sales by operation of law."[19] He writes,

> Antebellum sheriffs . . . had roles different from the gun-slinging crime-fighter of cinematic or operatic fame. The great bulk of sheriffs' work concerned civil litigation, not peace-keeping functions such as catching stagecoach robbers and horse thieves.[20]

Settling civil disputes led to public sales, especially of estates of people who died, and these estates included enslaved people.[21] The very mundaneness of the advertisements shows how deeply the system of slavery was embedded into the daily economy of the town's life. After the Civil War, McCurry continued to work in the sheriff's office, stayed active in his church, helping to build a Baptist church near his house, and continued his civic activities.

The Social Harp was first advertised in Athens newspapers in 1859 by Wm. N. White booksellers. The advertisement paired together *The Sacred*

Harp and *The Social Harp* in a shared advertisement; they ran versions of this ad until 1866. *The Social Harp* preceded *The Sacred Harp*, oftentimes as a headline, and sometimes in a larger font. In 1866, McCurry took out a series of advertisements with detailed descriptions, and where to find *The Social Harp*, specifically at Wm. N White in Athens and John B. Benson in nearby Whitehall.[22] In one of the final local ads, *The Social Harp* is featured along with turnip seed, a reminder of the county's agricultural history.[23] In contrast to the frequent advertisement of *The Social Harp* in the Athens area, I found very few additional advertisements in a search of statewide newspapers.

The reception of McCurry's book during his lifetime was perhaps mixed. On February 2, 1856, *The Social Harp* was reviewed in *The Organ*, a musical newsletter published in Hamilton Georgia, started and edited by B. F. White. White writes, "This work . . . we are sorry to say, is compiled by a Georgian."[24] The critique of the work centers on the issues he takes with the rudiments of music but ends with an accusation of plagiarism from *The Sacred Harp*, as several tunes were used from it without permission of the compilers.[25] Two months later, however, *The Organ* published a positive review of *The Social Harp* in a letter to the editor. B. F. White, to his credit, published the letter:

> Musical brothers in Georgia and elsewhere, you ought to have it in connection with the Sacred Harp, The Hesperian Harp, and all good Harps. There is one or two new pieces in the Social Harp that is richly worth one dollar—Come boys, test what I say. To brother John G. McCurry, I wish to say that he has my best wishes for his present and future prosperity through life. Amen.[26]

The Social Harp was also mentioned several times in Aldine Kieffer's newsletter *The Musical Million* (1870–1914).[27] Aldine Kieffer (1840–1904) was the grandson of the music teacher, publisher, and hymnal compiler Joseph Funk (1778–1862), who worked in Singers Glen, Virginia. Together with Ephraim Ruebush (1833–1924), Kieffer continued his grandfather's publishing company, continuing to publish hymnbooks, creating *The Musical Million* journal to draw attention to hymns and singing schools across the southeast, and leading singing schools across the south known as "Normal Music Schools."[28] *The Social Harp* is listed in *The Musical Million* alongside other shape-note hymnals in 1879.[29] In 1880, A. J. Showalter (1858–1924) (singing school teacher, composer, and author of "Leaning on the Everlasting Arms") mentioned attending a singing in which *The Sacred Harp* and *The Social Harp* were used side by side.[30] In 1882, an article discussed collaboration between the newsletter and McCurry, who planned to teach a Normal Music School in Elberton with Isham Dyar (a singing school teacher) at some point in the near future.[31]

In 1883, Kieffer visited McCurry, a visit discussed by George Pullen Jackson. A. J. Showalter, Thos. C. Hayes, and Isham Dyar were also present. Kieffer wrote warmly, "Then came an evening of song whose influence will linger around the hearts of all who were present so long as reason holds her throne, or love maintains her hold upon the heart. The *sterling* melodies found in Social Harp, with their *crude* harmonies, were discussed by our voices, accompanied by a small parlor organ."[32] Note the use of "crude" in reference to the harmonies, historicizing the hymns and suggesting that though Kieffer continued the use of shaped-notes for teaching singing, his preference was for the sweeter, chordal harmonies associated with newer gospel tunes.

While Aidan Kieffer visited McCurry near the end of his lifetime, he had a strong influence on another Athens-area hymn writer and compiler at the beginning of his career, J. B. Vaughan (1862–1918), another farmer who became a hymn writer and compiler.[33] Though Vaughan did not publish oblong hymnbooks in the tradition of the nineteenth-century hymnbook compilers, he included hymns from these traditions in his compilations and self-published numerous seven-shaped hymnbooks.

Vaughan and McCurry probably met at a Normal Music School conducted in Hart County. Vaughan is listed as one of the attendees at the first Georgia Normal Music School in 1881, conducted in Hart County by Kieffer, Hayes, and Dyer.[34] This was a formative experience for the nineteen-year-old Vaughan. *The Musical Million* advertised an upcoming singing school to take place beginning on July 24, 1882, in Hart County, conducted by Dyer and McCurry.

Vaughan corresponded with and contributed to *The Musical Million* as he continued his working writing hymns and teaching music. The Normal Music Schools that Kieffer encouraged, promoted, and participated in functioned as a bridge from the earlier musical styles associated with McCurry and the antebellum tunebooks and their "crude" harmonies into the gospel-style harmonies associated with hymns into the turn of the century. Even if it can't be proven that McCurry and Vaughan met personally, their connection through Kieffer, Dyer, and others who participated in these schools points to a continuous Athens-area tradition. Another connection between them was McCurry and Vaughan's mutual connection with A. J. Showalter, evidenced by Vaughan's assistance with compiling Showalter's hymnbook *Good Tidings* (1884).[35]

In addition to the biographical evidence, Vaughan's republication of McCurry's hymns further demonstrates the continuity of the Athens-area hymn tradition. In particular, the volume *Resurrected Songs* (1904) shows this continuity. In the introduction, Vaughan discusses his impulse toward creating this volume:

For years I have been vividly impressed to compile, revise, arrange and rewrite the old songs that our fathers and mothers chanted with happy hearts and inspiring voices. I have no desire or inclination to resurrect, recall or revise anything of the past unless it is more desirable and useful than such as the present affords us. But I do believe in clinging to all that is good and that may be productive of good, regardless of age or sect.[36]

This led him to solicit contributions of older hymns that people still loved to sing.

In the year 1896 my mind was peculiarly directed to the task of republishing the old songs that had long been favorites; this inclination of my mind was encouraged by repeated calls from all sections of the South and West for a work of this kind. I began advertising and searching for the old and tried songs that were used and are still being used with gospel power for good in the homes, churches and singing schools.[37]

Unfortunately, two intervening fires delayed his intentions, in 1896 and in 1902. He moved to Athens with his wife in 1903.[38] An afternoon walk inspired him to try again and resulted in the publication of the hymnbook. In his introduction, Vaughan specifically cites the work of well-known hymnbook compilers of the previous century, "Most of the old revival songs . . . were gathered largely from the old books edited by Walker, White, McCurry, and others."[39]

For many of the hymns, he identifies its source, the composer, and the author and/or compiler of the hymn. However, many of the songs lack identification, and their presence in multiple hymnals makes it difficult to determine their precise source. Considering the comparative rarity of McCurry's *The Social Harp* in comparison with those released by the other authors, the Athens connection is writ large. Within the hymnal, he attributes four of the hymns to McCurry ("Come Over and Help Us," "River of Jordan," "Raymond," and "We'll Land on Shore"); other hymns are present in *The Social Harp* but are unattributed. Though most of the book consists of the older hymns, he completes the work with a small section of hymns composed by himself or other contemporary hymn writers drawn from his earlier publications.[40] Interestingly, the older hymns are set in round-notes, while the hymns inserted at the conclusion of the hymnbook from his earlier publications feature a different font, and the seven-note shape system.

His stated desire was to preserve the structural integrity of the old tunes and their harmonies, whether or not they follow current theories of musical practice.

92   *Joanna Smolko*

Heretofore, publishers of music books have not considered it a good business venture to republish these old songs. The most tedious and difficult work consisted in trying to harmonize and arrange the old, unique tunes without making a change in the melody. Many of these old, cherished songs are very peculiar in make-up and are not theoretically constructed; therefor can not be harmonized correctly and according to the rules of composition. So rather than make any changes in the tunes that have so many sacred associations on memory's page, we have let stern, uncompromising theory bend to the convenience of the old lovely melody. Music students and critics are at liberty to vindicate or condemn.[41]

In many of the hymns drawn from the earlier tradition, he preserves some of their distinguishing features, such as open harmonies, fuging sections, etc. However, he could not resist tinkering with the modal minor tunes from the earlier period. For example, in both "Wondrous Love"[42] and "Idumea,"[43] Vaughan introduces leading tones into the melody and harmony that eliminate the implied and traditionally practiced Dorian of the former and the Aeolian mode of the latter.[44] The harmonization, however, does not consistently use the leading tone, so tricky cross-relationships are created between the voices (for example, the E and E# in "Idumea," measure 6, and the E and Eb in measure 1 of "Wondrous Love"). At times the choices between the leading tone and the b7 of the natural minor/Aeolian mode seem arbitrary. For both tunes, the perfect fifth motion between the voices are eliminated in favor of common practice voice leading.

Figure 4.4a. *Southern Harmony and Musical Companion* (1835), "Idumea."

Shape-Note Hymn Traditions in Athens, Georgia

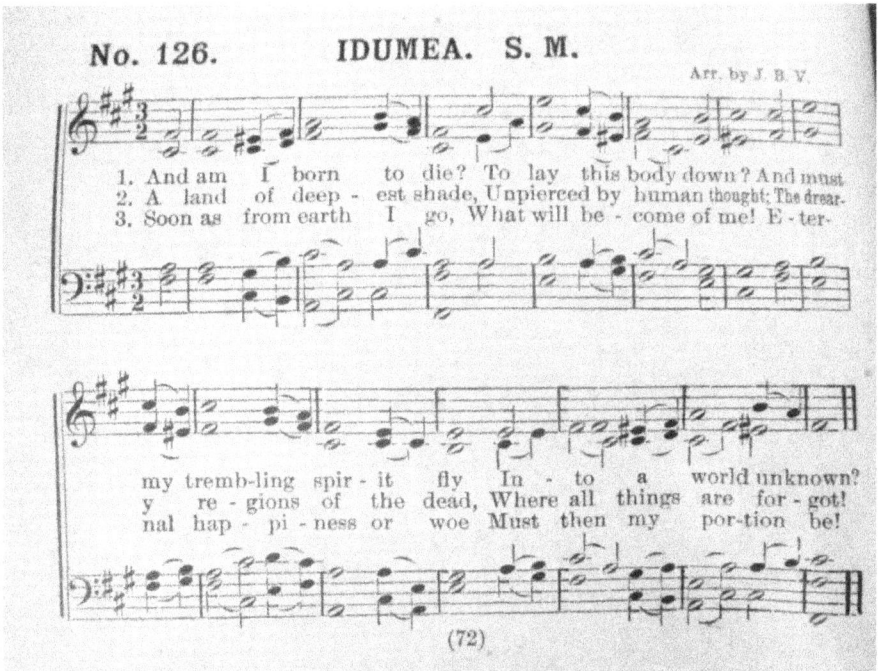

Figure 4.4b.   J. B. Vaughan, *Resurrected Songs* (1904), "Idumea."

Figure 4.4c.   *Southern Harmony and Musical Companion* (1835), "Wondrous Love."

Figure 4.4d. J. B. Vaughan, *Resurrected Songs* (1904), "Wondrous Love."

However, in John McCurry's major-keyed "We'll Land on Shore," most of the tune and harmonization is intact, with some small changes: a fourth alto part is added to the three-voice setting by McCurry, and the bass part is simplified harmonically.[45]

Vaughan continued to use his musical networks to help form the North Georgia Singing Convention together with his colleagues. The first large "singing fest" was set for October 3, 1914, in Athens. The event was significant enough that it vied for top headline with news from the Allied front of The Great War/World War I.[46]

Figure 4.5. *The Athens Daily Herald* (Athens, Georgia), September 28, 1914. World War I and all-day singing headlines.

Though it was not its first meeting, the group organized itself officially, with the election of officers on October 3, 1914.[47] Singers across several Georgia counties were elected to the board, with J. B. Vaughan as "permanent president." This was intended to be a large singing festival, but the weather led to poor turnout so Vaughan worked with his colleagues to organize an all-day singing planned for October 24, 1914.[48]

Athenians and others were called to "mobilize for singing not for fighting" for the convention. Over a thousand singers from numerous Georgia counties, as well as South Carolina, were expected to attend.[49] The event was scheduled for the University of Georgia's Moss Auditorium.[50] The committee negotiated with the local train lines to secure discount tickets for singers, "Seaboard and Southern are going to give special train rates."[51] Rather than a traditional "dinner on the grounds," the committee worked with local cafés to organize lunches for the singers; the singers were given identifying badges in order to obtain their lunches.[52]

Over a thousand singers did come to town for the event and the organizers were pleased enough with the success of the event that they planned another statewide singing for June 4 and 5, 1915.[53] Once again, the organizers negotiated with local train lines. "Attempts have been made to get various rail roads leading into Athens to put on reduced rates."[54] Merchants advertised their wares directly to the singers and were urged to attend the events.[55] An even larger number of singers were expected this time: three thousand or more.[56] The mayor was asked to introduce the event. This time, rather than sending singers out to the local cafés, they arranged a women's committee to feed the incoming singers; this committee asked women from the town to contribute as part of their civic duty.

> The following dinner has been planned and the merchants of Athens and its ladies and all others are asked to contribute anything they will to these dinners, and telephone Mrs. A. O. Harper, Mrs. J. B. Vaughn, Mrs. S. J. Tribble or the presidents, of any of the above organizations of the city.[57]

The list of suggested food followed: "Brunswick Stew. Ham. Pickles. Loaf Bread. Biscuit. Cake. Coffee."[58]

A four-note shape-note singing was planned (and presumably executed) as a demonstration of the older styles: "A little boy and little girl will show how naturally little folks can sing and then there will be examples of the old fa, sol, la singing, given by some of the old people."[59] This demonstrates both a *continuance* of the tradition during this time (a living oral/aural history practice) and a historicization of the process, this is what the "old people" do, in contrast with modern singing practices.

The crowds do not appear to have been as large as anticipated, but the singing was considered very successful.[60] Though all-day singings and conventions continued in nearby areas, I have not found evidence of the kind of civic involvement that took place within the 1914 and 1915 singings in Athens itself. After Vaughan's death in 1918, the goal to have an annual singing, and perhaps even the North Georgia Singing Convention itself, appears to have died out, perhaps in response to the 1918–1919 outbreak of the Spanish Flu, which led to the cancelation of many large-scale events. However, Vaughan's widow continued to attend gospel singings, sometimes leading songs, and even publishing hymnals after her husband's death.

The reference to the fa-so-la singing demonstration is the last direct reference I have found to the public practice of Sacred Harp and similar traditions within Athens during the period, though it is likely to have continued in smaller venues, perhaps not advertised within the local newspaper; this is suggested by a 1909 advertisement for an "old Sacred Harp" singing at the West End Baptist Church and in a 1917 ad for a demonstration of "the old time fa so la singing led by Mr. Frank P. Griffeth" at an Athens-area church.⁶¹ The evidence for local singers and continued interested in Sacred Harp is found through the inclusion of events outside of the local Athens area within the local newspapers. For example, there are a couple announcements of Nicholson-area Sacred Harp singings in 1915, presumably extending an invitation to Athens singers.⁶² Perhaps the most interesting is the announcement of a road trip by Lawrenceville-area singers, a town roughly halfway between present-day Atlanta and Athens.

> The Lawrenceville brass band will lead the procession, and will be accompanied by one of the most noted fa-sol-la choirs in Georgia. The fa-sol-la choir will be composed of famous Sacred Harp singers, who know just what it takes to make good old time [*sic*] music, and they will sing strictly by note too. . . . Seventy-five automobiles loaded down with boosters; the brass band dispensing inspiring music; the choir of fa-sol-la singers lifting their voices over the fields and woods; everybody boosting for "the good old county of Gwinnett, the best place to live beneath the stars"—this is what will happen on Thursday, June 24, 1915, in the county of Gwinnett.⁶³

The last mention of anything directly related to Sacred Harp or other shape-note singings in Athens-area newspapers during this period was a brief note on September 25, 1923, where it was noted that "Sacred Harpers plan meeting in Columbus Georgia."⁶⁴ This leaves a nearly fifty-year gap until discussions appear in 1973 around the republication of *The Social Harp*. It can be inferred, if not proven, that there continued to be informal practices of older shape-note singing at least for a time, especially as there were regular singings in other regions of Georgia. However, I have found no evidence that Athens or its immediate vicinity continued to use *The Social Harp* hymnal, and given the rarity of the hymnal when George Pullen Jackson encountered it in the 1930s, it can be inferred that singing from this hymnal had diminished significantly, perhaps continuing in small gatherings in churches or perhaps through travel to other community singings.

How did Athens become a node within the network of late twentieth-century/early twenty-first century shape-note singing practices? To consider that, we will turn to the roles of singers and scholars (like John Garst, discussed earlier) who played active roles as singers, hosts, editors, collaborators, and researchers. Like the nineteenth century, this time period is also shaped by Athens's position as both a rural southern town and a university town.

Sometime in the late 1950s or early 1960s in California, John Garst settled down in his living room to peruse Gilbert Chase's book *America's Music*, perhaps finding comfort and mental stimulation from thinking outside of his field of chemistry, melodies instead of formulas, harmonies instead of compounds.[65] He was drawn to the sound of shape-note hymns prior to this reading as he heard the haunting sounds included on the 1952 Folkways LP set *An Anthology of American Folk Music* and eagerly devoured Chase's accounts of the "fa-so-la" folk.[66] His wife Edna cooked their dinner in the kitchen as he immersed himself in his reading. He recalls:

> Something in Chase's book implied that north Mississippi was a place where there was Sacred Harp singing. Well my wife is from north Mississippi. So she was in the kitchen fixing supper. I just yelled from the adjacent room, "You ever heard of Sacred Harp singing?" And she yelled back, "The old people around home do that all the time." And it turned out to be true." Following up on the information, they attend a singing during their next vacation home to see Edna's folks, and were entranced by the sound.[67]

Moving to Athens in 1963, Garst sought out information on local singings in the area and found singings near Atlanta. They began attending singings, getting to know local singers, such as Hugh McGraw, a life-long Sacred Harp singer and advocate for the tradition. Returning one day to Chase's *American Music*, Garst was struck by the mention of *The Social Harp*, especially Chase's quotation of Jackson's description: "If ever a book grew out of its native soil, that book was McCurry's Social Harp."[68] Obtaining a couple of rare, original copies, Garst set to work on getting it reprinted, enlisting his friend Daniel Patterson, folklorist and professor at the University of North Carolina. They convinced the editors at the University of Georgia Press of the value of the project, and the edition was published in 1973.

Recognizing the importance of this endeavor, Hugh McGraw talked Garst into hosting a singing to celebrate its release, enlisting numerous Georgia Sacred Harp singers to participate. It took place at the University of Georgia Memorial Hall ballroom on March 4, 1973, and was well attended by singers across the region. It became the first of the annual University of Georgia singings, now regularly held on the fourth Sunday of February. Singing from *The Sacred Harp* was added to the practice, and it became known as "The Old Harp Singing," distinguishing it from most singings that typically used a single hymnal (usually *The Sacred Harp*). Over time, the singing moved to the Georgia Botanical Gardens, where it is held at the airy visitor's center. The open space and glass exterior of this greenhouse area magnifies and echoes the sound similar to a wooden church, but with its own unique resonance.

Our next story is that of the Hollingsworth family. In 1967, John Hollingsworth and his family moved to Danielsville, Georgia, to teach mathematics at the University of Georgia. Hollingsworth sang these songs as far back as he can remember from his childhood in Mississippi; they were passed down from his grandparents to his parents.[69] In his own words, "It was the music of the good old songs that we sang in church. We were farmers and it was all very local and the shape-note books that were used were *The Christian Harmony* and later when we got a car, we would go to Sacred Harp singings."[70] Together, he and his family attended singings all around the region, from Georgia to Mississippi, and he also helped to chair the UGA Botanical Gardens singing over the years.

In 2006, John and his wife Elsie began to host their annual New Year's Eve singing, ringing in the new year through song. The first singing included both *The Christian Harmony* and the 1991 edition of *The Sacred Harp*. The year 2008 was a landmark because the Hollingsworths hosted the inaugural singing for *The Georgian Harmony* on February 16, a brand-new hymnal containing songs by longtime singer and composer Raymond Hamrick (1915–2014).[71] John and his son Bill worked carefully with Raymond to compile and publish the hymnal, using their skills as researchers and with computer programming to facilitate its publication.[72] In 2009 this singing expanded to include a full day of singing the following day, a two-day marathon to celebrate the new year, singing from *The Sacred Harp* and *The Christian Harmony* on New Year's Eve, with the New Year's Day singing drawn from *The Georgian Harmony*. In 2010, a significant expansion to *The Georgian Harmony* was published and incorporated into subsequent singings.[73]

John and Bill Hollingsworth's family also collaborated on the republication of *The Christian Harmony* (2010), along with Michael Spencer of nearby Bishop, Georgia, and others.[74] This edition synthesized elements of the book's second edition (1873) with updates that were found in the 1958 revision. It also exchanged the distinctive Walker style of seven shaped-notes for the more frequently used Aiken shapes.[75] John Hollingsworth writes of the significance of this republication,

> You ask if the revision contributed to the growth of the tradition. Certainly! The Georgia State Convention and Camp DoReMi are direct consequences, and the Saturday night singing at Camp Do and the Georgia Conventions were unusually good singings. In fact, they were perhaps the best Christian Harmony singings I have attended in the last forty years. Perhaps more important is the impact on the spread of the tradition. . . . Christian Harmony is now sung in England, Ireland, Germany, Oregon, and other places. We believe the revision gets credit for this growth.[76]

Shannon Primm is another vital node in the Athens singing network. She has continued the practice of hospitality shown by the Hollingsworth family, inviting singers into her home for monthly singings and using social media to tap into the singing diaspora. She moderates a Facebook page and a listserv to disseminate information about local singings, and frequently visitors from out of town, or country, will attend local singings because of her outreach. She compares the networks fostered through social media to the roles of penpals in the past.[77] They provide an opportunity to strengthen the bonds created through the face-to-face singing communities. Like John Garst, she first came into contact with Sacred Harp as an adult. Her first exposure was through a demonstration concert in the 1970s by Dewey Williams and the Wiregrass Sacred Harp Singers. But it wasn't until moving to the Athens area in the 1990s that she became involved in singing the tradition. She was drawn to it through the sound of the music, but even more so because of the egalitarian nature of singings. She recounts,

> It's sort of this family, this network that's very far-reaching and it's a lovely experience. To listen to someone talk about a singing friend they lost . . . you know this is really a significant thing, it's an important community event. And everybody is welcome to be a part of it, no matter what your religious affiliation is or your talent. You only have to be a person, that's it. That's the only requirement. How can you beat that?[78]

After a brief stint in Florida, where she sang with groups in north Florida, she returned to Athens and was welcomed back by the singers. On her return, Shannon began to play a more active role in organizing local singings. She travels all over the southeast and even as far as England to attend singings (sometimes traveling to thirty or more within a single year). From 2010 on, Shannon has hosted monthly singings, at local churches, at her house, and at a local bowling alley.

A project of note that Shannon masterminded is the screening of Matt and Erica Hinton's documentary *Awake, My Soul* at the Athens local arthouse theater, Athens Cine, on February 24, 2011.[79] This was a great moment of collaboration between a local institution and traditional singers. The screening of the documentary was followed by a singing demonstration by local singers and those who traveled, mostly from the Atlanta area, to participate, as well as a question-and-answer session with the directors.

Surveying the post-1973 phase of shape-note hymn singing in Athens, there are several characteristics that distinguish it. First is its use of multiple books. Four books are used regularly in local singings, *The Sacred Harp*, *The Christian Harmony*, *The Social Harp*, and *The Georgian Harmony*, the last three of which feature the work and collaboration of Athens-area researchers and participants. Second is its collaboration and links with other Georgia traditions, especially Atlanta-area singers. This is mostly clearly seen in the February "mega-singing" weekend. On the fourth Sunday of February, singers can sample from seven different shape-note books, including different versions of *The Sacred Harp*, beginning in Decatur on Saturday morning, moving to the Hollingsworth house on Saturday evening, and concluding with the Botanical Gardens singing on Sunday. Finally, Athens demonstrates the possibilities of collaboration between university resources and local singers, as the university has supported the continuance of the tradition through hosting, publishing, and supporting research. A culminating moment for Athens was its invitation in 2019 to host the Georgia Sacred Harp Convention for the first time in the convention's nearly sixty-year history, a recognition of Athens's vital role in the continuance of the tradition.

It is difficult, at this moment in time,to predict how shape-note singing in Athens will continue to unfold. After J. B. Vaughan's death in early 1918, no one picked up his mantle to organize a large-scale hymn-singing event in Athens perhaps because the Spanish flu pandemic hit the area by that October.[80] In 2020, the voices of singers have again been silenced by a pandemic. As COVID-19 quickly spread, Sacred Harp singings around the world ground to a halt. The mixed generational groups, cross-community travel, loud volume of the singing, and directionality of performance practice as singers face each other in a tight square have made the practice particularly dangerous in this time.

In internet groups that host the Sacred Harp diaspora, such as "Sacred Harp Friends," singers have shared their grief over not singing and their stories of singings past.[81] Some use recording technologies to fuse together the voices of those singing in their own homes; others have tried widely distanced singings in places like deserted parking lots. But for most, including singers in the Athens community, they see the community created by singing as something that transcends the physical presence at singings. For now a singer may say, in the words of an old hymn, that though for this time "duty makes me understand that we must take the parting hand," soon we may be able to sing together again,

> Ye mourning souls, lift up your eyes
> To glorious mansions in the skies;
> Oh trust His grace—in Canaan's land
> We'll no more take the parting hand.[82]

NOTES

1. Ernest C. Hynds, *Antebellum Athens and Clarke County, Georgia* (Athens: University of Georgia Press, 1974), 158.

2. Ibid., 159.

3. Athens Music Project, University of Georgia, https://willson.uga.edu/research/research-clusters/amp/.

4. J. B. Vaughan, *Resurrected Songs* (Athens, GA: J. B. Vaughan, 1904).

5. *The Social Harp*, [compiled] by John G. McCurry, edited by Daniel W. Patterson and John F. Garst (Athens: University of Georgia Press, 1973).

6. Kiri Miller, *Traveling Home: Sacred Harp Singing and American Pluralism* (Urbana: University of Illinois Press, 2008), 28.

7. Hynds, *Antebellum Athens and Clarke County, Georgia*, 95.

8. *The Hesperian Harp*, [compiled] by William Houser (Philadelphia: Printed by T. K. and P. G. Collins, 1848).

9. "Prospectus of a New Music Book in Patent Notes Called the Hesperian Harp," *The Southern Whig* (September 16, 1847): [3], https://gahistoricnewspapers.galileo.usg.edu/lccn/sn82015107/1847-09-16/ed-1/seq-3/print/image_632x817_from_1820,550_to_3674,2944/.

10. "Sacred Harp. 50 Copies New Improved and much Enlarged Edition. McAllister and Johnston, Broad Street, Athens, Georgia," *The Southern Watchman* (October 17, 1866): [3], https://gahistoricnewspapers.galileo.usg.edu/lccn/sn82014669/1866-10-17/ed-1/seq-3.pdf?fbclid=IwAR0teZX42HUTOy1DKhxI21m3e3VanuyNhgpQAhJWWaUNytl5CGBYocil5VA.

11. "New Music Book," *The Southern Watchman* (December 25, 1867): [3], https://gahistoricnewspapers.galileo.usg.edu/lccn/sn82014669/1867-12-25/ed-1/seq-3.pdf.

12. "Christian Harmony," *The Southern Watchman* (May 5, 1875): [2], https://gahistoricnewspapers.galileo.usg.edu/lccn/sn82014669/1875-05-05/ed-1/seq-2/print/image_596x817_from_3369,531_to_4731,2398/.

13. "West End Baptist Church," *The Athens Banner* (June 13, 1909): [5],
https://gahistoricnewspapers.galileo.usg.edu/lccn/sn88054098/1909-06-13/ed-1/seq-5.pdf.

14. "'Big Foot Ben' Collier of Jackson Some Singer," *The Weekly Banner* (July 20, 1917): [6], https://gahistoricnewspapers.galileo.usg.edu/lccn/sn88054112/1917-07-20/ed-1/seq-6/#date1=01%2F01%2F1763&nottext=&date2=12%2F31%2F2018&words=Ben+Big+Collier&searchType=advanced&sequence=0&index=8&proxdistance=1&rows=12&ortext=&proxtext=Big+Ben+Collier&andtext=&page=1.

15. D. G. B., "The Old-Time Songs," *The Athens Banner* (August 17, 1913): 4, https://gahistoricnewspapers.galileo.usg.edu/lccn/sn88054098/1913-08-17/ed-1/seq-4/.

16. Patterson and Garst, *The Social Harp*.

17. Ibid., ix.

18. Thomas D. Russell, "South Carolina's Largest Slave Auctioneering Firm—Symposium on the Law of Slavery: Criminal and Civil Law of Slavery," *Chicago-Kent Law Review* 68 (June 1993): 1241–81, https://scholarship.kentlaw.iit.edu/cgi/viewcontent.cgi?article=2908&context=cklawreview; J. D. Thomas, "The Slave Market (1830–1860)," *Accessible Archives* (October 21, 2015), taken from Albert Bushnell Hart's *The American Nation: A History, Volume 16, Slavery and Abolition, 1831–1841* (New York; London: Harper & Bros., 1906), https://www.accessible-archives

.com/2015/10/the-slave-market-1830-1860/; "Hart Sheriff's Sale," *Daily Chronicle & Sentinel* (January 10, 1856): [3], https://gahistoricnewspapers.galileo.usg.edu/lccn/sn82015215/1856-01-10/ed-1/seq-3/print/image_540x817_from_4615,3909_to_6253,6384/ [figure].

19. Russell, "South Carolina's Largest Slave Auctioneering Firm," 1241.

20. Ibid., 1245.

21. Ibid., 1244.

22. "Social Harp," *The Southern Watchman* (July 25, 1866): [3], https://gahistoricnewspapers.galileo.usg.edu/lccn/sn82014669/1866-07-25/ed-1/seq-3/print/image_614x817_from_1767,4117_to_3120,5916/.

23. "Fresh Turnip Seed," *The Southern Watchman* (October 2, 1866): [4], https://gahistoricnewspapers.galileo.usg.edu/lccn/sn82014669/1866-10-02/ed-1/seq-4/print/image_609x817_from_4649,6157_to_5331,7071/.

24. B. F. White, "Musical," *The Organ* (February 2, 1856), https://gahistoricnewspapers.galileo.usg.edu/lccn/sn90052353/1856-02-02/ed-1/seq-2.pdf.

25. David Warren Steel with Richard H. Hulan, *The Makers of the Sacred Harp* (Urbana: University of Illinois Press, 2010), 136.

26. Edmund Dumas, "For *The Organ*," *The Organ* (April 5, 1856), https://gahistoricnewspapers.galileo.usg.edu/lccn/sn90052353/1856-04-05/ed-1/seq-2.pdf.

27. Aldine Kieffer, ed., *The Musical Million* (Dayton, VA), https://virginiachronicle.com/?a=cl&cl=CL1&sp=MSM&e=-------en-20--1--txt-txIN-------.

28. Harry Eskew, "Aldine S(illman) Kieffer," in *Grove Music Online*, retrieved July 9, 2020, from https://www.oxfordmusiconline.com/grovemusic/view/10.1093/gmo/9781561592630.001.0001/omo-9781561592630-e-0000014992.

29. J. C. Byars, "News Along the Line," *The Musical Million* 10, no. 7 (July 1, 1879): 106, https://virginiachronicle.com/?a=d&d=MSM18790701.1.10&srpos=1&e=-------en-20--1-byDA-txt-txIN-%22social+harp%22-------.

30. A. J. Showalter, "Messrs. Ruebush, Kieffer & Co.," *The Musical Million* 11, no. 7 (July 1, 1880): 103, https://virginiachronicle.com/?a=d&d=MSM18800701.1.7&srpos=4&e=-------en-20--1-byDA-txt-txIN-%22social+harp%22-------.

31. "Notice," *The Musical Million* 13, no. 7 (July 1, 1882): 105, https://virginiachronicle.com/?a=d&d=MSM18820701.1.9&e=--1882-----en-20-MSM-1-byDA-txt-txIN-%22Isham+Dyar+%22-------.

32. Aldine S. Kieffer, "A Visit to the Home of a Southern Musician," *The Musical Million* 14, no. 5 (May 1, 1883): 72, https://virginiachronicle.com/?a=d&d=MSM18830501.1.8&srpos=7&e=-------en-20--1-byDA-txt-txIN-%22social+harp%22-------.

33. Special thanks to Dr. Kevin Kelly, who generously shared his original research into J. B. Vaughan's life.

34. Aldine S. Kieffer, "A Complete Success," *The Musical Million* 13, no. 1 (January 1, 1882): 8, https://virginiachronicle.com/?a=d&d=MSM18820101.1.8&srpos=1&e=01-01-1882-----en-20-MSM-1-byDA-txt-txIN-%22vaughan%22-------.

35. *Good Tidings: For Sunday-Schools, Prayer, Praise and Gospel Meetings*, [compiled] by A. J. Showalter, assisted by J. B. Vaughan [and others] (Dalton, GA: A. J. Showalter, 1884).

36. J. B. Vaughan, *Resurrected Songs: Prepared for the Church*, ed. J. B. Vaughan (Athens, GA: J. B. Vaughan, 1904), 2.

37. Ibid., 2.

38. "Prof. J.B. Vaughan Moves to Athens," *Athens Banner* (October 22, 1903): [3], https://gahistoricnewspapers.galileo.usg.edu/lccn/sn88054098/1903-10-22/ed-1/seq-3/.

39. Vaughan, *Resurrected Songs*, 3.

40. Ibid.

41. Ibid.

42. Ibid., 96.

43. Ibid., 72.

44. William Walker, *The Southern Harmony and Musical Companion*, revised edition (Philadelphia: E. W. Miller, 1835). Reprint edition in the Federal Writers' Project of Kentucky, Works Progress Administration, *The Southern Harmony Songbook* (New York: Hastings House, 1939), "Idumea" (31) and "Wondrous Love" (252).

45. Vaughan, *Resurrected Songs*, 118.

46. "Singing Fest Here Next Saturday," *The Athens Daily Herald* (September 28, 1914): [1], https://gahistoricnewspapers.galileo.usg.edu/lccn/sn88054118/1914-09-28/ed-1/seq-1.pdf.

47. D. P. Hazleton, Dr. J. L. Pendley, and J. B. Vaughn, "Will Hold Second Singing Fest Here Saturday, Oct. 24," *The Athens Daily Herald* (October 5, 1914): [1], https://gahistoricnewspapers.galileo.usg.edu/lccn/sn88054118/1914-10-05/ed-1/seq-1.pdf.

48. Ibid.

49. Ibid.

50. "All Day Singing," *The Athens Banner* (October 21, 1914): [1], https://gahistoricnewspapers.galileo.usg.edu/lccn/sn88054098/1914-10-21/ed-1/seq-1.pdf.

51. "All-Day Singing Will Bring Many Visitors to City on Next Saturday," *The Athens Daily Herald* (October 22, 1914): [1], https://gahistoricnewspapers.galileo.usg.edu/lccn/sn88054118/1914-10-22/ed-1/seq-1.pdf.

52. Ibid.

53. "Singing Convention," *The Athens Daily Herald* (February 26, 1915): 3, https://gahistoricnewspapers.galileo.usg.edu/lccn/sn88054118/1915-02-26/ed-1/seq-3/print/image_609x817_from_504,1148_to_2340,3610/.

54. "Two Days Singing Convention Here on June 4 and 5," *The Athens Daily Herald* (May 26, 1915): [1], https://gahistoricnewspapers.galileo.usg.edu/lccn/sn88054118/1915-05-26/ed-1/seq-1.pdf.

55. "Suburban Shoppers and Visitors to the Singing Convention," *The Athens Daily Herald* (June 3, 1915): 8, https://gahistoricnewspapers.galileo.usg.edu/lccn/sn88054118/1915-06-03/ed-1/seq-8/print/image_605x817_from_0,0_to_3739,5044/.

56. "Singing Convention."

57. "Preparations by Committee of 140 for Song Convention," *The Athens Banner* (May 29, 1915): 6, https://gahistoricnewspapers.galileo.usg.edu/lccn/sn88054098/1915-05-29/ed-1/seq-6.pdf.

58. Ibid.

59. "Singing Convention Here in June Will Be Important Event," *The Athens Daily Herald* (May 29, 1915): 3, https://gahistoricnewspapers.galileo.usg.edu/lccn/sn88054118/1915-05-29/ed-1/seq-3.pdf.

60. "Words of Praise," *The Athens Daily Herald* (June 8, 1915): 3, https://gahistoricnewspapers.galileo.usg.edu/lccn/sn88054118/1915-06-08/ed-1/seq-3.pdf.

61. J. P. Cooper, "West End Baptist Church," *The Athens Banner* (June 13, 1909): 5, https://gahistoricnewspapers.galileo.usg.edu/lccn/sn88054098/1909-06-13/ed-1/seq-5.pdf; "Choir Meets," *The Athens Daily Herald* (August 18, 1917): 6, https://gahistoricnewspapers.galileo.usg.edu/lccn/sn88054118/1917-08-18/ed-1/seq-6/print/image_609x817_from_1475,1402_to_2407,2652/.

62. "Nicholson," *The Athens Daily Herald* (July 1, 1915): 2, https://gahistoricnewspapers.galileo.usg.edu/lccn/sn88054118/1915-07-01/ed-1/seq-2/print/image_529x817_from_543,1363_to_1401,2686/.

63. "Booster Trip," *The Athens Banner* (May 30, 1915): 8, https://gahistoricnewspapers.galileo.usg.edu/lccn/sn88054098/1915-05-30/ed-1/seq-8.pdf.

64. "Sacred Singers Plan Meeting," *The Banner-Herald* (September 25, 1923): 6, https://gahistoricnewspapers.galileo.usg.edu/lccn/sn88054099/1923-09-25/ed-1/seq-6/print/image_632x817_from_381,1493_to_1306,2687/.

65. Gilbert Chase, *America's Music: From the Pilgrims to the Present* (New York: McGraw-Hill, [1955]).

66. *Anthology of American Folk Music*, ed. Harry Smith, Folkways Records FA 2951--FA 2953, 1952, 6 LP box set.

67. John Garst, interview with author, Athens, Georgia, September 25, 2014.

68. George Pullen Jackson, *White Spirituals in the Southern Uplands: The Story of the Fasola Folk, Their Songs, Singings, and "Buckwheat Notes"* (Chapel Hill: University of North Carolina Press, 1933), 80.

69. John Hollingsworth Jr., "Shape Note Singing: Christian Harmony in Newton County, Mississippi," *Newton County, Mississippi Historical and Genealogical Society*, https://www.nchgs.org/html/shape_note_singing.html.

70. John Hollingsworth, Roundtable Discussion at "Music in Athens: A Sacred Harp Symposium" (Athens, Georgia), October 30, 2014.

71. "Inaugural Singing from the Georgian Harmony by Raymond C. Hamrick," from *A Homepage for Christian Harmony Singings* webpage, http://www.christianharmony.org/harmony/minutes/2008minutes/Georgian01.html; Raymond C. Hamrick, *The Georgian Harmony: A Collection of Hymns and Fuging Tunes in the Shape-Note Tradition* (Georgia: Hamrick, 2008).

72. John Hollingsworth, "The Making of the Georgian Harmony," *Sacred Harp Publishing Company* (December 31, 2016), http://originalsacredharp.com/2016/12/31/the-making-of-the-georgian-harmony/.

73. Raymond C. Hamrick, *The Georgian Harmony: A Collection of Hymns and Fuging Tunes in the Shape-note Tradition*, second edition (Georgia: Hamrick, 2010).

74. *The Christian Harmony*, 2010 Edition (Bishop, GA: Christian Harmony Music Company Inc., 2010).

75. "About Shaped-Note Singing and the Christian Harmony," http://www.christianharmony.org/harmony/about.html.

76. John Hollingsworth, email with author, May 22, 2020.//
77. "AMP-001. Shannon Primm interviewed by Joanna Smolko. November 25, 2014" (Athens, Georgia), https://www.youtube.com/watch?v=X-7xXXyGTMY.
78. Ibid.
79. *Awake, My Soul: The Story of the Sacred Harp*, a film by Matt and Erica Hinton, written by Matt Hinton with John Plunkett, an Awake Productions film, produced in association with Digital Maps (Atlanta, GA: Awake Productions AP-001, 2006), DVD.
80. Victoria Swyers, "100 Years After the 1918 Quarantine of Athens, the Flu Continues to Plague Society," *The Red & Black* (October 7, 2018), https://www.redandblack.com/athensnews/100-years-after-the-1918-quarantine-of-athens-the-flu-continues-to-plague-society/article_22bb9610-ca58-11e8-9cfc-57597b19bd71.html.
81. "Sacred Harp Friends," Facebook group, https://www.facebook.com/groups/288062357886428/.
82. John Blaine, "Parting Hand" (1818), ("My Dearest Friends, in Bonds of Love"), *Hymnary.org* website, https://hymnary.org/text/my_christian_friends_in_bonds_of_love_wh.

FURTHER READING

Athens Music Project, University of Georgia, https://willson.uga.edu/research/research-clusters/amp/.

Awake, My Soul: The Story of the Sacred Harp. A film by Matt and Erica Hinton. Written by Matt Hinton with John Plunkett. An Awake Productions film. Produced in association with Digital Maps. Atlanta, GA: Awake Productions AP-001, 2006, DVD.

Bithell, Caroline, and Juniper Hill, eds. *The Oxford Handbook of Musical Revival*. Oxford and New York City: Oxford University Press, 2014.

Cobb, Buell. *The Sacred Harp: A Tradition and Its Music*. Athens: University of Georgia Press, 1978.

Hynds, Ernest C. *Antebellum Athens and Clarke County, Georgia.* Athens: University of Georgia Press, 1974.

Jackson, George Pullen. *White Spirituals in the Southern Uplands: The Story of the Fasola Folk, Their Songs, Singings, and "Buckwheat Notes."* Chapel Hill: University of North Carolina Press, 1933.

Miller, Kiri. *Traveling Home: Sacred Harp Singing and American Pluralism*. Urbana: University of Illinois Press, 2008.

Steel, David Warren, with Richard H. Hulan. *The Makers of the Sacred Harp*. Urbana: University of Illinois Press, 2010.

Chapter Five

The Hymn Tunes of Thomas Hastings

David W. Music

Thomas Hastings was one of the most active church musicians in the United States during the nineteenth century, teaching singing schools and musical conventions, compiling tunebooks, composing music, writing hymn texts, authoring books, and editing newspapers. Together with his slightly younger contemporary, Lowell Mason, he was also one of the chief figures in the major reform that occurred in US church music practice during the early nineteenth century.

Hastings is the subject of three substantial dissertations, a book-length biography, and several journal articles.[1] Most of the notice he has received has dealt with the tunebooks he compiled and his writings on behalf of church music reform. However, relatively little attention has been paid to the actual music he wrote. When mentioned at all, his compositions are often dismissed as bland, uninteresting, sentimental, or worse.[2]

While it is true that Hastings's works do not have the rhythmic vigor of a William Billings anthem, the contrapuntal interest of a Daniel Read fuging tune, or the modal inflection of a *Southern Harmony* folk hymn, his music does not deserve the near-total neglect that has been its lot in American music scholarship. The hymn tunes of Hastings and Mason appeared widely in US hymnals during and after their lifetimes, and between them the two men established a hymn tune style that became the standard for urban church music in the United States in the last half of the nineteenth century and well into the twentieth. Furthermore, some pieces are still familiar to many Americans today through their use in churches, Sacred Harp sings, movies, and other venues.[3] If Mason is perhaps slightly better known today than Hastings, thanks particularly to his work in public school music education and his congregational arrangements of "Antioch" ("Joy to the World") and "Hamburg"

("When I Survey the Wondrous Cross"), as well as several original tunes, this does not lessen the need at least to acknowledge the important role Hastings played as a composer of reform church music. The present essay describes and evaluates a group of Hastings's hymn tunes in an effort to understand and illustrate one practical outgrowth of the reform philosophy of church music he espoused, a philosophy that became quite influential in the United States during the nineteenth century.[4]

THOMAS HASTINGS

Thomas Hastings was born in Washington, Connecticut, on October 15, 1784. His father, a medical doctor, moved the family to a farm in Oneida County, New York, when Thomas was thirteen years old. Around age twenty-two, Thomas began teaching singing schools in the Oneida County area, leaving this occupation for unknown business pursuits about 1810–1811, then becoming manager of his father's farm in 1812.[5]

In 1816, Hastings left the farm and returned to music as a vocation. He spent the rest of his life attempting to reform church music in the United States by extensive teaching, writing, compiling of tunebooks, and composing/arranging of music. Based primarily in New York, he taught singing schools throughout that state and well beyond. His book *Dissertation on Musical Taste* (1822, second edition 1853) was the first major publication by a US author on the philosophy of music; toward the end of his life he issued *Sacred Praise: An Earnest Appeal to Christian Worshippers, in Behalf of a Neglected Duty* (1856), another major document on church music philosophy. He also served as the editor for two newspapers, the *Western Recorder* and the *Musical Magazine*. In recognition of his services to music, New York University conferred upon him the Doctor of Music degree in 1858. Hastings died in New York City on May 15, 1872.

CHURCH MUSIC REFORM

In his attempt at reform, Hastings took special aim at two types of music then common in Christian churches of the United States, New England psalmody of the William Billings/Oliver Holden/Daniel Read type and folk hymnody. In Hastings's view, despite the popularity of the New England psalmodists of the previous generation, their music was full of melodic and harmonic ineptitudes and was too complex for effective performance by a congregation.[6] The last-named feature was particularly characteristic of the fuging tune, in which at least one phrase of the piece contained overlapping entries of the voices preceded by rests; this, of course, also obscured the words, which Hastings thought should be primary. The often driving or dance-like rhythms were another area of concern, in his mind making the music generally unsuitable for the purposes of devotion.

Even worse in his view were the folk hymns that circulated in the rural areas of the country. These pieces were often derived from secular ballads or songs; in the mere singing of them, Hastings believed, parishioners could not help but call to mind their previous associations with words that were sometimes bawdy or perhaps harmless enough but still were not "sacred."

Hastings was born during the era when "standard harmonic practice" became fully established in the works of such composers as Handel, Haydn, Mozart, and Beethoven. It was the belief of Hastings and other American reformers that this was the harmonic idiom that was best suited for congregational music. However, he was also critical of the sacred music of the European art music composers because of its complexity and what he considered to be its nondevotional character. He especially objected to the use of music with sacred texts in settings other than worship (as was the case, for example, with oratorio performances), especially when the music seemed to be too intricate or intended to show off the skills of the composer and/or performers. In his own words, "Worship and amusement are both legitimate objects in music; but they ought never to be *united in the business of expression*: and this circumstance alone, should form the line of distinction between Sacred and secular music: and between music of the church, and the concert and oratorio."[7] Furthermore, he noted that

> if sacred words are set to music for the purpose of display; for the sake of their beauty, pathos, or sublimity, irrespectively of moral consequences; if the emotions they are found to excite, are chiefly such as result from gratified taste; and if they do not, under the most favorable circumstances, serve to impress upon us as rational and sentient beings, through the medium of our sensibilities, those solemn truths and considerations of religion, which they were originally intended to convey; then it is evident, that in respect to us, if not to others, the composition, or execution, or both, must be regarded as a failure.[8]

MUSIC PUBLICATIONS AND COMPOSITIONS

Hastings was a prolific compiler of tunebooks, both by himself and in association with other reformers, such as Lowell Mason and William B. Bradbury. His first tune book, *Musica Sacra*, probably published in its complete form in

1816, was combined with Solomon Warriner's *Springfield Collection* (1813) in 1818, and this joint venture went through at least ten editions and several reprints under the title *Musica sacra: or Utica and Springfield Collections United.*[9] Hastings went on to publish many additional tunebooks, the specific number of which is difficult to categorize because he sometimes issued the same work under different titles; for example, the *New York Choralist* (1847) and the *Sacred Choralist* (1847) have the same musical contents and differ only in their titles and publication information. In some instances, he incorporated one collection into another, as when a small tunebook, *Congregational Harmony* (1849), became an appendix to the larger *Mendelssohn Collection* of the same year. Altogether, the compiler was responsible in whole or in part for about thirty-five collections of music, not counting various editions or reprints of the same work.[10]

Hastings's individual compositions are also challenging to catalog because he frequently published them without an attribution or under a pseudonym. In cases where he did sign a tune, he usually did so by simply using the letter "H." Several of his pseudonyms have been positively identified, but there are several other suspects that have thus far eluded verification.[11] In many instances, he published a tune anonymously, then, in later collections, simply credited the book where it first appeared.

Still, Hastings can be positively identified as the composer of nearly nine hundred original compositions that were signed in at least one tunebook with his name, initial, or a known pseudonym or that appeared in *Hastings's Church Music*, which contained only music by the compiler.[12] Because this figure does not count unattributed items or arrangements of pieces by other composers, and because a few editions or collections are no longer extant or otherwise not available, the total number of his compositions is surely much higher. His works include cantatas, anthems, service music, children's songs, secular glees, and other genres, but by far the largest category is that of hymn tunes.

HASTINGS'S HYMN TUNES

Hymn tunes by a composer such as Thomas Hastings are difficult to categorize for several reasons. The first challenge, of course, is the sheer number of his compositions. Closely allied to this obstacle is the problem of distinguishing hymn tunes from other short forms that are somewhat similar in character to congregational hymns but were perhaps intended primarily for choirs or singing schools. The composer's labels are sometimes, though not always, helpful in this regard. As was the custom of the day, Hastings usually gave hymns a tune name and designated other pieces as an "anthem," "introit," "motet," etc., or simply titled pieces of the latter sorts by a textual incipit. However, the relationships between the labels or titles and the actual pieces are not always clear cut. For example, "Zion" and "Sabbath Eve," both of which appear in *Hastings's Church Music*, are named for aspects of their texts and both titles sound like typical hymn tune names. That, indeed, is true for "Zion," but in the case of "Sabbath Eve" the title disguises the choral nature of the piece.[13] The categorization of a piece such as the strophic "dirge" "Go to Thy Rest," which includes a "symphony" between each stanza and again at the end, brings its own set of challenges. A conservative estimate is that Hastings composed at least six hundred pieces that could be denominated as "hymn tunes."

And, of course, there are difficulties in analyzing hymn tunes of any composer or era. The small scope of the hymn tune compared with, say, a symphony or a sonata means that there is relatively little material with which to work. The tunes are meant for singing by a congregation, so they are often constructed of relatively uncomplicated materials. This is particularly true of Hastings, who, as a reformer, strove to keep his tunes as simple as possible. The strophic nature of the music, not to mention the fact that tunes can frequently be sung to different sets of words, implies that word-tone relationships are generally of lesser importance than in through-composed pieces.

The procedure followed in this study is to examine the tunes that Hastings himself published most often in his various collections. Presumably, these are the pieces that the composer himself thought were among his most successful ones, those that his tunebooks could not do without. Nine tunes that Hastings issued at least ten times have been chosen for analysis, to which one item ("Rock of Ages," published eight times) has been added because of its subsequent use and popularity.[14] It is assumed that his latest publication of the tunes represents the composer's final version of the pieces, and thus they are primarily analyzed from *Hastings's Church Music* (1860), which served as a compendium of much of his work in the hymn tune genre. The ten tunes, their original sources, and the number of printings they received in Hastings's collections are listed in table 5.1.

Table 5.1. Hastings's collections

Tune	First Known Publication	Number of Printings
"Chester"	*Musica Sacra*, 1831 edition	11
"Child of Sin and Sorrow" (also "Ava" and "Newburyport")	*Spiritual Songs*, 1833 edition	10
"Haven"	*The Musical Miscellany*, 1837	11
"Hemans" (also "Hark 'Tis the Tem'prance Call")	*The Psalmodist*, 1844	11
"How Calm [and Beautiful]" (also "Calm" and "Hastings")	*Spiritual Songs*, 1833 edition	10
"Laight Street" (also "Invocation")	*Spiritual Songs*, 1833 edition	10
"Ortonville"	*Manhattan Collection*, 1837	12
"Retreat" (also "Mercy-Seat")	*Juvenile Songs*, 1841	10
"Rock of Ages"	*Spiritual Songs*, 1832 edition	8
"Zion"	*Spiritual Songs*, 1832 edition	13

TEXTS

Six of the ten tunes in *Hastings's Church Music* employed texts by British hymn writers of the eighteenth or early nineteenth centuries.[15] A seventh lyric, "From every stormy wind that blows," was also by a British author but is of special interest because it was contemporary with the composer himself; indeed, it was first published in the version used by Hastings only nine years before he composed his tune "Retreat" for it.[16] This suggests that Hastings was familiar with contemporary developments in hymnody from across the Atlantic.

The three remaining lyrics were all written by the composer himself.[17] In addition to his work as a writer of music, Hastings has been credited with the writing of six hundred original hymn texts.[18] In *Hastings's Church Music*, each of the three items was labeled simply "Words and Music," indicating that both elements were by the compiler of the book.

TUNE NAMES

Six tunes were named for some element of their associated text: "Child of Sin and Sorrow," "Haven," "How Calm," "Retreat," "Rock of Ages," and

"Zion." In every case but one, the word or words of the title are found in the text itself; the exception is "Haven": while that word is not used in the hymn, it is implied by the text, particularly in the line "The Christian's bark will reach the shore."

The reasons for the names of the other four tunes are less obvious. It is possible that Hastings chose the name "Chester" in hopes that his tune would replace William Billings's piece of the same name. "Hemans" might have been titled for the English poet Felicia Hemans (1793–1835), though why Hastings would use this designation for a tune that sets words by another author (James Allen) is not evident. "Laight Street" was almost certainly named for the Laight Street Presbyterian Church in New York City.[19] No reason for the title "Ortonville" has been discovered.[20]

KEYS

One of the most notable features of the tunes is that they are all in major keys (see figure 5.1). According to *The Autobiography of Lyman Beecher* (1864), this use of major keys by the reform composers was in keeping with the optimistic evangelical flavor of the times.

> The music of New England had originally been plaintive and mournful to a remarkable degree. It was the natural tendency of persecution and exile to tune the harp of the daughter of Zion in the minor key; but, under the exhilaration of anticipated conquest, minor airs became distasteful and went out of date, and music assumed a bolder, livelier, more triumphant character.[21]

Whether or not Hastings's tunes are "bolder," "livelier," or "more triumphant" in character than those by the earlier New England composers may be debatable. Hastings himself observed that "in either scale [major or minor] there are great varieties of sentiment embraced; and therefore the simple question whether a hymn [text] is of a joyous or plaintive character, does not alone suffice for the purposes of adaptation [of tunes to words]," nor did he disdain composing in minor keys.[22] Nevertheless, the overwhelming bulk of his works, including his most popular tunes, appear in the major mode, in contrast to the frequent use of minor keys and modes in earlier American psalmody and contemporary shape-note folk hymnody. It seems likely that the tunes of Hastings (and Mason, whose tunes are likewise mainly in major keys) played an important part in developing or at least reinforcing the views of many American parishioners that major keys are "happy" and minor keys are "sad," an implication that can already be seen in the earlier quote from Beecher's autobiography.

Figure 5.1.

Figure 5.1.

METER AND RHYTHM

Hastings's ten tunes show a balance between simple triple meters (3/4, 3/2; four tunes), compound duple meters (6/8, 6/4; three tunes), and simple duple meters (2/2; three tunes). Six of the pieces are entirely syllabic; the rest include a few slurred notes but never more than two at a time. The melodies generally use no more than three-four note values (sometimes only two, as in "Laight Street") and are without syncopation, hemiola, or other rhythmic complications.[23] "Rock of Ages" and "Zion" make considerable use of dotted-quarter/eighth-note or dotted-eighth/sixteenth-note patterns. Once a rhythmic pattern has been established, there is often little variation from it; "Hemans," "Ortonville," and "Retreat" are particularly clear examples (see figure 5.1).

MELODY AND HARMONY

Hastings did his work during a period when the placement of a hymn tune melody was in the process of transitioning from the tenor to the soprano part.[24] Generally speaking, this transition occurred as the oblong tunebook began to give way to the hymnal with music, a development that began with the publication of Darius E. Jones's *Temple Melodies* (1851) and Henry Ward Beecher, Charles Beecher, and John Zundel's *Plymouth Collection of Hymns and Tunes* (1855). Before the collections by Jones and Beecher, American hymnals typically contained words only, the music being found in tunebooks, which, however, usually did not include full texts. Hymnals with music maintained the upright shape of the words-only hymnal, and because these books typically included the music in closed score, the melody was now placed in the soprano.

The change in the position of the melody was, however, neither sudden nor consistent. For example, when Hastings first published his tune "Retreat" (under the title "Mercy-Seat") in *Juvenile Songs* (1841), the melody was in the top voice with a three-part harmonization. In its next appearance (*Sacred Songs*, 1842), the tune was on three staves, with the middle stave containing two parts, the upper of which is the melody. For the next two publications, *The Psalmodist* (1844) and *The Mendelssohn Collection* (1847), Hastings placed the melody in the top part with a four-part harmonization. In *The Presbyterian Psalmodist* (1852), he returned to traditional practice by giving the melody in the tenor. Thereafter, the melody was placed in the soprano until its last publication by the composer in *Hastings's Church Music* (1860), where it was again in the tenor.

An examination of these printings confirms that, for Hastings, the position of the melody depended mainly on whether the tune was printed in open or closed score. All the four-part settings in closed score placed the melody in the top part, while the two four-part settings in open score gave it in the tenor (or, when only three staves were used, the upper voice of the middle stave).

It should be noted, however, that Hastings's expectation was that the melody (wherever it was located on the printed page) should be sung by treble rather than tenor voices; as the composer pointed out in the 1818 edition of *Musica sacra*, "The Air . . . is . . . designed for treble voices" but was "placed next to the base" "for the convenience of those who practice on finger-keyed instruments."[25] It is this expected accompaniment by keyboard that accounts for the difference in placement of the melody between closed and open score: in the former, the keyboardist could easily see and play all the parts at once, while in the latter, having the melody immediately above the bass enabled the player to fill in the harmonies in basso continuo-like fashion.

As would be anticipated in almost any four-part hymn tune, the melody part is the most prominent one in Hastings's pieces. However, there are several aspects of the composer's work that make the melody particularly conspicuous. Among these features are the range and active nature of this part. Each of the melodies covers at least an octave and several encompass a tenth ("Chester," "Child of Sin and Sorrow," "Hemans"). Some of the melodies primarily use conjunct motion ("Haven," "Hemans"), but others contain many leaps, some of them quite large ("Child of Sin and Sorrow," "Laight Street"; see figure 5.1).

These aspects of the melody contrast significantly with the other voices, which often have only a four- or five-pitch compass with many repeated notes. Perhaps the most extreme example in this regard is "Haven": apart from the "Coda for last verse," the alto voice never leaves the pitch E except to sing a neighbor tone on either side, and it functions essentially as a "filler"; the soprano part is slightly more active but also includes numerous repeated notes, while the bass has a range of only a sixth (again, except for the coda; see figure 5.2). The same is generally true of all the tunes: the upper harmonizing parts employ a small range and many repeated notes, the bass mostly moves by chord roots, and the melody stands out because of its greater activity.

Another important feature in the prominence of the melody is the plainness of the harmonic background. The harmonies of all ten tunes are composed principally of primary chords, and because the tunes are all in major keys this means that a minor or other quality chord is seldom found.[26] In "Retreat," for example, the only pitches in the bass are the tonic, subdominant, and dominant, and the harmony never moves outside the chords implied by these roots. "Zion" is similarly inactive harmonically, though it does include a few first inversion chords (figure 5.3). Dissonances are mostly mild and employed only in passing, and full chords predominate. While "Retreat" and "Zion" are the most unusual examples, none of the tunes demonstrate what might be called an active harmonization. The static nature of the harmony tends to throw the more active melody into relief and make it stand out above the other parts.

A distinctive feature of the ten melodies is that they all begin on either the third (five tunes) or fifth degree (five tunes) of the musical scale; not one

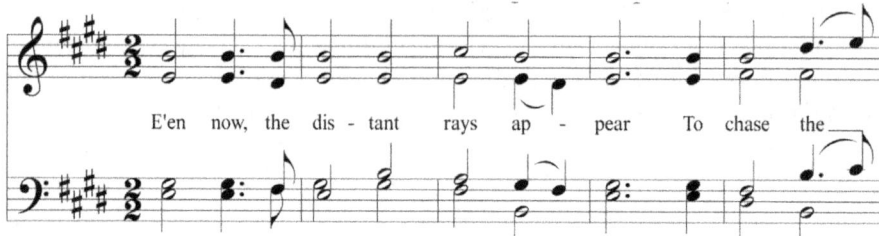

Figure 5.2.

starts on the tonic. It is not uncommon for hymn melodies to begin on the fifth degree, usually as a pick-up to the tonic, but three of Hastings's tunes do not use it in that manner. A start on the third degree is often considered to be a "weak" beginning to a tune because this is the "color" note of the chord. In any case, all but one of the melodies ("Zion") migrates to the tonic for the last note.[27]

Another characteristic of Hastings's tunes is that they are almost invariably diatonic in all their parts. The only accidentals in the tunes (other than those of the key signature or for cautionary or cancellation purposes) are found in "Haven," "Hemans," and "Laight Street." "Haven" and "Hemans" each use a single accidental to form a secondary dominant, while "Laight Street" employs a natural (twice) to lower the leading tone and provide a temporary

Figure 5.3.

modulation to the subdominant. The static nature of the harmony, relative lack of movement of the harmonizing parts, and absence of chromatic alterations gives the settings a plainness of character that contrasts significantly with the early American psalmody and folk hymnody that Hastings sought to replace.

The simple nature of the harmony in Hastings's tunes is offset to a degree by the interest provided by their melodies. It is obvious that though he preferred that the parts be sung by the specific voices for which they were written, even if they were also accompanied by a keyboard instrument, he recognized that a mixed congregation would primarily sing the principal melody.[28] This practice would allow not only for all to be involved in the singing but would also provide the "distinct, earnest, and impressive" declamation of the text that Hastings believed was the scriptural model for church music.[29] For Hastings, the expression of the words was uppermost in the church's music and he wrote his hymn tunes in such a way that they could be articulated plainly and intelligibly.

The melodic and harmonic characteristics that have been described might strike us today as more or less "standard" hymnic practice, but in Hastings's own time they represented a distinct change from the usual presentation of congregational song in the United States. The earlier American psalmody Hastings sought to replace often included open fifths (especially at cadences), parallelisms, contrapuntal (or at least active) harmonizing parts, and nonfunctional chord progressions, with the principal melody frequently being only slightly more prominent than its surroundings (and, of course, buried in the tenor).

Nineteenth-century collections of folk hymns had many of the same characteristics but carried them to even further extremes, were frequently modal in character, and added such "ineptitudes" as beginning a tune with a chord in second inversion. The work of Hastings and his fellow reformers established a melodic and harmonic style for hymn tunes that became widely practiced in the United States from about the middle of the nineteenth century until well into the twentieth and influenced not only the regular congregational hymn but also the development of the Sunday school and gospel song.

FORM

In addition to their active melodies, the greatest interest in Hastings's tunes is provided by their form, which is perhaps their most creative aspect. While the form of a hymn tune is, of course, largely determined by the text, Hastings often found ways to vary the shape or repetitions of the tune to give it a distinctive quality. Four pieces extend the tune by repeating the last line or two of the text ("Chester," Laight Street," "Ortonville," "Zion").[30] Another tune, "Haven," repeats the last line as a coda for the final stanza. The five phrases of "Laight Street" approach a through-composed design, ABCDE, though the last phrase can also be seen as a variant of B. "Hemans" is similarly through-composed except for a repetition in the middle of the tune (ABCD-DEF), but there is a subtlety that does not show up in such a bare listing in that E is a sequence of D. "Rock of Ages" follows the form ABCCAB, while "Chester" is written as ABACD, but phrase C contains a reminiscence of B. The other tunes show similar imagination and generally avoid frequently used approaches for hymn tunes such as bar form or rounded bar form.[31]

OTHER FEATURES

Several additional features are designed to give interest to Hastings's tunes. Though he does not use metronomic markings, the composer occasionally indicates a general tempo or the character in which the piece should be sung. Thus "Chester" is to be sung "Tenderly," while "Hemans" should be "Bold. Staccato. Quick." "Ortonville" is marked "Quick and Joyous," with the added note that "this tune is too often sung in a drawling manner," a comment that suggests that it was already well known and widely sung, albeit not in a manner that Hastings approved. "Retreat" should be sung "Gently" but "Not too Slow." From these designations it appears that Hastings generally preferred a moderate or brisk tempo rather than a slow one for his music.

Three of the tunes give dynamic indications. The first two phrases of "Chester" are marked m (mezzo or medium) and p respectively, the third and fourth phrases return to m, and the last phrase (a textual repeat of phrase four) is indicated "*Last line p*"; decrescendos are indicated in two places. "Laight Street" does not include letter designations for dynamics but incorporates two crescendo-decrescendo marks, as well as a third decrescendo mark at the end of the third phrase. The second phrase of "Ortonville" is to be sung p with a decrescendo into the last note, and a crescendo-decrescendo occurs later in the tune, the crescendo leading directly into the climax of the melody. These dynamic markings and tempo indications are invariably omitted in congregational hymnals.

Another method Hastings used for varying the performance of the tunes was to change the texture by temporarily omitting one or more of the voice parts, a procedure that had also been used by the earlier American psalmodists. This textural change occurs in three pieces. In "How Calm," the bass part rests for one phrase, leaving only the upper three parts, while "Retreat" and "Zion" both reduce the texture to two parts for a phrase—alto and tenor in "Retreat" and soprano and tenor in "Zion." In both cases, notes for an instrument are cued into the bass part.

TEXT SETTING

For the most part, Hastings seems to have considered his pieces to be "proper" tunes, ones that were associated with a specific text. He invariably published four of the tunes with the same lyrics: "Chester," "Child of Sin and Sorrow," "How Calm," and "Rock of Ages"; it will be recalled that the second and third of these had words by Hastings himself.

Four other tunes were printed with a different text in *The Presbyterian Psalmodist* (1852), for which Hastings served as music editor: "Haven" ("How sad our state by nature is"), "Ortonville" ("O for a closer walk with God"), "Retreat" ("Jesus is gone above the skies"), and "Zion" ("O'er the gloomy hills of darkness"). In these instances, the text that Hastings originally set did not appear in *Psalms and Hymns Adapted to Public Worship* (1830), the official hymnal of the Presbyterian Church in the United States, for which *The Presbyterian Psalmodist* served as a companion. This fact undoubtedly explains the use of a different text in these collections.[32]

The two remaining tunes, "Hemans" and "Laight Street," were employed by Hastings as "common" tunes and were set to a variety of texts. In fact, Hastings's ten printings of "Laight Street" were associated with five different texts. In some cases, the use of a different hymn was called for by the nature of the collection in which the tune appeared, as when "Hemans" was set to "Hark, 'tis the temperance call" in *The Crystal Fount* (1847), a collection of temperance songs; in other instances, the reason for the change is not evident.

Whether used as a "common" or a "proper" tune, however, Hastings sought to link his tune with words whose character was in general accord with that of the music. The graceful neumatic groupings and cadential sighing figures of "Chester" well match the tenderness of "How sweet the name of Jesus sounds." The earnestness of "Child of Sin and Sorrow" is suitably plain and inviting for an appeal to accept Christ, and "Retreat" is appropriately restful for a text about "a calm, a sure retreat" "from every swelling tide of woes." "Laight Street" expresses the celebratory nature of "Come, ye that love the Saviour's name, / And joy to make it known,"[33] and "Rock of Ages" reflects the same prayerful attitude as Augustus Toplady's text, while the dotted rhythms of "Zion" suggest the trumpet of the "sacred herald" mentioned in the first stanza. On the whole it can be said that Hastings followed his own advice that "the sacred themes which the musician chooses as the subjects of musical adaptation, must always be treated in such a manner as to heighten their interest strictly in accordance with their religious character" and that "every possible variety of sentiment, which is suggested by the words of a psalm or hymn, must be taken into account" when setting them to music.[34]

USE OF HASTINGS'S TUNES

The website http://www.hymnary.org contains a comprehensive list of publications of hymn texts and tunes in North American hymnals from the colonial period to the twenty-first century.[35] The figures given on the website must be handled with caution because it does not index every printed North American collection of religious song, and some categories of publication are largely excluded (gospel song and tunebooks, for example). Nevertheless, the website is the best available resource for tracking publications of a hymn and giving at least an approximate indication of the usage of individual texts and tunes.

Of the ten tunes that Hastings himself printed most often, only four appear to have been widely employed in other collections: "Toplady [= "Rock of Ages"] (479 times), "Ortonville" (315), "Retreat" (204), and "Zion" (219). The others range from two ("Laight Street") to approximately twenty publications ("How Calm") each.[36] Altogether, these ten tunes were printed at least 1,276 times.

Casting a wider net, the website catalogues many other tunes by Hastings, some of which actually saw more use than several that he himself printed most often. Among these are "Armenia" (29), "Bremen" (28), "Byefield" (36), "Luther" (40), and "New Haven" (29), though the aggregate of all these other tunes totals only 318.[37]

In recent years, the number of Hastings tunes in circulation has declined significantly. Indeed, only one of his four most commonly printed tunes, "Rock of Ages"/"Toplady," still appears to be widely used. A check of seven US hymnals published in the early twenty-first century shows that this piece is found in five of the books: *Baptist Hymnal* (2008), *Evangelical Lutheran Worship* (2006, Evangelical Lutheran Church in America), *Glory to God* (2013, Presbyterian), *Lutheran Service Book* (2006, Lutheran Church—Missouri Synod), and *Worship and Rejoice* (2001, nondenominational). Only one of the volumes, *Baptist Hymnal*, contains another tune by Hastings, "Ortonville," used twice for different texts. The remaining two hymnals, *Celebrating Grace* (2010, Baptist) and *Lift Up Your Hearts* (2013, Reformed), do not include any Hastings tunes.

A comparison of these figures with those of four hymnals published fewer than sixty years earlier, all of which were predecessors to ones listed in the previous paragraph, is instructive. *Baptist Hymnal* (1956) included all four of Hastings's "big tunes," with "Zion" being used twice and "Ortonville" no fewer than three times. *The Hymnbook* (1955, Presbyterian/Reformed) and *Hymns for the Living Church* (1974, nondenominational) contained "Ortonville," "Retreat," and "Toplady," while the *Service Book and Hymnal* (1958, Lutheran) printed "Ortonville" and "Toplady."

There are probably several reasons for the decline in publication of Hastings's tunes. Inevitably, the works of a popular hymn author or composer will gradually diminish in use over time, as can be seen even with such hymnic luminaries as Isaac Watts, Charles Wesley, and Ralph Vaughan Williams.

In some cases, there may be problems with the tune's associated text. For instance, Hugh Stowell's "From Every Stormy Wind that Blows," to which Hastings's "Retreat" is set, makes frequent allusion to the "mercy seat" and refers to Jesus shedding "The oil of gladness on our heads," Old Testament images that will probably be unfamiliar to most parishioners of the twenty-first century. Indeed, the entire text is somewhat vague, and it does not contain a call to action or commitment. In the more prosaic twentieth and twenty-first centuries, where directness of expression tends to be valued over typology and where knowledge of the Old Testament on the part of parishioners is often rudimentary, texts such as this tend to be omitted from hymnals. As a result, the associated tune is lost as well.

The explosion of new hymnody and contemporary Christian popular music in Great Britain and North America during the late twentieth and early twentieth centuries is probably another cause for the dropping of tunes by Hastings: room must be made in the hymnals for these new productions, and, in some cases, hymnals (and their repertory) have been abandoned altogether. Finally, the very plainness of the tunes perhaps works against them in comparison with the harmonic daring and rhythmic drive of twentieth and twenty-first-century hymn tunes and Christian popular music

HASTINGS'S LEGACY

Thomas Hastings's two principal concerns were that sacred music be "correct" and that it should reflect "sentiment" (feeling or emotion). The composer and his fellow reformers lived during a time of scientific discovery, and in their view musicians of the previous generation had finally defined the "science" of music, the immutable laws of harmony that should govern any compositional activity. Hastings's adoption of this "scientific" approach shows most clearly in his use of "correct" harmonic progressions and voice leading (emphasis on the primary chords and generally stepwise motion of the accompanying parts) as well as the clarity and plainness of the harmony. "Correctness" also meant that the words should be clearly understood, a feature that is articulated not only by the plainness of the harmony but also by the lack of contrapuntal elaboration or other features that might obscure the text.

The "sentiment" of Hastings's tunes lies mainly in their expressive melodies and the forms in which they were cast. The melodies are generally evocative of the words that they set, reflecting both the mood of the texts and, in some cases, specific aspects of their subjects (for example, "Zion"). Hastings believed that sacred music should be properly "devotional" in character and the goal in his own hymnic compositions was to write a melody that was not only pleasing to sing and hear but that expressed the mood and meaning of the text. Though he occasionally stumbled in achieving this goal, his music certainly met his aim of giving prominence to the words to which it was set.

The influence exerted by the many compositions and tunebooks of Hastings, not to mention his writings on sacred music, was enormous, and, linked with the work of Lowell Mason, he helped create a style that became synonymous with "hymn tune" in the United States during the late nineteenth and early twentieth centuries. If later commentators have not found Hastings's tunes to be particularly interesting *as music*, Hastings would not have been unduly concerned (though he would surely not want to have them labeled as "bland" or "uninteresting") because their purpose was to provide material in which all could join in singing with a clear articulation of the text. That Hastings succeeded in his quest to provide singing congregations with text-driven music in which all could participate is evident from the widespread use his tunes enjoyed in the nineteenth and twentieth centuries and, to a lesser degree, that they continue to receive in the early twenty-first century.

Apart from Hastings's tunes themselves, a number of which are attractive and are well worth revival (including several of the ones studied in this article), the composer's legacy includes several lessons that could be taken to heart by congregational song composers and leaders today. The primacy of the text, the provision of music that is simple enough for participation by the whole congregation, and the proclaiming of "those solemn truths and considerations of religion" through the act of singing to God are all legacies that Hastings has bequeathed to posterity and that we would do well to heed.[38]

NOTES

1. James E. Dooley, "Thomas Hastings: American Church Musician" (PhD diss., Florida State University, 1963); Lynette M. Roth, "Heaven, Harmony, and Home: Thomas Hastings's and Joshua Leavitt's Dueling Tunebooks" (PhD diss., University of Wisconsin–Madison, 1996); John Mark Jordan, "*Sacred Praise*: Thomas Hastings and the Reform of Sacred Music in Nineteenth-Century America" (PhD diss., Southwestern Baptist Theological Seminary, 1999); Hermine Weigel Williams, *Thomas Hastings: An Introduction to His Life and Music* (New York: iUniverse, 2005); Anson D. F. Randolph, "Thomas Hastings," *The New-York Evangelist* (November 21, 1872): 2; Mary Browning Scanlon, "Thomas Hastings," *The Musical Quarterly* 32, no. 2 (April 1946): 265–77; Lee Hastings Bristol, "Thomas Hastings, 1784–1872,"

The Hymn 10, no. 4 (October 1959): 105–10; and Mary D. Teal, "Letters of Thomas Hastings," *Notes* 34, no. 2 (December 1977): 303–18.

2. For example, in 1933, George Pullen Jackson sneered at Lowell Mason and his ilk (including Hastings) as "Better Music boosters" (*White Spirituals in the Southern Uplands* [Chapel Hill: University of North Carolina Press, 1933], 17), while in 1955, the first edition of Gilbert Chase's *America's Music: From the Pilgrims to the Present* (New York: McGraw-Hill Book Company, 1955), 161, characterized Hastings as rivaling Lowell Mason "in productivity, success, influence, and mediocrity." To his credit, by the revised third edition of the book (Urbana: University of Illinois Press, 1987), 138, Chase had left off the pejorative term: "Outdoing Mason in longevity and rivaling him in productivity, influence, and success was his older contemporary and colleague, Thomas Hastings (1784–1872)." Dooley, "Thomas Hastings," 185–90, gives a brief description of some of the features of Hastings's music, including particularly his early hymns.

3. See, for example, "Ortonville" in *The Sacred Harp: 1991 Revision* (N.c.: Sacred Harp Publishing Company, 1991), 68. In the 1969 film *Support Your Local Sheriff*, Joan Hackett hums the Hastings tune "Rock of Ages" while preparing dinner, and in 1988's *Ernest Saves Christmas* Jim Varney sings it while delivering "snakes" to a movie studio. For notice of other movies that include the tune, see https://en.wikipedia.org/wiki/Rock_of_Ages_(Christian_hymn), accessed January 9, 2020. "Rock of Ages" is also known as "Toplady" (after the author of the text to which it is usually sung) but will be referred to throughout this article by the former name, which is the one Hastings himself gave it.

4. Throughout this article the word "tune" will be used to describe an entire composition (melody and harmony), while "melody" will be used in reference to the principal voice part.

5. The information on Hastings's biography is summarized from the sources listed in endnote 1.

6. See particularly Hastings's article "Musical Authors and Publications of the United States," *The Musical Magazine* 1, no. 3 (July 1835): 85–91, and the commentary on this article in David W. Music, "Early New England Psalmody and American Folk Hymns in the Tune Books of Thomas Hastings," *Journal of the Society for American Music* 10, no. 3 (August 2016): 272–73.

7. [Thomas Hastings], "Expression, No. II," *Western Recorder* 1, no. 22 (October 26, 1824): 88.

8. Thomas Hastings, *Dissertation on Musical Taste* (New York: Mason Brothers, 1853), 246–47.

9. Though dated 1815 on both the title page and the copyright notice, the first edition of the book was probably not issued in its final form until the fall of 1816. See the introduction to *Thomas Hastings: Anthems*, ed. David W. Music, Recent Researches in American Music 83 (Middleton, WI: A-R Editions, 2017), viii.

10. For an annotated bibliography of Hastings's works, see Dooley, "Thomas Hastings," 199–262. It is possible that *Congregational Harmony* began as an appendix to the *Mendelssohn Collection* and was then published separately, but that does not seem likely.

11. Among his known pseudonyms are "Carameni," "K—lff," "Nomeni," "Zinceti," and "Zol—ffer." These can be identified with Hastings chiefly because in a later tunebook he sometimes republished a tune and included his real name or initial, or because the piece was contained in *Hastings's Church Music* (1860), all the contents of which were by the compiler. For example, the tune "Abode," published under "Carameni" in *Selah* (1856), reappeared in *Hastings's Church Music* without an attribution, but because this whole volume consisted of Hastings pieces, it can be safely assigned to him. Another probable pseudonym, "G—ky," appears to have been used only one time (in *The Manhattan Collection*, 1837), and its associated tune, "Palermo," does not seem to have been reprinted. Various other initials or symbols appear in the tunebooks from time to time and may also have been Hastings's pseudonyms (for example, "H. I." ["Amietta" in the *Mendelssohn Collection*]) and "?—" ["Essex" in *Selah*, 1856]).

12. When a piece in *Hastings's Church Music* represented his arrangement of a tune by another composer, he always included the original composer's name. Dooley, "Thomas Hastings," 184, estimated that Hastings had written approximately one thousand pieces of music, a projection that seems to be generally accurate.

13. "Sabbath Eve" is listed in the index among the "larger pieces."

14. A tune is counted only once for each volume, even if the book went through multiple editions. For example, if a tune appeared in each of the ten editions of *Musica Sacra* it was counted only one time. However, if a tune appeared in only a single edition of *Musica Sacra* but was included in at least nine other collections, it is dealt with here.

15. "Chester" ("How sweet the name of Jesus sounds," John Newton), "Hemans" ("Glory to God on high: / Let heaven and earth reply," James Allen), "Laight Street" ("Come, ye that love the Saviour's name," Anne Steele), "Ortonville" ("Majestic sweetness sits enthroned," Samuel Stennett), "Rock of Ages" ("Rock of Ages! Cleft for me," Augustus Toplady), and "Zion" ("Zion stands with hills surrounded," Thomas Kelly).

16. "From every stormy wind that blows" was first published in 1828 but was rewritten for the author's *Selection of Psalms and Hymns* (1831); see John Julian, *A Dictionary of Hymnology*, second edition (1907; repr. New York: Dover Publications, 1957), 399. In *Hastings's Church Music*, the composer dated "Retreat" "1840."

17. "Child of Sin and Sorrow" ("Child of sin and sorrow"), "Haven" ("Earth's stormy night will soon be o'er"), and "How Calm" ("How calm and beautiful the morn").

18. In his privately printed *Thomas Hastings* (N.c.: By the author, n.d.), Anson D. F. Randolph claimed to own "a clean, clear manuscript, a part of the revised, completed copy of his [Hastings's] 600 original hymns, with his name and date inscribed on the cover Thomas Hastings, May 2, 1872" (p. 29); quoted in Dooley, "Thomas Hastings," 116.

19. Hastings himself was a Presbyterian, and the Laight Street church was one with which he worked when he moved to New York City in 1832; see Dooley, "Thomas Hastings," 62–63. "Laight Street" was dated "1832" in *Hastings's Church Music*.

20. There is a village named Ortonville near Detroit; Hastings's brother Eurotas lived and worked in the latter city, but the village of Ortonville was not established until about ten years after Hastings wrote the tune. There is also an Ortonville Cemetery at Lisle in Broome County, New York.

21. Barbara M. Cross, ed., *The Autobiography of Lyman Beecher*, vol. 2 (Cambridge: Belknap Press of Harvard University Press, 1961), 112. The "autobiography" was actually written by Beecher's children, particularly his son Charles (see Cross's introduction, vol. 1, pp. xi–xii). The "anticipated conquest" was Beecher's "full belief that the millennium was coming, that it was at hand, that the Church was just about to march with waving banners to final and universal dominion" (vol. 2, p. 112).

22. The quotation is from Hastings's unsigned article "Practical. Adaptation," in *Musical Magazine* (April 1837), 183. For an example of a minor key tune by Hastings, see "Wilberforce" (G minor) in *Psalmista* (1852), 178.

23. "Laight Street" uses only half and quarter notes, except that the last measure has a dotted half note. "Child of Sin and Sorrow" is similar.

24. See Dennis M. Weber, "The Transition of the Cantus Firmus from the Tenor to the Soprano in Anglo-American Hymnody," *The Hymn* 51, no. 3 (July 2000): 11–23, especially pp. 20–22.

25. Thomas Hastings and Solomon Warriner, *Musica sacra*, revised edition (1818), vi.

26. "Chester" (in B flat) includes two C minor chords (mm. 3, 11) and "How Calm" (C major) uses a single D minor chord in passing (m. 7).

27. "Zion" ends on the third scale degree.

28. See Jordan, "Sacred Praise," 293–94.

29. Thomas Hastings, *Sacred Praise: An Earnest Appeal to Christian Worshipers, in Behalf of a Neglected Duty* (New York: A. S. Barnes, 1856), 57.

30. This type of "extended tune" was also characteristic of early American psalmody. See Karl Douglas Kroeger, "The Worcester Collection of Sacred Harmony and Sacred Music in America 1786–1803" (PhD diss., Brown University, 1976), 256–57.

31. The main exception among the ten tunes is "Child of Sin and Sorrow," which is in rounded bar form.

32. The lyrics used with "Ortonville," "Retreat," and "Zion" in *The Presbyterian Psalmodist* all appeared in *Psalms and Hymns*, while the words employed with "Haven" were not in the hymnal. "Haven" was also used for "How sad our state by nature is" in Hastings's *Sacred Songs* (1842). It will be recalled that "Haven" was originally written for a text by Hastings himself. *The Presbyterian Juvenile Psalmodist* (1856) set "Zion" to "Lord, dismiss us with thy blessing"; all the texts for the *Juvenile Psalmodist* were taken from the Presbyterian Board of Publication's *New Hymns for Youth* (1855).

33. "Laight Street" seems less well suited to some of the other texts to which Hastings had set it earlier, including "Come, Holy Spirit, heavenly Dove," "O for a closer walk with God," and "Jerusalem, my happy home." The only other text used with this tune, "Lord, when my raptured thought surveys," is similar in character to "Come, ye that love the Saviour's name."

34. [Thomas Hastings], "Vocal Execution," *Musical Magazine* 2, no. 9 (January 1837): 135; [Thomas Hastings], "Choice of Tunes," *Western Recorder* 6, no. 42 (October 20, 1829): 168.

35. https://www.hymnary.org, accessed November 7, 2019. The website incorporates the Hymn Society in the US and Canada's Dictionary of North American Hymnology.

36. The information on the website is sometimes inconsistent and confusing. For example, Hastings's "How Calm" is listed under that title as having been published in twenty-two collections, but it is also indexed under the title "Hastings" as appearing in twenty books; the lists of hymnals for the two titles are identical, but both contain twenty-one items. "Child of Sin and Sorrow" is catalogued under the title "Ava," and "Hemans" is indexed as "Composer Unknown."

37. The tune "Holy Cross," listed as having been published in sixty-four hymnals, is not an original piece by Hastings but an arrangement of a melody by Felix Mendelssohn. It is interesting to compare these figures with those for Hastings's protégé and sometime rival, Lowell Mason, on the same website. Six Mason tunes are credited with at least 200 publications each: "Bethany" (424), "Boylston" (367), "Laban" (233), "Missionary Hymn" (297), "Olivet" (482), and "Work, for the Night Is Coming" (230), for a total of 2,033 separate printings. Mason is said to have composed some 1,210 original hymn tunes—about twice as many as Hastings—so the proportion of "popular" tunes between the two composers seems appropriate. On the number of tunes by Mason, see Henry Lowell Mason, *Hymn-Tunes of Lowell Mason: A Bibliography* (Cambridge, MA: University Press, 1944), vi.

38. See the quotation from Hastings's *Dissertation on Musical Taste* earlier.

FURTHER READING

Crawford, Richard. "Ancient Music and the Europeanizing of American Psalmody, 1800–1810." In *A Celebration of American Music: Words and Music in Honor of H. Wiley Hitchcock*, edited by Richard Crawford, R. Allen Lott, and Carol J. Oja, 225–55. Ann Arbor: University of Michigan Press, 1970.

Music, David W. "Early New England Psalmody and American Folk Hymns in the Tune Books of Thomas Hastings." *Journal of the Society for American Music* 10, no. 3 (August 2016): 270–303.

Music, David W. "Tunes by Lowell Mason and Thomas Hastings in Southern United States Shape-Note Tune Books of the Early Nineteenth Century." *Journal of Musicological Research* 25, no. 4 (October–December 2007): 325–52.

Music, David W., and Paul Westermeyer. *Church Music in the United States 1760–1901*. Saint Louis: MorningStar Music Publishers, 2014.

Ogasapian, John. *Church Music in America, 1620–2000*. Macon, GA: Mercer University Press, 2007.

Pemberton, Carol A. *Lowell Mason: His Life and Work*. Ann Arbor: UMI Research Press, 1985.

III

CONTEMPORARY WORSHIP

Chapter Six

"Além do *gospel*"
A History of Brazil's Alternative Christian Music Scene

Marcell Silva Steuernagel

In 1999, Expresso Luz released their fourth studio album, *Bom Dia*.[1] The last track, "Mamãe, Eu Sou *Gospel*," composed by Carlinhos Veiga, portrays a young Brazilian Christian complaining to his mother:

Ó, mammy, porque eu vim nascer	Oh, mommy, why was I born
Em pleno terceiro mundo	In a third-world country
Com esse povo atrasado	With this backward people
Que ainda vive sem computador	That still lives without computers
Ó, mammy, e ainda ter que curtir	Oh, mommy, and I still have to listen
Canções tupiniquins	To Brazilian songs
Eu quero ouvir rock'roll	I want to hear rock and roll.[2]

Expresso Luz performed "Mamãe, Eu Sou *Gospel*" on stages throughout Brazil, positioning themselves against *gospel*, a popular umbrella term for Brazilian Christian music not to be confused with, and indeed unrelated to, its North American counterpart.[3] Almost two decades later, composer and pastor Gerson Borges still echoed the sentiment of "Mamãe, Eu Sou *Gospel*": "The whole [*gospel*] thing became big business. The underworld takes over big media, FM radios, the major stadiums, million-dollar contracts. The form, the presentation, the aesthetics, become professionalized in the wake of, and in imitation of, [American] Contemporary Christian Music [CCM]."[4]

Veiga and Borges's stances highlight a gap between the stylistic, theological, and market aspirations of the *gospel* phenomenon in Brazil and the themes, sounds, and audiences that artists such as Veiga and Borges engage with.[5] This gap is reflected in scholarship on the rising Christian music cultures that surfaced in Brazil since the mid-twentieth century, Brazilian Christian Music (I will use MCB, *música cristã brasileira*, as an umbrella term for Christian musics in Brazil). Well-documented in Portuguese and mentioned (at least in passing) in English, historical accounts do not portray the "B-side" of MCB: artists that, although historically connected to the rise of MCB, developed an "indie" circuit instead of collaborating with the *gospel* "majors" that came to dominate the *gospel* industry.[6]

In this essay, I use oral accounts, historical scholarship, and my own participant-observer experience to trace the development of this "indie" MCB scene.[7] I interviewed Guilherme and Sandra Kerr, along with Jorge Camargo and Nelson Bomilcar, who represent an early generation of MCB artists involved since the 1970s with Christian music in Brazil. Carlinhos Veiga and Claudia Barbosa, along with (slightly younger) Gerson Borges, Nelson Rios, and Zé Bruno, represent a generation active since the mid-1980s that witnessed the rise of *gospel* music. Finally, Marcos Almeida offers a more recent perspective into how artists continue to negotiate issues of identity and music in Brazilian Christianity.

This investigation focuses on the historical development of the alternative MCB scene and concludes with a few analytical considerations. I start with a summarized account of the development of MCB in what can be called the "pre-*gospel*" period, between the 1960s and early 1980s. I then focus on the late eighties, at the moment when the *gospel* industry and the independent scene went in different sonic and theological directions. My conclusion identifies topics for further research in the hope that others might use this historiography in further inquiry.

"ANTES DO *GOSPEL*": MCB FROM THE 1960s TO THE 1980s

The MCB phenomenon is linked to the rise of *evangélicos* in Brazil.[8] Early in the second half of the twentieth century, *evangélicos* represented less than 10 percent of the population (they now represent roughly 30 percent of Brazil's population).[9] As Brazil's urban concentrations grew, artists such as Luís de Carvalho, Washington Alves, Feliciano Amaral, and others (many tied to Pentecostal churches) began to introduce the *corinho* influence to audiences previously accustomed to the hymnodic legacy of Western Protestantism.[10] These *corinhos* were marked by the use of popular North American rhythms, percussion, and wind instrument accompaniments, and simple, repeatable melodies for congregational singing.[11] According to composer and pastor Nelson Bomilcar, in São Paulo, Conde de Sarzedas Street specialized in marketing this repertoire. The street's commerce was fueled by Bompastor, a label established in 1975 that featured solo artists and the quartets favored by Pentecostals.[12] Early labels such as Bompastor had connections to denominations but were not owned by them. Therefore Bomilcar argues (along with others) that MCB did not start with *gospel*, noting that "the market already existed, and it was a rising market," even if it did not bear that specific moniker.[13]

The Brazilian music industry had become intertwined with its North American counterpart decades before, and international major labels such as CBS and Continental signed many of these early artists. But by the mid-1970s these two markets were growing apart. According to Brazilian scholar Eduardo Vicente, the relationship between *evangélico* artists and major music industry labels "seems to never have consolidated" even as *evangélicos* conquered space in Brazil's communication networks, such as radio and TV.[14]

This early scene grew in parallel with the establishment of para-ecclesiastical organizations (PEOs) in Brazil, intent on evangelism and Christian education in Latin America. Many of these PEOS were North American, and their influence converged with that of the corinhos, which already reflected the emotionalist tone and simple melodic and harmonic structures of North American revivalist repertories in the nineteenth century.[15] The following list shows the main PEOs active at the time:

Portuguese Name	Abbreviation	Translation of Name
Aliança Bíblica Universitária do Brasil	ABUB	University Biblical Alliance of Brazil
Jovens da Verdade	JV	Youth of Truth
Mocidade para Cristo	MPC	Youth for Christ
Organização Palavra da Vida	OPV	Word of Life Organization
Vencedores por Cristo	VPC	Winners for Christ

Among these, JV is the only Brazilian PEO.[16] These organizations sponsored retreats, conferences, and campaigns, partnered with churches for theological education, and produced music that reflected North American theology and sounds.

Many of the artists I interviewed were influenced by the theological outlook of these organizations, which could diverge significantly. While OPV and VPC leaned more toward a North American proclamationist approach and rarely engaged with Brazilian social and political realities, MPC and ABUB grappled with Latin American issues. Singer Jorge Camargo remembers how the first teams at OPV were "very closed, hermetic."[17] Jaime Kemp, the Californian missionary who founded VPC, defended a less conservative theology than OPV, but the group's itinerant performers did not comment on Brazilian social or economic realities.[18] Bomilcar, who collaborated with Kerr and Camargo at VPC, was influenced as much by his experience there as by his work with university students in ABUB and MPC, which made him "realize the importance of [Latin American theology]."[19]

In the 1970s, these PEOs were influenced by the Jesus Movement. Theologians Swee Hong Lim and Lester Ruth describe the phenomenon as "a "Christian element in the hippie counterculture of the late 1960s" whose "perspective became mainstreamed into larger evangelicalism" in the United States.[20] As the movement grew in the United States, its strategies of public preaching, performing skits, and using contemporary musics were exported by missionaries and pastors to Brazil.[21] Jaime Kemp, who led VPC, was one such missionary. Guilherme Kerr says that Kemp wanted similar transformations to happen in Brazil "and came over with a project to leverage this new language."[22] Kemp would translate imported material, and VPC would then record it. For him, while VPC was certainly influenced by the "youth choir" models prevalent in North America, the influence of the Jesus Movement was stronger. Bomilcar concurs.[23]

Overall, PEOs adopted imported strategies and cultural trends unevenly. OPV resisted the hippie fashion trend but updated its musical offerings to reflect the influence of Jesus music. MPC, in contrast, gave participants freedom to explore musical expressions both international and local, along with the fashion and language that came with them. For Claudia Barbosa, who plays flute and sings with Veiga, MPC wanted to explore "music and the arts, and this is the way we found to do something different."[24] Her involvement with contemporary theater, for instance, was not well-received in her local church but was accepted and encouraged at MPC.

The 1960s were a culturally charged period throughout Latin America. Brazil's authoritarian takeover in 1964 was, according to ethnomusicologist Werner Ewald, "explosive in terms of politics, economy, theology, music, and culture."[25] The military coup generated widespread reaction from a generation of Brazilian musicians engaged in shaping the soundscape of Brazil in different directions, after the bossa nova craze of the 1950s and 1960s. Artists such as Chico Buarque in Rio de Janeiro; the *Tropicália* movement, including Novos Baianos, Gilberto Gil, and Caetano Veloso in Bahia; and Milton Nascimento and the Clube da Esquina collective in Minas Gerais became icons in the fight for democracy.[26]

Significant sectors of Brazil's historic Protestant denominations aligned themselves with the military government and closed down seminaries and Christian youth movements.[27] This vacuum was filled by the PEOs, which welcomed a slew of young Christians influenced by the music of popular artists such as Buarque and Veloso. According to scholar Daniel Hunger, with the advent of this so-called Música Popular Brasileira (MPB), a generation of Christian composers engaged with the reality of Brazil's poor and oppressed by writing music "inspired by the oppression of the dictatorship, by the *Tropicália* movement, by the MPB festivals and rock."[28]

This soundscape was at times enriched by musics from neighboring countries and also by theological perspectives that lay outside the curatorship of North American organizations, especially at the intersection of Liberation Theology and the protest music wave that swept Latin American. According to Vicente, discussions about Latin American identity and Liberation Theology after the Second Vatican Council birthed "a Catholic music of strong political sense, that reflected this approximation of the church to the popular movements through the association of regional rhythms and sonirities to liturgical celebration."[29] The protest music of artists like Violeta Parra and Mercedes Sosa, as well as the theological perspectives of Gustavo Gutierrez, fed the maelstrom of influences that disturbed the waters of the Americanized, Protestant soundscape that PEOs and churches were accustomed to.

PEO engagement with these sonic and theological worlds varied. OPV and VPC did not, according to Bomilcar, "engage head-on with what was happening in the political structure," wary of being associated with more progressive undertakings.[30] Kerr admits that VPC's main goal "was not to transform society, to make a preferential option for the poor . . . this political underlining was absent."[31] But even in the more conservative PEOs, exposure to the social and economic realities of Brazil was inevitable. Musical styles crossed geographical boundaries as groups picked up songs in different locales and performed them elsewhere, as Sandra Kerr recalls.[32]

Moreover, if nonchurch styles such as samba, bossa nova, and the music of artists that were exploring new ways to be "Brazilian" in music during this authoritarian regime were considered out of bounds by certain denominations and PEOs, they nevertheless found their way into MCB. Claudia Barbosa recounts that within MPC, besides listening to Christian music, they heard Chico Buarque, Tom Zé, and "popular Brazilian music artists that were in evidence at the time. We heard their music to get our references. But we also listened to what was being released by VPC; they were trying to establish a link with MPB."[33] ABUB and MPC were actively engaging in conversations about Liberation Theology and listening to Latin American protest songs. Bomilcar admits to being influenced by *Vamos Cantar*, a hymnal published by ABUB in 1973 that compiled several popular Christian songs at the time, including a number of pieces from other Latin countries.[34] When ABUB and VPC partnered for a year-long ministry initiative in 1975, VPC missionaries were faced with the task of engaging university students, which took them further out of their cultural and theological comfort zone. According to Bomilcar, "we were pushed [to develop a new approach] because the poetic, biblical discourse we had did not make sense in the university. So, we had to sing Brazilian music."[35]

Overall, these artists described living in a liminal space fed, on the one hand, by the North American perspective, and, on the other, by Latin American reality. Thus artists such as Bomilcar and Barbosa were influenced by North American sounds even as they at times resisted it. Barbosa recounts that she began to listen to Mercedes Sosa and Tarancón in an active attempt to resist the influence of Amy Grant and what she calls "that American bunch."[36] She and her friends gathered to listen to Latin American music, to study *maracatu*, and resisted foreign influences by mixing them with their own traditions.

This amalgam of Tropicália, bossa nova, the Beatles, and the Rolling Stones mixed with intense political and theological activity survived into the 1980s.[37] Zé Bruno, singer and guitarist of Resgate, one of the first nationally acclaimed *gospel* rock bands, describes how they were influenced by the bands that he was listening to, such as Rita Lee, Mutantes, and Joelho de Porco. For him, subtle critiques of the country's political situation were embedded in at least a portion of this repertoire, such as the music of Chico Buarque and Caetano Veloso.[38] At this intersection of PEOs, churches, Brazilian, and Latin musics, Christian artists experienced theological, political, and musical influences flowing across boundaries and traditions.

Transition: The 1980s and the Split of MCB

As Brazil's *evangélico* population increased throughout the 1980s, churches realized the potential of media. They began investing in radio stations and television channels and started Christian record labels. New labels arose that, from their inception, were founded by specific denominations in connection with larger media projects. Among the many labels in the Brazilian *gospel* market, three stand out historically: MK Music, Line Records, and Gospel Records.[39] Of these three, two are tied to Neopentecostal churches.[40] Gospel Records, established in 1990, belongs to Igreja Renascer em Cristo (IRC/Reborn in Christ Church). Line Records, established in 1992, connected to Igreja Universal do Reino de Deus (IURD/Universal Church of the Kingdom of God). The third major label, established in 1986 as MK Publicitá (today's MK Music), is the only independent among the three majors of this early period. These labels, supported by radio stations and television networks, imprinted an industrial style to the production and distribution of music across the country. After this shift, according to Robson de Paula, "*evangélico* music, especially that produced in the country's Southeastern region, began to reach a large audience" and coalesced into what is known as the Brazilian *gospel* market.[41] I now turn to the history of the term and of its transformation into a synonym for MCB.

Igreja Renascer em Cristo (IRC), or simply Renascer, holds a central place in the narrative of my interviewees because Renascer is considered to be responsible for popularizing the name *gospel* as an umbrella term to designate "Christian" music tailored for consumption by *evangélicos*. Lead pastor Estevam Hernandes Filho, along with São Paulo businessman Antônio Carlos Abbud and other partners, wanted to leverage youth culture to establish a national presence. According to Brazilian scholar Jacqueline Dolghie, using this strategy Renascer was able to offer a "new liturgical product" to its members.[42] The church launched the term *gospel* to differentiate this new music from other genres.[43]

Thus I must emphasize that Brazilian *gospel* is not a musical style per se. The term itself was transplanted from North America without regard for its connection to the African American heritage, in order to brand a burgeoning market. Robson de Paula describes *gospel* music as

> *evangélico* songs released by record companies for mass consumption. In other words, more than a designator of melodic and rhythmic singularities, as in its North American counterpart, in [Brazil] the term gospel is used as a category that establishes borders, distinguishing the music industry of the *evangélicos* from others and, in effect, identifying the phonographic sector that produces it.[44]

In Brazil, *gospel* culture is closely tied to *evangélico* identity. Being *gospel* is a lifestyle, a place to belong, and also a market. This conflation affects the commercial aspects of *gospel*, which enjoys some of the lowest piracy rates in Brazil's music industry (a fact that international majors such as Sony and EMI have not overlooked).[45] Thus I agree with Dolghie that to "talk about gospel is to talk about the market, and all of its consequences."[46] The *gospel* conflation of industry and identity was a recurring theme in my interviews. Bomilcar distinguishes *gospel* from its North American counterpart, "articulated when Estevam Hernandes decided to make it a marketing strategy for the growth of his church."[47] Gerson Borges calls *gospel* "a hoax. It's a con. While in American gospel you have the legacy of the black church, . . . here in the eighties we have Gospel Records, Renascer, and in Rio de Janeiro Marina de Oliveira and MK. This isn't really *gospel*, it's contemporary Christian music. It's CCM that they started calling *gospel* in Brazil."[48]

While Bomilcar's and Borges's comments reflect a critical stance toward the current state of affairs, in the late 1980s an aura of optimism surrounded this burgeoning enterprise. Many of my interviewers mentioned a "kickoff" gathering of Christian artists and producers convened by Abbud, Hernandez, and partners at Abbud's house in Alphaville, an upscale neighborhood in São Paulo. According to Kerr, the meeting was informational:

[They didn't want to] ask for permission, but to let us know: we're going to enter the radios with full force. We have the money, the capital, we have the backing of the churches for what we want to do. . . . We are going to change [MCB] to *gospel*. They invited us, and said that if we wanted to catch the train of history, this is what was going to happen. For me, it was shocking.[49]

Many artists accepted the call to action. João Alexandre and Nelson Bomilcar were the label's first producers.[50] Jorge Camargo coordinated Renascer's radio station, Gospel FM. Renascer leased twelve hours from a radio station, drawing the repertoire from available contributors:

Everyone donated records, and they hired me as the station's programmer. . . . I gathered all of these materials, and started playing them. And what happened? It grew, the hours started increasing, and then they began recording people. They recorded Resgate, João Alexandre, and established a label. Then, when the whole thing was set up, they fired me. And removed all of our programming from the radio to play only what was theirs. That was their vision: "we want to make the history of Christian music from now on."[51]

Camargo's account aligns with others: "There was no reverence to what came before. So much so that if you listen to their narrative, this is what they say: that the history of Brazilian Christian music starts with them."[52] Thus from afar it might appear that the history of MCB ran along a continuous line from the Pentecostal scene in the mid-twentieth century to early 1990s *gospel*. In fact, while the *gospel* phenomenon assumed center stage in the narrative, a handful of performers and composers that were heirs to the pre-*gospel* scene of MCB were pushed toward the margins, a dynamic that the literature on the history of MCB fails to portray.

The narrative of the split between *gospel* and these alternative streams relies primarily on oral history and participant observation. For Veiga, "it was a tractor that ran everything over," including musics from outside the Rio de Janeiro–São Paulo axis.[53] While Kerr decided not to be a part of the *gospel* project, he recognizes that "it was a tsunami" and that the radio stations "began to abuse their financial power to only play their own catalog."[54] He summarizes what happened: "We were not the alternative scene. They were. We were the narrative, they were the alternative. But, if you look at it today, *gospel* is the narrative. And our music is, if anything, the alternative."[55] For him, MCB was in fact moving toward more Brazilian expressions, and there came a moment when the *gospel* enterprise took over the market.[56] This split is the epicenter of Brazil's alternative MCB scene. While in previous decades these artists had been protagonists, they suddenly found themselves at the fringes of a consolidated, market-oriented initiative able to leverage communication networks and cater to rising *evangélico* demographics. As a result of this marginalization, a new network developed that connected the pre-*gospel* scene to an independent or "alternative" Christian music scene, populated by many of the artists active in that period and convening at events such as Som do Céu (SdC), a yearly music retreat sponsored by MPC that started in the 1980s.

When I first performed at SdC in 2001 with my band Golgotha, I was struck by the variety of music at the event. Instead of encountering a roster of *gospel*-infused offerings, we were exposed to a mosaic ranging from Christian disco to *baião* and *frevo* from Brazil's northeast. Furthermore, many of the conversations between artists and audience revolved around the pre-*gospel* history of MCB and the use of Brazilian sounds and poetry. It was at SdC that I met Camargo and Bomilcar and where I first saw Carlinhos Veiga perform "Mamãe, Eu Sou *Gospel*." They considered themselves an alternative to the Americanized sounds of *gospel*, heavily influenced by North American pop-rock with a touch of *brega*.[57] Borges, who performed frequently at SdC, shared with me that "the music [he] decided to make was never commercial like *gospel*, this aesthetic that is so manipulative, so tied to prosperity."[58] I will address such theological critiques later.

The mixed soundscape at SdC led to unique collaborations. In 2002, Golgotha collaborated with Sal da Terra, a northeastern ensemble, to perform a rock-baião version of "Glória, Glória, Aleluia," a Portuguese hymn set to "Battle Hymn of the Republic." Such (frequent) collaborations draw on a shared understanding of being independent and being Brazilian, in contrast to the international sound of *gospel*. According to Borges, this interest in a Brazilian aesthetic created collaborative networks.[59] These artists were not concerned with "purity" or the preservation of a "typical" Brazilian sound in Christian musicking but in preserving the best of the legacy that the pre-*gospel* years had to offer and in the mashups that resulted from "mixing it up": old and new, north and south, coastal and inland Brazil. They celebrated the influence of Brazilian music in their own work, not only today but since the 1970s.[60] An example is *De Vento em Popa*, an album that Kerr produced for VPC in 1977.[61] At the time, the record was not well received, but has left a legacy that most, if not all, of my interviewees acknowledge as the first release to overtly engage with Brazilian styles and rhythms in MCB. Borges, for instance, considers it "the first album of Brazilian song, of Brazilian popular [Christian] song."[62]

It is possible that the *gospel* takeover of the MCB scene led to a galvanization of these independent artists' resolve to emphasize Brazilianness in their work, precisely because of how *gospel* became the sonic norm. According to Veiga, the rise of *gospel* throttled burgeoning local scenes across the country, in a pattern familiar to cultural activity in Brazil: from São Paulo and Rio de

Janeiro to the rest of the country. Veiga says: "The kids would imitate the bands from São Paulo's Renascer em Cristo."⁶³ Veiga's "Mamãe, Eu Sou Gospel" was a reaction to this sonic takeover. As time went on, the *gospel* trend moved beyond pop-rock and entered "a wave of worship music, this syrupy music, emotional music," says Veiga.⁶⁴

Veiga, Kerr, Camargo, Bomilcar, and others also believe their scene was independent because the *gospel* industry was not interested in their music. The notion that *gospel* music was devoid of Brazilianness has been passed on to subsequent generations (such as myself). When I interviewed Marcos Almeida, an up-and-coming artist, he told me he was not interested in being *gospel* and used "Brazilian music with Christian roots" to describe his work.⁶⁵ Like his predecessors, he celebrates the fact that his search for musical identity led him to engage with MPB.

Even so, certain artists were involved in both worlds, transitioning between the *gospel* pop-rock world and the Brazilian-infused independent scene. I first met Nelson Rios at SdC, playing bass with Veiga. On one hand, Rios played with groups on the independent side of the spectrum, such as Estilo de Vida and Cântaro, and produced a number of independent bands, including my own, Golgotha. On the other, he was involved in the *gospel* scene and played with Livre Arbítrio, which he considers the first *evangélico* heavy rock band, at S.O.S da Vida, a yearly event sponsored by Renascer in São Paulo.⁶⁶

Before moving on to an analysis of this independent scene, two caveats are necessary. First, I must emphasize that SdC was not the sole event in the alternative circuit. SdC was mentioned frequently in my interviews, along with Acampamento Louvor and other events. Moreover, for decades artists have performed around the country in Protestant congregations and denominational events historically associated with the pre-*gospel* scene. This circuit was at least partly established before the *gospel* explosion, as many of those involved with the PEOs came from these denominations.

Second, I do not mean to imply that releases from *gospel*-affiliated labels were completely devoid of Brazilian expressions. Veiga, Bomilcar, and others acknowledged certain early artists released by *gospel* labels that featured Brazilian expressions. João Alexandre's album *Simplesmente João* came out on Gospel Records in 1991, with Bomilcar on backing vocals, and achieved significant success. But according to Camargo, after Gospel Records initially released albums by João Alexandre, Quarteto Vida, Edson e Tita, and a few others, they later decided to stick to pop.⁶⁷ As the industry grew, these became niche sounds with limited marketability. For Zé Bruno, a former *gospel* industry insider, when major labels did release *samba* and *pagode* records, while the sound was stylistically distinct from *gospel*'s international pop-rock, the message in the music reflected the *gospel* perspective, including its triumphalist and prosperity-oriented theology.[68] Most of my interlocutors agree that while there may have been early flirtations with Brazilian musics in the *gospel* enterprise, the market concentrated on international pop-rock, designed to cater to a wide variety of audiences and tastes instead of featuring regional, localized musics.

Even today the *gospel* phenomenon is closely connected to international pop-rock, and the industry has now incorporated the "worship sound" of international names such as Chris Tomlin, Hillsong, and Bethel. In contrast, many of the artists associated with this independent scene continue to advocate for a Brazilian sound and a different theological approach to congregational musicking. I now turn to an analysis of certain dynamics that sustain this configuration, both in terms of "why" and "how" these scenes coexist.

THE SOUNDSCAPE AND THEOLOGY OF BRAZIL'S ALTERNATIVE MCB SCENE

As we have seen, while at first the legacy of pre-*gospel* MCB was incorporated into the burgeoning *gospel* project, it was later marginalized. This shift undergirds how my interlocutors see their work: they were cast to the margins and had to operate in ways that distinguished them from mainstream *gospel*. They needed to redesign performance, recording, and publishing networks. Some artists reenvisioned their careers to intersect with the secular market. Barbosa mentions that the exclusion from the *gospel* media networks became, for her and Veiga, "a privilege, an opportunity to do what we always wanted to do, which was to bring music with Christian themes to the 'outside.'"[69]

From within the *gospel* context, this dynamic of marginalization was construed differently. I asked Zé Bruno, vocalist and guitarist of Resgate, what he thought of this divide between *gospel* and non-*gospel* artists, and he told me he didn't notice the distinction at the time. Bruno continued to enjoy the music of VPC and other pre-*gospel* artists even as Resgate's career took off under Gospel Records. He lamented that they hadn't "jumped on the bandwagon" because the scene was good and would benefit everyone. The nascent Neopentecostal theology of leaders such as Estevam Hernandez, which would later drive him and his bandmates away from Renascer, was not immediately apparent.[70] For those on the inside, this process of marginalization was certainly not construed as purposeful exclusion by the leadership of the *gospel* enterprise.

Between the margins and the center of the *gospel* scene, distinctions in style and soundscape began to crystallize. While *gospel* later fragmented into myriad styles and theological/denominational expressions, I agree with Vicente and other scholars that "songs with a slower tempo, strongly influenced by North-American romantic songs, predominate in [the *gospel*] segment and serve as the basis for the works of its main sellers."⁷¹ Olívia Bandeira, in a review of Brazilian literature about *gospel*, suggests that part of the difficulty lies in the methodological distinctions that underlie the theological, economic, and ecclesiastical aspects of this market. What one denomination might consider profane in terms of style, another might find completely acceptable.⁷² She mentions that if one examines the lineup of the eight largest current labels in Brazilian *gospel*, a vast majority fall under the "louvor e adoração" ("praise and worship") category, while other genres such as rap, rock, and samba "circulate in more peripheral and strategic fashion in churches."⁷³ In other words, I argue that the sonic heritage of *gospel* is recognizable even if it is increasingly varied not only through style but also through performance practices that can be traced to the early formative years of *gospel*.

Moreover, as the market grew, producers and artists were under increased pressure to create music tailored to particular audiences. As I have stated elsewhere, commercially viable artefacts of material religious culture are surrounded by market considerations that shape them in specific ways.⁷⁴ If early proponents of the *gospel* project relied on North American strategies to establish their market, and if this reliance entailed mirroring the sounds of North America's burgeoning Christian music market, it seems only natural that *gospel* became associated with international pop-rock idioms. In this sense, if earlier artists did experiment with Brazilian sounds in Christian music (such as with *De Vento em Popa*), the events of the mid- to late 1980s redirected (or derailed) MCB back into the pop-rock fold.

While many independent artists compete for space in the *gospel* market and also perform in these international styles, it is also true that the majority of artists I interviewed or interacted with over the years preserve an authorial voice distinct from *gospel* sounds. At the margins, market expectations are less compelling, and artists have freedom to pursue alternative themes and sounds and engage with Brazil's geography, history, society, and culture. If *gospel* references to Brazilian social life and politics are frequently general in nature, artists like Veiga go for specifics.⁷⁵ They use harmonic and rhythmic elements not found in traditional Brazilian church music (which, not surprisingly, reflects its colonial and missionary heritages). They use instruments like the *viola caipira*, name locales and fruits, and engage in regional forms of poetry (such as *cordel*).⁷⁶ Ensembles such as Sal da Terra perform in typical northeastern garb. These regionalizations are markers of identity that connect them to particular localities and position them in contrast to the general "internationalness" of *gospel*.

Moreover, independent artists might be encouraged to perform Brazilianness by their fans. At SdC, Brazilianness is a key component of discourses of identity. Veiga says that, at SdC, "the idea was to raise up popular *evangélico* Brazilian music. That was the banner." It was a scene where experimentation was appreciated and encouraged, where according to Veiga, "a rock band would get up, perform, and the following act would be a *baião* group from the Northeast. These partnerships were possible at SdC."[77] But they were not accepted in the broader *gospel* market because, according to Borges, the labels "did not want to produce that type of music anymore. So, we had to do it independently."[78]

Finally, this gap between *gospel* and alternative scene follows theological and ecclesiological lines. The *gospel* phenomenon became increasingly associated with Neopentecostal theology and ecclesiology in Brazil, which is not surprising considering the roster of churches behind its major labels. Renascer, IURD, and other Neopentecostal churches have historical connections to the rise of prosperity theology in Latin America.[79] Zé Bruno, who lived this transformation personally, says that *gospel* was not originally connected to these theologies:

> When we left Renascer in 2010, it was not the church we had originally joined [in 1991]. When we started there were no apostles, no prosperity craziness. There was no sacred commerce, campaigns based on artefacts, prayer, and miracles. There was no push to buy something, to conquer. That triumphalist strain began, in my opinion, in 1998.[80]

Bruno describes a slow process of theological transformation that did not necessarily shock the church leadership (of which he was a part). Finally, Resgate decided to leave Renascer, and stepped into a theological world that they hand not been exposed to for two decades while immersed in Neopentecostalism. The band members started a new church, Casa da Rocha.[81] "According to Bruno, when they left, they "didn't know what kind of church we were going to be, but I had absolute conviction about the kind of church we weren't going to be. I immediately stopped preaching about triumphalism, prosperity, and went back to preaching the gospel." Bruno later received a Master of Divinity from Servos de Cristo, an independent seminary.[82]

Theologically and ecclesiologically, many of these independent artists intentionally distance themselves from the *gospel* market in their critiques of Neopentecostalism. When asked to describe what *gospel* meant to him, Veiga said, "It is a style, a culture, a way of doing things that is intimately connected to the Neopentecostal way of being," marked by "its use of media, radio and TV, this aspect of not respecting and trampling others, a confusing theology. That's what *gospel* music was for me."[83] As the *gospel* phenomenon grew, these artists remained active in the theological and denominational worlds historically associated with the pre-*gospel* era. Some, like Veiga, Borges, and Bruno, are pastors. Many of the pre-*gospel* artists with ties to historic Protestant denominations in Brazil continued to operate within these networks. Their pre-*gospel* experience was marked by Protestant theology, along with Latin American Liberation Theology and *missão integral*, a rearticulated theology of social justice that resists North American proclamationist views. Veiga began to write music that was politically engaged, referencing environmental issues and government corruption. He remembers that the SdC context was a place where he could engage with such themes, which was not the case in the *gospel* scene.[84] Such negotiations continue to permeate MCB. Artists and denominations resist, learn to accept, and negotiate the reality of Neopentecostal Christianity in Brazil and across Latin America, both in terms of theological thought and the ecclesiological networks with which they are connected or refuse to collaborate with.

BRIDGING THE GAP

This essay is not an exhaustive history of MCB. It is meant as an initial foray into some of its marginalized narratives. Much remains to be done, and I identify here two areas (among many) that warrant further investigation. The first relates to questions of musical and theological flows between Brazil and Latin America. The second is a call to include other protagonists in this account, particularly female perspectives and voices from recent generations who are writing new chapters in this history.

The connection between Liberation Theology and *missão integral* as developed in the Latin American context, the *canção de protesto* tradition that developed against the backdrop of Latin American dictatorships, and MCB, remains unexamined.[85] While this connection appears at certain points in my research, further work is necessary in order to understand how Protestant theology (in its European and North American expressions), Latin American theologies, local churches and denominations, PEO festivals and camps, and the cultural scenes have interacted to shaped the current MCB scene.

In addition, further research must integrate female perspectives into a narrative that, up to this point, is heavily patriarchal. This problem appeared in my search for interlocutors and is reflected in the disproportion between male and female interviewees. Sandra Kerr and Claudia Barbosa's involvement with PEOs was marked by a protagonism not reflected in their local church experiences. Kerr describes what it was like to be on equal ground with her male counterparts in VPC's ministry.[86] Barbosa laments the silence of female composers even today.⁸⁷ Both recognize that women's roles in Latin American Christianity have expanded significantly, and further research into how women are helping to reconfigure the MCB scene is important because some of the biggest artists in the *gospel* scene today are "cantoras" or female solo singers.

Finally, a number of developments from the past forty years have not made their way into this essay. The role of charismatic transnational worship phenomena such as Vineyard and Hillsong in shaping contemporary worship in Brazil warrant further scholarly attention. Marcos Almeida's interview emphasized the importance of the rise of Brazil's "adoração extravagante," or "extravagant worship" movement, modeled on the bands of the "British Invasion" that influenced North American worship in the late 1990s, such as Delirious and Matt Redman.⁸⁸ Moreover, very little has been written about how the rise of Brazil's independent congregations, or *comunidades evangélicas*, helped shape Brazilian MCB since the pre-*gospel* era and continue to do so. Recent events such as Rock no Vale and Nossa Música Brasileira, sponsored by JV, inherited the legacy of pre-*gospel* PEO-sponsored events such as Acampamento Louvor and SdC. Artists like Almeida do not respect the dividing lines of sacred and secular, *gospel* and independent worlds, that previous generations of artists and market considerations drew in the sand of Brazil's ever-shifting MCB scene.

The Brazilian MCB phenomenon is a complex and flourishing example of contemporary musical practices in the Americas. Guilherme Kerr frames it thus: "there is a lot of good material coming out. So, something good is happening. This distinction between *gospel* and the [independent] scene is a fragile distinction."⁸⁹ As these historical divides continue to fuse into current expressions in MCB, my hope is that this research may contribute to church music scholarship that strives to depart from a North Atlantic, colonial narrative and shift instead toward increased hospitality to phenomena of Christian music throughout the world at large, and across the Americas in particular.

NOTES

1. Expresso Luz, *Bom Dia* (Expresso Luz, 1999), Compact Disc.
2. Carlos Veiga, "Mamãe, Eu Sou *Gospel*," track 13, *Bom Dia*. All translations from Portuguese and Spanish to English in this essay are my own unless otherwise indicated.
3. To distinguish African American gospel from the Brazilian *gospel* phenomenon, I will italicize the latter. I have chosen to not capitalize these terms to avoid association with the biblical Gospels.

4. Gerson Borges, *Ser evangélico sem deixar de ser brasileiro* (Viçosa, MG: Editora Ultimato, 2016), 67.

5. My use of "Brazilianness" is not meant to essentialize the diversity of musical expressions in Brazil but to highlight how these senses of being Brazilian through music are articulated by artists in the alternative Christian music scene in contrast to *gospel*.

6. Contributions to the history of MCB (to name but a few): Magali do Nascimento Cunha, "Vinho novo em odres velhos. Um olhar comunicacional sobre a explosão gospel no cenário religioso evangélico no Brasil" (dissertation, São Paulo: SP; Universidade de São Paulo, Escola de Comunicação e Artes, 2004); Jacqueline Ziroldo Dolghie, "A Igreja Renascer em Cristo e a consolidação do mercado de música gospel no Brasil: uma análise das estratégias de marketing," *Ciencias Sociales y Religión/Ciências Sociais e Religião* 6, no. 6 (August 25, 2007): 201–20. Contributions from outside Brazil include: John Burdick, *The Color of Sound: Race, Religion, and Music in Brazil* (New York: New York University Press, 2013).

7. I use "independent" and "alternative" interchangeably. Both terms were used by interviewees to describe their scene.

8. The Brazilian *evangélico* does not equate to its North American counterpart, *evangelical*. In Brazil, Christians who identify in contrast to Catholicism, the majority religion, would be considered *evangélicos*. This includes Pentecostals, Neopentecostals, historic Protestant denominations (immigrant based and missionary established), and nowadays might tentatively include Seventh-Day Adventists and Mormons. According to Paul Freston, a discussion of Latin American Christianity must acknowledge that "the preferred self-definition of Latin American Protestants is as *evangélicos*." Paul Freston, ed., *Evangelical Christianity and Democracy in Latin America, Evangelical Christianity and Democracy in Latin America* (Oxford: Oxford University Press, 2008), 6.

9. Guilherme Esteves Galvão Lopes, "500 Anos De Reforma Protestante: Os Desafios Contemporâneos Dos Evangélicos Do Brasil," *Revista Dia-Logos* 12, no. 1 (2018): 108–22; Adair Nelo Pereira and Maria do Socorro Freire de Sá, "Os Batistas e o Crescimento Evangélico," *Revista Summae Sapientiae* 1, no. 1 (October 31, 2018): 140–65; André Ricardo de Souza, "Pluralidade cristã e algumas questões do cenário religioso brasileiro," *Revista USP*, no. 120 (March 11, 2019).

10. Cunha, "Vinho," 123.

11. Ibid.

12. Nelson Bomilcar, interview by the author, January 10, 2020.

13. Ibid.

14. Vicente, "Música e Disco," 34

15. Cunha, "Vinho," 123.

16. "Youth of Truth." "Jovens Da Verdade—Contato," accessed April 10, 2020, https://www.jovensdaverdade.com.br/contato/quem_somos. OPV was founded by American Jack Wyrtzen: "Palavra da Vida | Quem Somos," accessed April 10, 2020, https://www.pvnordeste.com/quem-somos. VPC was led by Californian Jaime Kemp, a missionar of service for the Evangelization of Latin America/SEPAL, founded by

American Dick Hillis: "História," *Sepal* (blog), accessed April 10, 2020, https://sepal.org.br/historia/. MPC was founded by American Torrey Johnson: "Trajetória—MPC Brasil," accessed April 10, 2020, https://mpc.org.br/trajetoria/. ABUB is the Brazilian branch of International Fellowship of Evangelical Students/IFES. "História | ABUB—Aliança Bíblica Universitária Do Brasil," accessed April 10, 2020, http://abub.org.br/historia.

17. Jorge Camargo, interview by the author, December 18, 2019.
18. Ibid.
19. Bomilcar, interview.
20. Swee Hong Lim and Lester Ruth, *Lovin' on Jesus: A Concise History of Contemporary Worship* (Nashville, TN: Abingdon Press, 2017), 20.
21. Cunha, "Vinho," 128.
22. Guilherme Kerr, interview by the author, January 22, 2020.
23. Bomilcar, interview.
24. Claudia Barbosa de Souza Feitoza, interview by the author, February 26, 2020.
25. Werner Ewald, *Música e Igreja: Reflexões Contemporâneas Para Uma Prática Milenar* (São Leopoldo, RS: Editora Sinodal, 2010), 183.
26. Tropicália refers particularly to the Tropicalismo movement. More information about the relationship between popular music and the military coup in Brazil can be found in Anaïs Fléchet and Marcos Napolitano, "Musique Populaire et Dictature Militaire Au Brésil: Dynamiques Contestataires et Logiques de Marché (1964–1985)," *Nuevo Mundo—Mundos Nuevos*, June 1, 2015, https://doi.org/10.4000/nuevomundo.68081.
27. Cunha, "Vinho," 132–37.
28. Daniel Hunger, "Produção Musical No Morro Do Espelho: Um Resgate Histórico Da Música No Campus Da Faculdades EST," *TEAR ONLINE* 3, no. 1 (2014): 46. Instead of using its translation, Popular Brazilian Music, I will adhere to the practice in English-language scholarship of referring to Brazilian music using the Portuguese, MPB. See Sean Stroud, Stan Hawkins, and Lori Burns, *The Defence of Tradition in Brazilian Popular Music: Politics, Culture and the Creation of Música Popular Brasileira* (Abingdon, UK: Routledge, 2008).
29. Eduardo Vicente, "Música e Fé: A Cena Religiosa No Mercado Fonográfico Brasileiro," *Latin American Music Review* 29, no. 1 (August 8, 2008): 31.
30. Bomilcar, interview.
31. G. Kerr, interview.
32. Sandra Kerr, interview by the author, February 28, 2020.
33. Barbosa, interview.
34. Cena América da Silva and John Griffin, *Vamos Cantar* (São Paulo, SP: ABU Editora, 1973); Bomilcar, interview.
35. Bomilcar, interview.
36. Barbosa, interview.
37. G. Kerr, interview.
38. "Resgate" means "rescue" in Portuguese. José Antônio Bruno, interview by the author, March 17, 2020.

39. These are certainly not the only labels worth investigating, but there is some consensus that, historically, they set the stage for the *gospel* scene, followed by others. Top Gospel was established in 1996, Graça Music in 1999, Central Gospel Music in 2005, and Sara Music in 2010. This configuration has changed as labels team up with international majors, establishing brands such as Sony Music Gospel. For further detail into these label mergers, see Vicente, "Musica e Disco"; Nina Rosas, "Cultura Evangélica e Dominação Do Brasil: Música, Mídia e Gênero No Caso Do Diante Do Trono" (Belo Horizonte, MG, Universidade Federal de Minas Gerais, Faculdade de Filosofia e Ciências Humanas, Programa de Pós-Graduação em Sociologia, 2015); Olívia Bandeira and Olívia Bandeira, "Música gospel no Brasil—reflexões em torno da bibliografia sobre o tema," *Religião & Sociedade* 37, no. 2 (December 2017): 200–228; Edson Ramos de Oliveira Costa, "Mercado de música gospel: como nasce uma indústria cultural" (São Cristóvão: SE, Universidade Federal de Sergipe, 2017).

40. My use of Neopentecostal draws on Allan Anderson's typology of Latin American Protestantism. He equates the terms "Neo-Pentecostal" and "neo-Charismatic," describing these churches as "influenced by both classical Pentecostalism and the Charismatic movement." Anderson recognizes that the term is fluid, used in different ways over the past half-decade to refer chronologically to "older church Charismatics," then to "independent Charismatic churches [and] Third Wave churches," and in more recent cases "to a wide range of newer independent Pentecostal churches that embrace contemporary cultures, use contemporary methods of communication, media, and marketing, form international networks or 'ministries,' and often have a prosperity emphasis." Allan Anderson, "Varieties, Taxonomies, and Definitions," in *Studying Global Pentecostalism*, ed. Allan Anderson et al., first edition, Theories and Methods (University of California Press, 2010), 19–20.

41. Robson de Paula, "'Os Cantores Do Senhor': Três Trajetórias Em Um Processo de Industrialização Da Música Evangélica No Brasil," *Religião & Sociedade* 27, no. 2 (December 2007): 59.

42. Dolghie, "A Igreja Renascer," 209.

43. Jacqueline Dolghie, "O gospel da Renascer em Cristo e suas relações com o campo protestante brasileiro," *Revista Ciências da Religião—História e Sociedade* 3, no. 1 (May 21, 2009): 75.

44. Robson de Paula, "O mercado da música gospel no Brasil: aspectos organizacionais e estruturais," *Revista Uniabeu* 5, no. 9 (April 23, 2012): 142–43.

45. Lamia Oualalolou, "El poder evangélico en Brasil," *Nueva Sociedad; Caracas*, no. 260 (December 2015): 127.

46. Dolghie, "O Gospel da Renascer," 74. Sant'Ana makes a similar argument: Raquel Sant'Ana, "A música gospel e os usos da 'arma da cultura.' Reflexões sobre as implicações de uma emenda," *Revista Intratextos* 5, no. 1 (July 15, 2014): 23–41.

47. Bomilcar, interview.

48. Gerson Borges Martins, interview by the author, March 6, 2020.

49. G. Kerr, interview.

50. Bomilcar, interview.

51. Camargo, interview.

52. Ibid.

53. Carlos da Veiga Feitoza, interview by the author, December 19, 2019.
54. G. Kerr, interview.
55. Ibid.
56. Ibid.
57. In Portuguese, *brega* denotes the tacky, outdated, unfashionable. It is also a musical style that draws from Brazil's Jovem Guarda scene and romantic pop. An analysis of *brega* can be found in Samuel M. Araújo, "Brega: Music and Conflict in Urban Brazil," *Latin American Music Review / Revista de Música Latinoamericana* 9, no. 1 (1988): 50–89.
58. Borges, interview.
59. Ibid.
60. Ibid.
61. Vencedores Por Cristo, *De Vento Em Popa* (São Paulo, SP: Vencedores Por Cristo, 1977), Vinyl.
62. Borges, interview.
63. Veiga, interview.
64. Ibid.
65. Marcos Oliveira de Almeida, interview by the author, March 3, 2020.
66. Nelson Rios, interview by the author, March 17, 2020.
67. Camargo, interview.
68. Bruno, interview.
69. Barbosa, interview.
70. Bruno, interview.
71. Eduardo Vicente, "Música e Fé: A Cena Religiosa No Mercado Fonográfico Brasileiro," *Latin American Music Review* 29, no. 1 (August 8, 2008): 34.
72. Bandeira, "Música Gospel no Brasil."
73. Ibid., 221.
74. Marcell Silva Steuernagel, "Profetizando do Palco: Performances Políticas na Música *Gospel* Brasileira," in *Linguagens Litúrgicas e Artísticas Na América Latina: Memórias e Identidades*, ed. Renato Ferreira Machado and Júlio Cézar Adam (Canoas, RS: Editora Unilasalle, 2019).
75. For more about how Brazilian *evangélicos* engage in sociopolitical critique through MCB, see Silva Steuernagel, "Profetizando."
76. *Cordel* is a form of popular Brazilian literature that draws from medieval minstrelsy traditions. A good English-language introduction to *cordel* can be found in Candace Slater, "Brazilian Popular Literature (the Literatura de Cordel)," in *The Cambridge History of Latin American Literature*, ed. Roberto Gonzalez Echevarría and Enrique Pupo-Walker, first edition (Cambridge: Cambridge University Press, 1996), 315–28.
77. Veiga, interview.
78. Borges, interview.
79. Eric Kramer, "Making Global Faith Universal: Media and a Brazilian Prosperity Movement," *Culture and Religion* 3, no. 1 (May 1, 2002): 21–47.
80. Bruno, interview.
81. http://www.acasadarocha.com.br/.

82. Bruno, interview.
83. Veiga, interview.
84. Ibid.
85. Various "protest song" or *canção de protesto* movements erupted in Latin America in reaction to authoritarian politics: Caio De Souza Gomes, "'Por Toda América Soplan Vientos Que No Han de Parar Hasta Que Entierren Las Sombras': Anti-Imperialismo e Revolução Na Canção Engajada Latino-Americana (1967–69) * Anti-Imperialism and Revolution in Latin American Protest Song (1967–69)," *História e Cultura* 2, no. 1 (August 1, 2013): 146–65.
86. S. Kerr, interview.
87. Barbosa, interview.
88. Monique M. Ingalls, "Transnational Connections, Musical Meaning, and the 1990s 'British Invasion' of North American Evangelical Worship Music," in *The Oxford Handbook of Music and World Christianities*, ed. Suzel Ana Reily and Jonathan Dueck (New York: Oxford University Press, 2016), 425–45.
89. G. Kerr, interview.o

FURTHER READING

Borges, Gerson. *Ser evangélico sem deixar de ser brasileiro*. Viçosa, MG: Editora Ultimato, 2016.
Burdick, John. *The Color of Sound: Race, Religion, and Music in Brazil*. New York: New York University Press, 2013.
Cunha, Magali do Nascimento. "Vinho novo em odres velhos. Um olhar comunicacional sobre a explosão gospel no cenário religioso evangélico no Brasil." Dissertation, São Paul, SP: Universidade de São Paulo, Escola de Comunicação e Artes, 2004. http://www.teses.usp.br/teses/disponiveis/27/27134/tde-29062007-153429/.
Dolghie, Jacqueline Ziroldo. "A Igreja Renascer em Cristo e a consolidação do mercado de música gospel no Brasil: uma análise das estratégias de marketing." *Ciencias Sociales y Religión/Ciências Sociais e Religião* 6, no. 6 (August 25, 2007): 201–20.
Ewald, Werner. *Música e Igreja: Reflexões Contemporâneas Para Uma Prática Milenar*. São Leopoldo, RS: Editora Sinodal, 2010.
Freston, Paul, ed. *Evangelical Christianity and Democracy in Latin America*. Evangelical Christianity and Democracy in Latin America. Oxford: Oxford University Press, 2008.
Kramer, Eric. "Making Global Faith Universal: Media and a Brazilian Prosperity Movement." *Culture and Religion* 3, no. 1 (May 1, 2002): 21–47. https://doi.org/10.1080/01438300208567181.
Mendonça, Joêzer de Souza. "O Gospel é Pop: Música e Religião Na Cultura Pós-Moderna." Thesis. São Paulo, SP: Universidade Estadual Paulista "Júlio Mesquita Filho," 2009. http://repositorio.unesp.br/handle/11449/95139.

Paula, Robson de. "'Os Cantores Do Senhor': Três Trajetórias Em Um Processo de Industrialização Da Música Evangélica No Brasil." *Religião & Sociedade* 27, no. 2 (December 2007): 55–84. https://doi.org/10.1590/S0100-85872007000200004.

Rosas, Nina. "Cultura Evangélica e Dominação Do Brasil: Música, Mídia e Gênero No Caso Do Diante Do Trono." Dissertation. Belo Horizonte, MG: Universidade Federal de Minas Gerais, Faculdade de Filosofia e Ciências Humanas, Programa de Pós-Graduação em Sociologia, 2015. https://www.academia.edu/11094827/Cultura_evang%C3%A9lica_e_domina%C3%A7%C3%A3o_do_Brasil_m%C3%BAsica_m%C3%ADdia_e_g%C3%AAnero_no_caso_do_Diante_do_Trono.

Silva Steuernagel, Marcell. "Profetizando do palco: performances políticas na música *gospel* brasileira." In *Linguagens Litúrgicas e Artísticas Na América Latina: Memórias e Identidades*, edited by Renato Ferreira Machado and Júlio Cézar Adam, 37–50. Canoas, RS: Editora Unilasalle, 2019. https://revistas.unilasalle.edu.br/index.php/books/issue/view/274.

Vicente, Eduardo. "Música e Disco No Brasil: A Trajetória Da Indústria Nas Décadas de 80 e 90." Dissertação. São Paulo, SP: Universidade de São Paulo, 2002. http://www.abpd.org.br/wp-content/uploads/2015/01/doutoradoEduVicente.pdf.

Discography

Alexandre, João. *Simplesmente João*. Gospel Records, GRCD 106, 1991. Compact Disc.

Expresso Luz. *Bom Dia*. Expresso Luz, 1999. Compact Disc.

Vencedores Por Cristo. *De Vento Em Popa*. Vencedores Por Cristo, VPCLP-023, 1977. Vinyl.

Interview List (Alphabetized by Artist's Last Name)

Marcos Oliveira de Almeida, March 3, 2020.
Nelson Bomilcar, January 10, 2020.
Gerson Borges Martins, March 6, 2020.
José Antônio Bruno, March 17, 2020.
Jorge Geraldo de Camargo Filho, December 18, 2019.
Guilherme Kerr, January 22, 2020.
Sandra Kerr, February 28, 2020.
Claudia Barbosa de Souza Feitoza, February 26, 2020.
Carlos da Veiga Feitoza, December 19, 2019.
Nelson Rios, March 17, 2020.

Chapter Seven

Ethics, Justice, and Politics in Contemporary Worship Music

Jeff R. Warren

In this essay I examine the musical, theological, and political structures surrounding the creation of contemporary worship music (CWM) and identify the ideas of justice that accompany CWM. An underlying question is how the devotional practice of singing praise to God relates to strong political affinities, yet how at the same time CWM retains the ability to be sung by evangelicals with diverse political leanings. While CWM makes claims that it is about spirituality and beyond politics, this essay argues that CWM participates in ethics, justice, and politics wrapped up in issues of race, class, gender, and citizenship. The essay concludes by asking if CWM might also be a future site for justice and resistance.

On December 6, 2019, a group of evangelical worship leaders and pastors gathered in the White House in Washington, DC. Representing some of the most influential churches and contemporary worship music groups in the United States and the world, these leaders posed for a photo in the Oval Office surrounding President Donald Trump, received a briefing from Vice President Mike Pence, and held a musical worship session in the White House.[1] Many leaders represented neo-Charismatic churches, specifically a subset described by sociologists Brad Christerson and Richard Flory as Independent Network Charismatic (INC) Christians.[2] In short, these churches do not fall under traditional denominations and are led by individuals often self-identified as "apostles."[3] This segment of Christianity is the fastest growing in the United States, and its music has even wider influence.[4] One church with significant musical influence and several representatives at the December White House visit is the Redding, California–based Bethel Church. Among their delegation was Sean Feucht, a Bethel songwriter and music pastor who ran for Congress in 2020 as a Republican. In one of the White House photographs, Feucht leans in and touches Trump's arm, reflecting how Feucht's political positions also lean toward those of Trump's Republican Party.

In the fall of 2019, Feucht posted a campaign video that begins with a voiceover asking the question, "What is happening to the identity of America?" paired with images of an American flag burning and news footage of demonstrations.[5] The opening section climaxes with the claim that "family values are being eroded, the unborn are sacrificed, morals are low, and taxes are high." Shortly after, the intensity of the music decreases and a synth pad with shimmer reverberation introduces a worship song that we later learn is sung by Feucht.[6] The voiceover then turns to how these problems can be fixed: "America is not just a country. It's a legacy built on a foundation of hope and truth. A beacon to the world." After featuring a woman wrapped in an American flag, the narrator asks, "If we lose our identity how will the world learn from our greatness?" We learn that the narrator is Feucht's wife, and she describes him as "a man who knows what feeding the hungry, protecting the vulnerable, and fighting for one's beliefs is all about. A man with a guitar and a purpose," and that purpose is "to restore the identity, values, and morals of this great nation." The video cuts to a church service, and now the background music becomes diegetic. Feucht, with guitar in hand, leads a congregation with raised hands singing the title lyric of the song: "until the whole world looks like heaven."

Feucht's political campaign provides an exemplary link between evangelical worship music and ideas of ethics, justice, and politics. It vocalizes a Christian nationalism that sociologists Andrew L. Whitehead and Samuel L. Perry note "conceptually blur[s] and conflate[s] religious identity (Christian, preferably Protestant) with race (white), nativity (born in the United States), citizenship (American), and political ideology (social and fiscal conservative)."[7] While the cultural framework of Christian nationalism is not limited to white evangelicals, Feucht's political stances resonate with the way the vast majority of white evangelicals voted in the 2016 US election. Over 80 percent of those identifying as white born-again or evangelical Christians voted for Trump.[8] Reasons to vote for Trump included the political party, positions on particular issues such as abortion, and potential judicial appointments.[9] Others, however, are convinced that if Christians or supporters fill enough positions of power, it will enable the transformation of earth into heaven. In this view, Christians in leadership positions bring about a just world, and worship music can both give a glimpse of that world right now and create the conditions for this utopia. In this context, support of Trump is justified in two ways: that he is a Christian or that he supports Christians. Some established evangelical leaders have vouched for Trump's faith.[10] Those who question the veracity of his faith compare Trump to the biblical story of King Cyrus, who was not an Israelite but was used by God to benefit the Israelites.[11] Politics, however, is only one area that requires Christian leadership in this framework. Equally important is the influence of artistic and cultural production. The Oval Office photographs and Feucht's campaign provide links between politics and CWM, the music that dominates evangelical church services.

CONTEMPORARY WORSHIP MUSIC

Millions of people across the world regularly sing contemporary worship music. CWM is a musical practice that believes "congregational song should be set to the musical style of the surrounding culture."[12] It is dominant within evangelical churches, and its influence includes albums that regularly reach the *Billboard 200* charts.[13] One influential group is Hillsong Worship, a group affiliated with Hillsong Church. Hillsong Music has released forty-six albums since 1992 and claims that each week their songs are "sung by an estimated 50 million people in 60 languages" in church services.[14] Hillsong's other musical groups include Hillsong United and Hillsong Young and Free. The church organization has released a combined sixty-six albums, and in 2018 reported over $103 million in revenue.[15]

CWM is the music many believers use to perform their faith. In a recent article I analyzed the ways that ethical and spiritual values are performed in CWM.[16] CWM is usually understood as a medium for personal devotion or for a church congregation to worship. This style of music is, however, performed in churches that are dominated by a few major producers. The church groups most influential to CWM are theologically neo-Charismatic and include the aforementioned Hillsong and Bethel. This centralization of production is noted by a music industry whose model has shifted from sales revenue to streaming revenue. Ethnomusicologist Andrew Mall published a roundtable discussion with executives in the Christian music industry during which one executive noted the unique reach of CWM: "One of the things that people like to say in our industry is that we're the only genre where we know where every buyer and listener is for three hours every Sunday morning. No other form of music can say that."[17] If particular songs are performed regularly in church, their popularity is already known, and it is therefore easier to promote the song through other avenues. This has led to CWM taking over a larger segment of the wider Christian music industry. As CWM's influence includes performance in churches, streaming, and radio, it becomes associated with other products that by extension become affiliated with Christianity. One industry executive goes so far as to claim that music contributes to the claim that "Christianity is a lifestyle brand."[18] This brand of music and faith often affiliates with political leanings.

In the conclusion to my article on ethical and spiritual values performed in CWM, I question the implications of the centralized production of CWM sung across churches with wide theological beliefs. While it may signal a new musical ecumenical movement, centralized and standardized CWM production and strong neo-Charismatic influence on CWM might affect Christian responses to events such as the Syrian refugee crisis.[19] One step toward investigating the relation between CWM and justice is to examine both the theology and politics of the neo-Charismatic groups that dominate CWM production and work to understand how their musical practices are positioned within their views of justice and politics.

INDEPENDENT NETWORK CHARISMATIC CHRISTIANITY

Drawing upon interviews and attendance at church-related events, Christerson and Flory's book *The Rise of Network Christianity* aims to "explain the phenomenal growth rates of one particular subgroup of independent neo-Charismatic believers that we have labeled 'Independent Network Charismatic.'"[20] Although the authors note the presence of music at INC events, they do not provide much detail about the music of these groups or the influence of their music, so I supplement their description with additional details about the specifically musical influence of INC. I argue that CWM plays an important role in fulfilling neo-Charismatic aims for social justice. Additionally, these social justice ideals from a relatively small group of independent Charismatic churches may be gaining influence through their musical outputs. In 2019 an overwhelming percentage of singing across Protestant church denominations came from music disseminated by a relatively small group of independent Charismatic churches.[21] The authors argue that "this group is the fastest-growing Christian subgroup in America and that its unique practices and governance structures account for its success in the American religious market."[22] This growth is particularly notable at a time when, according to a Pew study, most other traditions of Christianity are shrinking.[23]

INC groups find a common history in the Pentecostal movement, which Christerson and Flory suggest "typically refers to the denominational groups that emerged from Los Angeles's Azusa Street Revival in 1906."[24] Neo-Charismatic churches are a branch established after 1960, and two of the most influential early movements were Calvary Chapel and Vineyard.[25] Both of these groups were also influential in the rise of contemporary worship music.

California-based Calvary Chapel was home to the "Jesus Movement." The movement's musical influences include the folk rock–influenced use of the acoustic guitar as the lead instrument and helping establish the Christian music recording industry through the launch of Maranatha! Music in 1971. Vineyard was prominent in the worship music movements of the 1990s and early 2000s and remains influential in the songs churches sing currently. American studies scholar Randall J. Stephens argues that Calvary Chapel and Vineyard were "both prime promoters of Christian rock" and "were instrumental in the growth of nondenominational Christianity."[26] Christerson and Flory claim that many INC churches have important links to Vineyard through movement leader John Wimber.[27] Wimber was a part of the Calvary Chapel until he was removed for some of his "experiments" with the Holy Spirit (which he also did at Fuller Theological Seminary). Wimber then joined Vineyard and was instrumental in establishing Vineyard Music in 1982. As the Vineyard movement spread, its musical influence grew significantly in the 1990s through songwriters such as Kevin Prosch and Brian Doerksen. Vineyard Worship leader Carl Tuttle details how Wimber passed leadership of the group to him despite Wimber's stronger musical background.[28] After establishing a musical group with a consistent sound and vision, Vineyard Music began putting songs composed at other Vineyard churches onto their albums. This model of a core band with a recognizable sound performing songs written by a wider network of composers seems to have helped establish a model that several CWM groups continue today.

While Wimber and Vineyard were instrumental in the spread of Charismatic Christianity and developing many future INC leaders, the groups identified by Christerson and Flory as INC Christianity "have broken off from the rest of Pentecostal/Charismatic Christianity in significant ways."[29] One notable split was the Toronto Airport Vineyard Church leaving the Vineyard denomination in 1995. The Toronto church began to "experiment" with the Holy Spirit, and the results ranged from fainting while being "slain in the spirit" to barking, laughing, and practicing miraculous healing.[30] Ironically, it was Wimber, who was himself removed from Calvary Chapel from his own "experiments," who disaffiliated the Toronto church from Vineyard.[31] Bethel's head pastor Bill Johnson's 1994 visit to the Toronto church was a turning point, and his experience of that church may have been influential on his choice to preemptively remove Bethel from the Assemblies of God denomination.[32] In place of a denomination as governance, control of the church is passed to a pastor who is considered endowed with a mandate from God. Peter Wagner's teaching on "apostolic leadership" is important here, and his term "New Apostolic Revolution" (NAR) is one of the terms associated with this rise of independent Charismatic churches.[33] Christerson and Flory do not adopt Wagner's term because they aim to expand their description beyond groups that identify with Wagner's ideas. They identify the following four distinguishing factors of INC Christianity:

1. *They do not seek to build a "movement"* or to create affiliated franchise congregations using a particular name.
2. *They are not primarily focused on building congregations* in the traditional sense but rather seek to influence the beliefs and practices of believers regardless of congregation or affiliation, including those who are not affiliated with any congregation or religious group.
3. *They seek to transform society as a whole* rather than saving individual souls and building the church.
4. Instead of being formally organized into a "movement" or "denomination," the various leaders and ministries in this category are highly connected by networks of cooperation.[34]

The authors claim to expand their scope by moving from NAR to their broader term INC, however the grouping of neo-Charismatic churches into INC highlights some connections to the exclusion of others. Their approach, for example, is structured by highlighting the ways these groups market or grow their influence. In short, INC focuses on institutional structure at the church level. An alternate approach to examine relations between neo-Charismatic groups could focus on their influence in CWM and accompanying musical structures. While worship music does not feature highly in Christerson and Flory's text, it is one of the strongest influences of these churches upon evangelicalism, if not Christianity as a whole. Focusing on CWM highlights similarities between Bethel and other independent churches. Hillsong, for example, is ignored by Christerson and Flory because Hillsong appears invested in creating its own denominational movement and franchised group of churches. As I discuss later, Bethel Music, the music publishing arm of Bethel church, is structured more like a branded movement and has many parallels to the structure of Hillsong Music. In short, Bethel church is an exemplar INC organization for Christerson and Flory, but the structure of Bethel Music does not always fit their four distinguishing factors of INC. The point here is that music is a crucial way that these churches strive toward their goals of wider influence and social transformation, and here I aim to expand upon the work of Christerson and Flory by examining how these groups position CWM within their wider ethical, social justice, and political aims. Throughout the following sections I detail Christerson and Flory's arguments about INC and then expand upon and challenge these arguments by showing similarities between Bethel and Hillsong.

One way to measure the influence of independent neo-Charismatic churches in CWM is through examining what music churches use. The company Christian Copyright Licensing International (CCLI) administers rights for churches to sing copyrighted songs in church services. Churches pay a yearly license for legal access to display song lyrics and perform copyrighted works. The group uses an intermittent sampling method to determine the frequency of performance and distribution of royalties.[35] Twice a year CCLI updates their "CCLI Top 100" list with songs congregations performed most over the time period.[36] I examined the top twenty-five songs in the United States in early 2019, looking at the publishing company as well as the church affiliation of the songwriter. The vast majority of songwriters are part of neo-Charismatic churches. The only church affiliation exceptions I could find are one Catholic, one Vineyard, and one Anglican songwriter. Eleven of the 25 songs came from Bethel and Hillsong. If Chris Tomlin and Matt Redman, two influential CWM composers and worship leaders with close ties to the Passion church and Passion conferences, are added to Bethel and Hillsong, these three groups make up the majority of the top twenty-five most performed songs in churches across the United States. Or, to put it another way, a handful of people with particular theologies of musical worship and social justice have an extraordinary reach across American and increasingly across global Christianity. Previously fringe theologies of worship are becoming dominant through the increased influence of these groups. In the next sections, I discuss the Bethel and Hillsong church groups in more detail, with a focus on how their musical output relates to their positions on justice and politics.

INFLUENCE AND JUSTICE

For Christerson and Flory, a key element of INC churches is an emphasis on building a network of influence. But more important than the network structure is the concept of social justice that underpins the structure. They argue that "Bethel is not concerned with franchising congregations or building a denomination, but rather with transmitting their 'culture of heaven on earth.'"[37] These ideals are reflected in their music. Earlier I mentioned Bethel songwriter Sean Feucht's song "Until the Whole Earth Looks Like Heaven," and Bethel Music's annual conference is called "Heaven Come."[38] One high-profile INC leader told Christerson and Flory their vision is to

> bring heaven's culture here on earth, to bring heaven down to earth. We've been praying that for 2,000 years, praying, "Thy kingdom come, thy will be done on

earth as it is in heaven." So I think we're not just about planting churches, but we want to do what we can to eradicate systemic poverty . . . so there's a whole transformational element to what we're doing and our vision.[39]

Bringing heaven to earth, then, is linked to a transformed and just society. The eradication of poverty is a worthy goal, but crucial here is understanding how INC envisions social change taking place. Another informant provides background about why and how this is to happen:

> So the idea behind it theologically is that they believe that they need to retake the dominion that Satan stole from Adam in the Garden of Eden. Now, since Jesus came, now they believe that they can retake that dominion and advance the kingdom of God socially, not just making individual converts. They are advancing the idea of what they call the "seven mountains mandate." The seven mountains are seven sectors of society—family, government, arts and entertainment, media, business, education, and religion, and Christians are supposed to permeate each mountain and rise to the top of each mountain. They believe if Christians permeate each mountain and rise to the top of all seven mountains, then society will be completely transformed. Society would have biblical morality, people would live in harmony, there would be peace and not war, there would be no poverty. It's really almost a utopian vision.[40]

In short, social change takes place when right-believing Christians take places of social power. Christians in power may be the preconditions for a just society, but little is detailed about the concrete ethical values guiding a just society or the political policies required to eradicate poverty. This view represents a shift from the more common evangelical aim of saving souls for the next life to saving the world in this life. Theologically it is a shift to postmillennialism, a view that Christ's second coming will follow a time when Christian ethics create a utopian society. In other words, as Christerson and Flory note, "God has empowered believers through the Holy Spirit to literally create heaven on earth through their gaining power in the various sectors of society."[41] Postmillennialism was once dominant within American Christianity but had declined strongly after World War I. Historian James H. Moorhead, writing about the erosion of postmillennialism between 1865 and 1925, concludes that "experience simply had not sustained postmillennialism. The product of an era when evangelicalism enjoyed cultural dominance, it could not survive when that ascendance waned."[42]

Neo-Charismatic groups revive postmillennialism by reenvisioning how the utopian age will come about. This change comes about by Christians achieving power and also through asking God for this change through prayer and (musical) worship. Christerson and Flory note the dual methods of prayer and power to achieve these aims:

Because they see the cause of social ills as spiritual, rather than structural, it makes sense they would not have a poverty-reduction policy agenda, for example, other than putting kingdom-minded, spirit-filled believers at the top of the mountains of business and government, which would then allow God's spiritual and material blessing to flow into society through them.[43]

INC followers believe leaders in positions of power will result in social justice, but just as important are the prayer and worship that establish the model of heaven on earth and are thought to provide a glimpse into that future world.

CWM AS PRAYER

Neo-Charismatic churches consider contemporary worship music a form of prayer where God sometimes responds miraculously. Bethel worship leader Jeremy Riddle, who moved to Bethel from the Vineyard church, is perhaps best known for his co-composition of "This Is Amazing Grace," a song released in 2012 that has been near the top of the CCLI charts for several years.[44] Filmmaker Darren Wilson released an interview with Riddle about a supernatural experience at Bethel.[45] In the segment, Riddle states, "I've experienced those moments where I know something else has come over me."[46] That "something" is later described as the Holy Spirit, and Riddle describes one particular miraculous experience in which a "glory cloud or cloud of gold dust" identified as a "manifestation" of God appeared above the stage during congregational singing. The interview is followed by cell phone footage of one of Bethel's worship services showing sparkling dust in the air.[47] This event took place during a time of musical worship, and this particular manifestation reportedly took place multiple times during corporate singing of CWM.

Another video released by Bethel TV in 2011 includes similar footage and is accompanied by head pastor Bill Johnson talking to the Bethel congregation during a service interrupted by this "glory cloud." Johnson states that "the church has been gathering together for decades around a sermon. Israel camped around the presence."[48] He argues that the future will hold some "dramatic shifts" around "how we do life and how we do church" and states that his "church is camping around the presence . . . finally, the main thing has become the main thing."[49] Johnson's argument seems to be that worship during CWM manifests God's presence, and that presence will lead the church, and the world, to become more like heaven. Just as the manifested presence of God led Israel to the promised land, the CWM manifestation of God will bring heavenly justice.

In a recent article I analyzed how several elements of CWM perform spiritual and ethical values.[50] CWM lyrical themes include right belief and also identification of singing as the responsibility of the faithful. These integrate into key Protestant themes, such as the articulation in the Westminster Shorter Catechism that "man's chief end is to glorify God, and to enjoy him forever," and Donald Hustad's argument that "worship is the 'work of the people.'"[51] Additionally, I argued that lyrically and performatively CWM identifies that the ideal form of experiencing God is singing praise to God with others. Monique Ingalls details the variety of ways that CWM is used, from personal listening to YouTube lyric videos to mega conferences, but multiple aspects of CWM from lyrics to sonic properties communicate the ideal of collective singing.[52] Bethel's "manifestation" of the Holy Spirit reinforces this ideal.

Taken together, for many neo-Charismatic Christians and increasingly other evangelicals, CWM provides a glimpse of heaven on earth. And at least within neo-Charismatic churches, worship is an end in itself for achieving social justice because it provides a model of the utopian world to come. In a nutshell, Bethel's perfect society of "heaven come" is performed and enacted through CWM.

CWM AS POWER

Not only does CWM do the work of performing the sort of spirituality that supposedly brings heaven to earth but the increasing popularity and centralized production of CWM make it a site for fulfilling the "seven mountains mandate" of establishing powerful leaders in arts and entertainment.[53] Despite many CWM leaders publicly eschewing the trappings of celebrity, the structure of musical production and distribution within Bethel, Hillsong, and other groups reveals a centralization of influence that pervades Christianity within the United States and increasingly throughout the globe. Emphasizing the concentration of power within Bethel Music provides an alternative description to one key category Christerson and Flory identify in Bethel and other INC churches: the "network" wherein groups do *not* look to spread their name brands or institutions. While the model of multiple church campuses is followed by Hillsong but not by Bethel, the methods of consolidation and influence within musical production tell a different story. Even with a different church structure, Bethel promotes its musical brand in a manner consistent with Hillsong and before that Vineyard.

As discussed earlier, Vineyard Music established a model that continues with Hillsong and Bethel. Vineyard Music began with a core team recording first their own music, then recording music composed by others across the denomination, and finally expanding to multiple leaders and songwriters. Hillsong continues this format, with a central team selecting songs from a range of writers and then taking turns leading songs in performance. To the credit of the INC argument, Bethel is more loosely organized, with members being part of an "artist collective." Former Bethel leaders launched another church in Sacramento and began another label called "Jesus Culture Music."[54] The musical products of Bethel may not appear as centrally organized as Vineyard or Hillsong, but their organization is more sophisticated. Hillsong Music's main outputs are Hillsong-branded acts, including Hillsong United, Hillsong Worship, and Hillsong Young and Free. Although the Bethel Music label releases albums under the group name Bethel Music, these are not the only outputs of the label. Bethel Music releases are credited as featuring Bethel Music and Jesus Culture Music artists. These artists in turn release their own albums under the Bethel Music, Jesus Culture Music, or other labels. The result is an approach that appears to be a loosely related network of artists but retains centralized control and power through the label. When examining CCLI charts, Hillsong-produced songs are prominent through the credited group, but affiliations of Bethel artists are only found by seeking additional information about the record label. Bethel's influence is less apparent on the charts, but their influence is slightly larger than Hillsong's.

There are other parallels between Hillsong and Bethel. Each of them is led by three generations of church leaders, and the youngest generation leads CWM endeavors. Bethel head pastor Bill Johnson's father was previously the pastor of Bethel. Bill's son Brian Johnson now serves as the president of Bethel Music. Frank Houston founded the church that would eventually become Hillsong church under current lead pastors Brian and Bobbie Houston. Their three children all have leadership positions in the church, with two of them part of prominent musical movements. Joel Houston leads Hillsong United, Laura Toggs is a member of Hillsong Young and Free as well as a pastor in Hillsong youth ministry in Australia, and Ben Houston is the lead pastor of Hillsong Los Angeles. Both groups have educational facilities: the Hillsong International Leadership College and the Bethel School of Supernatural Ministry. These schools leverage their musical influence by providing training in worship leadership, training leaders that bring the influence of these churches to affiliated and unaffiliated churches, and also write music for the label.

Both groups also left Assemblies of God denominations. As mentioned earlier, Bethel left the Assemblies of God in 2005 shortly after Bill Johnson took over. In 2018, Hillsong left the Australian Assemblies of God denomination and created their own denomination. Brian Houston explained it this way:

As Hillsong Church has continued to grow, we no longer see ourselves as an Australian Church with a global footprint, but rather a Global church with an Australian base—our global office now resides in the USA. Two thirds of the people attending Hillsong Church each weekend live in countries beyond Australia. We have pastoral staff in twenty-four nations around the world, representing 123 campuses and locations, with 263 different church services on any given weekend. We consider it to be "One House, with many rooms."[55]

Christerson and Flory might see a significant difference in approach between Bethel's commitment to remaining a church with influence and Hillsong's creation of a denomination and desire to credential their own pastors (it is worth noting that Christerson and Flory wrote their book before Hillsong created its own denomination). Despite these differences, however, there is significant similarity between these two self-governing groups that share a neo-Charismatic theology and have built significant influence through CWM.

CWM AND POLITICS

Thus far, the ideas linking neo-Charismatic CWM to justice involve prayer and power. CWM is prayer and worship that is thought to do the work of bringing heaven to earth, sometimes leading to miraculous manifestations of God. CWM also develops power in arts and culture, one of the "seven mountains" that require Christian leadership. This utopian rhetoric includes a fully just world, but the content of what justice looks like and the methods of how it is achieved are not always clear. A discussion of political affiliation and support provides more explicit ideas about how these neo-Charismatic groups imagine what a just society looks like.

Turning back to the opening example, CWM leaders are influential enough to be invited to the White House and would likely aim to use their power to influence any president. With over 80 percent of white evangelicals voting for Trump in the 2016 election, this seems to delineate the acceptable lines of what faith-based justice looks like.[56] Neo-Charismatic leaders have significant influence through their networks and through CWM, and despite the distinctiveness and independence of these neo-Charismatic churches, their political stances are not far from older "moral majority" evangelicals, even if their particular theologies differ.[57]

Shortly after Trump was elected, Bethel's head pastor Bill Johnson posted on Facebook describing why he voted for Trump.[58] Johnson's post provides an example of the melding of neo-Charismatic and Christian nationalist views of social justice. Unsurprisingly, Johnson cites positions on abortion and same-sex marriage as important issues in determining his vote. He also discusses immigration and social welfare, using faith-based arguments to defend Republican positions. He states that "compassion for aliens (visitors to a nation) is vital, but here again the responsibility to provide safety for its citizens comes first." In this context, globalization is, according to Johnson, "nothing more than a modern Tower of Babel." Johnson also criticizes social support systems as a "failed liberal agenda," stating that "God gives us the ability to make wealth, and that merely giving people money without work can create a lifestyle of dependency that is dangerous for them and our government."

Johnson parrots Republican talking points about the faults of Trump and his rival, Hillary Clinton. He argues that Trump's accusations of racism were "ill-founded" and that "Trump was never called a racist until he ran against Clinton." He argues that "accusation is a trick of the devil to create fear" and "the devil himself is called the accuser," implying the real identity of Trump's political opponent. Clinton also violated honesty, a "core value of God's kingdom," in the email scandal.[59] On the other hand, Trump's actions are minimized. Johnson claims Trump's treatment of women is "inexcusable, but not unforgivable," and that he faces challenges such as political correctness that "Jesus Himself faced."

At least for Bill Johnson, the social justice of bringing heaven to earth seems to not be as radical as it may have first appeared and integrates into narratives of American Christian nationalism that include "assumptions of nativism, white supremacy, patriarchy, and heteronormativity, along with divine sanction for authoritarian control and militarism."[60] CWM seems to become one way to achieve this vision of social justice, even if the weekly times of worshipful singing with other believers seem far removed from political policies. Even if the structures surrounding CWM have these political affiliations, CWM lyrics generally focus on God and say very little about loving your neighbor or social justice.[61] CWM's silence on ideals of justice and politics enable these songs to be sung in a wide variety of churches that may be at odds with the political and social justice ideas espoused by the neo-Charismatic churches that birthed these songs. The dominance of neo-Charismatic churches within CWM may influence American Christianity as a whole, but perhaps there remains space for resistance to the links between CWM and these particular views of justice. Perhaps there are Christians who sing praises to God with Bethel-composed worship songs but disagree with Johnson's political views and who today echo Frederick Douglass's 175-year-old statement that "between the Christianity of this land, and the Christianity of Christ, I recognize the widest possible difference."[62] This requires an alternative relationship between ethics, justice, and politics.

CWM, ETHICS, JUSTICE, AND RESISTANCE

In *Music and Ethical Responsibility*, I argued that musical experience involves ethics because music always involves others, drawing specifically on the work of philosopher Emmanuel Levinas.[63] Levinas develops his ethical philosophy through describing an encounter with another person. He argues that ethics is responding to the needs of the other and develops his argument in dialogue with Jewish and Christian concepts of loving your neighbor.[64] Yet Levinas recognizes that we live in a world with many others and that deciding how to respond to multiple others involves institutions of justice. We are never in a world with two people, so it is with "the third" that "justice begins."[65] Institutions of justice are often at odds with ethics. Levinas writes that "politics is opposed to morality, as philosophy is to naiveté," and that "a state in which the interpersonal relationship is impossible, in which it is directed in advance by the determinism proper to the state, is a totalitarian state. So there is a limit to the state."[66] Instead Levinas argues that institutions of justice should be grounded in ethical responses to others: "Justice, exercised through institutions, which are inevitable, must always be held in check by the initial interpersonal relationship."[67] For Levinas, ethics necessitates justice but always remains in tension with justice and politics.[68] These tensions can challenge too easy associations between music and justice.

Sociologist Gerardo Martí, writing a foreword to a book on the Hillsong movement, claims that Hillsong music "provides a sonic religious identity, one that is portable and reproducible, such that immersion in the tribe can be relived again and again."[69] Hillsong music may play that role for some people, but this claim misses the fact that millions of people outside of Hillsong churches sing Hillsong music every Sunday. But is it possible that the same music that "provides a sonic religious identity" could also be used to resist the political structures associated with the creation of the music? While over 80 percent of white evangelicals voted for Trump, "only half (50%) of evangelical Protestants under the age of 30 are white, compared to more than three-quarters (77%) of evangelical Protestant seniors (age 65 or older)."[70] Will support for Trump's Christian nationalist ideas of justice continue to permeate the church and be spread by CWM or will the changing demographics of evangelicals change ideas about justice? If ideas about justice change, will the music also change? Can churches continue to sing "until the whole world looks like heaven" without imagining that heaven on earth looks like what Sean Feucht presents in in his campaign video? Perhaps resistance already exists within evangelicalism.

In this essay I showed close connections between CWM and ideas of Christian nationalism, the ideology Whitehead and Perry argue "comprises beliefs about historical identity, cultural preeminence, and political influence."[71] Whitehead and Perry argue, however, that "Christian nationalism should not be thought of as synonymous with 'evangelicalism' or even 'white evangelicalism.'"[72] Christian nationalism is undoubtedly influential within white evangelicalism but is a powerful mythology influential beyond those of faith. The authors draw upon their sociological data to argue that Christian nationalism is often at odds with religious belief. For example, they argue that "religious practice is powerfully related to views of morality that emphasize ideas of care for the vulnerable, social justice, and even reducing one's consumption patterns for the sake of environmental stewardship," while "Americans who embrace Christian nationalism are less likely to believe actively seeking social and economic justice is important to being a good person."[73] Similarly, "The more Americans adhere to Christian nationalist views, the less willing they are to acknowledge police discrimination against black Americans. But as people more frequently attend church, pray, or read their sacred scriptures, they become more likely to recognize racial discrimination in policing."[74] In other words, there are CWM-singing Christians who see a gulf between "the Christianity of this land and the Christianity of Christ."[75] CWM's ubiquity seems to rely upon nonspecificity as it leaves each congregation to sing about the social justice of their own imagination. Specifying support or criticism for Christian nationalism in CWM may be seen to be distracting from focus on worshipping God, but silence on themes is worth noting. CCLI's online tool that lists worship songs by theme has over a hundred fold more entries for "heaven" than "justice."[76] Therefore churchgoers and leaders should carefully consider their musical worship. Their examination of lyrics should go beyond what they say and consider what they are silent on. They should consider the affiliations of the music. They should consider how it contributes to justice for the problems of today, from the COVID-19 pandemic to institutional racism. Martin Luther King Jr. criticized the white moderate who "prefers a negative peace which is the absence of tension to a positive peace which is the presence of justice."[77] Like Levinas, King identifies the tension of justice. It is a tension that is too often absent from CWM.

NOTES

1. Samuel Smith, "Brian Houston, Christian Worship Leaders Pray for Trump, Visit Oval Office," *The Christian Post*, 2019, accessed June 8, 2020, https://www.christianpost.com/news/brian-houston-christian-worship-leaders-pray-for-trump-visit-oval-office.html.

2. Brad Christerson and Richard W. Flory, *The Rise of Network Christianity: How Independent Leaders Are Changing the Religious Landscape* (New York: Oxford University Press, 2017).

3. Ibid., 31.

4. Ibid., 5.

5. Sean Feucht, "Let's Take Action," 2019, accessed June 8, 2020, https://www.youtube.com/watch?v=TckczL3f6yo; Caleb Parke, "Worship Leader Runs for Congress in California: 'Morals Are Low, Taxes Are High,'" *Fox News*, 2019, accessed June 8, 2020, https://www.foxnews.com/politics/california-congress-worship-leader-sean-feucht.

6. For more on shimmer, see Jeff R. Warren, "'That Worship Sound': Ethics, Shimmer Reverberation, and Contemporary Worship Music," in *Ethics and Christian Musicking*, ed. Nathan Myrick and Mark Porter (Abingdon: Routledge, 2021).

7. Andrew L. Whitehead and Samuel L. Perry, *Taking America Back for God: Christian Nationalism in the United States* (Oxford: Oxford University Press, 2020), x.

8. Jessica Martínez and Gregory A. Smith, "How the Faithful Voted: A Preliminary 2016 Analysis," *Pew Research Center*, 2016, accessed June 8, 2020, https://www.pewresearch.org/fact-tank/2016/11/09/how-the-faithful-voted-a-preliminary-2016-analysis/.

9. Whitehead and Perry, *Taking America Back for God*, 74.

10. James Dobson, for example, suggests that Trump may be a "baby Christian" in the early stages of his faith in a post encouraging Christian voters to vote for Trump. See "Dr. James Dobson on Donald Trump's Christian Faith," 2016, accessed June 8, 2020, https://drjamesdobson.org/news/dr-james-dobson-on-trumps-christian-faith.

11. Christerson and Flory, *Rise of Network Christianity*, 5; Brad Christerson and Richard W. Flory, "Rick Perry's Belief That Trump Was Chosen by God Is Shared by Many in a Fast-Growing Christian Movement," *The Conversation*, 2019, accessed June 8, 2020, https://theconversation.com/rick-perrys-belief-that-trump-was-chosen-by-god-is-shared-by-many-in-a-fast-growing-christian-movement-127781.

12. Monique Ingalls, "Contemporary Worship Music," in *Continuum Encyclopedia of Popular Music of the World, Volume 8*, ed. David Horn and John Shepherd (London: Continuum, 2012), 147.

13. Hillsong Worship, for example, has sixteen albums on the *Billboard 200*, Bethel Music has thirteen, and Chris Tomlin reached number one. Hillsong Worship chart history, accessed June 8, 2020, https://www.billboard.com/music/hillsong-worship; Bethel Music chart history, accessed June 8, 2020, https://www.billboard.com/music/bethel-music; Keith Caulfield, "Chris Tomlin Scores First No. 1 Album on Billboard 200 Chart," *Billboard.com*, 2013, accessed June 8, 2020, https://www.billboard.com/articles/news/1496483/chris-tomlin-scores-first-no-1-album-on-billboard-200-chart.

14. "Hillsong Fact Sheet," accessed June 8, 2020, https://hillsong.com/fact-sheet/.

15. "Hillsong Annual Report," 2018, accessed June 8, 2020, https://hillsong.com/policies/annual-report-australia/.

16. Jeff R. Warren, "Performing Spiritual and Ethical Values in Contemporary Worship Music," *Verge: A Journal of the Arts and Christian Faith* 3 (2019),

accessed June 8, 2020, https://create.twu.ca/verge/2019/09/25/performing-spiritual-and-ethical-values-in-contemporary-worship-music/.

17. Andrew Mall, "'As for Me and My House': Christian Music Executives Roundtable," *Journal of Popular Music Studies* 32, no. 1 (2020): 18.

18. Mall, "'Me and My House,'" 24. More specifically, Tom Wagner argues that "Hillsong is a lifestyle brand" in *Music, Branding and Consumer Culture in Church* (Abingdon: Routledge, 2019), 4.

19. Warren, "Spiritual and Ethical Values."

20. Christerson and Flory, *Rise of Network Christianity*, 6.

21. "CCLI Top 100," accessed April 19, 2019, https://songselect.ccli.com/Search/Results?List=top100.

22. Christerson and Flory, *Rise of Network Christianity*, 6.

23. Ibid., 3.

24. Ibid., 7.

25. Ibid., 8.

26. Randall J. Stephens, *The Devil's Music: How Christians Inspired, Condemned, and Embraced Rock 'n' Roll* (Cambridge: Harvard University Press, 2018), 188.

27. Christerson and Flory, *Rise of Network Christianity*, 18.

28. Carl Tuttle, "History of Vineyard Worship—1976–1997," 2009, accessed June 8, 2020, https://worshiptherock.com/profiles/blogs/history-of-vineyard-worship.

29. Christerson and Flory, *Rise of Network Christianity*, 7.

30. Ibid., 20, 28.

31. Ibid., 24.

32. Ibid., 35–36.

33. For example, see C. Peter Wagner, *The New Apostolic Churches* (Delight, AR: Gospel Light Publications, 1998).

34. Christerson and Flory, *Rise of Network Christianity*, 8.

35. Warren, "Spiritual and Ethical Values."

36. "CCLI Top 100."

37. Christerson and Flory, *Rise of Network Christianity*, 113–14.

38. Caleb Parke, "Thousands Seek Revival at 'Heaven Come' Conference in Los Angeles: 'God Wants to Do It Again,'" *Fox News*, 2019, accessed June 8, 2020, https://www.foxnews.com/faith-values/california-heaven-come-revival-los-angeles.

39. Christerson and Flory, *Rise of Network Christianity*, 92.

40. Ibid., 91–92.

41. Ibid., 92.

42. James H. Moorhead, "The Erosion of Postmillennialism in American Religious Thought, 1865–1925," *Church History* 53, no. 1 (1984): 77.

43. Christerson and Flory, *Rise of Network Christianity*, 138.

44. Number two in 2015, number one in 2017, number four in 2019, and number six in 2020.

45. Martin Saunders, "Has a Film-Maker Really Captured Footage of a Golden 'Glory Cloud' at Bethel Church?," *Christian Today*, 2018, accessed June 8, 2020, https://www.christiantoday.com/article/has-a-film-maker-really-captured-footage-of-a-golden-glory-cloud-at-bethel-church/124751.htm.

46. Darren Wilson, "WP TV Exclusive—the Bethel Glory Cloud," 2018, accessed June 8, 2020, https://youtu.be/VcOPXLKAqL0.

47. Wilson, "Glory Cloud."

48. Bethel TV, "Glory Cloud at Bethel," 2011, accessed June 8, 2020, https://www.youtube.com/watch?v=lvJMPccZR2Y.

49. Bethel TV, "Glory Cloud."

50. Warren, "Spiritual and Ethical Values."

51. Donald P. Hustad, *Jubilate II: Church Music in Worship and Renewal* (Carol Stream, IL: Hope Publishing Company, 1993), 448.

52. Monique Ingalls, *Singing the Congregation: How Contemporary Worship Music Forms Evangelical Community* (Oxford: Oxford University Press, 2018).

53. See Mike Jacobs and Cindy Jacobs, "The Seven Mountains of Societal Influence," 2020, accessed June 8, 2020, https://www.generals.org/the-seven-mountains; Bill Johnson, Lance Wallnau, Alan Vincent, C. Peter Wagner, Ché Ahn, and Patricia King, *Invading Babylon: The 7 Mountain Mandate* (Shippensburg, PA: Destiny Image Publishers, 2013).

54. Jesus Culture Music, accessed June 8, 2020, https://jesusculture.com/music/.

55. Leonardo Blair, "Hillsong Church Becomes Own Denomination, Splits from Australia's Largest Pentecostal Group," *The Christian Post*, 2018, accessed June 8, 2020, https://www.christianpost.com/news/hillsong-church-becomes-own-denomination-splits-from-australias-largest-pentecostal-group.html.

56. Martínez and Smith, "How the Faithful Voted."

57. For a brief overview of the "moral majority," see Patrick Allitt, *Religion in America Since 1945: A History* (New York: Columbia University Press, 2003), 152–53.

58. The Facebook post is quoted in Carey Lodge, "Bethel Church's Bill Johnson: Why I Voted for Trump," *Christian Today*, 2016, accessed June 8, 2020, https://www.christiantoday.com/article/bethel-churchs-bill-johnson-why-i-voted-for-trump/100306.htm.

59. Ibid.

60. Whitehead and Perry, *Taking America Back for God*, 10.

61. Warren, "Spiritual and Ethical Values."

62. Frederick Douglass, *Narrative of the Life of Frederick Douglass, an American Slave* (Boston: Anti-Slavery Office, 1849), 118.

63. Jeff R. Warren, *Music and Ethical Responsibility* (Cambridge: Cambridge University Press, 2014).

64. See Warren, "That Worship Sound," for a more detailed discussion of Levinas, CWM, and Christian ethics.

65. Emmanuel Levinas, *Otherwise Than Being* (Pittsburgh: Duquesne University Press, 1981), 150.

66. Emmanuel Levinas, *Totality and Infinity* (Pittsburgh: Duquesne University Press, 1969), 21, and Emmanuel Levinas, *Entre Nous: Thinking-of-the-other* (London: Continuum, 1998), 104.

67. Emmanuel Levinas and Philippe Nemo, *Ethics and Infinity* (Pittsburgh: Duquesne University Press, 1985), 90.

68. See Jeff R. Warren, "Music Ethics Politics," *New Sound* 50 (2018): 30–31.

69. Gerardo Martí, "Foreword," in *The Hillsong Movement Examined: You Call Me Out Upon the Waters*, ed. Tanya and Tom Wagner Riches (London: Palgrave MacMillan, 2017), ix.

70. Ingalls, *Singing the Congregation*, 13.

71. Whitehead and Perry, *Taking America Back for God*, x.

72. Ibid., 20.

73. Ibid., 14.

74. Ibid., 21.

75. Dougglass, *Narrative*, 118.

76. Songselect by CCLI, "Themes," accessed June 28, 2020, https://songselect.ccli.com/search/themes.

77. Martin Luther King Jr., "The Negro Is Your Brother," *The Atlantic Monthly* 212, no. 2 (August 1963): 78–88.

FURTHER READING

Ingalls, Monique. *Singing the Congregation: How Contemporary Worship Music Forms Evangelical Community*. Oxford: Oxford University Press, 2018.

Myrick, Nathan, and Mark Porter, eds. *Ethics and Christian Musicking*. Abingdon: Routledge, 2021.

Routledge's "Congregational Music Studies" Book Series. https://www.routledge.com/Congregational-Music-Studies-Series/book-series/ACONGMUS.

Wagner, Tom, *Music, Branding and Consumer Culture in Church: Hillsong in Focus*. Abingdon: Routledge, 2019.

*IV*

PARALITURGICAL MUSIC

Chapter Eight

"Resignation" and Virgil Thomson's *Hymns from the Old South*

Zen Kuriyama

Virgil Thomson's *Hymns from the Old South* is a collection of four Southern hymn tune arrangements published as separate octavos in 1949.[1] While well known today (somewhat infamously) for his scathing music criticism, Thomson was also a prolific composer. Integral to understanding Thomson's idiosyncratic musical language and his contribution to American classical music is the influence of shape-note hymnody, which reached full maturity in the composition of *Hymns from the Old South* (also known as *Four Southern Folk Hymns*). This shape-note seed planting began in 1937 when the composer was commissioned to write music for *The River*, a documentary film on the Mississippi River and its environmental threats. In *The River*, listeners hear a tune several times that becomes eerily familiar and haunting. Thomson came across this tune, titled "Resignation," in an 1854 edition of William Walker's *Southern Harmony*, which served as the inspiration for his *Hymns from the Old South* over a decade later.

My analysis of Thomson's anthem "My Shepherd Will Supply My Need" (set to the "Resignation" tune) will be in two parts: inspiration and synthesis. Thomson was not alone in drawing inspiration from shape-note hymnody: American composers Aaron Copland and Randall Thompson likewise integrated the singable and spirit-filled melodies of shape-note hymns into their compositions. In my analysis, however, I will argue that Thomson's synthesis of the "Resignation" tune is distinct, most notably in his particular use of harmony, contrapuntal texture, affect, and declamation. An excursus on reception/performance notes for concert or liturgical service follows, reframing the analytical mode of this study into one concerning issues of functional programming, performance practice, and significance to the sacred music canon. A brief overview of the critical reception of *Hymns from the Old South* is also provided, underscored by additional comments on its place within Christian worship by prominent American church musicians, thereby situating this work within the aesthetic tastes of twentieth-century American sacred music.

INSPIRATION

Thomson's treatment of shape-note hymnody can be contextualized within the inherited musical traditions present in twentieth-century American culture. Kip Lornell's exhaustively thorough 2012 book on musicking in America lists the many and varied influences on musical culture in the United States, of which shape-note hymnody is but one.[2] Within the panoply of players, we can distill two primary branches of "authentic" sacred music in America, provided that one acknowledges that Native American peoples engaged in music making but did not influence mainstream concert music composition in major ways during the first half of the twentieth century.[3] Anglo-American and African American musical traditions are generally seen as the defining progenitors of what eventually evolved into a distinctive brand of American sacred music; in this "brand," shape-note hymnody played a critical role as its inception and integration were equal parts pedagogical and spiritual. The tradition had its beginnings in the gallery music of English parish churches and was first established on the East Coast of the United States in the late eighteenth century.[4] Protestant ministers saw it as an alternative to the "old way" of psalm singing that had come to dominate in eighteenth-century Protestant traditions of worship.[5] As the tradition evolved, various shapes of the note heads represented specific pitches within a musical scale, and a theoretical pedagogy supported the teaching of the musical system. The most common system employed four-shape "fa sol la" notation, and this became widely known in the South of the United States as Sacred Harp singing due to the popular shape-note hymn book *The Sacred Harp*, first published in Georgia in 1844.[6] As with any device used for music literacy, in the beginning, Sacred Harp singing used the shapes for practical purposes (that is, to alleviate the tedious teaching by rote of tunes by those who "were not conversant with standard Western notation").[7] The use of shapes was a rather ingenious invention: a form of elementary-style musical education that could eventually be removed or done without.

Calling any musical tradition "unique" is dangerous and often inaccurate, yet several scholars, including Buell Cobb, have suggested this label for shape-note hymnody. The practice played a significant role in community development, in addition to liturgical worship.[8] In fact, traditional Sacred Harp practices included a "regular sing," where groups got together at specific times to sing shape-note hymnody as a community, separate from any type of church-designated worship.[9] There was an additional entrepreneurial aspect with the establishment of singing schools and the employment of Sacred Harp tunesmiths, whose anthem contributions greatly expanded the repertory.[10] There is also a colloquially accepted view of the actual sound associated with Sacred Harp singing, which is generally thought to be primal, raw, and rather unfinessed. This style of singing in Sacred Harp is unlike any European hymn singing tradition, perhaps only rivaled by the West Gallery music tradition in England.[11] Modern studies in affect and ethnomusicology have extensively studied the phenomenological emotional impact that the primal cries of Indigenous singing create.[12] The appeal of singing traditions like Sacred Harp is that they descend from a type of musicking that united disparate communities into a singular congregational and worshipping body.[13] Theologically, of course, hymnody and the community within the context of liturgy stretches back as far as the monasteries of the Middle Ages, and indeed the chorale singing tradition of the Lutheran church has cemented the uniting and binding power of hymns in Christian fellowship.

Thomson's exposure to shape-note hymns took place at an early age. Although he lived and worked in New York City for most of his life, Thomson was raised in Missouri and had strong Baptist ties since childhood. It has been observed in recent scholarship that the infusion of Southern hymnody into his compositional style was more than simply satisfying an aesthetic taste. Musicologist Joanna Smolko has made a case for nostalgia in Thomson's affinity for these tuneful melodies, noting that its influence on the composer was not elective but rather ingrained since childhood where he participated in these hymns: "hymnody had left an indelible mark on his musical language, a mark that he did not attempt to erase or suppress."[14] Smolko's observation is important when discussing both music traditions in the Americas and more broadly American classical music in the early 1900s. The amalgamation and synthesis of various types of music traditions in the United States are as eclectic as they are distinct. Therefore tracing the motives behind the music composition in works like *The River*, *Hymns from the Old South*, or *Symphony on a Hymn Tune* allows us to advocate for the authenticity of any type of national or uniquely American school of music. Thomson said it best in a 1977 interview: "When you reach down into your subconscious, you get certain things. When Aaron [Copland] reaches down, he doesn't get cowboy tunes, he gets Jewish chants. When I reach down I get Southern hymns."[15] It is not surprising, then, that when asked to supply the music for a film about the Deep South, Thomson already knew where to begin.

Virgil Thomson's film score to *The River* has been labeled by David Bordwell and Kristin Thompson as "distinctly American" and is widely regarded as one of the finest examples of early film scoring.[16] Establishing national music and a distinctly American sound is problematic, yet Bordwell and Thompson's claim focuses on Thomson's source of inspiration for the score: Southern hymnody. Thomson took great interest in reaching back into America's musical heritage and was not alone in the first half of the twentieth century in looking to the past in order to fortify a new genre in the present. In an interview with Diana Trilling in 1980, Thomson said, "the courage to use your own grass roots is the big American acquisition, if you can make it."[17] This reclaiming of national heritage through music during the early 1900s was pronounced in many countries around the world, such as in England with the English Musical Renaissance (c. 1850–1950), in which composers sought to establish a distinctly English sound. This 1980 interview also exposes Thomson's anti-German sentiments, which was no doubt a response to the Germans' own contempt toward a rising French school of music in the early twentieth century.[18] During this long century of nationalism, musical styles thrived on drawing from characteristically regional traits of language and expression. While using nineteenth-century European musical nationalism is helpful in terms of understanding the efficacy of creating an idiomatic style of composition unique to a region, it is not to say that the reasons were the same for twentieth-century Americanism in music. Indeed, the motivations spurring nationalism in Europe in the mid- to late 1800s were a type of centuries-long catalytic thrust on a continent marred by monarchical claims to rule and the particular religious rites that sanctioned them to do so. Since its founding, America has in many ways served as the antithesis to the primary motivations of this type of nationalism. The mingling of diverse peoples in the United States with their varied musical and cultural traditions in fact preclude an American sound from ever possessing the same type of inward-centric nationalism present in Europe.

Thomson needed to provide music for a film that depicted the destruction of the beauty and natural resources of the Mississippi River and the government's solution to the problem. While Thomson had never before written a score for film, director Pare Lorentz was keen to enlist the composer's aid, noting "the combination of his clarity of style with his previous musical use of Midwestern songs and hymns."[19] A film about the desecration of a land region should contain music from that area, and Thomson found this in William Walker's *The Southern Harmony and Musical Companion* (1835) and E. J. King's *Sacred Harp* (1844). These hymns were an integral part of the Christian Deep South. The sacredness of these hymn tunes also juxtaposed the desecration of God's creation represented in the film's visual imagery, a sentiment that would have been widely shared throughout the region, especially by residents. *The River* was a form of propaganda, designed to support the government's agenda on the conservation of natural resources. In this sense, the hymn tunes also played a persuasive role, appealing to the pathos of the white Protestants that made up most of the region, influencing their views on the government by targeting their ingrained spirituality. While the film score was purely instrumental, listeners may have found themselves singing the words to the familiar tunes, subconsciously guiding their opinion on the issue.

Several shape-note hymns are used in the film, such as "Foundation" (which opens and closes the film) and "Mount Vernon." The "Resignation" tune ("My Shepherd Will Supply My Need") is prominently featured and, according to film theorist Claudia Widgery, "is used at two pivotal points as well as in various permutations."[20] While incorporating the hymn tunes of the Mississippi region was important to Thomson and to Lorentz (one of the tune names is actually "Mississippi"), Thomson was more concerned with the affective power of the sonic aesthetic than with any symbolic nature of tune names correlating with the plot.[21] To help depict the altering of the natural landscape, Thomson occasionally alters these hymn tunes, using techniques such as chromaticizing the melody, which he does in the third verse of "My Shepherd Will Supply My Need." The use of this tune functions throughout the film like a quasi-Leitmotif; the harmony and orchestration changes at each occurrence, sonically telling the story in tandem with the visual imagery on screen. Notably, Thomson incorporates elements of the African American musical tradition in some of the tune's harmonic alterations, such as incorporating ragtime-like syncopations and a call-and-response texture (also found in shape-note "fuging tunes") among different sets of instruments. This is a crafty and powerful synthesis in itself, weaving together into a single vocabulary these hymns with black spirituals, which were also products of the Deep South. Such a commingling is potentially problematic, given that black spirituals carry with them the stories of slavery and oppression that these hymns do not. With the prominent history of slavery in the South still tinging the air in the 1930s, Thomson's musical reconciliation of these two separate, indeed segregated, genres is curious indeed. Thomson was a product of his time and place of birth; both the film and the musical score were fashioned during a time of intense discrimination toward the African American community.

SYNTHESIS

Thomson was among the first American classical music composers to synthesize shape-note hymnody into modern choral music and whose works in this genre have become staples in sacred music repertoire.[22] Thomson wrote his arrangement of "My Shepherd Will Supply My Need" for four-part a cappella chorus the same year *The River* premiered, indicating that his devoted study to these hymn tunes made its way into his creative psyche. Conductor David Guthrie correctly notes that "over the next several years this single choral work was to become Thomson's most popular and commercially successful composition."[23] Twelve years later, in 1949, the composer set three more shape-note hymns for a cappella chorus, creating a collection he called *Hymns from the Old South*.

While all four Southern hymn tune arrangements are noteworthy examples of Thomson's shape-note choral synthesis, "My Shepherd Will Supply My Need" (No. 1) is particularly rich for analysis because of its comparative success over the other arrangements in the set. The other three pieces in *Hymns from the Old South* ("The Morning Star" [No. 2], "Green Fields" [No. 3], and "Death, 'tis a Melancholy Day" [No. 4]) are all suitable candidates for both compositional appreciation and musical analysis. In particular, the harnessing of minor key–area affect in "Death, 'tis a Melancholy Day" resembles the same type of homophonic and contrapuntal ethereality of oscillating minor chords that is heard in other well-known twentieth-century works. Thomson wrote a great deal about music, but it must not be forgotten that he was a protégé of Nadia Boulanger and therefore had superb compositional training. Nevertheless, for the scope of this study, the "My Shepherd" octavo presents fertile ground for the type of synthesis I wish to explore.

Thomson's setting (with text by Isaac Watts based on Psalm 23) offers a fresh presentation of the lyrical and curving melody of "Resignation," in addition to providing shades of contrast through a wider harmonic vocabulary than the original setting. Composer and theorist John Cage notes that the harmonization of "My Shepherd Will Supply My Need" in Walker's *Southern Harmony* is based solely on the pentatonic scale, but Thomson's arrangement uses the full breadth of the diatonic harmonic arsenal.[24] This diatonicism is executed through prominent use of the fourth- and seventh-scale degrees, and what results is a study in four-voice polyphonic counterpoint that is also simultaneously largely homorhythmic. As Guthrie observed, another interesting feature of Thomson's setting is his extension of each phrase ending by a measure.[25]

Thomson sets each verse in an AABA form, repeated strophically three times. While homophony appears, at times imitating Walker's setting quite closely, polyphony provides the textural timbre for the work, strengthening phrases at their entrances.[26] Thomson alters the mood and affect of the originally pentatonic composition by changing the harmony, both at phrasal midpoints and at cadences. Most significant are the iii and vi chords that Thomson lands on at the most important parts of the text, such as on "Je-HO-vah" and "name" in the first line (see figures 8.1 and 8.2). Important structural downbeats occur on these minor mode tonalities, emphasizing a solemn tone that permeates the entire composition.

Table 8.1. "My Shepherd Will Supply My Need," text by Isaac Watts, 1719

1. My Shepherd Will Supply My Need, Jehovah is His name; In pastures fresh He makes me feed Beside the living stream. He brings my wand'ring spirit back When I forsake His ways; He leads me for His mercy's sake, In paths of truth and grace. 2. When I walk through the shades of death, Thy presence is my stay; One word of Thy supporting breath Drives all my fears away.	Thy hand in sight of all my foes, Doth still my table spread; My cup with blessings overflows; Thine oil anoints my head. 3. The sure provisions of my God Attend me all my days. O may Thy house be my abode, And all my work be praise! There would I find a settled rest, While others go and come. No more a stranger or a guest But like a child at home.

Figure 8.1. Opening of Thomson's "My Shepherd Will Supply My Need"; observe the iii chord. (Roman numeral analysis added by the author.)

In *The River*, this tune is associated with the full and flowing "living stream" of the Mississippi. Understanding this connection immediately reframes the spiritual narrative of the motet: the forsakenness of precious earth and the sadness when parted from the Shepherd are washed away by the Lord's mercy.

The B section of each verse begins and ends on a vi chord, with the only other primary function chord being a dominant V. The B section is also where Thomson uses a bell-like "chanting" motif, in which a vocal part sings several words of the text on the same pitch. The bell-like reference is meant

Figure 8.2. End of second A section, beginning of B section; observe the vi chords. (Roman numeral analysis added by the author.)

to emphasize the lingering and ringing sonority that the repeated notes create within the vocal texture. The bass voice begins this every time, followed by the alto and tenor simultaneously (see figures 8.3 and 8.4).

At one point toward the end of the B section, all three lower voices have this bell-like chanting motif, creating a quasi-drone-like homophonic texture under the soprano's concluding B-section melody.

The result is a four-voiced texture of great forward momentum until the caesura before the return of the A-section material (see figure 8.4). The caesuras play a pivotal role in the dramatic nature of the piece, taking on a different affective quality in the drastically different B sections of the three verses.

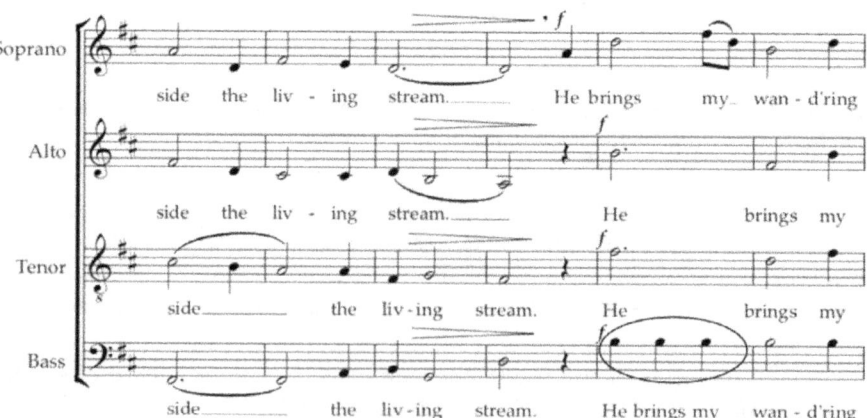

Figure 8.3. Beginning of verse 1 B section; notice motif in the bass part. (Circle added by the author.)

"Resignation" and Virgil Thomson's Hymns from the Old South 185

Figure 8.4. End of B section of verse 1. (Circles added by the author.)

What is perhaps most compelling about Thomson's synthesis of this shape-note hymn into a modern compositional language is his taste for declamation. Visually and sonically, the octavo is finely crafted, using controlled counterpoint to decorate and subsequently heighten the moments where homophony dominates the texture. Thomson also capitalizes on using a wide vocal range and tessitura in nearly all of the voices. For instance, if one considers the final low D at the end of the piece, the bass part spans an astounding two octaves (D2–D4). The choral texture this creates is one of vastness and expanse. Another timbral device Thomson uses to great effect is that of a five-beat-long F#2 drone in the bass part, creating a two-and-a-half-octave homophonic sonority with the soprano. Ever so subtly, Thomson incorporates syncopation by accenting beat 2 at nearly all the phrase endings, creating feigned suspensions before assuming root position at the downbeat of the following measure.

Traditionally, shape-note singing entailed "singing the notes" first on their solfège names, loudly and enthusiastically, and then adding in the words, making sure to not lose any verve in order to match the declamation of the text.[27] Likely aware that merely "singing the notes" would not be as efficacious as the plentiful nuance of text painting, Thomson created a dramatic and sensitive arc through his tempo and dynamic markings in correlation to the text, which come to a climax in the third verse. The pianissimo at the beginning of the second verse helps convey the initial trepidation of walking by faith, only to have those fears driven away by the Lord's "supporting breath." The B section of verse 2 is maintained in a piano dynamic, reverting back to pianissimo at the admission of the now-colloquial "cup runneth over" phrase (see figure 8.5).

Figure 8.5. End of B section and return of A section of verse 2; observe the pp after the caesura.

Given the rather fast moving tempo ("allegro ma sostenuto," with quarter note equal to 120) established in verse 1, Thomson's complete change of mood in the second verse reaches an almost unexpected peak at measure 60, where the half note on "OVER-flows" feels like it lasts for much longer.[28] This is real mastery in text painting, when a composer is able to convey affect through an almost phenomenological stretching of time rooted in the meaning of the word ("overflows"). One could argue that this highly finessed dynamic shaping of shape-note is not very authentic to the original Sacred Harp practice as it takes away the primal scream of heart-rendering praise. Nonetheless, it is safe to say that Thomson's goal was synthesis instead of recreation.

Thomson writes "Maestoso" ("majestically") at the beginning of verse 3, with a significant reduction in tempo (quarter note equal to 96). Up until this point, nearly every phrase ending was indicated with a decrescendo, but here Thomson writes "*non dim.*" throughout, signifying that this majestically slower tempo should not lose steam at any point. This is heightened tenfold at the B section, with the indications of *fortissimo, molto marcato* above the bass' bell/chant motif, and one final *non diminuendo* at the measure preceding the caesura, instructing the singers to all but wail in utter abandonment into a long, pregnant pause before the piano *dolce* that concludes the piece. In this sense, the previous caesuras only really make sense at the end, where the emotionally charged line is so intense as to warrant the enjoyment of silence. Given the extreme singing asked for during the B section of this verse, one cannot help but wonder if this was Thomson's homage to the "peel the paint off the wall" style of singing in Sacred Harp. The high tessitura of all the parts results in a wall of sound similar to what halls would have been accustomed to during a regular sing.

The final line of the text is indeed a moving paraphrase of the entire psalm: "no more a stranger or a guest, but like a child at home." This sense of coming home may have also had personal significance to Thomson, rooting itself in his Baptist Christian heritage and background. Compositionally, the four-part writing here is brilliance at its best (see figure 8.6): the slow-moving quarter note contrapuntal gesture in the tenor line in measure 94, the bass drone on a low F# for five beats under the tenors' lyrical stepwise descent to the dominant and the upper voices moving in thirds, culminating in the final cadence point, in a polyphonic subtlety with the sopranos/altos and tenors/basses ending in duets with one another.

Figure 8.6. The final line of Thomson's "My Shepherd Will Supply My Need."

In a sensitive and intuitive way, Thomson captures the aesthetic for which Sacred Harp singing has become known: melodic and homophonic crafting and declamation par excellence. Due credit must also be given to how the original Southern Harmony tune effectively complements Watts's text: the symbolism of the 3-2-1 mediant to tonic descent at "child at home" cannot be missed. Call it a Schenkerian-obsessed observation, but this final stepwise descent back to the tonic on these words is implicit text painting fused with the innate, affective pull of tonality.

EXCURSUS: RECEPTION/PERFORMANCE NOTES FOR CONCERT PERFORMANCE OR LITURGICAL SERVICE

In order to reliably depict the impact and lasting contribution of Thomson's shape-note choral synthesis, I have reached out to several prominent American church musicians to obtain their thoughts on the anthem.[29] The academic scholarship on *Hymns from the Old South* is sparse; no doubt Thomson's legacy as a music critic has overshadowed the scholarly attention on his compositional output. Given both the film inspiration and the artistic climate that the hymn tune arrangements were composed in, it is unlikely that Thomson intended these octavos to be performed exclusively within a liturgical or worship context. Even so, twentieth-century American sacred music is best analyzed within the setting that it thrives most in: the churches. Therefore analysis of the "My Shepherd" anthem by practicing church musicians who have established international reputations for excellence in the field are greatly beneficial to any academic analysis. To supplement these findings, recent critical reception will be offered by some of the work's recorded history, namely the select times *Hymns from the Old South* has been recorded for CD.

The Psalm 23 paraphrase by Watts is poetic in its interpretation of this most commonly known and oft memorized psalm and stirring in its affectual character. As David Eicher, editor of the *Glory to God* Presbyterian hymnal, notes, "The dynamics Thomson writes make the text come alive and take on additional power and emotion. That power and emotion is already there [in the original shape-note hymn], but Thomson uses dynamics to amplify the expression of those emotions."[30] Indeed, Thomson's setting captures this vividly; Gene Hinson writes, "The key to Virgil's treatment of the text is the observance of the specific and thorough expression markings (including a grand pause in m. 24). Each stanza begins with instructions which help to magnify its text."[31] The markings faithfully capture the affect of the text: *Allegro ma sostenuto* (quarter note = 120 at a mf dynamic) at "My shepherd will supply my need," *meno mosso* (quarter = 108, now pp) at "When I walk through the shades of death," and finally a grand, declamatory *Maestoso* (yet even slower, quarter = 96, but marked f) at "The sure provisions of my God." The third and final verse is perhaps the most striking, and Thomson, aware of performance tendencies in strophic works, aptly writes *non diminuendo* at three sections where the choir had previously tapered away. The most significant is the final *non dim.* before the caesura in the *fortissimo* B section of the third verse on "while others go and come." When this is closely observed (which goes against intuitive phrasing), the result is a deafening wail from the previously mentioned "wand'ring spirit," who once again finds his/her compass in the "sure provisions" of the Lord. This is then a contrast to the subito *piano dolce* on the final phrase, "no more a stranger or a guest but like a child at home," which must certainly rank as one of the most soul-stirring lines in the repertoire.

Hank Dahlman, in a March 2000 review of Thomson's recorded choral works, praised *Hymns from the Old South*, observing that it "reflects the composer at his best," singling out the choir's performance of "My Shepherd Will Supply My Need."[32] It would be wrong, however, to create the narrative that the other hymn arrangements in the set were unimpressive and completely glossed over; quite to the contrary. Another reviewer, Edward Greenfield, ends his assessment of *Hymns from the Old South* by stating, "'Green Fields' may be the loveliest hymn I've ever heard."[33] Another review from a CD featuring both Copland and Thomson's choral works speaks to the poignancy of Thomson's settings of Southern hymnody: "Virgil Thomson's vocal music remains largely underperformed and underappreciated, and the pieces on this disc are most welcome. The range of Thomson's choral writing is nicely demonstrated by the contrast of the direct, unmistakably American sound of the Hymns from the Old South."[34] After comparing the works of Copland and Thomson on the disc, Richard Burke concludes, "still, it is the Thomson pieces that stand out here, and one would hope that Patterson and her talented singers might give us more."[35] Traditionally, in the province of American classical music, supplanting Copland with Thomson is not often done, let alone ostensibly admitting that Thomson's choral writing is more interesting.

Both the accessibility and reverent tone of this piece make it an appropriate motet for any Christian liturgical service and for a variety of choir levels. Not a single accidental or modulatory sequence is present, making it a feasible a cappella option for even a small, amateur church choir. Both the homophonic and homorhythmic gestures complement the uncomplicated tonality, as does the clear-cut and finely crafted counterpoint. Much like the Lord's Prayer, Psalm 23 (or any paraphrase thereof) has become the great ecumenical bridge between different denominations, and Thomson's aesthetically beautiful and textually sensitive setting of the text has found its way into various Christian churches. It is an obvious choice for Good Shepherd Sunday (the Fourth Sunday after Easter in many calendars) but can appropriately be used for myriad other occasions, such as ordinations and any of the sacraments of initiation.[36] As Eicher further notes, "the piece is certainly one of the standards of American church choir libraries, and is also a favorite at choir festivals."[37] The devotional nature of this work can be used by nonliturgical traditions as well, and its brevity (four minutes) provides it with versatility and efficiency in any setting.

Kent Tritle and Jennifer Pascual provide valuable insights on the anthem.[38] Tritle writes:

> I have been so very, very grateful for Virgil Thomson's setting of "My Shepherd Will Supply My Need." In all my years as music director at St. Ignatius Loyola [NYC], it was the exquisite answer to a need for Psalm 23 at funerals. It embodied at once the simplicity of Americana, and the communication of a deep piece of classical music. As a work, it transcended any boundary, and was never refused by my clientele because of this.
>
> Additionally, I have been rewarded by experiencing this first through laborious teaching [of the anthem] to an amateur choir, and then having had the privilege of conducting it with a professional ensemble. With either, it bears the full weight of expectancy and musicality. While Virgil's tempi and dynamics are rather subtle, in the end they are incredibly powerful. I fear too many conductors nowadays do not attend to his tempo indications. They are incredibly important, and lend to the gravitas of salvation at the end of the work.[39]

In addition to his post at the Cathedral of St. John the Divine, Tritle is music director of both Musica Sacra and the Oratorio Society of New York, director of choral activities at the Manhattan School of Music, on the graduate faculty at the Juilliard School, and principal organist for the New York Philharmonic. His praise, then, of Thomson's anthem is noteworthy indeed. Pascual at St. Patrick's Cathedral in New York City complements Tritle's remarks, noting:

> Even though we are a Roman church, it is important as a model cathedral to try to incorporate an eclectic mix of choral music, and since we are supposedly "America's Parish Church," that should certainly include some Americana, in addition to the traditional Latin choral treasures and music from other time periods.
>
> And even though we are a semi-professional choir, I've used this piece with amateur choirs, as it is very accessible. Its melodic and harmonic simplicity also lends to ease of listening to the assembly, who are ultimately the people we aim to help pray through our music. Sometimes when choral music is too complex, overly academic or over accompanied, it can distract and turn into a form of sacred entertainment. The Thomson piece would never distract.
>
> There is also a sense of tranquility with this piece. There are some settings of Psalm 23 that can really put one in a sad mood and emphasize "the shadow of death," but this comforting setting enhances that indeed "My Shepherd will supply my need."[40]

Pascual's observation that Thomson's anthem "would never distract" is essential when discussing the function of sacred music today. Indeed, the ability and purpose of sacred music to complement liturgy and to unite and lift up souls needs to be emphasized and is rooted in teachings and documents on sacred music.

In the 1960s, the Roman Catholic Church produced a document sanctioning both the accessibility and use of polyphony in an anthem like Thomson's, allowing it to then enter seamlessly into many liturgically based denominations. *Sacrosanctum Concilium*, promulgated by the Second Vatican Council in 1963, is one of the defining documents on liturgical music in the twentieth century and has been used to advocate for the importance of sacred music across denominations.[41] The penultimate paragraph of Chapter VI, "Sacred Music," reads as follows: "Let them produce compositions which have the qualities proper to genuine sacred music, not confining themselves to works which can be sung only by large choirs, but providing also for the needs of small choirs and for the active participation of the entire assembly of the faithful."[42] These words laid down by Roman bishops in the 1960s are strikingly familiar to the needs and desires of eighteenth-century New England Protestants, the religious forefathers of shape-note hymnody. Not only does Thomson's anthem contain the requisite qualities of proper sacred music, it also harkens back to a congregational singing tradition in which all the faithful were encouraged to sing with full hearts and full voices. Shape-note hymnody was born from the Congregational hymn singing tradition, and New England Protestants would have sung this hymn and many others in four-part harmony. Modern-day Christianity has made ecumenism a great love feast, entreating and encouraging interdenominational dialogue at every turn. Music plays a critical role in these ecumenical relations. The versatility and innate diversity of Thomson's anthem continues to unite various Christians into one, great, regular sing.

While Thomson's background and influence from the shape-note tradition bore fruit in several compositions, a detailed study on Thomson's famous religious anthem would be incomplete without acknowledging that Thomson was not a Christian and did not hold Christianity in any high esteem:

> I never at any time took to religion. In the Baptist view I am not even a Christian, having never experienced conversion or undergone baptism. I have never felt inferior to believers, or superior; I simply am not one. Churches are not my home. In the choir room or in the organ loft I earn my fee. But I cannot be a customer; this was always so, is still so.[43]

Thomson's self-professed aversion to faith is clear. While this essay does make the claim that Thomson used shape-note hymnody as a form of American musical nationalism, I have been careful to not assert that it was Thomson's goal to create uniquely American *sacred music*. While the eventual fate of an anthem like "My Shepherd Will Supply My Need" inevitably found itself in the houses of the Lord, insight into Thomson's lack of religious conviction allows for a balanced and even impartial assessment of this piece.

Within recent decades, there has been renewed vigor in the Sacred Harp singing revival, with amateur groups meeting weekly, monthly, and annually around the world (the convention in Cork, Ireland, has been notably popular). Professional ensembles such as the former Chicago-based His Majestie's Clerkes, conducted by Paul Hillier, have recorded CDs of Sacred Harp hymns, and singing "from the shapes" has become a popular unit in courses on sacred music in the United States. Thomson integrated the "Resignation" tune in the *The River* such that the listener would not only hearken to its familiarity but would be propelled to action by the affective power that music has on the individual. Furthermore, sacred music contains the history and traditions and sometimes even the values of the faith system that brought it into existence. Like any composer constructing a sound world drawn from a nationalistic idiom, Thomson achieved more than mere aesthetic value in his choral arrangement of "Resignation." The language is nostalgia and comfort; indeed, just as the shepherd protects his flock, Thomson and others effectively preserved a tradition of American sacred music that is significant to the canon.

NOTES

1. The author wishes to express deep gratitude to Joanna Smolko, Tim Smolko, Susan Youens, Margot Fassler, Paula Musegades, Joseph Smith, Ryan Peteraf, and Andrew Shenton for their extremely helpful and exacting guidance in producing the final version of this essay. Special thanks to the Jubilate Music Group, LCC, for the permission to use the musical examples from Thomson's anthem.

2. Kip Lornell, *Exploring American Folk Music: Ethnic, Grassroots, and Regional Traditions in the United States* (Jackson: University Press of Mississippi, 2012); "musicking" is a now-popular term coined by Christopher Small that is heavily used in ethnomusicological scholarship and discussions on music and culture.

3. Still, several composers were deeply influenced by their understanding of Indigenous music; publications by Wa-Wan Press (existing from 1901 until 1912, when it was acquired by Schirmer) are good examples of this so-called Indianist movement in classical music. See also Edward S. Curtis and Mick Gidley, *The Vanishing Race: Selections from Edward S. Curtis' The North American Indian* (New York: Taplinger Publishing, 1977).

4. Nicholas Temperley, *The Music of the English Parish Church*, Cambridge Studies in Music (Cambridge: Cambridge University Press, 1979), 151.

5. Nicholas Temperley, "The Old Way of Singing: Its Origins and Development," *Journal of the American Musicological Society* 34, no. 3 (1981): 511.

6. Harry Eskew, "Sacred Harp," in *The New Encyclopedia of Southern Culture, Volume 12, Music*, ed. Bill C. Malone and Charles Reagon Wilson (Chapel Hill:

University of North Carolina Press, 2008), 128. While first published in Georgia, it was printed in Philadelphia.

7. Lornell, *Exploring American Folk Music*, 119.

8. See Buell E. Cobb, *The Sacred Harp: A Tradition and Its Music* (Athens: University of Georgia Press, 1989).

9. These "regular sings" still exist; for example, the author belongs to "Boston Sacred Harp," which holds regular sings every Wednesday.

10. Wallace McKenzie, "Anthems of the Sacred Harp Tunesmiths," *American Music* 6, no. 3 (1988): 247.

11. See Andrew Gant, *O Sing Unto the Lord: A History of English Church Music* (Chicago: University of Chicago Press, 2017).

12. See, for example, Donovan Schaefer, *Religious Affects: Animality, Evolution, and Power* (Durham: Duke University Press, 2015).

13. Temperley, *The Music of the English Parish Church*, 158.

14. Joanna Smolko, "Reshaping American Music: The Quotation of Shape-Note Hymns by Twentieth-Century Composers" (PhD diss., University of Pittsburgh, 2009), 15.

15. John Rockwell, "A Conversation with Virgil Thomson," *Parnassus: Poetry in Review* 5, no. 2 (Spring–Summer 1977): 423. Cited in Smolko's "Reshaping American Music," 16.

16. David Bordwell and Kristin Thompson, *Film Art: An Introduction* (New York: McGraw Hill, Inc., 1993), 115.

17. Virgil Thomson, "An Interview with Virgil Thomson," in Diana Trilling, *Partisan Review* 47, no. 4 (1980): 550.

18. Thomson/Trilling, "An Interview with Virgil Thomson," 552.

19. Claudia Joan Widgery, "The Kinetic and Temporal Interaction of Music and Film: Three Documentaries of 1930's America" (PhD diss., University of Maryland, College Park, 1990), 198.

20. Widgery, "The Kinetic and Temporal Interaction of Music and Film," 201.

21. Ibid., 205.

22. Along with Randall Thompson, Aaron Copland, and others.

23. David Guthrie, "Shape-Note Hymnody as Source Material for Modern and Post-Modern Choral Art Music" (DMA thesis, University of South Carolina, 2014), 41.

24. John Cage, "His Music," in *Virgil Thomson: His Life and Music*, ed. Kathleen Hoover and John Cage (Freeport, NY: Books for Libraries Press, 1959), 181.

25. Guthrie, "Shape-Note Hymnody as Source Material for Modern and Post-Modern Choral Art Music," 43.

26. See William Walker, *The Southern Harmony and Musical Companion*, revised edition (Philadelphia: Miller and Burlock, 1854).

27. Kiri Miller, "'First Sing the Notes': Oral and Written Traditions in Sacred Harp Transmission," *American Music* 22, no. 4 (2004): 484.

28. Note: The musical content for this is the same as the first five bars in figure 8.6. Unfortunately, due to copyright issues, an excerpted musical example of this specific moment cannot be included.

29. The following views included were not deliberately chosen among a panoply of responses: out of the several prominent American church musicians contacted in nearly all mainstream Christian denominations, three responded: David Eicher (the Presbyterian Church of the United States), Kent Tritle (the Protestant Episcopal Church of the United States), and Jennifer Pascual (Roman Catholic Church). Their responses are all included.

30. David Eicher, personal email correspondence with the author, January 2020. Used by permission. *Glory to God* is currently the official hymnal of the Presbyterian Church of the United States.

31. Gene Hinson, "An Investigation of Common Stylistic Traits Found in Selected Sacred Choral Works of Randall Thompson and Virgil Thomson" (DMA thesis, New Orleans Baptist Theological Seminary, 1992), 55.

32. Hank J. Dahlman, "Compact Disc Reviews," *Choral Journal* 40, no. 8 (2000): 64.

33. Edward Greenfield, "Hymns from the Old South," *American Record Guide* 64, no. 2 (2001): 86.

34. Richard Burke, "Classical Recordings," *Fanfare Magazine* 3 (2001): 152.

35. Ibid.

36. For liturgical Christians, this would be Baptism, First Holy Communion, and Confirmation.

37. Eicher, email correspondence with author, January 2020. Used by permission.

38. Kent Tritle is director of cathedral music and organist at the Cathedral Church of Saint John the Divine in New York City, the mother church of the Episcopal Diocese of New York. Jennifer Pascual is director of music and organist at St. Patrick's Cathedral in New York City, the seat of the Roman Catholic cardinal archbishop of New York and a widely visible symbol of Catholicism in the United States.

39. Kent Tritle, personal email correspondence with the author, January 2020. Used by permission.

40. Jennifer Pascual, personal email correspondence with the author, January 2020. Used by permission.

41. As many American liturgical scholars have noted, the reforms of the liturgy in the Roman Catholic Church that resulted from Vatican II (1962–1965) influenced the sacred music of nearly all mainstream, liturgical Christian denominations. In the United States during the 1970s and 1980s, the music of the Catholic Church was *significantly* less traditional than other liturgical Christian denominations. By the 1990s, a widespread synthesis occurred in which some sacred music common in Catholic services (for example, the hymn "On Eagle's Wings") suddenly became canonic. With the issuing of the motu proprio *Summorum Pontificum* by Pope Benedict XVI in 2007, Gregorian chant and traditional polyphony has seen a resurgence, largely due to the removal of the *Ecclesia Dei* (1988) mandate that required presbyters to seek permission from the local ordinary in order to celebrate the so-called Tridentine Latin Mass.

42. *Sacrosanctum Concilium* 121, Second Vatican Council, 1963.

43. Virgil Thomson, *Virgil Thomson* (New York: Da Capo Press, 1966), 19–20.

FURTHER READING

Arnold, Jonathan. *Sacred Music in Secular Society*. Farnham: Taylor and Francis Group, 2016.

Garrett, Charles Hiroshi. *Struggling to Define a Nation*. Berkeley: University of California Press, 2008.

Marini, Stephen A. *Sacred Song in America: Religion, Music, and Public Culture*. Public Expressions of Religion in America. Urbana: University of Illinois Press, 2003.

Phillips, Christopher N. *The Hymnal: A Reading History*. Baltimore: Johns Hopkins University Press, 2018.

Steel, David Warren. "Secular Music in Shape Notes." In *Rethinking American Music*, 50. Urbana: University of Illinois Press, 2019.

Svec, Henry Adam. *American Folk Music as Tactical Media*. Amsterdam: Amsterdam University Press, 2017.

White, Harry, and Michael Murphy. *Musical Constructions of Nationalism: Essays on the History and Ideology of European Musical Culture, 1800–1945*. Cork, Ireland: Cork University Press, 2001.

Chapter Nine

Rock of Ages

Jesus in American Popular Songs, 1969–2019

Delvyn Case

> [Jesus], being in very nature God, did not consider equality with God something to be used to his own advantage; rather, he made himself nothing by taking the very nature of a servant, being made in human likeness.
>
> —Philippians 2: 5–11 (ESV)

This powerful Christological statement has its origins in a hymn of the early church.[1] Since then, Christians have continued to use sacred music as a terrain in which to explore the nature, identity, and meaning of Jesus.

Over the past fifty years, however, something has changed. Jesus no longer shows up just in songs used in church but also those heard in new and unexpected places: the disco, honky-tonk, blues bar, and even the strip club. These songs are secular, intended for anyone who listens to pop music. They are written by artists who may or may not be Christians and for reasons ranging from spiritual exploration to social commentary to self-aggrandizement.

Working outside of the church or the Christian music industry yet profoundly influenced by the ideas and conceptions about Jesus woven through American society, these artists have depicted him in ways that range from the orthodox to the profane. In order to understand him in ways that are relevant to their own lives, they've compared him to figures as diverse as a soldier, hippie, and presidential candidate. They've imagined him as gay, black, female, and Korean; as a friend, lover, and romantic rival; and even as the offspring of Mary and Hitler.[2]

Taken as a whole, these songs testify to the willingness of artists to explore the meaning and significance of Jesus in ways that are not necessarily restricted to the ideas inherited from the Christian tradition. Their work shows that, by at least the latter half of the twentieth century, Jesus had become a cultural figure as well as a religious one, available and recognizable to all yet having any number of possible meanings, "liberated," as religious historian Stephen Prothero writes, "from divinity, dogma, and even Christianity itself."[3]

But this does not mean that the Jesus of popular music is absolutely free of the influence of the Christian tradition. The truth is in fact the opposite. The Jesus of popular music remains a solidly traditional figure at his core. These songs reveal fundamental conceptions of Jesus that have been accepted by most Christians since the time of the early church.

This study identifies and describes major trends in the ways that popular music has understood Jesus over the past fifty years.[4] These trends emerged through a heuristic process of analysis of almost 450 songs in virtually all secular genres.[5] By exploring the tensions inherent in popular songs about Jesus, this study provides a glimpse into the uniquely secular nature of religion in contemporary America. In doing so, it provides a fascinating and surprising example of the paradox described in Philippians 2: that it is through Jesus's humanity that we glimpse his very deity.

INCARNATIONS

From Scott Stapp's "Jesus Was a Rock Star" to Bobby Bare's "Dropkick Me, Jesus, Through the Goalposts of Life," some of the most famous (and infamous) of these songs are those that compare Jesus to a character from contemporary society. In these songs, Jesus assumes the attributes of a particular stock figure or specific individual whose cultural meaning is generally shared and understood among members of their interpretive community. Examples of the former include the cowboy or the hippie; examples of the latter include Martin Luther King Jr. or Hank Williams Jr. Because this allows us to imagine Jesus "in human likeness," I am calling this songwriting technique *incarnation*.

This technique is quite popular among songwriters, appearing in 100 songs among the 435 studied for this essay. A small collection of "incarnations" makes up almost half of these songs: celebrity (16), musician (10), friend (12), and lover (9). If we also consider the handful of songs that compare Jesus to alcohol or a drug, we see what links them to each other: they all belong to the mythical world of the popular musician. As such, they provide a contemporary example of what theologian Albert Schweitzer said about those who had undertaken to write a "Life of Jesus": "it was not only each epoch that found its reflection in Jesus; each individual created Him in accordance with his own character."[6]

We see even better examples of artists recreating Jesus in their own image when we look at specific genres. For example, it is very common for rappers to liken themselves to (or even identify themselves as) Jesus; I will discuss this more extensively shortly. In country music, the most common incarnation is, of course, the country musician, usually someone from the pantheon of country stars. Examples include George Jones (Trace Adkins's "Jesus and Jones"), Hank Williams (Cadillac 3's "Hank and Jesus"), Hank Williams Jr. (Kid Rock's "Jesus and Bocephus"), and Elvis (Kenny Chesney's "Jesus and Elvis.")

These songs do more than just serve as oblique self-aggrandizement on the part of the artist. They also highlight the reflexive nature of the process of "incarnation" itself. These songs simultaneously describe Jesus in terms of the country musician and the country musician in terms of Jesus. They attribute traditional evangelical Protestant attributes of Jesus, such as his constant and palpable presence in one's life, to the country musician. At the same time they attribute certain values of Southern working-class culture, like the importance of "plain-talking" and a suspicion of institutions, to Jesus.[7]

Perhaps the best example of this reflexivity occurs in Eric Church's anthemic "Country Music Jesus," whose chorus ends with the line, "There'll be screamin' and there'll be shoutin' When my country music Jesus comes."[8] As the music builds to a rock-gospel-bluegrass breakdown, it becomes increasingly difficult to know exactly what is being described. Is it a church service, a concert, or both? Is this song about the need for a revival in country music, led by a singer whose salvific power is described in terms of Jesus, or about the need for revival in society, led by an apocalyptic Jesus whose salvific power can only be fully realized by channeling a country musician? Though Church indicates that his intention was the former, the song still depends on a process of reflexivity (or even fusion) for its poetic conceit and its musical success.[9]

The "incarnation" technique provides the songwriter with a particularly powerful way to argue for a specific interpretation of Jesus. It is a quick way for an artist to immediately place Jesus in a familiar category, which then grounds the song's poetic conceit and guides it as it unfolds. James Otto's "Soldiers and Jesus" is an example. But, of course, the process of comparison only works because it proceeds from a set of meanings for its signifier that are familiar and shared widely within the song's interpretive community. As Otto's song shows, in the world of country music both soldiers and Jesus are heroes who are willing to sacrifice their lives for freedom. But if this were a folk song with the same title, it would proceed from a very different shared understanding of the meaning of the soldier (and probably of Jesus as well).

Thus songs that use the "incarnation" strategy function to both reveal and reconfirm the values in a particular community. Because the meanings they share are often so deep-seated and seemingly unimpeachable (soldiers are heroes!), these songs carry significant rhetorical power. It is partly for this reason that we see it used by popular musicians pursuing a wide variety of agendas, from testifying about their faith (Lance Miller's "George Jones and Jesus"), to challenging believers to defend said faith (NOFX's "Pods and Gods"), to simply advocating for another claim or idea by using Jesus as a foil (Jeff Bates's "Momma Was a Lot Like Jesus").

In Matthew 16, Jesus's disciples report that the people of Judea had been doing the same thing: describing Jesus by comparing him to John the Baptist, or Elijah, and Jeremiah. Perhaps it is because Jesus recognized this potential means of understanding him that he ultimately rejected this strategy, turning instead to Simon Peter for a better answer. Or maybe it was because he knew that any contemporary incarnation would be too limiting, revealing more about the ideas of the first-century Judeans than anything else. For these reasons, finding a more satisfying answer to the question "Who is the Jesus of popular music?" requires us to look at a broader range of songs than just those that present Jesus "in human likeness." We need to look at all of the songs assembled for this study, regardless of the strategies they use, the opinions they express, or even the depth to which they focus on Jesus at all, and ask one simple question: How does the artist conceive of Jesus? Or, in other words, "What is the fundamental understanding of Jesus that the song reveals?" We will call these fundamental understandings or conception "images" because, like a great portrait, they reveal something profound about the character or essence of our subject.

IMAGES

The rest of this essay focuses on these various "images." It proceeds by presenting and then exploring a taxonomy of these images, derived heuristically, then uses case studies of certain songs to illuminate interesting trends and patterns among them.

The highest level of this taxonomy is made up of three "domains," defined by the general ways songwriters engage with the meaning of Jesus. A song falls in the Person domain when the artist considers Jesus *solely* as a human. It belongs in the Paragon domain when the songwriter invokes Jesus principally as symbol, not as a human or a theological figure. It appears in the Presence domain, which is by far the largest of the three, when the artist engages with Jesus in a way that is significant, complex, or compelling.

Person Domain (Twenty-One Songs)

Songs in the Person domain treat Jesus exclusively as a human figure, shorn of any theological characteristics.[10] Some depict him as a character in the narrative world of the song. In so doing they present compelling and sensitive explorations of the distinctly human side of Jesus's existence. A good example is Richard Shindell's "The Ballad of Mary Magdalene." This moving song allows us to consider Jesus from Mary's perspective, as a man whom she loves who has suddenly and inexplicably left her. The tantalizing idea of Jesus as a romantic figure is explored in two other songs about his relationship with Mary Magdalene: Chris DeBurgh's "Just Another Poor Boy" and the well-known "I Don't Know How to Love Him" from *Jesus Christ Superstar*.[11]

Another subset in the Person domain consists of those whose approaches to depicting him are decidedly less sensitive or nuanced. They can be comical (Screaming Blue Messiahs's "Jesus Chrysler Drives a Dodge"), simplistic (ZZ Top's "Jesus Just Left Chicago"), or intentionally provocative or offensive (Jello Biafra's "Are You Drinking With Me, Jesus?"). Most of these songs are generally positive or at least agnostic in their judgment of Jesus. Of course, this is not the case for those that are intended to offend. For example, Jello Biafra's song makes its point by emphasizing certain rarely imagined aspects of Jesus's physical existence, such as his ability to urinate.[12] The best example might be the song "Jesus Entering from the Rear" by the punk band Feederz, which depicts Jesus in perhaps the most "human" way possible: as a corpse.

Despite their silliness or offensiveness, these songs actually do highlight an orthodox Christian belief: that Jesus was fully human. Of course, imagining Jesus as *only* human is a way to deny the central claim of Christianity. But these songs still demonstrate the prominence of the idea that Jesus was in fact a human figure, not just a spirit, ghost, or idea. By emphasizing his corporeal existence, they function, unintentionally, as antidotes to the Docetism against which the Church has fought for two millennia. In fact, though I have found many songs that reject Jesus's claims by pointing to things like the hypocrisy of his followers or the unbelievability of his miracles, I have found none that do so by denying his actual corporeal existence. This is interesting, as it would seem to be a very simple and effective rhetorical strategy for those artists (like the punk band Bad Religion) who rail against Christianity consistently and vigorously throughout their careers.

Paragon Domain (Seventy-One Songs)

Categories:
  Power (46)
  Other (25)[13]

While songs in the Person domain consider Jesus principally as a human, songs in the Paragon domain do the opposite. They present him as a symbol, usually of an abstract idea or character trait. As the name of the category suggests, Jesus is usually invoked as the ultimate signifier of whatever is being signified. Though the variety of attributes is quite broad, it is the view of Jesus as the ultimate symbol of power that is most common.

Hip-hop songs dominate the Paragon domain as a whole (thirty-nine of the seventy-one songs) and within the *power* subcategory as well (thirty-five of the forty-six songs.) In hip-hop, power is usually manifested in a certain limited number of ways that represent the "gangsta" image, discussed shortly. For example, in "Black Jesus," The Game raps:

> Black presidential Rolls [Rolls Royce], black pieces [guns]
> You know why, cause I'm the young black Jesus.[14]

This song is representative of the dozens of "boasting" songs in which rappers compare themselves to Jesus.[15] It demonstrates two attributes common to most of these songs. First: Jesus appears only briefly. Unlike the many powerful hip-hop songs that appear in the Presence domain, these songs rarely take Jesus as their subject or grapple with his meaning or identity in any significant way. For example, in this song The Game's use of the adjective "black" does not function to interrogate the issue of race, pointing us toward a deeper consideration of how Jesus's identity relates to it. Instead the adjective refers to himself, and he references Jesus in order to boast about his worldly success and power. Other songs that work the same way are Ghostface Killah's "Black Jesus," Kanye West's "I am a God," Nas's "The Cross," Everlast's "Black Jesus" (an interesting song from a white rapper), the female rapper Lil B's "Look Like Jesus," and "Korean Jesus" by the Korean hip-hop group Dumbfounded.

These songs also share a second attribute: they all invoke Jesus as an example of a specific, limited, and culturally determined set of attributes—physical strength, wealth, access (to drugs and weapons), artistic skill, and sexual prowess. These values emerged as particular symbols of power in hip-hop as a result of historic and persistent oppression of African Americans. As religion scholar Ebony Utley writes, they are those of the "gangsta," an "enduring identity that allows youth to imagine themselves as authoritative figures" and that "empower[s] rappers whose aggressive posturing earns not only money but also respect."[16] When faced with an extremely narrow and prescribed path toward respect, and therefore power, boasting plays a huge role in the self-mythologizing of the hip-hop artist. In Utley's words, "envisioning oneself as God is a very necessary fantasy for constitutors whose real world is often too bleak to promise personal advancement or empowerment."[17]

Of course, the Jesus of the gospels did not emphasize wealth, sexual prowess, or physical strength as avenues of respect. Nor did he embody those in his earthly ministry. But if we see these values as the ways a specific culture interprets and represents Jesus's power, we can indeed see how they point toward an understanding of Jesus that we can indeed recognize in the Bible: the Jesus of Revelation. That Jesus is the one who manifests a kind of power before which every knee shall bow, and who will return to exact judgment on behalf of the oppressed, serving up the kind of righteous vindication only possible in a "gangsta's" dreams. For rappers, the attraction to this conception of Jesus is understandable. As Utley writes, "Oppressed people who appropriate Jesus become invincible."[18]

Presence Domain (343 Songs)

Images:
  Heavenly Savior (53)
  Judge (22)
  Source of Truth (180)
  Worldly Savior (88)

The third domain, Presence, comprises over 80 percent of the songs on the list. This domain is composed of four images: Heavenly Savior, Judge, Source of Truth, and Worldly Savior. Each of these is further divided in into additional categories.

Heavenly Savior Image (53/435)

Categories:
  Source of forgiveness of sins (30)
  Source of eternal life (11)
  General source of salvation (12)

This image focuses on Jesus as a divine figure who forgives sins and/or offers eternal life. Fifty-three songs reveal this image, including famous and commercially successful songs in a variety of genres, such as Norman Greenbaum's "Spirit in the Sky," Pacific Gas and Electric's "Are You Ready," and Donna Summer's "I Believe in Jesus," all top singles.

There are three categories of this image. The most common is that of Jesus as a *source of forgiveness of sins*. Many of these songs present such an orthodox understanding of Jesus as savior that they could easily find their place in the devotional lives of Christians. Unsurprisingly, many are country songs, including Toby Keith's "If I Was Jesus," Tucker Beathard's "Momma and Jesus," and Lance Miller's "George Jones and Jesus Listen." Several songs from Bob Dylan's "gospel period" fall into this category as well, as do many songs written by secular artists who are Christians (U2, Mumford and Sons, Nick Cave, and Kanye West, among others). The most surprising song in this category is perhaps Black Sabbath's "After Forever," which, though somewhat idiosyncratic in its poetic style, is one of the most straightforward and even apologetic rock songs that I have ever encountered.

The second category of the Heavenly Savior image is composed of songs that view Jesus as the *source of eternal life in heaven*. Unsurprisingly, this includes songs written by a number of artists who are Christians, including Prince ("The Christ"), U2 ("Tomorrow"), and many country artists. Some of these songs are quite simple, such as Bobby Bare's "Dropkick Me, Jesus, Through the Goalposts of Life" and Donna Summer's "I Believe in Jesus," while some are quite profound, such as the female rapper Rapsody's "Jesus Coming."

The final category includes songs in which Jesus is presented as a *general source of salvation*, but in which it is unclear exactly what that means. Some of these are songs quite powerful, especially Chance the Rapper's "How Great," which combines a statement of faith in Jesus's salvation with trenchant political critique.

The Heavenly Savior image also includes several songs that, though viewing Jesus primarily as a source of salvation, ultimately question or even reject him. Some songs do so from a perspective of faith, including Concrete Blonde's "Jesus Forgive Me for the Things I'm About to Say" and "Jesus Couldn't Love Me" by Chloe Lilac. Another group of songs, however, rejects Jesus's offer of forgiveness outright. This includes four powerful alternative rock songs, Nirvana's "Jesus Doesn't Want Me for a Sunbeam" (a version of the punk band Vaseline's "Jesus Wants Me for a Sunbeam"), Cake's "Jesus Wrote a Blank Check," Smashing Pumpkins's "Jesus Is the Sun," and Brand New's "Jesus Christ." This last song ends in a way that echoes the moment in the liturgical reading of the Passion when the congregation says, "Crucify him!" together: "I know you think that I'm someone you can trust / But I'm scared I'll get scared, and I swear I'll try to nail you back up."[19] At the end, the narrator doubts that even Jesus will forgive or accept him for the hate that is in his heart and in that of society, repeating over and over the crushing line, "But we all got wood and nails."

The songs just mentioned are some of the most emotionally powerful among those in this study. Regardless of whether they ultimately accept or reject Jesus as a "savior" (whatever that may mean for their narrator), they describe in particularly raw terms a host of authentic responses to the claims of Jesus. Their power is perhaps because the subjectivism that is central to the popular music genre is in some ways specifically appropriate to the idea of "salvation." As theologian Maeve Louise Heaney writes,

In honest, felt, and expressed human experience something happens. Something is transmitted. And something implies an artist "behind" the song who is not afraid, not only to express love, laughter, deep happiness, pain, and suffering, but also to *feel* it. Contemporary sensibility describes the effect of this kind of honesty as somehow "salvific."[20]

These songs are epigrammatic yet highly personal explorations of the meaning of salvation and its relationship to Jesus. As such, they model the unique challenges facing those honestly considering the salvific power of Jesus in contemporary secular society.

Judge Image (22/435)

Categories:
Personal (10)
Apocalyptic (12)

Another image of Jesus that conceives him as essentially a heavenly figure is that of Judge. In some songs, Jesus appears as one who judges humans for their sins, that is, as a *personal judge*. This subset includes songs in which the artist recognizes their sins and expects some sort of judgment from Jesus, including Bob Dylan's "Gonna Change My Way of Thinking," Hobo Johnson's "Jesus Christ," and two particularly powerful songs by contemporary artists who are quite different: J. Cole's "Chaining Day" and The 1975's "Jesus Christ 2005 God Bless America."

In the second category, *apocalyptic judge*, Jesus appears as the Christ of the Second Coming. A dozen songs from various genres imagine Jesus returning to judge the world, either at the Apocalypse or some other point. Interestingly, this event appears in similar narrative detail in three different songs from three different genres: country artist Will Hoge's "Jesus Came to Tennessee," metal band Black Label Society's "Doomsday Jesus," and punk band NOFX's song "I'm Going to Hell for This One." In Will Hoge's song the narrator speaks from a position of faith, while those in the others do not. But the message is the same: Jesus is going to come back, and he won't be happy because of what he sees.

Source of Truth Image (180/435)

Categories:
Rejected (74)
    False/failure (22)
    Negative impact on the individual believer (19)
    Negative impact of Christians on the world (33)

Affirmed (106)
    Generally positive (75)
    Seeker (16)
    Prophetic (15)

The most common image of Jesus in popular music is that of Source of Truth, appearing in almost one-third of all the songs. Here Jesus is understood as a spiritual teacher or founder of a religious tradition. Of course, this image of Jesus does not in any way correlate to an artist's judgment of his message or the religion he inspired. In fact, half of the songs have negative views of Jesus's message: that is, while they conceive of Jesus primarily as a teacher or religious leader, they actually reject his message.

The songs that *reject* Jesus as a source of truth are some of the most interesting because they reveal a veritable taxonomy of reasons for unbelief. Some of these songs view Jesus as false, that is, they see Jesus's message as simply wrong. These are songs that evangelize for atheism and are dominated by punk and metal bands, including Fucked Up ("Son the Father") and Slayer ("Jesus Saves"). A number of artists instead see Jesus as a failure, either as a man who mistakenly thought he was divine or whose followers did. Again, we see rock bands dominating this category, including Jethro Tull ("My God") and Bad Religion ("The Answer"). Some of the most provocative songs in this category present Jesus as an actual divine figure, yet one who is either powerless to accomplish what he promises or refuses to do so. Rock bands again feature prominently, including Deicide ("Death to Jesus"), Lostprophets ("Jesus Walks"), and The Project Hate MCMXCIX's "I Smell Like Jesus . . . Dead."

The second category of the Source of Truth image features songs that reject Jesus by focusing not on the content of his message per se but rather on the *negative impact of that message on the individual believer.* The most common reason cited by the songs is that Jesus keeps one from living an authentic human life. Sometimes these songs present Jesus as one who keeps individuals from having faith in themselves and recognizing their own power (and responsibility) to make their own choices. For example, in "Gold Soul Theory" the hip-hop group Underachievers rap, "You's a fucking livin' God, why you bowin' down to Christ."[21] Madonna, in "X-Static Process," considers following Jesus but fears that she will lose herself if she does. The metal band Nunslaughter writes, "It is time to rise and think for yourself; Be strong inside and don't ask for help."[22]

This reasoning for the rejection of faith is consistent with popular music's subjective and individualistic focus, emerging from its historical emphasis on rebellion against institutions and structures. It is also reminiscent of the importance of "authenticity" as an ideological value for many genres of popular music, with punk being perhaps the best example. Thus one particular explanation for this reasoning may be that it is not simply about Christianity's power to erase individuality (or any other system's potential to do so) but also that the very specter of an individual losing her or his ability to make free choices is fundamentally frightening. Though this may seem ironic when one considers that Jesus was executed partly because he challenged dominant structures in society, once he is viewed as the founder of a religion he becomes a threat to individuality and authenticity, violating what Michael Iafrate calls "punk's kerygmatic statement": *"You have one life. Live it with intentionality. Don't go through life as a mere spectator."*[23] Though Iafrate describes this ethos regarding punk, it is present in all genres of popular music, and it is Jesus's presence in a variety of songs that often reveals it clearly.

The songs mentioned here focus on the negative influences of Jesus's message on individuals. But another significant category rejects Jesus's message by pointing to the negative influences of his message on society. Essentially, they highlight the sins of his followers. Some songs hold Jesus accountable as inspiring a religion whose followers who are guilty of myriad social evils, including war ("Golden Boys" by NOFX, "Cathedral" by Crosby, Stills & Nash, and "Killing for Jesus" by Circle Jerks) and intolerance/racism ("White Jesus, White AmeriKKKa" by Tokunbo, "Gay Jesus for President" by World's Scariest Police Chases, "East Jesus Nowhere" by Green Day). However, according to popular music, the most grievous sins of Jesus's followers are hypocrisy and judgmentalism. That issue has inspired powerful invectives by a number of major artists, including 2Pac ("Blasphemy"), Ben Folds ("Jesusland"), Jethro Tull ("Hymn 43"), and Tom Waits ("Jesus Gonna Be Here"). The specific focus for many of these songs is the greedy, hypocritical preacher. That cultural trope appears in Soundgarden's "Jesus Christ Pose," Nick Cave's "Red Right Hand," and Ray Stevens's "Would Jesus Wear a Rolex?" as well as the pop hits "Jesus He Knows Me" by Genesis (with its memorable video of a despicable televangelist) and "Modern Jesus" by Portugal. The Man.

One fascinating trend that emerges among the subset of songs that reject Jesus is that it is not he himself who is the object of their ire. Instead it is the falseness of his message or its negative effects. Almost no songs charge Jesus with knowingly misleading his followers, having ulterior motives, or being malicious in his heart. Again, doing so would seem to be an obvious strategy for artists with an anti-Christian agenda. The fact that it rarely occurs is evidence in a culture of a deep-seated positive view of Jesus—or at least his intentions. This is yet another example of a fundamentally traditional conception of Jesus that lies at the root of popular music.

Songs that *affirm* Jesus as a source of truth form the second largest category of this image. About two-thirds of these songs present a generally positive evaluation of Jesus's message without referring to specific elements of it. These are songs that reveal a confident Christian faith. As songs of worship, praise, and even evangelism, they often affirm Jesus's message in broad terms, communicating a general sense of joy or thanksgiving about the truth they have discovered. This is a surprisingly large group of songs, comprising at least seventy of the songs in this study, and is created primarily by artists who are known to be Christians, including Lecrae, Twenty-One Pilots, Violet Femmes, P.O.D., U2, Nick Cave, Mumford and Sons, Bob Dylan, and Kanye West.[24] These songs present a fascinating example of clearly "Christian" music that has found acceptance among millions of fans who (presumably) do not share the beliefs of the artists. Their presence in the world of popular music points yet again to the bright streak of Christianity that still runs through America; they are the musical analog to the displays of Bibles at Wal-Mart, culturally accepted manifestations of Christianity in an otherwise secular environment. As songs that have become religiously meaningful for a wide range of Christians, they can be considered in many ways "sacred." But the breadth of their impact is also perhaps a reason to continue to consider them "secular." Their existence outside of the Christian music industry points to the continued erosion of the exclusive claim of institutions and other discursive structures on the lives of Christians, something that is a central feature of modern secular life. That position allows them to mediate religious claims and ideas in ways that speak to a much broader range of Christians than if they were subject to the control of specific institutions and structures. At the same time, these songs present unapologetic (pun intended) claims of Christian truth, usually expressed in distinctly subjective terms, which nonetheless appear alongside an extensive menu of other songs making competing truth claims. As such, they exist as resources for those engaged in the highly anthropocentric process of spiritual exploration that is unique to the secular world.[25]

Songs that demonstrate this process of spiritual exploration form the remaining one-third of songs that affirm Jesus's message. Some of these songs function *prophetically*, in that they criticize Jesus's message from a position of faith. Others take an unflinching view of Jesus's message as part of a process of genuine spiritual *seeking*.

The 1975's "If I Believe You" is a moving example of a song in this second category. Opening with a raw statement of spiritual emptiness, the chorus builds up to the cry: "And I'm broken and bleeding. . . . And I'm asking you Jesus, show yourself."[26] At first hearing the song's musical landscape points directly to gospel: slow triplet subdivisions, the use of the organ, the call-and-response phrases structure, and of course the gospel choir. But its musico-dramatic structure shows that it is not. The call of the gospel choir in the chorus ("And if I believe you") is followed only by silence: singer Matty Healy does not fill in the space with the improvised vocal responses that, in gospel, serve the crucial subjectifying function of connecting the singer with the message of the song. As result, he maintains a significant personal distance from the emotional intensity of the song, essentially rejecting the opportunity to fully give in to movement of the Spirit. However, the pain and subjectivity of the lyrics make it clear that he is not keeping his distance out of ironic detachment. Instead I believe it is because his own perceived lack of faith does not allow him to do so authentically. We see this most powerfully as the chorus continues. As Healy sings "And I'm asking you," the choir joins him on the word "Jesus," lifting up his prayer on their wings. The music swells and the harmonic rhythm accelerates, setting us up for the traditional moment of emotional release in a gospel song: the vocal cadenza that will complete the transformation of singer into preacher, song into testimony. But that does not happen. Instead the band drops out, and there is nothing but the simple phrase "show yourself." There is no vocal melisma, no dramatic release, no dramatic dominant chord. In fact, the phrase is actually missing two beats, removing even the chance that the singer could fully inhabit that moment. Instead of a singer floating on the wings of the congregation, we are left with just a single voice, alone in a church at the very moment when he needs the support of a cloud of witnesses, releasing a small prayer into the ether, hoping that Jesus will hear him.[27]

This extraordinary song is an example of the fundamentally anthropocentric nature of the spiritual search in a secular age. Unlike our forebears, today we bear the full and individual responsibility for our own belief. Our modern understanding of our place in the cosmos and the contingent nature of any belief system place us, ultimately, where Matty Healy is, alone with the question that ends the song: "If I'm lost then how can I find myself?" The line is repeated nine times over a subdominant pedal: the first half of a plagal cadence, an "Amen" whose second syllable never occurs. The song ends with the listener waiting in vain for an answer.

This song understands Jesus principally as a source of truth, crying out to him to provide a sense of meaning that will provide healing or even "salvation." Unlike the songs that reject Jesus, it does not approach his message from a logical or rational perspective, asking Jesus to explain or defend what he has preached or what his followers have done in his name. Rather, it asks simply for his presence, confident in the sufficiency of Jesus's revelation. Like Paul on the road to Damascus, it reveals a central soteriological claim of Christianity: that the experience of Jesus as Word necessarily precedes the understanding of his words. This is what makes this a song not of doubt but of faith, albeit a kind of faith that seems nearly impossible to believe in.[28]

A final subset of songs that affirm Jesus's message is composed of those that do so in a *prophetic* manner. Though written by Christians, they are not songs of praise, thanksgiving, or joy. Instead they are songs that critique Christianity and modern "Christian" America, often focusing on the hypocrisy of fellow believers. This includes two country songs that challenge the materialism of contemporary Christians, "Would Jesus Wear a Rolex" by Ray Stevens and "Jesus Was a Carpenter" by Johnny Cash. Two compelling examples from contemporary folk music are "Explaining Jesus" by Jordy Searcy and "Ring the Bells" by JOHNNYSWIM and Drew Holcombe and the Neighbors.[29] In this latter song, we see echoes of the long American tradition of attempting to reclaim "true" Christianity by charging fellow believers with perverting Jesus's message.

Worldly Savior Image (68/435)

Categories:
Social justice warrior (18)
Personal helper (70)

The second most common understanding of Jesus among the songs studied for this essay is as Worldly Savior. It focuses on Jesus's ability to provide healing, comfort, or deliverance from the problems in one's daily life rather than forgiveness of sins or eternal life. Some of these songs merely make a passing reference to Jesus's ability to help, but many are nothing short of faith-filled prayers to Jesus in times of desperate need. As such, though they are some of the least theologically complex songs in our study, they are some of the most spiritually powerful. As in the psalms, however, their power is not just a function of the faith of the writer. Because many of these songs represent a highly subjective spirituality that exists outside of traditional structures of church and community, they often reveal doubts about Jesus's willingness to help, his ability to do so, and even his very existence. Regardless of the degree or type of faith represented in individual songs, as a group these songs present an understanding of Jesus as an active, interventionist figure who may be approached without a mediator and who can provide specific types of salvation for individuals and the world.

There are two main categories of this image that together form a comprehensive understanding of the ways in which Jesus may intervene in the world. First, there is the Jesus who can redeem society, either through impacting politics or by inspiring individuals to act in ways that will better their world. He appears in this way, as a *social justice warrior*, in a handful of songs spread among various genres. An interesting example is "Jesus Christ" by Woody Guthrie. (This is one of the very few secular songs featuring Jesus written before the end of the 1960s.) Here Guthrie presents Jesus as a martyr in a Marxist mold, put to death by the powerful in response to his radical notions about economic rights and his solidarity with the poor.

The image of Jesus as a figure who can intervene in the world to effect political or structural change is actually quite rare, but when it does occur it is limited to white artists. In contrast, when Black artists imagine Jesus as a figure who addresses himself to the problems of the world, their gaze is instead local, personal, and powerful, focusing upon problems facing Black urban communities. Denzel Curry's 2019 song "SPEEDBOAT" is a good recent example. It features a hook that is an intercessory prayer directly to Jesus, ending with the lines: "What you see in life's illegal / I don't wanna use my Desert Eagle [a type of assault rifle]."[30] The meaning is somewhat ambiguous: Is Curry saying that he needs Jesus to help him control himself (so that his anger does not explode in violence), or that he believes Jesus has the power to accomplish what he, a human, could only accomplish through violence? Regardless, Jesus in this song is a living, accessible presence who has the power to change a broken society that is oppressing the Black community. But he is not a political figure who can make structural change, like the Marxist Jesus of Woody Guthrie. Even a decade after the election of Barack Obama, it seems impossible to imagine politics as a domain that even Jesus could reform society on behalf of African Americans.[31] Rather, in this hip-hop song and others, Jesus is a figure who exerts his power directly and personally in the lives of his people.

But is he really? Another way of interpreting the hook is that Curry doubts whether Jesus will in fact provide the deliverance for which he clamors. As such, the song is a contemporary example of a common trend in rappers' understanding of God: that God does not always choose to use his power. This provides another perspective on the common phenomenon of rappers identifying themselves with God. As Utley writes, "When God 'out there' refuses to account for the misuse of power in His name, God 'down here' [the rapper] takes over where He left off."[32] This provides a nuanced understanding of rappers' often contingent (and uneasy) belief in Jesus's worldly power.

The second subset of the image of Jesus as Worldly Savior is the most common, making up two-thirds of this category: that of a figure who can provide *personal help* to someone in need. Rather than focusing on Jesus's ability to make changes in society or the world or fixing large-scale problems like poverty or racism, this image describes a Jesus who can intervene in one's life to provide a specific solution to a specific problem. This image appears most commonly in country music, perhaps because of the historical and cultural indebtedness to the blues and gospel traditions. Indeed, among the seventy-five country songs on the list, twenty present this specific subset of the overall image of worldly savior. It is also significant that many of these songs were recorded by some of the genre's biggest stars. This includes Carrie Underwood's "Jesus Take the Wheel," which crossed over to hit number twenty-three on the *Billboard* pop chart in 2006.[33]

What kind of help do artists believe Jesus can provide? Unsurprisingly, the list includes challenges familiar to all humans: deliverance from despair or suicide; death, violence, or illness; addiction; and loneliness or heartache. Many of the songs in this category are actually addressed directly to Jesus: that is, they are prayers. They include Kris Kristofferson's "Help Me," Cupcakke's "Jesus," Kendrick Lamar's "Sherane," and the Indigo Girls's "Hey Jesus." As songs that are routinely sung loudly by thousands at clubs and concerts around the world, these sonic prayers provide an interesting challenge to a recent study indicating that most Americans say they pray silently and by themselves.[34] Kanye West's blockbuster song "Jesus Walks" (written before his conversion to Christianity) provides a uniquely powerful example of how such a "prayer song" can create a new space for religious practice in our secular world. This song is a prayer for worldly help and a meditation on the possibility of prayer itself. But it is more: it also functions as a fulfillment of that meta-prayer under the right circumstances. At the end of the song, West says that he hopes his song will "bring the day that I'm dreamin' about / Next time I'm in the club, everybody screamin' out 'Jesus Walk.'"[35] When dancers at a club add their voices to the diegetic gospel choir singing the hook, the song becomes the corporate prayer that West desires. This powerful epiphenomenon is an example of how secular prayer songs can challenge the strict distinctions between the sacred and secular in the contemporary world by providing an experience that is in many ways homologous to traditional religious ritual. Singing that hook with thousands of others (a hook that is in fact in the imperative mood, not the indicative used in the song's title) feels a lot like going to church, no matter one's beliefs.

As a scholar, I have found this vast collection of songs to be a fascinating example of the ways modern Americans have grappled with the meaning of Jesus in an increasingly secular world. That they exist at all seems somewhat surprising; that they consistently reveal theologically orthodox images of Jesus is even more so. Perhaps most surprising, though, is that few of them have a negative opinion of Jesus—either the man or his message. Instead the negativity in their songs tends to focus on the sins of Jesus's followers, especially their hypocrisy and judgmentalism.

As a Christian, these particular songs speak to me in discomfiting ways. They force me to confront difficult questions about my own faith and the sins my coreligionists and I have committed in Jesus's name. I am drawn as well to the songs that testify to their doubt about Jesus or that ask the tough questions about him that I often try to avoid. Ironically, it is those songs' secularity that has allowed them to address these ideas in ways that are spiritually valuable for me. Not limited to the religious standards or expectations of Christians or churches, they are free to grapple with questions about faith and doubt that long ago I learned needed to be conquered—or at the very least hidden. But artists don't deserve the title if they refuse to ask the questions and hide from the answers. The artist who confronts issues of faith in the secular world must do so with an unflinching honesty and authenticity to themselves.

If these songs manifest an authentic spiritual search, describe an honest response to the claims of Jesus, and challenge us to ask tough questions about our faith, then we have to ask the question: How are they *not* "sacred?" The answer, of course, is that they are. And as such, I believe that they can and should form an important resource not just for scholars of religion but also for Christians looking for ways to understand and articulate their faith in the modern world. These songs could form the basis of resources intended for Christian formation or discipleship sessions in an ecumenical array of churches, or even for personal devotion or study. They could also speak to those whose spiritual yearnings persist after having left Christianity or who are seeking a way to engage with Christianity outside of a specific denomination or tradition. Of course, the success of these resources would turn on the quality of the music they explore: songs that grapple with the meaning of Jesus in ways that are both relevant and authentic. As Maeve Heaney says, "Living at depth is for all Christians. Understanding it, intuiting it, finding meaning and expressing it in ways that open rich spaces to appreciate it is the artist's task."[36] If the artist does her job well, the Christian will benefit.

Long before St. Paul wrote his letter to the Philippians, he and his friends had been singing about Jesus. Since then sacred music has united Christians of all stripes. But in the religiously diverse world of today, perhaps it is the work of secular artists that is best positioned to provide the "rich spaces" where anyone interested in the claims of Jesus can gather in fellowship, not just Christians. This radical hospitality is a powerful way that secular music can contribute to the conversations about faith today.

NOTES

1. See "A Hymn to Christ? (Philippians 2:6–11) by Paul A. Holloway," accessed April 10, 2020, https://www.bibleodyssey.org/en/passages/related-articles/a-hymn-to-christ.

2. The specific songs referenced here include, among others, "Korean Jesus" by Dumbfounded, "Jesus Hitler" by Carnivore, and "Gay Jesus for President" by World's Scariest Police Chases.

3. Stephen Prothero, *American Jesus: How the Son of God Became a National Icon* (New York: Farrar, Straus and Giroux, 2003), 294.

4. An extensive database of these songs, indexed by their various images and categories, may be found at www.delvyncase.com.

5. This includes various genres of rock (including blues-rock, country-rock, and others): alternative rock, indie rock, rhythm and blues (including soul and disco), hip-hop, country, folk/singer-songwriter, electronic dance music (EDM), punk, metal, and mainstream pop. Because its goal is to identify large-scale trends, it is limited to artists with national profiles, defined as those who have released music on major labels and/or have achieved significant critical or commercial success. Songs made this list if Jesus appeared in them in any way, from those that take him as their subject (as in Kanye West's "Jesus Walks") to those that merely reference him in passing. This includes songs that feature his name, a clear reference to him, or that are generally understood to be about him. (I am grateful to my research assistant, Krystal Ssonko, for her help in discovering many of these songs.) Because my goal was to use music as a lens through which to view ideas about Jesus in mainstream American culture (not the American Evangelical Christian subculture), I excluded from this list songs released by Contemporary Christian Music (CCM) or gospel labels, or by artists who principally work in that genre. I did, however, include music by secular artists who are known to be Christians, including artists like U2, Nick Cave, and many country artists who make no attempt to hide their faith in their music or public personae. Though some of them, especially country artists, are certainly aware that there is an overlap between their listeners and fans of CCM or gospel, I included this set of artists in this study nonetheless. The reason is that their music is popular among a swath of listeners far broader and larger than CCM/gospel fans. That these songs have spoken to millions of (presumably) non-Christian listeners seems to be due in part to the ways the views of Jesus in these songs resonate with them. As a result, we can assume that the views of Jesus these songs reveal are acceptable, or at the very least not objectionable, to a large secular audience. Again, the implication is that these songs reveal something important about the ideas of Jesus that form a part of the fabric of American society.

6. Albert Schweitzer, *The Quest of the Historical Jesus* (London: Adam and Charles Black, 1910), PDF ebook, 10.

7. See Tex Sample, "'Help Me Make It Through the Night': Narrating Class and Country Music in the Theology of Paul," in *The Bible in/and Popular Culture: Creative Encounters*, ed. Philip Culbertson and Elaine M. Wainwright (Atlanta: Society of Biblical Literature, 2010).

8. "Eric Church—Country Music Jesus," *Genius*, July 26, 2011, https://genius.com/Eric-church-country-music-jesus-lyrics.

9. "Eric Church, 'Country Music Jesus'—Story Behind the Song," *The Boot*, January 16, 2015, https://theboot.com/eric-church-country-music-jesus-lyrics/.

10. Some songs that fall into the Person domain use the "Incarnation" songwriting technique discussed earlier. An example is Clay Walker's "Jesus Was a Country Boy," which principally imagines Jesus as a human being ("Swimmin' in the river, fishin' for his dinner"). Therefore it belongs in the Person domain. In contrast, James Otto's "Soldiers and Jesus" uses the comparison to highlight Jesus's role as sacrificial savior ("There's only two people who's ever died for me / Laid down their lives just so I could be free").

11. Philip Culbertson's essay in *Jesus in/and Popular Culture* explores a number of other songs that feature Mary Magdalene. See Culbertson, "'Tis a Pity She's (Still) A Whore: Popular Music's Ambivalent Resistance to the Reclamation of Mary Magdalene," in Culbertson and Wainwright, *Jesus in/and Popular Culture*.

12. A handful of songs allude to Jesus's sexual attractiveness, including Tee-Jay's "Clean Like Jesus," Lil B's "Look Like Jesus," and Denzel Curry's "Story: No Title."

13. Because "power" is the only category that appears extensively in the Paragon domain, this study will focus solely on that category. The "Other" category includes songs that view Jesus as a symbol of a wide variety of different concepts: kindness, martyrdom, love, piety, moral purity, forgiveness, and general uniqueness. It is significant that these are all positive attributes. But none of these specific symbols appears with enough frequency to warrant further treatment in this study.

14. "The Game (Ft. Dre)—Black Jesus," *Genius*, January 1, 2012, https://genius.com/The-game-black-jesus-lyrics.

15. While I have found few hip-hop songs in which a female rapper compares herself explicitly to Jesus by name, there are a number of songs in which a female rapper does so obliquely. Many of these are discussed in chapter 5 of Ebony A. Utley, *Rap and Religion: Understanding the Gangsta's God* (Santa Barbara, CA: Praeger, 2012).

16. Utley, *Rap and Religion*, chap. 5.

17. Ibid.

18. In chapter 3, Utley presents an impressive discussion of the ways rappers understand Jesus, organizing them into three categories: companion, crucified figure, and commodity.

19. "Brand New—Jesus Christ," *Genius*, November 20, 2006, https://genius.com/Brand-new-jesus-christ-lyrics.

20. Maeve Louise Heaney, "Musical Space: Living 'In Between' the Christian and Artistic Callings," in *Secular Music and Sacred Theology*, ed. Tom Beaudoin (Collegeville, MN: Liturgical Press, 2013), 26.

21. "The Underachievers—Gold Soul Theory," *Genius*, June 27, 2012, https://genius.com/The-underachievers-gold-soul-theory-lyrics.

22. "Nunslaughter—I Hate Christians," *Genius*, April 10 2020, https://genius.com/Nunslaughter-i-hate-christians-lyrics.

23. Michael J. Iafrate, "Punk Rock and/as Liberation Theology," in *Music, Theology, and Justice*, ed. Michael O'Connor et al. (Lanham, MD: Lexington Books, 2020), 25

24. In this category we do see a number of songs by artists who are not known to be Christians but who still affirm Jesus's message. This includes two bands seemingly caught up momentarily in the late 1960s vogue for Jesus as a source of spiritual truth

accessible through mystical union: the Rolling Stones ("Just Want to See His Face") and the Velvet Underground ("Jesus"). And for its sheer mind-blowing nature, there is the song "Nothing But Trouble (Instagram Models)" by the influential contemporary theologian Lil Wayne, which includes the line "I had to find Christ; Lord I had to, open up my eyes and find light." See Lil Wayne and Charlie Puth, "Nothing But Trouble (Instagram Models)," *Genius*, June 30, 2015, https://genius.com/Lil-wayne-and-charlie-puth-nothing-but-trouble-instagram-models-lyrics.

25. This is one of the main arguments of Taylor's *A Secular Age*.

26. "The 1975—If I Believe You," *Genius*, February 26, 2016, https://genius.com/The-1975-if-i-believe-you-lyrics.

27. This moment calls to mind David Brown's wonderfully comforting reminder: "God is present everywhere seeking a response. So, it is quite wrong to suppose that only explicit belief will meet with an answering echo." David Brown, *God and Grace of Body: Sacrament in Ordinary* (Oxford: Oxford University Press, 2011), 346.

28. This song demonstrates beautifully what Maeve Louise Heaney writes about the Christian artist: they "embrace and live *through* their sensibility, in both its strength and fragility; trusting in God's strength even when it is nowhere to be seen; risking new experiments although the old stuff 'kind of' works." Heaney, "Musical Space," 26.

29. "JOHNNYSWIM & Drew Holcomb & The Neighbors—Ring the Bells," *Genius*, April 6, 2018, https://genius.com/Johnnyswim-and-drew-holcomb-and-the-neighbors-ring-the-bells-lyrics.

30. "Denzel Curry—SPEEDBOAT," *Genius*, May 22, 2019, https://genius.com/Denzel-curry-speedboat-lyrics. I am grateful for my daughter, Alexandra Case, who introduced me to this powerful song.

31. For a nuanced discussion of this phenomenon, see Utley, *Rap and Religion*, 53.

32. Ibid., 93.

33. "Carrie Underwood," *Billboard*, accessed June 21, 2020, https://www.billboard.com/music/Carrie-Underwood/chart-history/ASI/song/488171.

34. "Silent and Solo: How Americans Pray," *Barna Group*, August 15, 2017, https://www.barna.com/research/silent-solo-americans-pray/.

35. "Kanye West—Jesus Walks," *Genius*, February 10, 2004, https://genius.com/Kanye-west-jesus-walks-lyrics.

36. Heaney, "Musical Space," 26.

FURTHER READING

Beaudoin, Tom. *Secular Music and Sacred Theology*. Collegeville, MN: Liturgical Press, 2013.

Cone, James H. *The Spirituals and the Blues: An Interpretation*. Maryknoll, NY: Orbis Books, 2000.

Culbertson, Philip Leroy, and Elaine Mary Wainwright. *The Bible in/and Popular Culture: A Creative Encounter*. Atlanta, GA: Society of Biblical Literature, 2010.

Gilmour, Michael J. *Call Me the Seeker: Listening to Religion in Popular Music.* New York: Continuum, 2005.

Heaney, Maeve Louise. *Music as Theology: What Music Has to Say about the Word.* Eugene, OR: Pickwick Publ., 2012.

Marsh, Clive, and Vaughn S. Roberts. *Personal Jesus—How Popular Music Shapes Our Souls.* Grand Rapids, MI: Baker Publishing Group, 2013.

Miller, Monica R., Anthony B. Pinn, and Bun B. *Religion in Hip Hop: Mapping the New Terrain in the US.* London: Bloomsbury Academic, 2015.

Prothero, Stephen R. *American Jesus How the Son of God Became a National Icon.* New York: Farrar, Straus and Giroux, 2006.

Sample, Tex. *White Soul: Country Music, the Church, and Working Americans.* Nashville, TN: Abingdon Press, 1996.

Spencer, Jon Michael. *Theological Music: Introduction to Theomusicology.* New York: Greenwood Press, 1991.

Utley, Ebony A. *Rap and Religion: Understanding the Gangsta's God.* Santa Barbara, CA: Praeger, 2012.

V

DIASPORIC MUSIC

Chapter Ten

The Folk Scholarship Roots and Geopolitical Boundaries of Sacred Harp's Global Twenty-First Century

Jesse P. Karlsberg

The state of Sacred Harp in 2018 would have been scarcely imaginable to those like folklorist George Pullen Jackson and singer and English scholar Buell Cobb, who questioned in the 1940s and 1970s, respectively, whether the style would survive past the year 2000. Both scholars pointed to its aging participants and a musical style seemingly irreparably out of fashion.[1] Even advocates set their sights on less ambitious targets than Sacred Harp's current geography. Georgia singer and clothing plant manager Hugh McGraw, who ceaselessly promoted Sacred Harp singing to new audiences, envisioned a national Sacred Harp community stretching across the United States, a goal that has been met and surpassed. As recently as 2008, the style was confined to the United States and pockets of England, Australia, and Canada. Today Sacred Harp is sung on four continents in twenty-five countries. By the time you read this essay, the landscape may have shifted yet again.

Sacred Harp in Europe, Oceania, East Asia, and the Middle East is both a global and local phenomenon. Though vastly expanded in geography and demographic variety, the style is still a "subcultural sound," a "micromusic," convening small groups of people with strong community bonds often beneath the level of broad cultural attention even as it regularly achieves local and sometimes national press coverage.[2] Despite its increasing reach, the new span of Sacred Harp singing is nonetheless limited in two respects: first, the style has spread only to developed countries where US popular culture and media have a large imprint and garner a comparatively favorable reception. The style continues to attract an overwhelmingly white group of participants, with the exception of singings in East Asia, which have drawn Asian and white American expatriate participants. In each country, for the members of a local singing network, Sacred Harp's reception follows and reacts to a history of economic and cultural relationships with America and with the Southern

United States. The outsize presences of these cultural and economic forces far exceed that of Sacred Harp and differently condition what participation in Sacred Harp means to new singers. Second, participation carries longstanding associations with deep roots in the "revival" of Sacred Harp in the United States. The style spreads abroad through transnational networks emulating practices associated with folk cultures of the Southern United States. It also travels along art music and academic networks engaged in the cultivated celebration, performance, and adaptation of material associated with these folk practices.

Even as economic and cultural relationships with the United States and an association with Southern folk culture direct Sacred Harp's spread, other factors facilitate the style's international transmission. Features of Sacred Harp music and associated cultural practice have transcultural appeal. Aspects of Sacred Harp singing's music culture engage participants in a full-voiced, participation-oriented, deeply spiritual, and accessible yet musically engaging practice and repertoire. Ethnomusicologist Ellen Lueck convincingly describes how the support of US-based Sacred Harp organizations, international singing groups' "charismatic and enabled leadership," and the affordances of the contemporary social media landscape have helped bolster Sacred Harp singing abroad.[3]

This essay documents the present scope of Sacred Harp singing outside the United States and examines the eighty-five-year-old folklore genealogies that factor into the style's recent spread. My focus is on how what I call "folklore's filter" made the expansion of Sacred Harp to new people and places possible.[4] I also touch briefly on other factors in the dissemination of Sacred Harp beyond North America: the unique musical features and practices that support Sacred Harp's adoption and the similarities and differences in the histories of transnational political, economic, and cultural exchange affecting the form of participation for many. These factors are critical to an understanding of Sacred Harp singing's new international reach. The contours and underpinnings of Sacred Harp's spread illustrate how academic genealogies, music cultural features, and geopolitics can influence the reception of sacred American cultural practices in new contexts. I begin by briefly recounting the history and practice of Sacred Harp singing itself.

SACRED HARP SINGING

Sacred Harp is a practice of sacred community singing from the tunebook *The Sacred Harp*. First compiled in 1844 by West Georgians Benjamin Franklin White and Elisha James King, *The Sacred Harp* has been revised every generation or so by Southern singer-teacher-composers. The book articulates a pedagogical system and adopts a bibliographic form, both of which have roots in eighteenth-century New England singing schools, and adopts a shape-note system of music notation dating to an 1801 Philadelphia tunebook called *The Easy Instructor*. The book features songs in three- and four-part harmony, mostly by American composers, in a variety of styles collectively described as dispersed harmony. The songs are settings of metrical poetry largely drawn from a corpus of English Protestant hymnody also widely incorporated into denominational hymnals. Since its publication, *The Sacred Harp* has been connected to group singing institutions called conventions, which spread across the South in the decades after the 1845 establishment of the Southern Musical Convention in West Georgia.[5] Conventions feature voluntary associations of singers seated by voice part in an inward-facing hollow square, at the center of which stand a succession of song leaders directing the group in one or more songs of the leader's choice from the tunebook. The proceedings frequently last from morning to mid-afternoon, punctuated by short breaks for refreshments, announcements, and a sumptuous mid-day meal called "dinner on the ground." The book's compilers envisioned its sacred songs as suitable for worship by any Christian denomination, and its singers spanned the nineteenth century's rural Southern denominational landscape, encompassing men and women and including both Black and white southerners. Yet race and gender affected the form of participation. Women rarely led songs in the nineteenth and early twentieth centuries, and Black singers were relegated to church balconies before emancipation; singings became largely segregated after Reconstruction when a resurgence of white supremacist political power curtailed Black participation in every aspect of Southern life.[6] *The Sacred Harp*'s connection to the music culture of singing conventions and its wide array of stakeholders committed to its success (thanks to their conscription in contributing to or revising the book) helped *The Sacred Harp* achieve wide adoption in a competitive landscape. *The Sacred Harp* outlasted an array of nineteenth-century competitors, surviving into the twentieth century as other books fell out of print and were supplanted by Sabbath School and gospel singing.[7]

By the early twentieth century, newer musical forms far exceeded Sacred Harp singing in popularity. To some, the style seemed outmoded and in need of modernization. Three competing groups revised the book in the wake of the original compilers' deaths. These revisers adopted different approaches to making *The Sacred Harp* new while retaining its distinctive qualities that had long endeared the book to devoted followers. In balancing old and new, these editors attempted to redefine participation in a historical tradition as modern. Embracing the conservative core of the style's music, the most successful reviser modernized aspects of the book's design and presentation, charting a path forward while setting the terms of what has remained an ongoing struggle for participants.[8] Like Sacred Harp's early twentieth-century tunebook editors, singers today regard participation in the style as an ongoing, evolving practice rather than the revival of something from the past, and sometimes struggle to articulate their relationship to this long and complicated history.

FOLKLORE'S FILTER

In the early twentieth century, participation in Sacred Harp singing was connected to a sense of local and personal belonging. The style's depiction as a form of folksong beginning in the 1930s, which also involved the selection of particular local Sacred Harp groups as representative of traditional practice (what I call the style's passage through folklore's filter), provided an avenue for people with no personal connection to Sacred Harp's original settings to imagine their active participation. To understand how Sacred Harp singing became folk music in the twentieth century, it is important to recognize that cultural phenomena do not objectively exist as folk practices. Instead a practice must be characterized as folk, usually by ideologically motivated cultural interveners. To describe a practice as folk entails detaching something occurring in the present and a casting it into what folklorist Barbara Kirschenblatt-Gimblett describes as folklore's "peculiar temporality."[9] This process is selective, a form of adaptation and rearrangement rather than a neutral transplantation.[10] Relocating present practices in the past also imbues music cultures with a new set of values associated with the folk label, such as oral transmission, cultural isolation, and key aesthetic concerns.[11]

George Pullen Jackson, a professor of German at Vanderbilt University, was the first to describe Sacred Harp singing as a folk culture. Jackson's scholarly interest in German Romanticism's elevation of all things Volk led him to wonder why Americans didn't care about their own folk culture. Despite vast historical and demographic differences between the United States and European nations, Jackson nonetheless "cast about" for a domestic Anglo-Celtic folk culture that might similarly serve as a foundation for American national "poetic and musical art-developments."[12] After stumbling upon Sacred Harp singing in 1926, Jackson immediately interpreted the style as a folk culture in need of promotion: under threat by modernity, on the verge of inevitable transformation, and in need of protection and publicity to affect the form of its transformation.[13] Jackson made saving Sacred Harp singing his mission through trumpeting its history to the world. Jackson also regarded Sacred Harp music as a source of germinal cultural matter of diverse but largely European and Anglo-Celtic origins transplanted and cultivated on American soil. This music, he believed, had matured in the imagined isolated cultural removes of the Southern upcountry and now sat ready for plucking and assimilating into a new national culture rooted in native American (but not Native American or African American) folksong.[14]

Jackson's project galls today, and even in its time it was controversial. Inspired by the attention he believed Northern philanthropists and a range of commenters on national American culture lavished on Black spirituals, Jackson named Sacred Harp and related shape-note music "white spirituals." Jackson argued that these songs were the source of Black spirituals on the mistaken premise that first publication implies prior composition, a position long since discredited.[15] He further suggested that these songs should thus be given pride of place over Black spirituals in the American cultural and musical landscape. This position aligned Jackson with racial nativists, such as Richard Wallaschek, who drew on claims of originary and derivative styles to depict African and other musics as the product of inferior races of savage capacities.[16] Jackson's positions also placed him in tension with scholars such as W. E. B. Du Bois, who championed Black spirituals as important expressions of the trauma of slavery and the middle passage.[17] Despite his bitterness at the lack of attention his "white spirituals" received, Jackson was an advocate for Black cultural life in his hometown of Nashville, supporting the Fisk Jubilee Singers. Jackson also championed the art music of the city's white elite (such as the Nashville Symphony Orchestra, which he founded).

Jackson did not achieve his ambitious goal of spawning a national culture rooted in Anglo-Celtic folk music. He did, however, publish widely on Sacred Harp, raising awareness of the style and carving paths along which future generations of scholars, festival promoters, and singers encountered the music, filtered through his folk characterizations. Jackson also presented Sacred Harp programs at numerous folk festivals and scholarly conferences, exposing the style to academics and folk music fans and locating it among other musics labeled as folk traditions. In addition, Jackson corresponded with leading composers such as Virgil Thompson, suggesting tunes to arrange, thereby contributing to the style's incorporation into other music genres. In so doing, Jackson laid the groundwork for successive generations of musicologists and listeners to encounter the style through art music inspired by the style's folk melodies.

Jackson's representation of Sacred Harp as "white spirituals" contrasts with the scholarship of John W. Work III, a Black professor of music at Fisk University, who also studied Sacred Harp in the 1930s. Although Work, like Jackson, described Sacred Harp as folksong, he instead wrote about the style as a form of Black cultural expression. Work faced racial discrimination and professional pressures that limited his capacity to fund and conduct research on Sacred Harp singing.[18] His lone publication on Sacred Harp, an article on a southeastern Alabama Black community of singers, failed to dislodge Jackson's misleading depiction of Sacred Harp as white with exceptional Black practitioners.[19] Nonetheless, Work's scholarship did log a representation of Black Sacred Harp in the scholarly record, which would lead successive generations of folk music scholars and folk festival promoters to the singers he documented.

FOLK FESTIVALS, NEW AUDIENCES

Folk festival promoters ventured through the channels that Jackson and Work carved to conduct fieldwork among Black and white Sacred Harp singers during the folk revival of the 1960s and 1970s. These efforts led to a new spate of scholarship, as well as opportunities for Black and white groups of singers to perform at folk festivals across the United States. White Sacred Harp singers made a memorable appearance in Newport in 1964, and Black and white groups sang together for the first time at the Smithsonian Festival of American Folklife in 1970 and 1976. Festival promoters like Ralph Rinzler and George Wein were invested in the civil rights movement and regarded integrated programming as a way folk music could help further racial harmony.[20] In this context, far removed from the still-segregated spaces where Sacred Harp singers gathered in the Southern United States, liberal and largely white festival audiences could associate Sacred Harp singing with idealized race relations and more easily identify with its white practitioners.[21] Hugh McGraw, leader of the white group at many of these festivals, drew on his considerable business savvy to reach out to audiences with the hope of attracting new participants to the tradition.

McGraw's outreach and the recontextualization of Sacred Harp at folk festivals led to increased interest and participation. Many new singers encountered Sacred Harp through folk music, at both large festivals and smaller gatherings. John Feddersen, a fifty-year veteran of Sacred Harp singing in North Carolina, first encountered Sacred Harp at the 1970 Festival of American Folklife.[22] Others first heard Sacred Harp in participatory folk song circles, such as those held at upstate New York's Fox Hollow Festival. The classical contexts in which Sacred Harp melodies could be heard, thanks to Jackson's earlier efforts, also drew newcomers into the style. Washington, DC, singer Steven Sabol, for example, first heard Sacred Harp melodies at a concert featuring an arrangement of a Sacred Harp tune by Samuel Barber and later found his way to Sacred Harp singing by perusing scores, recordings, and reissued tunebooks at university libraries.[23]

These choral, academic, and folk festival manifestations of Sacred Harp's rite of passage through folklore's filter contributed to the earliest institutionalization of Sacred Harp singing outside the Southern United States. By the time Alabama and Georgia singers performed at the 1970 Festival of American Folklife, folk music enthusiasts had already begun singing Sacred Harp at the Folklore Society of Greater Washington, leading Rinzler to promote the group's meetings to attendees from the festival stage.[24] Singings began at the Ark Coffeehouse in Ann Arbor, Michigan, before 1973. There folk music enthusiasts and academics sang together, embracing the longstanding history of University of Michigan musicology scholarship on American musics related to Sacred Harp.[25] The group instituted an annual all-day singing after later Sacred Harp revision consultant David Warren Steel arrived in 1973 as a musicology graduate student.[26] These academic, choral, and folk genealogies collided at Wesleyan University in 1976, where a planned concert by Vermont folkie and choral conductor Larry Gordon's Word of Mouth Chorus became the first annual New England Sacred Harp Convention, with McGraw as chairman and Wesleyan composer and music professor Neely Bruce as vice chairman. At this first Sacred Harp singing convention outside the South, these paths, the inheritance of Jackson's scholarship, converged.

The spread of Sacred Harp singing in the United States intensified through the 1980s and 1990s as Southern singers supported new participants in founding dozens of annual singings across the country.[27] Southern support for these fledgling conventions frequently arrived in the form of a bus full of singers, chartered by Jacksonville, Alabama, singer and retired schoolteacher Ruth Brown. Ruth Brown's bus helped forge networks of reciprocal travel that sustained these new singings by connecting singers, old and new. Many members of these burgeoning populations imagined their singings as outposts of a style with a homeland centered in the Southern communities that George Pullen Jackson's scholarship had enduringly marked as "traditional."

Like the folk festival audiences that heard Black and white renditions of what Jackson called "white spirituals," the late twentieth-century spread of Sacred Harp singing was largely white. However, thanks to folklore's, classical music's, and the academy's secularizing tendencies, Sacred Harp began to include participants of a much wider array of political and religious backgrounds. New participants were also increasingly economically and educationally diverse but skewed toward higher class and education levels than Southern singers thanks to this new population's overlap with the academy.[28]

TRANSPORTABLE FEATURES

The set of practices that have developed around singing from *The Sacred Harp* facilitated the music culture's growth in the 1980s and 1990s and its subsequent international expansion. These practices are emotionally and spiritually powerful, conducive to community formation, and particularly transportable. Ethnomusicologist Kiri Miller argues that the iconicity of Sacred Harp's hollow square seating formation, the emotional associations singers build around the configuration, and the ease with which it can be set up renders it a kind of "portable homeland."[29] Lueck articulates how a Sacred Harp singing convention "is a space that provides a familiar structure and social order across geographic and cultural distance" with a "shared event choreography which is legitimized through performative keys which rely on that choreography for interpretation, and social codes which police the space" while also affording a context "in which singers can express their belonging to the community-at-large."[30] Sacred Harp's participatory orientation, which includes not only the hollow square formation (in which singers sit facing each other rather than an audience) but also the rotation of leaders at singings and an openness to all who would wish to sing regardless of identity and singing ability, lends the style to community formation through music making.[31] Finally, for many participants in a variety of political contexts, Sacred Harp's full-voiced singing and status as a regular opportunity to gather with friends mean it can serve as a powerful source of emotional and spiritual renewal and as an antidote for perceived lacks in contemporary society.

The result as Sacred Harp continues to spread, Lueck argues, is a transnational community in which singers frequently articulate the style's capacity to bridge "vast differences" rendering singers akin to "family."[32] The transcultural appeal of these aspects of Sacred Harp's music culture are often what singers themselves offer in explaining their participation.

SPREAD TO EUROPE

The first flowerings of Sacred Harp in Europe grew directly out of the style's folk-inflected genealogies and histories, in particular the mix of folk music and its performance by choral ensembles, and were fed by the style's transportable features. Sacred Harp's "portable homeland" initially arrived beyond North America in the wake of workshops and performances held in the United Kingdom in the early 1990s and led by Northern Harmony, a touring ensemble based in Vermont and directed by Larry Gordon.[33] In the United Kingdom, English revivalists of the nineteenth-century congregational hymn singing practice known as "West Gallery music" taught each other to sing shape-notes, purchasing copies of *The Northern Harmony* (a shape-note tunebook Gordon had coedited in which New England and English tunes feature prominently), as well as *The Sacred Harp*.[34] In 1995, Neely Bruce led a quartet of young singers from Connecticut and Massachusetts on a United Kingdom tour. Like Gordon, Bruce mixed concerts with workshops during his English tour and encountered singers who recognized Sacred Harp singing as related to a shared legacy of nineteenth-century religious folk song. Those who attended Bruce's and Gordon's concerts came together with singers who encountered Sacred Harp in scholarly writing or available recordings to stage the first of what they styled a "singing day" in 1995. The following year, with the participation of New England Sacred Harp singers, English singers organized the first United Kingdom Shape-Note Convention, using *The Northern Harmony* and *The Sacred Harp* as tunebooks.[35] Sacred Harp singing grew steadily in England in subsequent years, largely among a population equally enthusiastic about folksong and folk dancing. Individual singers' pathways into Sacred Harp in England were diverse from the start, and in the late 1990s and into the 2000s the backgrounds of new English participants grew increasingly varied. But Sacred Harp singing's twentieth-century passage through folklore's filter made its journey across the Atlantic possible. Jackson's early associations between Sacred Harp and Anglo-Celtic folksong, as well as his promotion of the style as material for high-status art music performed by classical and elite choral ensembles, made possible the connections that first carried Sacred Harp to England and later fueled its subsequent growth. By 2018, English singers could attend twenty-five annual singings from *The Sacred Harp*, as well as an expanding list of monthly and weekly gatherings in cities across the country.[36]

The academic and performing legacy of Sacred Harp's folklorization also contributed to the establishment of Sacred Harp singing in Ireland, where the rapid growth of a young and enthusiastic population of singers in Cork precipitated increased transatlantic and intra-European travel to singings. As I recounted in 2011, "Sacred Harp singing was introduced to Ireland in 2009 with the founding of a music ensemble at University College Cork (UCC) led by ethnomusicologist Juniper Hill," a former student of Neely Bruce. "Hill's students soon established a singing at a community art space in downtown Cork," and interest in participating quickly outstripped the classroom where Hill had established the singing.[37] The first Ireland Sacred Harp Convention, held in March 2011, attracted unusually large contingents of American singers, as did subsequent annual sessions. Ethnomusicologist Jonathon Smith argues that these singers were drawn to Ireland in part because of a perception, more imagined than real, of Sacred Harp's (and of Sacred Harp singers')

Celtic roots.[38] Dating to George Pullen Jackson's articulation of Sacred Harp's "far southern fasola belt" populated by "Scotch-Irish and German, with a small ingredient of English," Sacred Harp singing's Celtic connection both detracts from equally significant historical influences at odds with Jackson's political project and lays groundwork for the style's valorization as tied to the music of the British Isles.[39] Most Irish singers recognized Sacred Harp singing's capacity for community formation, rather than its imagined Irish roots, as key to its success locally. Yet this geographical dimension of Jackson's characterization of the style as folksong contributed to the international appeal of early Ireland Sacred Harp conventions, in Ireland and beyond.[40]

Sacred Harp singing similarly reached Germany via the Northern Harmony tour that introduced Sacred Harp to England. Jutta Pflugmacher, a folk music enthusiast from Bündingen, Germany, attended one of these early concerts, singing briefly with English Sacred Harp singers. Back in Germany, she organized a stop on the 2010 Northern Harmony tour in her hometown. Motivated to bring Sacred Harp singing to Germany, Pflugmacher reached out to Keith MacDonald, an English expatriate and Sacred Harp singer. She also arranged for Aldo Ceresa, a New York–based singing school teacher, to present two workshops in her region, accompanied by a traveling group of English singers.[41] A fledgling group from Bremen who discovered Sacred Harp through the internet traveled to attend these workshops.[42] Young Sacred Harp singers from England and Ireland living temporarily in Germany added to these emergent groups. These singers hosted their first all-day singing in January 2012, followed by Germany's first convention in June 2014. Echoing Jackson, English singer Michael Walker noted in a report on the early German singing schools that Germany lacks the "natural points of connection with the British/Celtic origins of many of the tunes and with the religious poetry of *The Sacred Harp*."[43] The relatively few American visitors to the first German singings rarely describe their trips using the language of "returning home" that characterize some singers' motivations for visiting singings in Ireland. No Sacred Harp tour of Germany has yet materialized to match the 2007 tour of American Sacred Harp singers to England that included visits to the gravesites of prominent hymn writers whose poetry is included in *The Sacred Harp*. As singing in Germany has spread to new cities since 2014, the network has become an increasingly self-sufficient regional core accelerating central Europe's Sacred Harp growth.[44] According to singer Michael Walker, Germany "is a country with its own rich indigenous linguistic, cultural, musical, and religious heritage."[45] Yet despite the absence of a real or imagined connection to Sacred Harp's history, the beginnings of Sacred Harp in the country evince connections to the same folksong-inspired performing ensembles that facilitated the spread of Sacred Harp to England and Ireland.

Many of Poland's first Sacred Harp singers also encountered the style at events organized by individuals with connections to the spread of Sacred Harp in other parts of Europe and with roots in the academic study of Sacred Harp and related styles. Sacred Harp singing spread to Poland after a weeklong singing school at the Jarosław Early Music Festival taught by musician and ethnomusicologist Tim Eriksen.[46] An eclectic musician with roots in punk, grunge, folk, and world music, Eriksen first encountered Sacred Harp singing through the field recordings of folklorist Alan Lomax.[47] Eriksen, a former member of the quartet Bruce brought to England in 1995, later entered a doctoral program in ethnomusicology at Wesleyan University. Participants in the 2008 Jarosław singing school returned home to establish weekly Sacred Harp singings in Warsaw and Poznan. This growing group of singers collaborated with Alabama Sacred Harp singer and Camp Fasola cofounder David Ivey to arrange for a northern Poland location for a 2012 session of the annual singing school. Ivey organized the first session of the then nine-year-old singing school held outside Alabama in response to the growing interest in the style across the continent.[48]

Sacred Harp singing first reached Poland framed as "Early Music" rather than "folk music." Yet the possibility of this characterization also owes a great deal to the framing George Pullen Jackson introduced. Depicting Sacred Harp as "America's earliest music" was key to Jackson's hopes for inspiring a new national culture rooted in American Anglo-Celtic folk tradition. Singers and folklorists alike have championed Sacred Harp's antiquity in describing and promoting the style across the twentieth century. The rationale for including a contemporary music culture practiced across the United States and England in the Jarosław Early Music Festival, an event primarily featuring the music of seventeenth-century and earlier European music, relies on the folklorization of the style.[49]

Just as European and American singers helped establish Sacred Harp singings in England, Ireland, Germany, and Poland, traveling singers have contributed to the expansion of Sacred Harp singing across Europe and beyond since 2008. An Alabamian stationed in South Korea and a Cork singer there teaching English established shortly lived singings in South Korea in 2012.[50] Two Australians, Shawn Whelan and Natalie Sims, brought Sacred Harp to their country after encountering the style while Sims was completing a postdoctoral fellowship at a New England educational institution in 1998. Plans to hold an all-day singing came together in 2012, after Belfast singer Eimear Craddock, who first sang Sacred Harp in Cork, moved to Sydney.[51] Sacred Harp singing briefly flourished in Hong Kong after American singer Aaron Kahn, who had begun singing Sacred Harp stateside and briefly ran a singing in Paris, moved to the area. Tim Cook, long active in Sacred Harp and

Christian Harmony singing in Alabama, established the first singing in Japan in 2015 with Peter Evan shortly after moving to the country. Israel's Sacred Harp singing was founded by Israeli musician Ophir Ilzewski, who came across the style by chance in Norwich, England, and honed his skills at the fall 2014 second European session of Camp Fasola. As English, Irish, Polish, and American singers moved internationally, they crossed paths with individuals and small groups who first experienced Sacred Harp independently, connecting these singers to an emerging international network of singers and urging the adoption of practices associated with folksong, its revival, and the filters of its scholarly genealogies.

NATIONALISMS

The places that encompass the contemporary landscape of Sacred Harp singing feature dramatically different social and political contexts, but all are political allies of the United States where American popular culture has a large imprint. Sacred Harp singing operates subculturally, affecting the lives of small numbers of singers in each city or region. The massive commercial enterprises and political and economic ties that encourage adoption of American culture thus have little direct impact on Sacred Harp singing.[52] Despite its absence from popular awareness in the countries where singings are held, Sacred Harp's international reception refracts political and cultural relationships with the United States and its folksong. Each country's political allegiance with the United States makes possible the reciprocal travel that strengthens emerging singings, and the largely favorable conceptions of American culture form a background context in which Sacred Harp's "Americanness" does not seriously detract from and may even contribute to the singing's attraction and positive reception.

In England, perceived historical ties between Sacred Harp and English West Gallery singing intrigue a number of singers, particularly those from England and New England who were active during the period when Sacred Harp singings were initially established in the United Kingdom. Some English Sacred Harp singers are deeply involved in an English revival of West Gallery music. *The Northern Harmony* tunebook adopted alongside *The Sacred Harp* at early English singings gained popularity in part because it features arrangements of West Gallery tunes, their inclusion signifying to some an acknowledgment of a connection between the English and American practices. Relatedly, several early English Sacred Harp singers preferred New England fuging tunes to other songs in *The Sacred Harp*, drawing on the genre's historical relationship to the West Gallery repertoire. One English singer, Chris Brown, has examined music manuscripts to trace the migration of tunes from the United States to the United Kingdom around 1800, shedding light on a historical transatlantic exchange that parallels Sacred Harp's spread to the United Kingdom in the late twentieth and early twenty-first centuries.[53] He has also presented on the English roots of Sacred Harp singing, focusing not on the book's predominantly American tune writers but on its hymn writers, who are predominantly English.[54]

In Poland, a post–Cold War embrace of American and European cultural, economic, and political models introduces a narrative in which Sacred Harp's presence represents values identified with the United States, such as freedom of expression, as well as the allegiance between the two countries.[55] The location of the first two European sessions of Camp Fasola in Kashubia, a region in the country's north that is now expressing renewed celebration and revival of local cultural practices as well as ethnic folk traditions, facilitates a logic of cultural exchange with the West as a context for engaging with the presence of Sacred Harp singing in the area. In the fall of 2014, with Russia newly embroiled in conflict with Ukraine, tour guides for an American group visiting to participate in Sacred Harp singing placed the current conflict along the Russia-Ukraine border in the context of a centuries-long history of military and political domination of Poland by German and Russian forces. Their geopolitical narrative implicitly conscripted American tourists as Polish allies.[56] David Ivey, the camp director, articulated a similar cultural allegiance at the first Camp Fasola Europe in 2012. During a performance by a Kashubian folk music and dance troupe that emphasized the group's ability to celebrate Kashubian cultural heritage thanks to the absence of Soviet domination, Ivey stated that he never could have imagined Sacred Harp in Poland before the fall of the Iron Curtain.[57] Both Polish and American participants in the evening's cultural exchange pointed to its ability to celebrate and reiterate political ties between the two countries.

I offer these two examples of Sacred Harp's embeddedness in national political and cultural relationships with the United States to suggest that understanding folklorization's impact on the style's internationalization requires negotiating America's outsize presence and the effects of that presence on subcultural sound. Different national contexts, as well as the varied positions individual singers and their identity categories occupy with respect to these contexts, affect what Sacred Harp singing means to participants.[58] Understandings of Sacred Harp singing's practices as democratic and pluralistic also reveal the embeddedness of folksong-inspired rhetoric in geopolitically bounded Western political and cultural values. As Lueck notes, even the transportability of Sacred Harp's features "relies on the freedom of participants to create their own spaces of identity, and the freedom to pursue their affinity."[59] Further research might shed light on the ramifications of America's geopolitical alliances and cultural exports on musical subcultures abroad.

TRAVELING ON

As Sacred Harp singing continues to spread across the globe, the style can seem increasingly unmoored from the nostalgic, elegiac discourse that painted Sacred Harp singing as the dying art of an isolated "lost tonal tribe."[60] But the roots of this current transformation extend back to the style's passage through folklore's filter and to the networks of scholars and singers that flourished in its wake. Folklorization made the style's expansion beyond its southern and national boundaries possible and indelibly affected the form and direction of its growth.

Much ethnographic, theoretical, and archival work remains to be done to describe the social contexts in which Sacred Harp singing's ongoing geographical and demographic shifts are taking place. It is important to think about how scholars' characterization of the style as a folk music, and some singers' depiction of it as a venerable practice rooted in the antebellum Southern United States, may continue to affect the contours of its spread. It is equally necessary to ask how the style's association with America affects its reception in countries with varied political and cultural relationships with the United States. Even as many new singers emphasize the transcultural ability of Sacred Harp singings to serve as meaningful cathartic gatherings conducive to community formation, more research might shed light on how singers with different backgrounds in different parts of the globe respond to the style's practices. As Sacred Harp, now ascendant, travels to new corners of the globe, it is important to be mindful of who and where it does reach, and who and where it does not.

NOTES

1. George Pullen Jackson, *White Spirituals in the Southern Uplands: The Story of the Fasola Folk, Their Songs, Singings, and "Buckwheat Notes"* (Chapel Hill: University of North Carolina Press, 1933); George Pullen Jackson, *The Story of The Sacred Harp, 1844–1944: A Book of Religious Folk Song as an American Institution* (Nashville, TN: Vanderbilt University Press, 1944); Buell E. Cobb, *The Sacred Harp: A Tradition and Its Music* (Athens: University of Georgia Press, 1989).

2. Mark Slobin, *Subcultural Sounds: Micromusics of the West* (Wesleyan University Press, 1993).

3. Ellen Lueck, "Sacred Harp Singing in Europe: Its Pathways, Spaces, and Meanings" (PhD dissertation, Wesleyan University, 2016), vii.

4. Jesse P. Karlsberg, "Folklore's Filter: Race, Place, and Sacred Harp Singing" (PhD dissertation, Emory University, 2015).

5. On the roots and early history of Sacred Harp singing, see David Warren Steel, *The Makers of the Sacred Harp* (Urbana: University of Illinois Press, 2010); Cobb, *The Sacred Harp*.

6. On segregation's impact on Black participation in Sacred Harp singing, see Joe Dan Boyd, *Judge Jackson and the Colored Sacred Harp* (Montgomery, AL: Alabama Folklife Association, 2002); Donald R. Ross, "Black Sacred Harp Singing in East Texas," *Away Here in Texas*, June 1995, http://historical.texasfasola.org/blacksacredharp.html; Doris Jane Dyen, "The Role of Shape-Note Singing in the Musical Culture of Black Communities in Southeast Alabama" (PhD dissertation, University of Illinois at Urbana–Champaign, 1977); Jesse P. Karlsberg, "Folklore's Filter: Race, Place, and Sacred Harp Singing" (PhD dissertation, Emory University, 2015), 127–80, https://etd.library.emory.edu/concern/etds/n009w256n?locale=en.

7. Gavin James Campbell, "'Old Can Be Used Instead of New': Shape-Note Singing and the Crisis of Modernity in the New South, 1880–1920," *Journal of American Folklore* 110, no. 436 (April 1, 1997): 169–88; Karlsberg, "Folklore's Filter," 25–74.

8. Jesse P. Karlsberg, "Joseph Stephen James's *Original Sacred Harp:* Introduction to the *Centennial Edition*," in *Original Sacred Harp: Centennial Edition*, ed. Joseph Stephen James and Jesse P. Karlsberg, Emory Texts and Studies in Ecclesial Life 8 (Atlanta, GA: Pitts Theology Library, 2015), v–xvi; Duncan Vinson, "'As Far from Secular, Operatic, Rag-Time, and Jig Melodies as Is Possible': Religion and the Resurgence of Interest in the *Sacred Harp*, 1895–1911," *Journal of American Folklore* 119, no. 474 (October 1, 2006): 413–43.

9. Barbara Kirshenblatt-Gimblett, "Folklore's Crisis," *The Journal of American Folklore* 111, no. 441 (July 1, 1998): 281–327, doi:10.2307/541312.

10. David E. Whisnant, "Turning Inward and Outward: Retrospective and Prospective Considerations in the Recording of Vernacular Music in the South," in *Sounds of the South*, ed. Daniel W. Patterson (Chapel Hill: Southern Folklife Collection, Manuscripts Department, Wilson Library, University of North Carolina, 1991), 165–81.

11. Kirshenblatt-Gimblett, "Folklore's Crisis"; David E. Whisnant, *All That Is Native and Fine: The Politics of Culture in an American Region* (Chapel Hill: University of North Carolina Press, 1995); Benjamin Filene, *Romancing the Folk: Public Memory and American Roots Music* (Chapel Hill: University of North Carolina Press, 2000); Karl Hagstrom Miller, *Segregating Sound: Inventing Folk and Pop Music in the Age of Jim Crow* (Durham, NC: Duke University Press, 2010).

12. George Pullen Jackson, "Some Enemies of Folk-Music in America," in *Papers Read at the International Congress of Musicology Held at New York, September 11th to 16th, 1939* (New York: American Musicological Society, 1939), 77–83.

13. George Pullen Jackson, "The Fa-Sol-La Folk," *Musical Courier* 93, no. 11 (September 9, 1926): 6–7, 10.

14. On Jackson's designation of Sacred Harp as an American folk music, see also John Bealle, *Public Worship, Private Faith: Sacred Harp and American Folksong* (Athens: University of Georgia Press, 1997); Karlsberg, "Folklore's Filter."

15. Jackson makes this argument in George Pullen Jackson, "The Genesis of the Negro Spiritual," *American Mercury* 26 (June 1932): 243–55; Jackson, *White Spirituals in the Southern Uplands*; George Pullen Jackson, *White and Negro Spirituals: Their Life Span and Kinship, Tracing 200 Years of Untrammeled Song Making and Singing among Our Country Folk, with 116 Songs As Sung by Both Races* (New York: J. J. Augustin, 1943). Research debunking Jackson's claim includes William H. Tallmadge, "The Black in Jackson's White Spirituals," *The Black Perspective in Music* 9, no. 2 (October 1, 1981): 139–60, doi:10.2307/1214194; Dena J. Epstein, "A White Origin for the Black Spiritual? An Invalid Theory and How It Grew," *American Music* 1, no. 2 (July 1, 1983): 53–59, doi:10.2307/3051499.

16. Jackson himself did not hold such beliefs, and indeed argued that Black imitation of white practices was evidence of African Americans' equal abilities.

17. W. E. B. Du Bois, *The Souls of Black Folk: Essays and Sketches* (Chicago: A. C. McClurg, 1903), chap. 14.

18. John W. Work, Lewis Wade Jones, and Samuel C. Adams, *Lost Delta Found: Rediscovering the Fisk University–Library of Congress Coahoma County Study, 1941–1942*, ed. Robert Gordon and Bruce Nemerov (Nashville, TN: Vanderbilt University Press, 2005), 1–26; Nathan Frazier et al., *John Work III: Recording Black Culture* (Woodbury, TN: Spring Fed Records, 2008), Compact Disc; Karlsberg, "Folklore's Filter," 127–80.

19. John W. Work, "Plantation Meistersinger," *The Musical Quarterly* 27, no. 1 (January 1, 1941): 97–106.

20. Murray Lerner, *Festival!* (New York: Eagle Rock Entertainment, 2005); George Wein and Nate Chinen, *Myself Among Others: A Life in Music* (Boston: Da Capo Press, 2009).

21. Karlsberg, "Folklore's Filter," 181–264.

22. Dan Kane, "Archaic Sounds of Shape-Note Singing Resound in Raleigh," *News Observer*, March 22, 2015, https://www.newsobserver.com/news/local/counties/wake-county/article16035965.html.

23. Ted Johnson, email message to author, June 23, 2012; Steven Sabol, email message to author, February 4, 2016.

24. Sacred Harp Singers, *Festival Recordings, 1970: Wade and Fields Ward with Kahle Brewer; Sacred Harp Singers*, CD transfer, 1970, fp-1970-rr-0039, Smithsonian Center for Folklife and Cultural Heritage.

25. David Warren Steel, "Ann Arbor singings, was, Minutes and Question," Fasola Singings list, April 1, 2015. Pioneering University of Michigan musicology dissertations concerning early American psalmody include Allen Perdue Britton, "Theoretical Introductions in American Tune-Books to 1800" (PhD dissertation, University of Michigan, 1950); Richard Crawford, "Andrew Law (1749–1821): The Career of an American Musician" (PhD dissertation, University of Michigan, 1965).

26. Steel, "Ann Arbor singings."

27. On the geographical contours of this spread, see Jesse P. Karlsberg and Robert A. W. Dunn, "Mapping the 'Big Minutes': Visualizing Sacred Harp's Geographic Coalescence and Expansion, 1995–2014," *Southern Spaces Blog*, January 23, 2018, https://southernspaces.org/2017/mapping-big-minutes-visualizing-sacred-harps-geographic-coalescence-and-expansion-1995-2014/.

28. Kiri Miller, *Traveling Home: Sacred Harp Singing and American Pluralism* (Urbana: University of Illinois Press, 2008).

29. Miller, *Traveling Home*.

30. Lueck, "Sacred Harp Singing in Europe," 46.

31. Robert T. Kelley, "Harmonious Union: How Sacred Harp Brings People Together," *The Sacred Harp Publishing Company Newsletter* 2, no. 1 (March 14, 2013), http://originalsacredharp.com/2013/03/14/harmonious-union-how-sacred-harp-brings-people-together/.

32. Ellen Lueck, "The Old World Seeks the Old Paths: Observing Our Transnationally Expanding Singing Community," *Sacred Harp Publishing Company Newsletter* 3, no. 2 (November 12, 2014), http://originalsacredharp.com/2014/11/12/the-old-world-seeks-the-old-paths-observing-our-transnationally-expanding-singing-community/. These tropes, of seemingly unbridgeable differences and of the Sacred Harp network's status as a "family," implying greater closeness even than "community," frequently emerge in memorial lessons, in officers' remarks at the end of a day of singing, and in private conversations on car rides to and from singings and at social gatherings among singers.

33. Several English performing ensembles had recorded Sacred Harp songs prior to the Northern Harmony tour. Gordon's presence brought together several English singers interested in Sacred Harp thanks to these earlier performances and introduced additional key early organizers of English Sacred Harp singing to the style. Steve Fletcher, "Two Decades of Shape-Note Singing in the UK: A Personal Perspective" (Presentation, Sing Oxted, Oxted, United Kingdom, November 15, 2014). On Gordon's particularly influential 1994 tour of the United Kingdom, see also Lueck, "Sacred Harp Singing in Europe," 95–97.

34. Anthony G. Barrand, Larry Gordon, and Carole Moody Crompton, *Northern Harmony: Plain Tunes, Fuging Tunes, and Anthems from the New England Singing School Tradition* (Plainfield, VT: Northern Harmony Publishing Company, 1990).

35. Fletcher, "Two Decades of Shape-Note Singing in the UK."

36. "Calendar 2018," United Kingdom Sacred Harp and Shapenote Singing, accessed February 1, 2018, http://www.ukshapenote.org.uk/calendar/calendar.html.

37. Jesse P. Karlsberg, "Ireland's First Sacred Harp Convention: 'To Meet to Part No More,'" *Southern Spaces*, November 30, 2011, https://southernspaces.org/2011/irelands-first-sacred-harp-convention-meet-part-no-more/. On the establishment of Sacred Harp in Ireland and the first Ireland convention, see also Robert Wedgbury, "Exploring Voice, Fellowship, and Tradition: The Institutionalised Development of American Sacred Harp Singing in Cork, Ireland and the Emergence of a Grassroots Singing Community" (MA thesis, University College Cork, 2011); Alice Maggio, "Regional Report: First Ireland Sacred Harp Convention," *The Trumpet* 1, no. 2 (2011): vi; Lueck, "Sacred Harp Singing in Europe," 119–29.

38. Jonathon Smith, "Celtic Imaginaries: *The Sacred Harp*, Ireland, and the American South" (paper presentation, International Council for Traditional Music, Limerick, Ireland, July 17, 2017).

39. Jackson, *White Spirituals in the Southern Uplands*, 158–59. Jackson drew both population data about and support for his veneration of the group he identified as whites of the Southern Uplands from John C. Campbell, *The Southern Highlander and His Homeland* (New York: Russell Sage Foundation, 1921).

40. Karlsberg, "Ireland's First Sacred Harp Convention"; Smith, "Celtic Imaginaries."

41. Jesse P. Karlsberg, "New Writing on Sacred Harp in Europe," JPKarlsberg.com, March 14, 2013, http://jpkarlsberg.com/2013/03/14/new-writing-on-sacred-harp-in-europe/; Michael Walker, "German Singing Schools: Sacred Harp Comes to the Land of J. S. Bach," *The Sacred Harp Publishing Company Newsletter* 1, no. 1 (March 28, 2012), http://originalsacredharp.com/2012/03/28/german-singing-schools/.

42. Harald Grundner, "Wie Alles Begann," Sacred Harp Bremen, accessed August 24, 2015, http://www.sacredharpbremen.org/ueber-uns/persoenliches/harald/wie-alles-begann.

43. Walker, "German Singing Schools."

44. Jesse P. Karlsberg, "Regional Roots: Growing Sacred Harp in the Netherlands, Alaska, and British Columbia," *Sacred Harp Publishing Company Newsletter* 4, no. 2 (December 31, 2015), http://originalsacredharp.com/2015/12/31/regional-roots/.

45. Walker, "German Singing Schools."

46. Eriksen's Polish wife and manager Magdalena Zapendowska-Eriksen arranged for the workshop. I served as Eriksen's assistant. Then an English professor, Zapendowska-Eriksen had learned of Sacred Harp singing in 2003 through studying English hymnist Isaac Watts and first attended singings when visiting western Massachusetts in the United States to conduct research on Emily Dickinson in 2005. She began hosting a regular gathering to practice Sacred Harp songs at her home in 2006. A video recording of the singing that marked the conclusion of the singing school is at Timothy Eriksen, "Sacred Harp Singing in Jarosław, Poland," YouTube video (Jarosław, Poland, 2008), https://www.youtube.com/watch?v=-NkG7vm50Ns.

47. Lomax first encountered Sacred Harp singers during a 1942 recording session in Birmingham, Alabama, in collaboration with George Pullen Jackson.

48. Jesse P. Karlsberg, "'Come Sound His Praise Abroad': Sacred Harp Singing across Europe," *Country Dance and Song Society News* (Winter 2012): 9–12; Jesse P. Karlsberg, "Sacred Harp, 'Poland Style,'" *Southern Spaces Blog*, February 27, 2013, https://southernspaces.org/2013/sacred-harp-poland-style/; Gosia Perycz, "A Hollow Square in My Homeland: Bringing Camp Fasola to Poland," *Sacred Harp Publishing Company Newsletter* 2, no. 1 (March 14, 2013), http://originalsacredharp.com/2013/03/14/a-hollow-square-in-my-homeland-bringing-camp-fasola-to-poland/; Fynn Titford-Mock, "Celebrating Sacred Harp in Europe, September, 2012," *Sacred Harp Publishing Company Newsletter* 2, no. 1 (March 14, 2013), http://originalsacredharp.com/2013/03/14/celebrating-sacred-harp-singing-in-

europe-september-2012/. On Sacred Harp's arrival in Poland, see also Lueck, "Sacred Harp Singing in Europe," 108–19.

49. Jesse P. Karlsberg, "Resonance and Reinvention: Sounding Historical Practice in Sacred Harp's Global Twenty-First Century" (paper presentation, Stichting voor Muziekhistorische Uitvoeringspraktijk [Foundation for Historical Musical Performance Practice], Utrecht, Netherlands, August 29, 2015).

50. Brian Sears, email message to author, June 26, 2013; Brian Sears, "Sacred Harp in Korea!" Fasola Singings list, July 16, 2014.

51. Steven Levine, "Sacred Harp Down-Under: The First Australian All-Day Singing," *Sacred Harp Publishing Company Newsletter* 2, no. 1 (March 14, 2013), http://originalsacredharp.com/2013/03/14/sacred-harp-down-under-the-first-australian-all-day-singing/.

52. An important exception is the 2003 Hollywood film *Cold Mountain*, which featured two Sacred Harp songs. The film generated considerable publicity for Sacred Harp singing and attracted many new singers to the style. See Jesse P. Karlsberg, Mark T. Godfrey, and Nathan Rees, "The *Cold Mountain* Bump: Hollywood's Effect on Sacred Harp Songs and Singers," *Sacred Harp Publishing Company Newsletter* 2, no. 3 (December 31, 2013), http://originalsacredharp.com/2013/12/31/the-cold-mountain-bump/. In my fieldwork in Europe I have encountered several singers who trace their introduction to Sacred Harp singing to the film.

53. Chris Brown, "American Tunes in West Gallery Sources," *Sacred Harp Publishing Company Newsletter* 3, no. 2 (November 12, 2014), http://originalsacredharp.com/2014/11/12/american-tunes-in-west-gallery-sources/.

54. Chris Brown has taught classes on English hymn writers at sessions of Camp Fasola held in Poland and in Alabama in the United States.

55. See Derek E. Mix, "Poland and Its Relations with the United States: In Brief" (Washington, DC: Congressional Research Service, November 17, 2015), https://fas.org/sgp/crs/row/R44212.pdf.

56. I traveled as a member of the American tour group thanks to support from the Sacred Harp Musical Heritage Association and Emory University's Laney Graduate School's professional development support funds. On the September 2014 American Sacred Harp trip to Europe, see also Kathy Williams, "A Long Time Traveling: A Sacred Harp Tour to the UK Convention, Camp Fasola Europe, and the Poland Convention," *Sacred Harp Publishing Company Newsletter* 4, no. 1 (May 28, 2015), http://originalsacredharp.com/2015/05/28/a-long-time-traveling-a-sacred-harp-tour-to-the-uk-convention-camp-fasola-europe-and-the-poland-convention/.

57. Karlsberg, "Sacred Harp Singing across Europe."

58. Lueck notes that although singers celebrate the national diversity of major singings "as a sign of community growth and cooperation," actually expressing national identity can garner a mixed reception, as when singers "explicitly reference historical anti-British sentiments" through leading one of the handful of American patriotic songs in *The Sacred Harp*. See Lueck, "Sacred Harp Singing in Europe," 188, 190–91.

59. Ibid., 278.

60. Jackson, "The Fa-Sol-La Folk," 6.

FURTHER READING

Bealle, John. *Public Worship, Private Faith: Sacred Harp and American Folksong*. Athens: University of Georgia Press, 1997.

Bidgood, Lee. *Czech Bluegrass: Notes from the Heart of Europe*. Champaign: University of Illinois Press, 2017.

Cobb, Buell E. *The Sacred Harp: A Tradition and Its Music*. Athens: University of Georgia Press, 1989 [1978].

Filene, Benjamin. *Romancing the Folk: Public Memory and American Roots Music*. Chapel Hill: University of North Carolina Press, 2000.

Karlsberg, Jesse P. "Folklore's Filter: Race, Place, and Sacred Harp Singing." PhD dissertation, Emory University 2015. https://etd.library.emory.edu/concern/etds/n009w256n?locale=en.

Kirshenblatt-Gimblett, Barbara. "Folklore's Crisis." *The Journal of American Folklore* 111, no. 441 (July 1, 1998): 281–327. https://doi.org/10.2307/541312.

Laušević, Mirjana. *Balkan Fascination: Creating an Alternative Music Culture in America*. Oxford: Oxford University Press, 2007.

Lueck, Ellen. "Sacred Harp Singing in Europe: Its Pathways, Spaces, and Meanings." PhD dissertation, Wesleyan University, 2016.

Miller, Karl Hagstrom. *Segregating Sound: Inventing Folk and Pop Music in the Age of Jim Crow*. Durham, NC: Duke University Press, 2010.

Miller, Kiri. *Traveling Home: Sacred Harp Singing and American Pluralism*. Urbana: University of Illinois Press, 2008.

Slobin, Mark. *Subcultural Sounds: Micromusics of the West*. Middletown, CT: Wesleyan University Press, 1993.

Steel, David Warren. *The Makers of the Sacred Harp*. Urbana: University of Illinois Press, 2010.

Whisnant, David E. *All That Is Native and Fine: The Politics of Culture in an American Region*. Chapel Hill: University of North Carolina Press, 1995.

Chapter Eleven

Anglican Church Music in the United States

Tracing the Diaspora of English Traditions from the Eighteenth to the Twenty-First Century

Matthew Hoch

At the time of its founding in 1789 as the Protestant Episcopal Church in America, there was little distinction between the liturgy of the Episcopal Church and that of the Church of England. As a result, over the course of the next two centuries, many sacred English musical traditions endured, and Anglican repertoire can still be heard in many Episcopal churches throughout the United States, particularly in historic churches in the urban Northeast. In the past several decades, however, newer traditions have emerged that offer a distinctly American Anglicanism that merges the traditional liturgies of the Book of Common Prayer with the alternative sounds found in the New World. This essay examines the gradual Americanization of English church music over the course of the past two and a half centuries within the Episcopal Church while discussing distinctive new genres and liturgies that have established themselves alongside traditional ones. Select parishes are profiled that offer distinctly modern musical services while remaining true to Anglican liturgies.[1]

THE FOUNDATION: SACRED MUSIC IN THE ANGLICAN TRADITION

In order to fully understand the origins of Episcopal Church music, a rudimentary grounding in English church music is essential. Beginning with Henry VIII's split from the Catholic Church in 1534 via the Act of Supremacy, the newly established Church of England soon developed its own English-language liturgical traditions with the Book of Common Prayer. Anglican composers began writing vernacular settings of anthems, canticles for Morning and Evening Prayer, and Anglican chant psalm formulas, along with other genres essential to the liturgy. Distinct musical traditions developed in cathedrals and smaller parishes. Although a thorough history of English church music falls outside the confines of this essay, there are fortunately many resources available to explore this fascinating repertoire.[2]

THE NORTH AMERICAN EPISCOPAL CHURCH: ENGLISH TRADITIONS AND NEW DIRECTIONS

The Episcopal Church in North America can trace its roots to 1607 with the founding of the Jamestown colony in Virginia.[3] Robert Hunt (1568–1608) celebrated the first known Eucharist in the New World. In 1624, Virginia became a royal colony and was required to conform to the Church of England, including weekly prayers for the king. In 1701, Thomas Bray (1658–1730) founded the Society for the Propagation of the Gospel in Maryland, sparking the growth and spread of the Church of England throughout the colonies. In 1776, the Declaration of Independence was signed in Philadelphia, prompting the defection of many Anglican priests to England and Canada. The Revolutionary War officially ended in 1783 with the signing of the Treaty of Paris, and Samuel Seabury (1729–1796) was consecrated by the Episcopal Church of Scotland as the first American bishop in 1784. The Protestant Episcopal Church was founded in 1789, and the first American Book of Common Prayer (a revision of the 1662 prayer book) was published in the same year.

While the written liturgy of the Church of England was somewhat easy to adapt, replicating the music was another matter. One of the biggest challenges that presented itself to the early Episcopal Church musicians was the sheer lack of organs in the New World. With the exception of some unaccompanied choral works, mostly from the Tudor era, the organ was the instrument upon which all English liturgical music was based. There were several reasons for this shortage of organs. When the Episcopal Church was first established, there were few organ builders in America; organs had to be shipped from Europe, which made them cost prohibitive for most parishes. In fact, before 1800, there were fewer than twenty organs in New England.[4] Perhaps an even greater challenge, however, was that even if a parish was blessed with an organ, there would be no one available to play it, as there was little opportunity for organ training on the western side of the pond. This problem would remedy itself by the mid-nineteenth century.[5]

Thus, throughout most of its history, the music of the Episcopal Church was remarkably similar to the music of the Church of England. American choirmasters and organists largely performed the same repertoire by the same composers. From the Episcopal Church's earliest days, however, hymnody was emphasized to a greater extent due to an American prioritization of congregational singing. In 1919, the Joint Commission on Church Music was formed, the deliberations of which resulted in the publication of *The Hymnal 1940*. This hymnal was conceived to be used in tandem with the 1928 revision of the Book of Common Prayer. Half a century later, after the publication of the 1979 Book of Common Prayer, the hymnal was revised once again, resulting in the publication of *The Hymnal 1982* three years later. This hymnal, more than any of its predecessors, emphasizes the importance of congregational singing and expands the musical liturgy beyond its Anglican roots. Thus the initial impetus for a distinctly "American" musical tradition within the Episcopal Church came through its expanding hymnody.[6]

MULTICULTURALISM IN *THE HYMNAL 1982*

While *The Hymnal 1940* was a landmark achievement, the creators of *The Hymnal 1982* made a conscious effort to be significantly more culturally inclusive in their hymn selections. The final collection included eight songs from African American culture, four from the Judaic tradition, two from Hispanic cultures, two work songs from Africa, two folk songs from China, a Native American folk song, a French folk tune, and an Eastern Orthodox Slavonic chant. These multicultural additions to *The Hymnal 1982* are as follows:

African American Spirituals (6):
Hymn 99: "Go, Tell It on the Mountain" (GO TELL IT ON THE MOUNTAIN)
Hymn 172: "Were You There When They Crucified My Lord?" (WERE YOU THERE)
Hymn 325: "Let Us Break Bread Together on Our Knees" (LET US BREAK BREAD)
Hymn 468: "It Was Poor Little Jesus" (POOR LITTLE JESUS)
Hymn 648: "When Israel Was in Egypt's Land" (GO DOWN, MOSES)
Hymn 676: "There Is a Balm in Gilead" (BALM IN GILEAD)

Hymn Based on a Spiritual Tune (1):
Hymn 529: "In Christ There Is No East or West" (MCKEE)

Song of Inspiration (1):
Hymn 599: "Lift Every Voice and Sing" (LIFT EVERY VOICE)

Ghanaian Work Songs (2):
  Hymn 602: "Jesu, Jesu, Fill Us with Your Love" (CHEREPONI)
  Hymn 611: "Christ the Worker" (AFRICAN WORK SONG)

Communion Hymns Based on Chinese Tunes (2):
  Hymn 340: "For the Bread Which You Have Broken" (BENG-LI)
  Hymn 342: "O Bread of Life, for Sinners Broken" (SHENG EN)

Hymns Based on Native American Tunes (1):
  Hymn 385: "Many and Great, O God Are Thy Works" (DAKOTA INDIAN CHANT)

Native American Hymn Based to a French Folk Melody (1):
  Hymn 114: "'Twas in the Moon of Wintertime" (UNE JEUNE PUCELLE)

Hispanic Hymn (1):
  Hymn 113: "Duérmete, Niño Lindo" (À LA RU)

Hymn Based on Hispanic Tune (1):
  Hymn 277: "Sing of Mary, Pure and Lowly" (RAQUEL)

Judaic Hymns (4):
  Hymn 393: "Praise Our Great and Gracious Lord" (MOAZ ZUR)
  Hymn 425: "Sing Now with Joy unto the Lord" (ADON OLAM)
  Hymn 536: "God Has Spoken to His People" (TORAH SONG)
  Hymn 714: "Shalom Chavarim" (SHALOM CHAVARIM)

Eastern Orthodox Slavonic Chant (1):
  Hymn 355: "Give Rest, O Christ, to Your Servants with Your Saints" (KONTAKION)[7]

This multiculturalism, while modest in the year 2020, marked a major step forward from the Episcopal Church's previous hymnal (*The Hymnal 1940*). Nevertheless, it soon became apparent to the hymnal revision committee that additional supplements were needed to meet the needs of worshippers.

SUPPLEMENTS TO *THE HYMNAL 1982*

The Hymnal 1982 comprises 720 hymns and 449 settings of service music.[8] Nevertheless, the hymnal's one-volume size meant that there were certain limitations. In the decades following the publication of the hymnal, the

Episcopal Church released five additional volumes that were meant to be official companions of and supplements to *The Hymnal 1982*. Each of these collections revolved around a particular theme and efforts to expand and modernize the liturgy, as well as to address needs not adequately covered by *The Hymnal 1982*.

These supplemental volumes include *Lift Every Voice and Sing II* (1993), *Wonder, Love, and Praise* (1997), *El Himnario* (2001), *Voices Found* (2003), and *My Heart Sings Out* (2004). All are still in print and recognized as official hymnals of the Episcopal Church. Like *The Hymnal 1982*, all of these books are intended for use in liturgical worship. Therefore, like the hymnal, the musical contents are categorized thematically and according to the church year so that so that hymns can be appropriately selected for use in worship.

Lift Every Voice and Sing II (1993)

This is a collection of 280 pieces from African American and gospel traditions. The "II" in the title indicates that it is a sequel. It was preceded by a volume that was actually released before *The Hymnal 1982* titled *Lift Every Voice and Sing: A Collection of Afro-American Spirituals and Other Songs* (1981). The original volume, although out of print, is commonly referred to as *Lift Every Voice and Sing I.*

Lift Every Voice and Sing II was compiled under the supervision of the Office of Black Ministries of the Episcopal Church. The creators were inspired by similar volumes in other denominations, most significantly the Methodist *Songs of Zion* (1981) and the Roman Catholic *Lead Me, Guide Me* (1987). It includes African American spirituals, traditional and contemporary gospel songs, adapted protestant hymns, missionary and evangelistic hymns, and service music in alternative settings. With the exception of the title hymn ("Lift Every Voice and Sing"), *Lift Every Voice and Sing II* is an entirely new collection and avoids hymns that were already included in *The Hymnal 1982*.

Wonder, Love, and Praise (1997)

Beginning with Hymn No. 721, *Wonder, Love, and Praise* was conceived as an official addition to *The Hymnal 1982*. In fact, it is subtitled *A Supplement to The Hymnal 1982*. The General Convention passed a resolution in 1994 that stated:

> [Be it] resolved ... that the Standing Commission on Church Music be directed to continue preparing supplements to *The Hymnal 1982* that provide this Church with additional service music, inclusive language hymnody, additional texts in languages other than English, including texts printed in more than one language,

additional hymnody related to the lectionary and rites of the Book of Common Prayer, and texts and tunes written since the compiling of the present Hymnal.[9]

When compiling *Wonder, Love, and Praise*, the editorial committee followed three guiding principles: first, to prepare a resource that added to *The Hymnal 1982*; second, to strive for a musical simplicity that encourages immediate participation; and third, to offer a breadth of musical styles from many cultures. The result was an eclectic variety of 114 hymns and spiritual songs (Hymns 721–834) and seventy-two new pieces of service music (Hymns 835–906).[10] The service music section is particularly interesting, containing twenty-nine new canticle settings including six settings of the Gloria in Excelsis and two settings of the Te Deum. In addition, there are twenty-nine selections of devotional music that include table graces, rounds, acclamations, and selections from the Taizé community. The volume is permeated by congregational philosophy of music making:

> The church has entered a new frontier of inclusive hospitality, not only in welcoming all to the table, but also in providing rites, forms, and music which encourage the sharing of one's cultural story to foster the unity proclaimed in the gospel. This supplement honors that pilgrimage and affirms "the participation of all in the Body of Christ the Church, while recognizing our diverse natures as children of God."[11]

El Himnario (1998)

El Himnario is an ecumenical hymnal for Hispanic parishes. The Episcopal Church and several other mainline denominations sponsored this volume. In 2001, *El Himnario: Selecciones* was released. This collection is an inexpensive, words-only edition of favorite hymns and songs from the original *El Himnario* alongside translations of other hymns familiar to Hispanic congregations. In recent years, the Episcopal Church had prioritized making inroads into the Hispanic communities of the United States, and Spanish-language services are a big part of that effort. The Episcopal seminary at Sewanee: The University of the South offers several Spanish-language Eucharists each week, and seminarians are trained to deliver the Book of Common Prayer in Spanish as well as English.

Voices Found (2003)

Subtitled *Women in the Church's Song*, *Voices Found* is "a rich collection of hymns and spiritual songs by, for, and about women."[12] Most of the music is written in a congregational style and is intended for normal parish use. While some of the selections are written in traditional four-part harmony, many are in unison or two parts, making them especially appropriate to be sung entirely by women. According to the preface,

> *Voices Found: Women in the Church's Song* is a unique compilation of contemporary and historical materials that crosses boundaries of geography, time, and culture as it represents the diversity of the gifts of women and seeks to affirm and expand the spirituality of all women and men as they find new voices in the church's song.[13]

My Heart Sings Out (2004)

My Heart Sings Out is a hymnal designed for inclusive worship for people of all ages. Its specific goal is the full inclusion of younger children in weekly worship. It is organized into two main sections—the Eucharistic liturgy and the church year—with additional thematic sections, including songs for baptism and confirmation, songs of thanks and praise, and songs of suffering, healing, and assurance. The melodies are age appropriate, and the selections offer opportunities for adults to sing their parts in harmony, joining alongside the children's voices.

These resources collectively present a wide range of options for twenty-first century Episcopal worship, allowing individual churches to make decisions on what kind of music (and texts) they wish to prioritize in worship. When one attends an Episcopal Church service, it is not unusual to see one or more of these supplements in the pews alongside the Book of Common Prayer and *The Hymnal 1982*.

WHEN WILL THE EPISCOPAL CHURCH ADOPT A NEW HYMNAL?

Bearing the year of its conception in its title, *The Hymnal 1982* clearly dates itself. Almost forty years later, shouldn't the Episcopal Church adopt a new hymnal? This matter was studied carefully in 2011, and the result was "not now."[14] There simply wasn't significant support for a hymnal revision across any demographic: clergy, church musicians, or parishioners. The reasons varied, ranging from financial to a love of tradition. This reluctance to move forward from within the Episcopal Church, however, has not prevented musical liturgies from continuing to evolve.

EXTERNAL INFLUENCES: ALTERNATIVE AND NEW MUSICAL LITURGIES

Although the Episcopal Church has made internal efforts to look beyond the Anglican canon through its hymnal and hymn supplements, external influences have shaped the music of the church as well. Over the past several decades, disparate genres such as jazz, African American traditions, Celtic music, Iona traditions, Taizé, and others have also begun to shape the music of the modern Episcopal Church. The remainder of this essay will be devoted to an examination of these emerging and ever-evolving traditions.

JAZZ

Jazz is perhaps the most American of all musical genres. It is a style that combines African rhythms and European harmonies and could have only been invented in the New World with its unique fusion of cultures brought from two continents. Jazz has its roots in the spirituals, work songs, and field hollers of former African American slaves. Blues is the most significant forerunner of jazz and forms the basis of the genre's earliest experiments. Like European classical music, jazz went through many variations and styles over the course of its comparatively short history.[15] Improvisation is an essential element of jazz; virtually all jazz performers improvise regularly regardless of the specific jazz style they are performing.[16]

It is intriguing, then, that a secular style that had its roots in dance halls would find its way into liturgical worship, but that is precisely what is happening in some Episcopal parishes throughout the United States. While not altogether common, some churches have even begun regular jazz masses. For example, Canterbury House, the Episcopal student ministry of the University of Michigan, has earned a national reputation for their jazz masses, which have become highly successful over the past several decades.[17] Their story of how they have incorporated jazz into their liturgy has been documented in the book *Better Get It in Your Soul: What Liturgists Can Learn from Jazz*.[18] In this volume, the authors (who are both jazz musicians themselves) tell their story and offer practical advice on how to incorporate jazz into worship.

Jazz and jazz-related styles permeate every aspect of Canterbury House's worship services. The Eucharistic liturgy is still followed, but alternative musical styles are explored. Psalms, for instance, have formulas that seem to resemble Anglican chant, but upon closer inspection are revealed to be jazz progressions. Canterbury House also explores variety in their congregational singing styles, exploring Southern harmony and gospel singing in addition to traditional hymn singing. The result is a highly dynamic worship style that has created a vibrant worship experience for young people at the University of Michigan.

While Canterbury House's services have been pioneering in many ways, jazz, spirituality, and religion have been mingling with each other for decades. High-profile examples within the jazz industry include Louis Armstrong's *Louis and the Good Book* (1958), John Coltrane's *A Love Supreme* (1965), Duke Ellington's three sacred concerts (1965, 1968, and 1973), and Dave Brubeck's *To Hope! A Celebration* (1996). While these works and albums are not intended for liturgical use, the composers, all famous jazz musicians, wrote them to express something spiritual about themselves, thus distinguishing these works from the secular works that comprise their standard repertoire. Some churches began experimenting with jazz styles as early as the 1960s. Father John Garcia Gensel (1918–1998) established a jazz ministry at Saint Peter's Church in New York City in 1965. A quotation from Father Gensel serves as an appropriate conclusion to the powerful role that jazz can play in worship:

> I've learned that there is a *depth* to jazz that parallels scripture. Jazz is a music that is harmonically rich. Jazz melodies are intricate and take unexpected twists and turns. Jazz rhythms are vibrant and complex. Jazz honors diversity. Jazz requires a lifelong pursuit of understanding—there is always more to learn/discover. Yet there is something in jazz that touches and speaks to people.[19]

In 2012, Karen Noble Hanson (1943–2018) published her *Jazz Mass* with Church Publishing in New York, the same company that publishes *The Hymnal 1982* and all of its supplements. Hanson conceived authentically during one of her sabbaticals with the Metro Connection Jazz Group. Although a jazz combo replaces the organ accompaniment, Hanson intended for the work to be sung by a typical volunteer church choir, and her score consists of accessible four-part writing. This publication now offers church choirs in all parishes to experience jazz as a part of their weekly Eucharist celebration.

AFRO-CENTRIC LITURGICAL MUSIC

Closely related to jazz are several other distinctly African American musical styles, including Sacred Harp or shape-note singing, spirituals, and gospel. Each of these styles has been explored within Episcopal worship to various degrees over the past several decades. Some of these styles have also influenced hymnody. "Southern harmony" refers to a style of hymn singing that developed in the Southern United States in the eighteenth and nineteenth centuries.[20] The name derives from one of two major collections of these hymns: *The Southern Harmony and Musical Companion* by William Walker

(1809–1875) and *The Sacred Harp* by Benjamin Franklin White (1800–1879) and Elisha James King (1821–1844). Both of these collections employed "shape-note" singing.[21] Although shape-note singing is not practiced within the Episcopal Church, hymns from these two major collections are still a part of the repertory. Specific examples from *The Hymnal 1982* include Hymn 118 ("Brightest and Best of the Stars of the Morning," STAR IN THE EAST), Hymn 213 ("Come Away to the Skies," MIDDLEBURY), Hymn 439 ("What Wondrous Love Is This," WONDROUS LOVE), and Hymn 636 ("How Firm a Foundation," FOUNDATION). An ecumenical African American hymnal, *One Lord, One Faith, One Baptism*, was published by GIA in 2018 and is intended to be sung across denominations.

Spirituals are African American religious folk songs that date from the eighteenth and nineteenth centuries. During the nineteenth and early twentieth centuries, they were collected and introduced to the public at large by well-known composers and arrangers. Many of these tunes are easily recognizable, and some even appear as hymns in *The Hymnal 1982*. Stylistically, spirituals often employ a call-and-response format and refrains. Themes depict the struggles of a hard life combined with deep faith and a sense of determined optimism. Famous composers and arrangers of spirituals include Harry T. Burleigh (1866–1949), R. Nathaniel Dett (1882–1943), Hall Johnson (1888–1970), William Dawson (1899–1990), Jester Hairston (1901–2000), and Moses Hogan (1957–2003). Early versions of spirituals were also archived by nineteenth-century collectors in shape-note publications. Spirituals can be sung "concert style" (much like a classical art song) by a piano-accompanied soloist, and there are also many choral arrangements of spirituals available. Spirituals are now heard regularly in Episcopal churches across the nation. A descendent of the spiritual (with some blues thrown in), gospel is a distinctly African American style of sacred music that includes both choral and solo pieces. Conceived for worship, gospel music features simple melodies that are embellished through improvised harmonies, clapping, and movement.

In 2008, Carl MaultsBy published *Afro-Centric Liturgical Worship*, which contains full sung settings of Morning Prayer, Evening Prayer, and the Eucharist.[22] MaultsBy writes:

> The music used with BLSW [Black liturgical scripted worship] liturgies may have its roots in the European vernacular (folk), European conservatory, continental African vernacular, or the hybrid vernacular or hybrid conservatory music as found particularly in the Americas. For the purposes of this collection, this worship style is referred to as "Afro-Centric sacred." In short, the music of the Afro-Centric sacred tradition ranges from pre-Bach to post-Boyer [that is, Horace Boyer]. The music tradition also illustrates the struggle between the academic or conservatory influence and the vernacular or folk influence. In this

regard, the BLSW is but a microcosm of the music struggles in churches nationally and world-wide.[23]

This collection also contains two longer essays on Afro-centric liturgical worship. The reader is highly encouraged to seek them out and read them in their entirety. The influence that black Americans have had on music in the United States cannot be overstated, and in the twenty-first century Afro-centric repertoire is heard in sacred music contexts with ever-increasing frequency.

TAIZÉ

Taizé is an ecumenical monastic community located in Taizé, Saône-et-Loire, Burgundy, France.[24] It was founded in 1940 by the Swiss-born Brother Roger Schutz (1915–2005), who envisioned an inclusive community that emphasized prayer and meditation. Today Taizé is composed of more than one hundred men from many nations and denominations. Brother Roger was a prolific writer, and the philosophy of the Taizé community is well documented.

Although the term narrowly refers to the religious community itself, Taizé also defines a specific body of music composed by and for the Taizé community and the thousands who make a pilgrimage there each year. Based on chant, songs from Taizé feature simple repeated melodies, harmonies that can be easily improvised, and texts that lend themselves to use in liturgical worship. The founding composers of the Taizé repertoire included Jacques Berthier (1923–1994), a Parisian composer and organist at Église Saint-Ignace, the Jesuit church in Paris, and Joseph Gelineau (1920–2008). These two men are credited with conceiving and shaping the repertoire's style and liturgical use. Because the chants were designed to be used within an intentionally international community, a variety of languages are used (Latin, English, Spanish, and French). Each text is short and repetitive, allowing their use without singers requiring words or music in hand.

The musical simplicity of a Taizé service invites participation from the congregation. Because no musical scores are needed, participants are free to close their eyes and become a part of the musical fabric. The repetition of the same chant for an extended period of time makes the experience of singing the music of Taizé introspective and meditative. Prayer and scripture reading are also features of a Taizé service and, along with the music, often flow from one to another accompanied by periods of silence for reflection.

Parishes large and small throughout the world incorporate Taizé chants within their worship life. One of the most famous churches to adopt this model was All Saints' Episcopal Church in Beverly Hills, California, where Taizé services were pioneered by director of music Thomas Foster (b. 1958) over his long tenure from 1976 to 2003.[25] The music and liturgical format of the worship of the Taizé community today are being incorporated by many parishes within the Episcopal Church as well as other denominations. Whether individual chants are included in traditional Eucharistic or daily prayer liturgies or worship is designed to more fully focus on the music and format of a Taizé service, the spirit of Brother Roger and his philosophical emphasis on ecumenicalism, and an inclusive spirit make the Taizé chants appropriate in a variety of settings.

CELTIC MUSIC

The Celtic traditions of Ireland and elsewhere have also found their way into contemporary worship in the Episcopal Church. Every Sunday at 5:00 p.m., Christ Church Cathedral in Houston, Texas, offers "The Well": a Eucharist complemented entirely by Celtic music, the traditional music of Ireland.[26] Instead of an organ, three instrumentalists (harp, cello, and flute) and a cantor lead the congregation in song.[27] Harpist Becky Baxter (b. 1958), one of the founders of "The Well," describes their liturgy as a "hymnal in flux"; she is always seeking new Celtic music and texts to incorporate into the service.[28] Two sources that she frequently consults are the *Iona Abbey Music Book* and the *Celtic Hymn Book*.[29]

According to Baxter, the entire service lasts approximately fifty minutes, and music comprises thirty-five of those minutes.[30] There is an emphasis on congregational participation, and each service includes four hymns, which are led by the cantor and accompanied by the instrumentalists. These hymns often feature folk tunes from the British Islands, but on other occasions familiar hymn tunes are reimagined by the instrumentalists to sound Irish: there is an emphasis on authentic rhythm (including the "Scotch snap," which is technically not Irish), and the flutist utilizes a wooden head joint to imitate the sound of an Irish flute or pennywhistle.

The Well began on 9/11 in 2016, and since then it has rapidly become a fixture of Houston's ecumenical landscape, attracting worshippers across all denominations. Baxter explains why she believes Celtic music is so appealing to the Houston population:

> Houston is very multicultural port city, culturally diverse with many immigrants. We have Little Mexico, Little India, Chinatown, Taiwanese and Japanese neighborhoods . . . the list goes on and on. Street signs are often written in both English and the language of the community. While the Irish community

of course isn't as big as it is in New York City, there is a lot of interest in Irish music and culture. Several Irish pubs regularly feature traditional Irish music. The University of Saint Thomas even offers an Irish studies degree program. A New Yorker would feel surprisingly at home.[31]

The website of Christ Church Cathedral describes the significance of service's name and describes the ambiance of the liturgy:

> The Celtic tradition remembers that the world, is, indeed, enchanted by the flow of God's grace. The name of this service, The Well, also draws metaphorically and physically from the tradition. Ancient holy wells are found throughout Britain and Ireland, and in the Celtic tradition such wells were places of pilgrimage, gathering, and worship. Wells were not only the source of life-giving water, but also were places through which people connected to God. Genesis 1:2 says that the Spirit of God "moved over the waters" at creation. Holy wells served to remind the faithful that, like water from the earth, God flows from and into the center of our being. The Well features Celtic music played on harp, cello, and other instruments. It is contemplative, providing space for meditation and prayer. Lighting is muted, with the presence of many candles. The Eucharistic liturgy is thoroughly Episcopalian, but incorporates prayers from the Church of Ireland, the Iona Community in Scotland, and other sources.[32]

Of the service, Dean Barkley Thompson (b. 1972) says, "The Well provides a prayerful and peaceful way to center oneself in God at the end of the day and the outset of a new week. The Celtic tradition has enriched my own encounter with God's grace, and I hope many parishioners and newcomers will come and experience The Well."[33] Baxton offers a more colloquial rationale for why people continue to come back to the well, week after week: "People like the haunting Celtic tunes . . . they grab you!"[34]

IONA TRADITIONS

Closely related to Celtic music are Iona traditions, which are increasingly making inroads into the Episcopal Church. The Iona Community was founded in Glasgow and Iona, Scotland, in 1938 by George MacLeod (1895–1991).[35] Members of the community rebuilt and lived within the monastic quarters of a medieval abbey, where they established their principals of hospitality, inclusion, spirituality, social justice, human rights, environmental stewardship, peacemaking, nonviolence, healing, and reconciliation. Iona remains a center for tourism, hosting daily worship for anyone who makes the pilgrimage.

The Iona Community has fostered its own musical traditions as well. Its most well-known musician is John Bell (b. 1949), an influential writer and composer of hymns. He has published many collections through the Wild Goose Resource Group, the official publishing arm of the Iona Community (and available in the United States through GIA).[36]

Similar to the music of Taizé, the songs of Iona are often short, repetitive chants, easily sung and harmonized without the aid of words or music on paper. While Taizé chants are designed to encourage prayer and meditation, the texts of the Iona Community echo Iona's commitment to issues of social justice and faith. Worship in the Iona tradition may include full liturgies written by members of the community or simply the incorporation of Iona-related songs and chants into a parish's musical repertoire.

PAPERLESS MUSIC (MUSIC THAT MAKES COMMUNITY)

Closely related to the Taizé and Iona communities ideal of congregational music making is the recent American movement incorporating "paperless" music into worship. The concept of paperless music is based on folk traditions and building community through singing music that has been learned "by heart," free from traditional score-based notation systems. In his introduction to *Music by Heart* (2008), a collection of eighty-five paperless songs, Donald Schell (b. 1947) writes,

> What does singing "by heart" mean to you? To me it immediately suggests singing something known by memory and loved. It's also a feeling. Songs we know by heart come to us in a distinct recognizable way, their words and music seemingly flowing out of us, continuous, effortless, and whole. A crowd (church or secular) singing "Amazing Grace" knows where they're going. You can feel the music has come to mean more than the words, and that the moment connects to something more universal. And when it's by heart there's also something fresh and new in the moment, though the song is familiar. The music we sing by heart we've learned whole. Our memory connects mind, heartbeat, and breath. It makes us feel whole.[37]

Over the past decade, paperless music making has been encouraged by an organization called Music That Makes Community, which has developed a series of workshops designed to promote congregational singing within church communities.[38] Music That Makes Community was founded by Schell, Rick Fabian (b. 1942), and Emily Scott (b. 1980) as an extension of Schell and Fabian's liturgical work at Saint Gregory of Nyssa Episcopal Church in San Francisco, California. Collectively, they had a desire to have music for worship that would leave congregants "free to move around, use their hands, and be fully present to one another" in worship.[39] The theological spirit at the heart of their ministry is deep and inclusive:

> At Music That Makes Community, we're discovering how everyday life and worship are equally (and synergistically) labs or seedbeds for living fully human lives. We make liturgy to form a porous bond of solidarity. The bond is porous so that we can continue to welcome strangers, those "not like us" and "the unworthy"; the bond is stronger for it. This work is essentially a practice of hospitality that welcomes all into a group collaborating in making music. Within this bond of solidarity, we form our character as people: our leaders imitate Christ and we imitate our leaders, and in the process we move towards generosity, freedom and spontaneity, both in our liturgies and in our lives. To paraphrase Simone Weil, "absolute attention is prayer." We seek to engage our whole mental, physical and spiritual attention in worship. Our fully engaged presence is our best gift to one another and to God. In order to connect in a real, honest way, we must be vulnerable to one another. We take risks in our leadership, and when we choose the wrong pitch or our voices crack or a song doesn't work, we model forgiveness. We live into the dissonance and consider it all part of the holy work of coming together in song, in worship, in our life as the body of Christ.[40]

Although a recent phenomenon, the popularity of paperless music is rapidly spreading throughout the Episcopal Church. As of 2020, over nine hundred musicians, pastors, and lay parishioners have been trained by official Music That Makes Community workshops. The Saint Gregory's website is a rich resource to explore these alternative liturgies, with PDFs of their worship services available for other parishes to download and utilize.[41]

POP-INSPIRED "COVER" MASSES

Saint Paul's Episcopal Church in Mount Lebanon, Pennsylvania, has started a tradition of summer Eucharist services devoted to the catalog of a particular band or pop artist.[42] The original idea was to have a "U2charist," a Eucharist in which all of the music selections were U2 songs. Christin Cooper (b. 1989), director of these services, states that her music choices are entirely lyric driven, and hymn selections are made according to the Revised Common Lectionary.[43] For example, the gospel for that particular Sunday talked about being one with Jesus (John 17:20–26), which lent itself very well for U2's song "One" to be the sequence hymn.[44] She states, "For me, it has been an interesting project and has given me an opportunity to be creative when selecting texts. It is exciting to find new meaning or perspective in a song's lyric."[45]

The original U2charist was such a success that more "cover Eucharists" followed, including a Beatles mass, a Simon & Garfunkel mass, a Carole

King and James Taylor mass, and even a "showtunes" mass.[46] Cooper states that these unique services have been very popular during the summer months, attracting parishioners from Sunday mornings as well as new congregational participants. Cooper also organizes regular events at Saint Paul's called "Beer and Hymns." Parishioners gather at Caliente Piazza & Draft House in Mount Lebanon, where they eat, drink, and sing hymns together, fostering a unique opportunity for the worship community to bond with one another.

EMERGENT MUSIC (ECUMENICAL TRADITIONS)

Over the past two decades, a new form of worship has begun to take shape within the movement called the "emerging church." Fiercely ecumenical in nature, participants describe themselves as Protestant, post-Protestant, evangelical, postevangelical, liberal, postliberal, conservative, postconservative, Anabaptist, Adventist, Reformed, charismatic, neocharismatic, and postcharismatic. Emerging churches are spreading rapidly, with establishments in North America, Europe, Africa, and Australia. Emergent Christians seek to connect with ancient traditions as they have one eye fixed firmly on the future.

As emerging communities are both newly formed and (by their very nature) not denominational, there is no cohesive musical tradition within the emergent church. Rather, these worshippers draw upon a wide variety of resources. Isaac Everett (b. 1981), in the introduction to his book *The Emergent Psalter*, states that "with few exceptions, the emerging church has yet to create an identity for itself."[47] In this study, Everett discusses "new traditionalism" and notes the recent resurgence of interest in ancient forms of liturgy and spiritual practice:

> This return to ancient practice does not necessarily coincide with a return to theological orthodoxy. In fact, emerging Christians are discovering that the mystery and ambiguity of ritual meshes with a postmodern worldview in a way that their past experiences of worship haven't. This renewal of tradition doesn't signify a renewed commitment to religious institutions, either, which are often mistrusted by emerging Christians. Rather than adopt a single liturgical traditional wholesale, emerging Christians are drawing from a variety of traditions to create a personalized, à la carte spiritual practice, and I've seen emergent communities rediscovering everything from incense to alter calls. One common thread, however, is an emphasis on practices that "integrate body and spirit," focusing on actions rather than words, which engage an entire community in collaborative, interactive worship.[48]

Everett, a composer, goes on to discuss the process of capturing the essence of ancient texts through a contemporary musical language that draws upon a wide variety of sources. His magnum opus is an "emergent psalter," which explores new ways of singing and playing the psalms without the aid of an organ or four-part choir. Everett's approach offers a glimpse of what liturgical worship and church music itself might look like in a postmodern, emergent age.

HIP-HOP

Hip-hop has also found its way into the liturgy of the Episcopal Church. One highly successful experimentation is the Beyoncé mass, which has been mounted in many cities since its conception and inaugural performance in 2018.[49] Trinity Episcopal Church of Morrisania in the Bronx, New York City, has developed a liturgy called the "HipHopEMass":

> It's structured like any other Episcopal Eucharist and begins in the same manner—with one difference: it has a beat you can (and are encouraged to) dance to. In place of a choir there's likely a small table with two turntables set up side by side and a DJ, head bobbing to the prelude, with a hand on each, either syncing up the next beat, or putting the current track together. In a larger service there may be a full band providing the music, while in a smaller service as little as a powerful portable boom box may be doing the job. Leading the music, coming in generally when a choir would (and otherwise shouting encouragement when a choir would, likely, not) are a coterie of rappers. . . . The music is loud and exuberant. The rappers call out "God is in the House!"[50]

Timothy Holder (b. 1955), rector of Trinity Episcopal Church of Morrisania, developed the liturgy to draw a new community of worshippers into the church, particularly the youth for whom hip-hop culture is part of their daily lives. He writes,

> The HipHopEMass has introduced and made familiar the Good News of Jesus Christ to thousands of persons across the United States and Word. Hip hop communities have, in just a few years, sprung up North and South, East and West: in Atlantic City, New York, Cincinnati, all across Virginia, a "Hip Hop Hippo" (St. Augustine of Hippo) in Pennsylvania, a "Hip Hop Chapel" for the incarcerated in Missouri, a parish that presents graduating seniors with the first edition of *The Hip Hop Prayer Book* just outside Washington, D.C., and through big and small churches and communities in cities and towns all over the country. All opening their hears and doors to new life in search of the ages-old message of God's Love for All.[51]

Holder published these hip-hop liturgies in *The Hip Hop Prayer Book* (2006) and a revision two years later in *The Hip Hop Prayer Book: The Remix* (2008).[52]

POSTLUDE: THE FUTURE OF ANGLICAN CHURCH MUSIC IN AMERICA

The Episcopal Church has always been an institution of change, and liturgies are continuing to change, just as the world continues to evolve. As new generations replace older ones, values shift and new perspectives emerge. Social and theological shifts are often followed by musical ones: the revision of the Book of Common Prayer in 1979, for example, resulted in a more diverse and eclectic hymnal three years later.

In 1974, the "Philadelphia Eleven" became the first group of women ordained as priests in the Episcopal Church. In 2006, just thirty-two years later, Katherine Jefferts Schori (b. 1954) was elected the first presiding bishop of the Episcopal Church. In 2004, Gene Robinson (b. 1947) was installed amid controversy as the first openly gay bishop of the Episcopal Church. In 2012, just eight years later, the Episcopal Church authorized for trial use "The Witnessing and Blessing of a Lifelong Covenant." What is at first radical becomes not only accepted but celebrated as time passes.

What, then, are the implications for the future of music in the Episcopal Church? Will the next revision of the Episcopal hymnal include a hip-hop selection? My prediction is . . . perhaps. For decades, the Episcopal Church has positioned itself at the vanguard among progressive churches. Traditional theological views have been replaced by more nuanced ones, and "we have always done it this way" is rarely a winning argument when engaging with clergy or other worship leaders. At the same time, however, many people who worship at Episcopal churches choose to do so because it is one of the few denominations in the United States that still curates, in most cases, the traditional "organ and choir" music program. This combination of progressive theology with traditional music is a winning one for many parishioners.

One can often predict the future by studying the past. If this is true, music in the Episcopal Church will continue to include a unique blend of tradition and innovation within a strong liturgical framework. It is likely that Anglican chant and classic anthems will still be sung one hundred years from now. But it is equally likely that newer styles will merge with traditional ones to form creative new liturgies that we cannot yet imagine. Ultimately, sacred music is not measured by its form or style but by its effectiveness: music enhances worship, elevates texts, moves people to deep spiritual places, and evokes the spirit and power of God.

NOTES

1. Portions of this essay were previously published in the author's book *Welcome to Church Music & The Hymnal 1982* (New York: Morehouse, 2014) and have been reworked and reprinted here with permission.

2. See the "Further Reading" list at the end of this essay for selected core readings on the history of English church music.

3. The following paragraphs rely heavily on the information presented in Robert W. Pritchard's book, *A History of the Episcopal Church*, third edition (New York: Morehouse, 2014).

4. Corliss Richard Arnold, *Organ Literature: A Comprehensive Study*, third edition (Lanham, MD: Scarecrow Press, 1995), 283.

5. David Tannenberg (1728–1804), a Pennsylvanian, is perhaps the earliest recorded American organ builder; he built instruments in the German tradition. The leading organ builders for Anglican churches included George Hutchings (1835–1913), Hilborne Roosevelt (1849–1886), and the Hook brothers, Elias (1805–1881) and George (1807–1880).

6. For a thorough discussion of the history of Episcopal hymnody in the United States, see the essays collected under the heading "A Historical Survey of Christian Hymnody in the United States and Britain" in *The Hymnal 1982 Companion*, ed. Raymond F. Glover (New York: Church Hymnal Corporation, 1990), 319–634.

7. The S288 Rite II setting of the Te Deum canticle is also based on a Slavonic chant.

8. *The Hymnal 1982* designates musical settings of liturgies from the Book of Common Prayer as "service music." These settings can be found at the front of the hymnal and are labeled with an "S" preceding the respective numbers.

9. Preface to *Wonder, Love, and Praise* (New York: Church Publishing, 1997).

10. The "S" designation before service music numbers is curiously avoided in *Wonder, Love, and Praise*.

11. Preface to *Wonder, Love, and Praise*.

12. Preface to *Voices Found: Women in the Church's Song* (New York: Church Publishing, 2003).

13. Ibid.

14. The complete study, titled "The Hymnal Revision Feasibility Study: A Report to the Standing Commission on Liturgy and Music," can be found online at the Church Publishing Group website, www.cpg.org.

15. Some of these principal movements include ragtime, classic "New Orleans" jazz, hot jazz, swing, bebop, cool, hard bop, bossa nova, modal, and free jazz. Contemporary jazz since 1970 has consisted of many different types of fusion genres in addition to the blues.

16. For a practical history of jazz and an overview of jazz style, see Ted Gioia, *The History of Jazz*, second edition (New York: Oxford University Press, 2011).

17. http://www.umich.edu/~canter/jazz_mass.html.

18. Reid Hamilton and Stephen Rush, *Better Get It in Your Soul: What Liturgists Can Learn from Jazz* (New York: Church Publishing, 2008).

19. Richard Birk, "What About Jazz?," in *What Would Jesus Sing?: Experimentation and Tradition in Church Music* (New York: Church Publishing, 2007), 8.

20. Harry Eskew, rev. James C. Downey, "Shape-Note Hymnody," in *Grove Music Online*, Oxford Music Online, accessed April 4, 2020, https://www.oxfordmusiconline.com/grovemusic/view/10.1093.

21. Shape-note music, as the name implies, uses different shapes for each note in the musical scale as a pedagogical tool to increase sight reading facility. Sacred Harp songs are generally performed unaccompanied. Most of the texts are scripture oriented, and Sacred Harp singing usually occurs either at Sunday morning worship services or community social gatherings.

22. Carl MaultsBy, *Afro-Centric Liturgical Worship* (New York: Church Publishing, 2008).

23. Ibid., introduction.

24. Factual information in the following paragraphs is taken from Jason Brian Santos's book, *A Community Called Taizé: A Story of Prayer, Worship, and Reconciliation* (Downers Grove, IL: InterVarsity Press, 2008).

25. For detailed information about the music of this parish, see Thomas Foster's article titled "Taizé at All Saints' Episcopal Church, Beverly Hills, California," which is published in *What Would Jesus Sing?*, 163–68.

26. http://www.christchurchcathedral.org/worship/the-well/, accessed December 30, 2019.

27. There are only six Sundays in the liturgical year when The Well is not offered: Advent 1, Christmas 2 (or Epiphany 1), Lent 1, Palm Sunday, Pentecost, and All Saints Sunday. On these occasions, The Well is replaced with a 5:00 p.m. choral Eucharist.

28. Personal correspondence with Becky Baxter, December 30, 2019.

29. Iona Community, *Iona Abbey Music Book* (Glasgow: Wild Goose Publications, 2007); Ray Simpson, ed., *Celtic Hymn Book* (Stowmarket, Suffolk: Kevin Mayhew, 2004).

30. Personal correspondence with Becky Baxter, December 30, 2019.

31. Ibid.

32. http://www.christchurchcathedral.org/worship/the-well/, accessed December 30, 2019.

33. Ibid.

34. Personal correspondence with Becky Baxter, December 30, 2019.

35. For a detailed account of George Macleod and the founding of the Iona Community, see Ron Ferguson's book *George Macleod: Founder of the Iona Community* (Glasgow: Collins, 1990).

36. Some of these titles include *Heaven Shall Not Wait* (1987), *Enemy of Apathy* (1988), *Love from Below* (1990), *Cloth for the Cradle: Worship Resources and Readings for Advent, Christmas, and Epiphany* (1998), *Stages on the Way: Worship Resources and Readings for Lent, Holy Week, and Easter* (1998), *Innkeepers and Light Sleepers: Seventeen New Songs for Christmas* (2004), *Psalms of Patience, Protest, and Praise* (2005), and *We Walk His Way: Shorter Songs for Worship* (2008). The emphasis on all of these publications is spiritual community building through

congregational song. Bell has also offered several books, including *States of Bliss and Yearning: Marks and Means of Authentic Christian Spirituality* (1998), *The Singing Thing: A Case for Congregational Song* (2000), and *The Singing Thing Too: Enabling Congregations to Sing* (2007). He frequently travels as a clinician, giving workshops on congregational song as practiced by the Iona Community.

37. *Music by Heart: Paperless Songs for Evening Worship* (New York: Church Publishing, 2008), introduction.
38. https://www.musicthatmakescommunity.org/workshops.
39. https://www.musicthatmakescommunity.org/corevalues.
40. https://www.musicthatmakescommunity.org/worship_planning_resources.
41. https://www.saintgregorys.org.
42. https://www.stpaulspgh.org.
43. Cooper credits J. R. Ankley (b. 1958), with whom she worked at Saint James Episcopal Church in Lancaster, Pennsylvania, for giving her the inspiration for the U2charist. J. R. began a similar series of Saturday night masses, exploring not only the catalogs of various popular music artists but also masses centered on themes such as "addiction and recovery" and "the loss of a child." He called these Saturday night services "seeker's masses" as they regularly draw in worshippers who had no other association with the Episcopal Church or Saint James (personal correspondence with J. R. Ankley, January 7, 2020).
44. Personal correspondence with Christin Cooper, January 3, 2000.
45. Ibid.
46. Ibid.
47. Isaac Everett, *The Emergent Psalter* (New York: Church Publishing, 2009), introduction.
48. Ibid.
49. For more information, see the official Beyoncé mass website, https://www.beyoncemass.com/.
50. Lucas Smith, "The HipHopEMass at Trinity Episcopal Church, Morissania, Bronx, New York," in *What Would Jesus Sing?*, 181. It should also be noted that the HipHopEMass is not the only experimentation with liturgical hip-hop
51. Timothy Holder, ed., *The Hip Hop Prayer Book: The Remix* (New York: Seabury Books, 2009), xv.
52. Both of these volumes are published by Seabury Books in New York.

FURTHER READING

Bell, John. *What Would Jesus Sing?: Experimentation and Tradition in Church Music*. New York: Church Publishing, 2007.
Chapman, Mark. *Anglicanism: A Very Short Introduction*. New York: Oxford University Press, 2006.
Everett, Isaac. *The Emergent Psalter*. New York: Church Publishing, 2009.
Hamilton, Reid, and Stephen Rush. *Better Get It in Your Soul: What Liturgists Can Learn from Jazz*. New York: Church Publishing, 2008.

Hoch, Matthew, ed. *So You Want to Sing Sacred Music: A Guide for Performers*. Lanham, MD: Rowman & Littlefield, 2017.

Hoch, Matthew. *Welcome to Church Music & The Hymnal 1982*. New York: Morehouse, 2014.

Holder, Timothy, ed. *The Hip Hop Prayer Book: The Remix*. New York: Seabury Books, 2009.

MaultsBy, Carl. *Afro-Centric Liturgical Worship*. New York: Church Publishing, 2008.

Pritchard, Robert W. *A History of the Episcopal Church*. Third edition. New York: Morehouse, 2014.

Santos, Jason Brian. *A Community Called Taizé: A Story of Prayer, Worship, and Reconciliation*. Downers Grove, IL: InterVarsity Press, 2008.

VI

INDIGENOUS AND AFRICAN AMERICAN MUSIC

Chapter Twelve

"God with Me Speaking"

Envisioning the Study of Indigenous Christian Song in Brazil

Andrew Janzen and Meiry Yakawa

> I had only one song, but I sang it at every house meeting. I would sing it, and I would share with them how I experienced this song.
>
> —Georgine Takes Gun Falls Down (Crow Hymn Ministry Member)[1]

The first time Meiry Yakawa sang her song in public was in a packed room during an Indigenous Musicians Conference. In my video recording of the session, the camera slowly pans the room, showing conference participants seated in a large circle. Yakawa stands before them, speaking evenly into a microphone. She calmly recounts the circumstances of how this song came to her one night. Though several years have passed since receiving the song, Yakawa has never sung it for anyone beyond her own mother, my wife, and me. Having spoken for over half an hour, Yakawa now announces she wishes to sing her song for the group. After explaining the lyrics in Portuguese, she begins singing in her own language, Bakairi:

> Woman, arise and go speak
> Wake up and hear what I am saying . . .

While singing the traditional melody in an unhurried meter and steady voice, silent tears begin rolling down her cheeks. I recall looking around the room, noticing how many others were also in tears, including our recording engineer who had come from New York. Throughout her talk, Yakawa wonders at the fact that while she feels free to use Bakairi songs as a Christian, she seldom encounters in her travels within Brazil the use of Indigenous music among other Indigenous Christians. Though her song provides encouragement in her life and teaching, Yakawa struggled in the past against fear and shame in sharing her song and explaining its importance to others, even within her own church and community, often sensing resistance on both fronts.

This struggle to understand and come to terms with a combined Christian and Indigenous identity is also evident among scholars. A review of ethnomusicological literature shows that, in spite of the immense interest of anthropologists in Brazilian Indigenous peoples, there are relatively few ethnomusicological studies, and those that exist focus almost exclusively on two well-protected areas: the Xingu and the Upper Rio Negro region.[2] Furthermore, these studies predominantly consider only traditional music performed in traditional, ritual contexts.[3]

Within the field of the anthropology of Christianity, scholars now acknowledge that newly Christian populations have long been considered inappropriate subjects of study.[4] Correspondingly, Yakawa's experiences reflect the conflicted political and cultural position of Indigenous Christians in Brazil, caught between becoming modern citizens and sufficiently representing their indigeneity in order to maintain their Indigenous rights. Owing in part to this liminal positioning, there is an absence of literature documenting musicking by Brazilian Christian Indigenous communities, even though a quarter to a half of all Brazilian Indigenous people identify as Christian.[5]

CHRISTIAN *AND* INDIGENOUS?

Yakawa makes it clear that she sees no conflict in *being* both Indigenous (of the Bakairi Nation) and Christian. Yet for many within academia, society, and even the church, the circumstances and story of Yakawa's song are likely to raise serious questions. For instance, is this really an Indigenous song, considering the lyrics are laden with Christian meanings? In identifying as a Christian, is Yakawa in fact abandoning and rejecting her Bakairi traditions and cosmology, with its perspectives of the spirit world, and turning her back on that which makes her Indigenous?

Similar questions about Indigenous Christians have been considered elsewhere within North American Indigenous studies. In *The Jesus Road*, anthropologist Luke Lassiter collaborates with historian Clyde Ellis and Kiowa elder and singer Ralph Kotay to give an account of the history of Kiowa Christianity as expressed through Kiowa hymns. In his conclusion, Lassiter recommends that Indigenous Christian life experiences be described in more nuanced terms than simply through the optic of either forced assimilation and/or cultural genocide.[6] In a similar situation, linguist David Samuels remarks that while he studied Apache country musicians, many outsiders would ask: "How can this be?", how could Indigenous peoples possibly sing country songs?⁷ Samuels suggests that rather than such an alienating question, we can ask what singing such songs accomplishes for those who sing them.⁸ In other words, for this essay, we will ask how and why Yakawa's song is valuable to her.

Against this broader social and scholarly setting, we will use Yakawa's song "Deus Yagâ Aguely," or "God with Me Speaking," as a lens through which to examine Christian Indigenous music in Brazil. This essay explores two questions: What are the barriers impeding adequate representation of Indigenous Christian music in academic, social, and cultural circles, and how can the significance of one Indigenous song be measured? Thus in order to evaluate the worth of one song, we must first address certain barriers to adequate representation.

COLLABORATIVE METHODOLOGY

This essay employs collaborative methodology to develop an argument for the significance of Yakawa's song that privileges Indigenous ways of knowing, such as storytelling, by highlighting Yakawa's perspective of the spiritual, emotional, and culturally symbolic effects of her song.⁹ With this in mind, we present a shared reflection between an ethnomusicologist and an Indigenous musician regarding the experience and reception of just one Indigenous Christian song.

The authors' primary point of reference and reflection is a forty-five-minute recording of a talk given by Yakawa at Teruwah, a ten-day Indigenous musicians' conference my wife, Aimée Seng Janzen, and I initiated in 2014. Yakawa was a member of the Teruwah leadership team. Her presentation drew on years of reflection and teaching about Indigenous art and music. Additional ethnographic material comes from my years in Brazil, in particular the five years I worked as a teacher at the same college as Yakawa. For the purpose of this essay, we use the term *Indigenous songs* to refer to songs employing the Indigenous culture's musical style and language. According to Bakairi Christians from both Bakairi Indigenous areas, Yakawa's two songs are the first with Christian meanings that use both the Bakairi language and music.

FRAMEWORK

The following section begins by examining disciplinary barriers within music scholarship, drawing upon insights from the anthropology of Christianity. The understanding of Indigenous Christian song as sacred music is then discussed, and an explanation of the various categories of songs in use by Indigenous churches is given. This is followed by a description of Yakawa's song and accompanying testimony. In her testimony, she explains the powerful spiritual, cultural, and emotional aspects of her song. She also encourages others to remain strong in following Jesus, to overcome shame and fear, and to instill pride in Indigenous people's music, language, and identity. In conclusion, Yakawa's experience is compared with that of Georgine Takes Gun Falls Down, a Christian of the Apsáalooke (Crow) Nation, and the worth of one song is evaluated.

THEORETICAL BARRIERS TO STUDYING INDIGENOUS CHRISTIAN MUSIC

As mentioned earlier, a survey of anthropological and ethnomusicological studies of Brazilian Indigenous nations reveals an absence of descriptions of Indigenous Christian experiences, particularly in the area of music. Arguably, these omissions in scholarship may be caused in part by theoretical barriers within academia.[10] Among many possible reasons, the four most prominent issues, which will be described here, are (1) a social stigmatization of Christianity within the discipline of anthropology; (2) the assumption that Christian scholars lack objectivity due to their "problematic" subject position; (3) the assumed continuity of culture, for example, favoring hidden "resistance" over an acknowledgment of possible ruptures/discontinuities; and (4) the question of who is truly Indigenous.

The first and most significant theoretical barrier consists of sociocultural stigma within anthropology and related disciplines. In her book *Praying and Preying*, Brazilian anthropologist Aparecida Vilaça relates her struggles to describe the conversion of many Wari' during her years of fieldwork in the state of Rondônia. Vilaça reports feeling "bewilderment" and notes that in general, when confronted with Christianity "in the field," anthropologists have attempted to ignore or minimize reporting on such Christian influences.[11] Vilaça traces the roots of this to a historical rivalry between anthropology and Christian missions. Anthropology developed in the West in association with colonial projects, as Christian expansion was also taking place. Vilaça argues that anthropology is resistant to studying Christians because anthropology developed in antithesis to monotheistic religions.[12] As anthropologists discovered the exotic, different, or suffering, they tended to "ignore or reject" any influences of Christianity in those cultures.[13] Anthropologist and leading advocate for the anthropology of Christianity Joel Robbins, considering his own fieldwork with Urapmim charismatic Christians in Papua New Guinea, determines:

Christians are too similar by virtue of drawing on the same broad cultural tradition as anthropologists, and too meaningfully different by virtue of drawing on a part of that tradition that in many respects has arisen in critical dialogue with the modernist ideas on which anthropology is founded.[14]

Nevertheless, Robbins concludes that it is not intellectual reasons that restrain the anthropology of Christianity but cultural or social reasons. Robbins calls for the destigmatization of Christianity, suggesting that in the interest of developing the field of anthropology of Christianity, it is imperative "to have anthropologists who study Christianity be able to say that whatever else they are, they are also anthropologists of Christianity."[15] The same logic could apply to developing an ethnomusicology of Indigenous Christianity, whether the scholar is agnostic, like Muriel Reigersberg, or Christian, like myself.[16]

The second barrier to adequate representation is the subject position of Christian scholars. The same sociocultural barriers to studying Christian subjects extend to the position of Christian scholars. Assumptions exist that scholars who identify as Christian lack objectivity and fail to engage critically with their research. In her 1991 article titled "Representing Fundamentalism: The Problem of the Repugnant Cultural Other," secular anthropologist Susan Harding reported that she was repeatedly asked, "Are you now or have you ever been a born-again Christian?"[17] Scholars, including those within the anthropology of Christianity, now routinely mention this bias.[18] In another example, anthropologist Tanya Luhrmann admits that in her case, "[t]o hear that colleagues are Christian can be enough to cause one to dismiss them or at least to think about their intellectual questions quite differently."[19]

Such concerns expressed would seem to suggest that only secular researchers can be trusted to present objective research findings. Though these views are certainly common, they have been dealt with by feminist ethnography, which has fought successfully against the "presumed objective" perspective.[20] In fact, the "objective" stance of researchers was actually not objective but likely slanted, according to a combination of male, white, upper-class, and/or secular life experiences. In the 1980s, postmodern ethnography and standpoint theory clearly proved the impossibility of an objective view and showed how every scholar has a view grounded in a "particular time and place."[21]

If so, then what are the implications of an anthropologist writing from the subject position of a Christian? Scholars who hold to a shared Christian faith with their interlocutors are able to bridge the object/subject split in ways that a secular scholar with the same community would not be able to. Brian Howell gives the example from his fieldwork among Baptist congregations in the Philippines where he participated "as a fellow Christian believer" in worship, prayer, and teaching. In Howell's evaluation, this role opened up many opportunities with his interlocutors.[22] The fact that foregrounding one's perspective is not only a possibility but advantageous has, in time, also been applied to other subject positions: gender/sexual minorities, ethnic and racial identities, and Indigenous and/or non-Western subject positions. Howell's contribution then is to illustrate how "those committed to religious positions should be understood as occupying a subject position analogous to other subject positions which are characterized by moral/ethical commitments, for example, feminism."[23] In the end, though, Howell's concern is not to ask for a "position of privilege." Rather, he seeks to demonstrate how his position should not be seen as *harmful* but should be considered as *helpful*, considering, for example, that he shares with his interlocutors' Christian beliefs and practices. Like a performing musician undertaking fieldwork in another country who uses her musical skills and understanding as part of fieldwork, so too a Christian scholar studying Christian subjects is able to draw on shared knowledge and practices.

Third, anthropologists have also assumed continuity of culture based on transmission between generations and therefore struggle to account for total "ruptures," defined recently as "radical and often forceful forms of discontinuity."[24] Where drastic and complete cultural changes have occurred, anthropologists seek signs of continuity from the past. When that continuity is difficult to locate, anthropologists favor seeking "resistance" in its varied and hidden expressions, even to the extent of ignoring both the stated interests and lived experiences of a whole population. For instance, Lucas Bessire reports that when anthropologists are confronted with the testimonies of Ayoreode Christians, these are "either lamented as evidence of evangelical ethnocide or dismissed as a misleading appearance of change that conceals an unchanging core of continuous and pure cultural difference."[25] According to Robbins, Christians are difficult for anthropologists to "easily [make] sense of by the use of standard anthropological tools."[26] Vilaça, on her part, forcibly describes the difficulty in this way: "The notion of rupture intrinsic to Christianity (taking the conversion of Paul the Apostle as its 'mythic' reference model) . . . is challenging to conceptualize analytically."[27]

The fourth barrier is rooted in misunderstandings of who counts as Indigenous. The question of "who is truly Indigenous?" is often answered by tying Indigenous identity to traditional religions. Remarkably, religious belief as an identifying characteristic of who is Indigenous is not included in standard statements such as the UN definition of Indigenous peoples.[28] However, some scholars wrongly assume that "authentic" or "real" Indigenous peoples only follow Indigenous religions.

One possible reason for this understanding may emerge from an increased emphasis on *perspectivism*. In the past decade, anthropologists who study Indigenous peoples of the Americas have promoted the concept of perspectivism as a manner of framing an Indigenous cosmology, most famously proposed by Viveiros de Castro.[29] According to this theory, Amazonian societies view nature and culture as inseparable. Furthermore, what outsiders might consider "objects," such as jaguars, trees, tapirs, or birds, are actually "subjects" who see themselves as "people" who live in houses, hunt, eat, and drink.[30] However, in its essence, perspectivism, or the "ontological turn," merely represents updated descriptions of animism, shamanism, and structuralism. While perspectivism describes actual Indigenous experiences and spiritual beliefs, this theory is criticized by David Bond, Lucas Bessire, and Alcida Rita Ramos as essentializing Amerindian peoples as mysteriously "other" and by Anthony Seeger and Terrance Turner as overemphasizing similarities among the diversity of Indigenous cultures in the Americas.[31] Once defined as "other" and as inhabiting "radical alterity," Indigenous peoples can more easily be exiled from taking part in contemporary society and political debate.

Anthropologist Lucas Bessire's ethnography *Behold the Black Caiman* describes the real-life material results of such ideas. He contrasts the small numbers of highly sought-after "uncontacted" Ayoreode groups assumed to still be living in the forest with the thousands of Ayoreode in Bolivia and Paraguay who are generally despised by society. According to Bessire, this latter group chose on their own to "abandon nearly all of the past practices that count as authorized 'traditional culture' or ontological alterity in Latin America, such as shamanic rituals, curing techniques, magical songs, myth narratives, and ceremonial aesthetics," and instead joined an Ayoreode version of modernity "predicated on a shared Christian morality."[32] Bessire observes that due to their abandonment of traditional religion, these Ayoreode are regularly considered "ex-primitives" by state authorities, NGOs, and anthropologists and thus unworthy of citizenship rights or other material aid.[33]

Theories such as perspectivism intrinsically link a language and ethnic group with specific beliefs. Such a view, when held to the exclusion of ethnographic data, ignores the fact that Indigenous peoples, like non-Indigenous groups, also adopt new religious beliefs or cosmologies, including antagonism or secular convictions of different kinds. Furthermore, a theory like perspectivism leads to the categorization of Christian or secular Indigenous peoples as non-Indigenous. It can be argued that certain anthropologists are reessentializing Indigenous peoples as inherently understanding the world in certain ways. In this view, while non-Indigenous Brazilians are seen to adhere to a faith or to believe in a certain religion, Indigenous peoples hold animistic views as a part of their human nature and ancestry, not their culture.

In contrast to Indigenous peoples, it would be rare for scholars to state that African American Christian expressions are not truly African American or Black because they are linked to church or Christianity. John Burdick, for example, describes the use of gospel-influenced genres in Brazil by Black protestant believers, specifically Pentecostals.[34] In Trinidad, Timothy Rommen has described Afro-Creoles and Indo-Trinidadians singing a variety of Black gospel they made as their own.[35] Indeed, in the United States, studies of Black churches have been a mainstay of ethnomusicology for decades.[36] The widespread scholarly acceptance of a combined African American *and* Christian identity is all the more remarkable considering the original conditions of conversion during centuries of slavery and racism. Black music in the United States is commonly assumed to have its origins partly in the gospel music of African American churches. It is rare to encounter scholars expressing their doubts as to whether such music is authentic or suggesting Black Christians should return to a traditional cosmology, as happens within Indigenous communities in Brazil.

INDIGENOUS CHRISTIAN SONG AS SACRED MUSIC

While Western Christians typically conceive of *sacred music* as including genres of choral music presented by trained musicians for the rest of the congregation, Indigenous peoples of the Americas in general consider all songs to be sacred because songs are received from the spirit world. Ethnomusicologists Chad Hamil and Alan Merriam emphasize the centrality of "song" to Indigenous religious ceremonies in North America and worldwide.[37] According to Mark Clatterbuck, for Crow Christians in Montana, the term "sacred songs" came to refer to the Christian songs in Crow musical style sung in the Crow language, and sometimes in English.[38]

Among Kiowa, Cheyenne, and Comanche Christians, the singing of sacred or spiritual songs is well documented and illustrates how, for believers, these hymns are seen as a fulfillment and expression of Indigenous spirituality, not primarily as an aspect of a religion of outsiders.[39] Kiowa Christians note several characteristics of the songs that underline this. Individual songs were seen as being owned by specific people, arising from their experiences with God.[40] Furthermore, the words used in Kiowa are closely related and reflect the connections between "God's Spirit," "power," and "song." The Kiowa word for "Spirit" (Daw-kee) and the word for "song" (daw-gyah) both come from the root word "daw," meaning "power."[41]

INDIGENOUS CHRISTIANITY AND SONG TYPES IN WEST-CENTRAL BRAZIL

This study contemplates an area of West-Central Brazil, including the states of Rondônia, Mato Grosso, and Mato Grosso do Sul. Here the high plateau marks the division between the Amazonian drainage basin to the north and the Pantanal and the Paraguay River to the south. The landscape consists of the open and dry Cerrado, a savannah of grassland, stunted trees, and forested river valleys. In this sector of Mato Grosso, located in the southern Amazonian region, the Bakairi Nation occupies two separate Indigenous lands: Santana to the west, and to the east, Bakairi Indigenous Lands, where Yakawa's family lives.[42]

Though the Indigenous population of Brazil makes up less than 1 percent of the nation's total population, there are 254 Indigenous nations officially recognized and over 150 languages spoken.[43] West-Central Brazil contains a large concentration of Indigenous populations and is a hub of activity; it is a region where Indigenous Christians regularly travel to access further studies, health care, and to attend conferences.

In order to situate Yakawa's song within current practices, we will describe three categories of songs used within Indigenous churches. Depending largely on each particular Indigenous nation, churches sing a mix of translated or Portuguese songs as well as Indigenous songs. Based on our applied ethnomusicology work, songs are referred to in one of three ways: (1) *música traduzida*, or a translated song; (2), *música na língua mas no ritmo não indígena*, referring to a newly composed Indigenous language song based on a fusion of local and borrowed musical material; or (3) *música na língua indígena e no ritmo indígena*, or a song in an Indigenous language using Indigenous musical elements. The Portuguese word *ritmo* literally means rhythm in Portuguese, but it is used by Indigenous Brazilians to signify the song form, rhythm, melody, and dance all in one.[44] A ritmo may have associated lyrics, but it seems that it is relatively common to add new words to an existing ritmo, sometimes slightly changing the melody and tempo, resulting in a new composition.

The complexities of describing song types practiced by local churches worldwide has led scholars to employ terms[45] ranging from the more prescriptive, for example, *inculturation* and *contextualization*, to the more descriptive, for example, *indigenization* and *localization*, as well as to propose numerous taxonomies.[46] Swee Hong Lim, a liturgical scholar recognized for his work on Asian hymnody, identifies three types of congregational songs used in China, which are analogous to the three categories described earlier.[47] The first category is *Adopted Songs*, which have translated lyrics and "imported musical materials."[48] Adopted Songs, in his example, are hymns and choruses imported from Europe and America and translated into the local language. Though foreign, these songs eventually became beloved by local believers through repeated use. Lim gives examples from China, such as "How Great Thou Art," "Lord I Lift Your Name on High," and "How Great Is our God," all of which are also sung at the Bible college where Yakawa is director. Adopted Songs in Brazil often include hymns and choruses originally composed in English, German, or Portuguese and then translated into the Indigenous language.

Lim's second category of song is *Adapted Songs*, which are compositions "using local melodies" and "often affixed with Western harmonization,"[49] which is similar to what we call *música na língua mas no ritmo não indígena*. Sometimes someone will simply explain that such a song is played with guitar, or *é tocado com violão*. Possible examples of Adapted Songs could be the songs performed by Ticuna Christians in Manaus[50] or the more recent Xavante compositions sung in the Xavante language accompanied by guitar and using Western melodic material.[51]

Lim's third category is *Actualized Songs*, which "draw on the local culture for inspiration and idiomatic expressions."[52] Yakawa's song, under consideration in this essay, certainly would be classified in this category. Singing Actualized Songs often results in feelings of deep emotional and cultural intimacy.[53] Examples of Indigenous churches in Brazil with Actualized Songs would be the Xavante, Suruí, and Zoró churches, each with well-developed hymnodies of one hundred to several hundred songs. Other Indigenous churches such as the Paumarí, Kulina, Canela, and Kuikuru have at least a small number of songs.[54]

MEIRY YAKAWA'S SONG AND TESTIMONY

Meiry Yakawa, an artist and educator, is a single Christian woman from the Bakairi-Kurâ Indigenous Nation. The Bakairi, or Kurâ as they self-identify, have a population of about one thousand. Yakawa grew up in the Bakairi Indigenous area and only gained Portuguese fluency when she left home as a young adult to study. She graduated from a three-year Indigenous Bible college. In 2006, when my wife and I moved as a family to Brazil and started teaching at Yakawa's alma mater, she was already working there as one of the coordinators of the program for the children of students. Prior to that, she had worked as the head cook. During our time at the school, she slowly shifted into a full-time teaching role within the Bible college program. From 2007 to 2010, both Aimée and I cotaught courses with her and also collaborated closely with her on numerous local arts projects. After we left to teach at another school, Yakawa continued teaching, specifically a course called "Theology and Practice of Worship." This course includes a section on ethnomusicological research of Indigenous music and song writing. She also took a year-long sabbatical to complete further studies. Today Meiry Yakawa is the director of the Bible college.

Returning now to Yakawa's presentation mentioned in this essay's introduction, Yakawa recounted at length the song's creative process. After receiving the song from God, her initial fear was of how members of her community would react to Bakairi music being used in Christian worship, possibly criticizing it as a forbidden change in culture. She also felt fear because these songs, in the past, had a strong connection with evil spirits. The shame of being Indigenous also held Yakawa back from using her music. Yakawa states she has heard of many instances where Indigenous people were criticized for their Indigenous music. She cites examples of people saying to others, "Stop singing that music!" and "Your music is so ugly; how can you sing like that?" She says, however, that Indigenous Christians should not be influenced by fear or shame but by God's Word.

Yakawa explains that she was the first Christian in her family. After graduating from Bible college, she was unsure of what God wanted her to do. Years later, she returned to work at her alma mater, where she went through a difficult time of testing. Her dad, one grandmother, and a cousin all died within a short period of time. Yakawa felt isolated, angry at God, and hopeless. At the same time, she began teaching "Cultural Anthropology" and "Theology and Practice of Worship" at the Bible college. These classes made her think a lot about the deep spiritual issues in her personal life. She states that even as a teacher, she realized she still needed to confront issues of fear and shame in her own life.

As Yakawa began teaching specifically about Indigenous expressive arts, she strongly desired to create a song but felt unable to. She tells the audience of the tremendous confusion and weakness she felt during that time of intense struggle. She was not sleeping well and felt the enemy (Satan) was against her. However, she says, she and Aimée kept on talking and praying. Finally, God helped her finish the lyrics of her first song, "There Are Two Ways," along with an accompanying dance, which later was often performed at the school and elsewhere.

A few months later her other grandmother, with whom she was very close, passed away, and once again Yakawa experienced sleepless nights. She spent the nights praying, asking God to speak. Suddenly one night, a ritmo came to mind, one that she had not heard since infancy. Her grandmother had passed it on to her, but she could not recall all the lyrics. She knew it was a song of lament and the lyrics had something to do with insufficient paint and clothing for a ceremony. Yakawa explains that this ritmo was used in the past to sing and dance one week after someone's death. If the deceased was a woman, then all the women of the village would gather together. Hitting the ground with bunches of strong-smelling leaves, they would slowly follow the paths the deceased person had walked until reaching the cemetery where the ceremony would end. This was a way to "carry the soul along."

Later that same night, God gave her the new lyrics, which proved to be personally relevant. She then said to herself, "If this is from God, I will remember it in the morning," and promptly fell into a deep sleep. The next morning, she remembered it in its entirety.

As Yakawa finishes telling the story, she says she is feeling challenged and that now is the right time to publicly sing this personal song. In response, voices and cheers are heard from the audience. "This is God speaking with me," she says, "and I sing it now as a prayer":

> Woman, arise and go speak
> Wake up, come listen to what I am saying.
> Don't say it is late in the evening
> Don't say "Leave it 'til the morning."
> Come speak of me
> Tell about me to those who don't know me.
> I am telling you,
> If you speak of me
> With my blood I will paint you,
> With my clothes I will dress you.
> I am your Father who is speaking;
> I am your Creator who is speaking.

Yakawa testifies that through this song, God has continuously consoled and uplifted her when she is discouraged in her work. She recalls that before she began teaching "Theology and Practice of Worship," she thought, "How can I teach something I have never done or experienced?" This song helped her to inspire and motivate others. Her act of vulnerability was powerful and memorable for Yakawa and for all those participating in the musicians' conference.

In order to contextualize Yakawa's story within the experiences of other Indigenous Christians, I wish to compare it to a similar testimony of a Crow Christian woman from Montana, Georgine Takes Gun Falls Down.[55] Clatterbuck presents an interview with Georgine in which she tells of her Christian life, many difficulties, and the "one song" she received from God. I have chosen this account in part because so little else has been published on personal and/or women's songs within the ethnomusicology of Indigenous Christianity.[56]

Georgine now volunteers with the Crow Hymns Ministry with Crow singers who seek to teach, preserve, and perform the Crow "sacred song" hymnody.[57] She compares the sacred songs to the traditional medicine bundles, saying she "carries" the songs, and uses the songs as medicine and ministry while singing in homes and churches. Years before she began this work, Georgine was a struggling mother of four young children with a sick husband. The process by which she received a song began when her mother told her of a woman who had sung in church: "The Lord gave her a song. She sang it, and it was so beautiful that I wanted you to be there to listen at how the Lord worked in that woman's life."[58] Georgine was intrigued and began seeking a song from God. During a busy time of working and caring for her family, she suddenly had a melody that she began singing "in her heart." She tried to relax in the evening, but "that song was really coming strong" and "then I heard some words coming," she remembers.

Georgine, though very excited over the experience, was afraid of people's criticisms, so she held on to the song for a whole year. When some Pentecostal women came to her house to pray, she remembered the song, saying, "This song came to me and I was afraid of people. I should be afraid of the Lord, and here I am afraid of people, of what they would say. So, I've kept this for one whole year."[59] She began sharing "that one song" with others. Her husband's health finally improved, and her mother-in-law invited her to the Baptist church. When the pastor asked for testimonies, she finally gave in to what she felt was God's invitation: she sang her one song and "cried all the way through." Later Georgine began ministering with her songs and received many more songs, but she remembers that her song ministry began with receiving that one song. "I had only one song, but I sang it at every house meeting. I would sing it, and I would share with them how I experienced this song."[60]

What can be observed in comparing these two stories? Both accounts include waiting at night, asking God for a song, acquiring a melody followed later by the lyrics, and receiving one song with excitement but also with fear of what Christians or non-Christians would think. Then comes the challenge of sharing that one song accompanied by satisfaction at how people accept it and how it becomes part of a personal ministry involving speaking, singing, and relationships. My intent is not to claim definite transcultural Indigenous structures but simply to point out the power and striking similarity of experience in two personal songs.

"DEUS YAGÂ AGUELY" ["GOD WITH ME SPEAKING"]

Reflecting on the specificity of one song is useful in understanding Indigenous hymnody more generally. While many songs are based on a scripture verse or a general gospel message, this one is different, a reminder that not all Indigenous songs are the same.[61] Yakawa's song was based on her remembrance of a funeral song sung with the goal of "taking the soul along" after death. In Yakawa's understanding, God gave this song a new purpose: a personal song in which God speaks directly with her. The words are both commanding and comforting. The phrase "Woman arise and go speak" is a prophetic-like call to take courage. Yet the intimacy of this message is demonstrated by the lyrics "Wake up, come listen to what I am saying" and "I am your Father/Creator who is speaking."

The final lyrics, "If you speak of me, with my blood I will paint you, with my clothes I will dress you," are remarkable for their significance on multiple levels within a combined Bakairi and Christian worldview. "With my clothes I will dress you" reflects a theme common in the Bible and expressed in Christian songs.[62] By contrast, the phrase "with my blood I will paint you" is more startling to non-Indigenous ears. The reference to painting recalls the body painting done by most Indigenous groups, which carries numerous meanings within Indigenous worldviews.[63] A red fruit, *urucum*, is the source of an orange/red paste used to paint the body for ceremonies. Body painting is observed at both traditional dances/rituals as well as at contemporary celebrations, such as graduation ceremonies and April 19 Indigenous Day dances. During the preparation for an event, body painting generates excitement and careful planning. Without the painting, a celebration does not seem complete.

In personal conversations, Yakawa and Aimée reflected that while the original song was a lament and included lyrics about a lack of paint for celebrations, these new lyrics point to Christ's sufficiency and his provision for us, as Christians, to be able to celebrate. In a Christian understanding, being covered by Christ's blood is a central biblical theme signifying his sacrifice for the sins of humanity.[64]

THE WORTH OF ONE SONG

At the Teruwah Musicians Conference in 2014, Yakawa ended her talk asking the Indigenous participants present, "Why is it that during my travels, I see so few Indigenous churches using Indigenous songs?" With Yakawa's question in mind, I return to a query at the heart of this essay: What is the worth of one song? If, according to Yakawa's and my observations, most Indigenous churches sing hymns and choruses in Portuguese, without translation, why does Yakawa's one song even matter? Last year, when preparing to present her song in a college chapel service, Yakawa decided to change the title of her song from "Woman, Arise and Go Speak" to "God with Me Speaking." She made this change because the most relevant aspect of this song is that God speaks with her. The foremost reason Yakawa never presented her song in public before the Teruwah conference was that her song is so intimately personal she could not face singing it without being overcome with emotion.

Beyond personal reasons, this one song has emboldened Yakawa in her public speaking and bolstered her confidence in teaching and in encouraging the use of Indigenous music. As a result of Yakawa's experience and influence, various other Indigenous Christians have composed their own songs in their own language and musical style. Since receiving the song, Meiry Yakawa has developed her abilities in discipleship, teaching, and leadership in numerous ways as a teacher and now as director of the college, itself a remarkable position for an Indigenous woman in Brazil.

After interviewing Georgine about her songs, Clatterbuck remarked, "She illustrates her conviction that a passionate celebration of Crow culture is fully compatible with Christian faith."[65] An important theme of Yakawa's talk is how she understands her Christian faith to be expressed in and through her freedom to sing Bakairi songs. Undoubtedly, in Yakawa's case and for many other Indigenous people, there is no dichotomy between their own sense of indigeneity and their experience of a personal Christian faith.

In this essay, significant barriers impeding adequate representation of Indigenous Christian music were introduced. Further study is needed to explore the disciplinary and social factors within and outside Brazil and to envision a way forward with Indigenous Christian songs in a politically challenging, culturally fractured environment that includes rapid erosion of languages and cultural expressions. Nevertheless, given the drastic cultural and linguistic losses ongoing in many Indigenous nations, in addition to violence and forfeiture of lands, even "just one song" is very important.[66]

APPENDIX 1: SONG TRANSCRIPTION

Deus Yagâ Aguely
God with Me Speaking

Rosimeiry Paureky Yakawa
Bakairi Melody

Transcription: Aimée Seng Janzen
Mike Janzen

Figure 12.1. "Deus Yagâ Aguely"

APPENDIX 2: LYRICS AND WORD FOR WORD TRANSLATION

Title: Deus Yagâ Aguely [God with Me Speaking] Lyrics: Rosimeiry Paureky Yakawa Music: Based on Bakairi Melody	
Lyrics and Meaning	**Literal Translation**
Aukâ Pekodo idâ aguera (2x) [Woman, arise and go speak]	Aukâ = Arise, get up | Pekodo = Woman | idâ = go | aguera = speak
Âwaguegâ idakârâ auguely (2x) [Wake up, come listen to what I am saying]	Âwaguegâ = wake up | idakârâ = come listen | auguely = what I am saying
Kuetâji-enram tâkezeba ikâro [Don't say it is late in the evening]	Kuetâji = late in the evening | enram = already is | tâkezeba = don't say | ikâro = no adequate translation exists but similar to please or I hope.
Kopaelâga ise tâkezebane ikâro [Don't say "Leave it 'til the morning."]	Kopaelâga = tomorrow | ise = will be | tâkezebane = you better not say | ikâro = no adequate translation but similar to please or I hope.
Aguekârâ ywâgâ-ro [Come speak of me]	Aguekârâ = come speak | ywâgâ-ro = of me
Iegatugâ utudânry modoan-ha [Tell about me to those who don't know me]	Iegatugâ = tell about me | utudânry = who don't know me | modoan-ha = many (people)
Uguely kuru enram (2x) [I am telling you]	Uguely = I am telling | kuru = truly in the imperative sense | enram = already is
Ywâgâ amyguely watay [If you speak of me]	Ywâgâ = of me | amyguely = you speak | watay = if
Unugue âwenize urâ [With my blood, I will paint you]	Unu = my blood | gue = with | âwenize = paint you | urâ = I
Ietygue itydâze urâ [With my clothes, I will dress you]	Iety = my clothes | gue = with | itydâze = dress you | urâ = I
Unwy urâ agueim, [I am your Father who is speaking]	Unwy = your father | urâ = I | agueim = is speaking
Urâ agueim âugunipyry [I am your Creator who is speaking] (Previous two lines are repeated)	Urâ = I | agueim = is speaking | âugunipyry = your creator
Unwy urâ agueim, (2x) [I am your Father who is speaking]	Unwy = your father | urâ = I | agueim = is speaking

NOTES

1. The epigraph for this essay is from Mark Clatterbuck, "Singer, Healer, and Pow-wow Dancer: An Interview with Georgine Takes Gun Falls Down," in *Crow Jesus: Personal Stories of Native Religious Belonging* (Norman: University of Oklahoma Press, 2017), 206.

2. Bruna Franchetto and Tommaso Montagnani, "'When Women Lost Kagutu Flutes, to Sing Tolo Was All They Had Left!' Gender Relations among the Kuikuro of Central Brazil as Revealed in Ordeals of Language and Music," in "Ordeals of Language: Essays in Honor of Ellen B. Basso," *Journal of Anthropological Research* 68, no. 3 (2012): 339–55, accessed March 15, 2020, https://www.jstor.org/stable/23264639; Maria Ignez C. Mello, "Iamurikuma: Música, mito e ritual entre os Wauja do Alto Xingu" (PhD diss., Programa de Pos-Graduação em Antropologia Social, Universidade Federal de Santa Catarina, Florianopolis, Brazil, 2005), accessed March 14, 2020, http://repositorio.ufsc.br/handle/123456789/102877; Acacio Piedade, "O canto do Kawoka: Música, cosmologia e filosofia entre os Wauja do Alto Xingu" (PhD diss., Programa de Pos-Graduação em Antropologia Social, Universidade Federal de Santa Catarina, Florianopolis, Brazil, 2004), accessed March 14, 2020, http://repositorio.ufsc.br/xmlui/handle/123456789/86556.

3. Anthony Seeger, *Why Suyá Sing: A Musical Anthropology of an Amazonian People* (Cambridge: Cambridge University Press, 1987); Jonathan D. Hill and Jean-Pierre Chaumeil, eds., *Burst of Breath: Indigenous Ritual Wind Instruments in Lowland South America* (Lincoln: University of Nebraska Press, 2011); Ellen Basso, *A Musical View of the Universe: Kalapalo Myth and Ritual Performance* (Philadelphia: University of Pennsylvania, 1985).

4. Fenella Cannell, ed., *The Anthropology of Christianity* (Durham, NC: Duke University Press, 2006); Aparecida Vilaça, *Praying and Preying: Christianity in Indigenous Amazonia*, trans. David Rodgers (Oakland, CA: University of California Press, 2016); Aparecida Vilaça, "Reconfiguring Humanity in Amazonia: Christianity and Change," in *A Companion to the Anthropology of Religion*, ed. Janice Boddy and Michael Lambek (Hoboken: John Wiley and Sons, 2013), 363–86; Joel Robbins, "What Is a Christian? Notes Toward an Anthropology of Christianity," *Religion* 33 (2003): 191–99, accessed March 14, 2020, https://doi.org/10.1016/S0048-721X(03)00060-5; Lucas Bessire, *Behold the Black Caiman: A Chronicle of Ayoreo Life* (Chicago: University of Chicago, 2014).

5. Instituto Brasileiro de Geografia e Estatística. "Sistema IBGE de Recuperação Automática—SIDRA," 2018, accessed April 11, 2020, https://sidra.ibge.gov.br/Tabela/2094.

6. Luke E. Lassiter, Clyde Ellis, and Ralph Kotay, *The Jesus Road: Kiowas, Christianity, and Indian Hymns* (Lincoln, NE: University of Nebraska Press, 2002), 115.

7. David William Samuels, "Singing Indian Country," in *Music of the First Nations: Tradition and Innovation in Native North America*, ed. Tara Browner (Chicago: University of Illinois Press, 2009), 143.

8. Samuels, "Singing Indian Country," 147.

9. Beverley Diamond, *Native American Music in Eastern North America* (New York: Oxford University Press, 2008); Samuel Araújo, "Conflict and Violence as Theoretical Tools in Present-Day Ethnomusicology: Notes on a Dialogic Ethnography of Sound Practices in Rio de Janeiro," in "50th Anniversary Commemorative Issue," *Ethnomusicology* 50, no. 2 (Spring/Summer 2006): 310, accessed February 4, 2018, http://www.jstor.org/stable/20174454; Luke Lassiter, *The Chicago Guide to Collaborative Ethnography*, A Chicago Guide to Writing, Editing, and Publishing (Chicago: University of Chicago Press, 2005), 139.

Our collaborative methodology follows Samuel Araújo and Grupo Musicultura's practice of cosigning a text, as well as Luke Lassiter's "co-writing," which he lists as one of six approaches to producing a collaborative text (139). See note 2 in Araújo about cosigning. In his 2005 book, Lassiter provides an example of cowriting a chapter with Ralph Kotay for the book *The Jesus Road* (146). In our case, informed by our discussions about the song, I wrote the text based on a transcription of Yakawa's presentation, filmed in 2014. I then presented the Portuguese translation of the text to her, which we edited together.

10. Jonathan M. Dueck and Suzel Ana Reily, "Introduction," in *The Oxford Handbook of Music and World Christianities*, ed. Suzel Ana Reily and Jonathan M. Dueck (New York: Oxford University Press, 2016), 3; Aparecida Vilaça and Robin Wright, eds., *Native Christians: Modes and Effects of Christianity among Indigenous Peoples of the Americas* (Farnham: Ashgate, 2009).

11. Vilaça, *Praying and Preying*, 8; Peter Gow, "SIL in the Piro Lived World," in *The Anthropology of Christianity*, ed. Fenella Cannell (Durham, NC: Duke University Press, 2006), 214.

12. Vilaça, "Reconfiguring Humanity in Amazonia: Christianity and Change," 365.

13. Ibid.

14. Robbins, "What Is a Christian?" 192.

15. Ibid., 195.

16. Muriel Swijghuisen Reigersberg, "Applied Ethnomusicology in Christian Indigenous Contexts: Ontologies, Frameworks and the Christianity of Ethnomusicology" (Lecture at the 62nd Annual Meeting of the Society of Ethnomusicology, Denver, Colorado, October 28, 2017).

17. Susan Harding, "Representing Fundamentalism: The Problem of the Repugnant Cultural Other," *Social Research* 58, no. 2 (1991): 375, accessed March 10, 2020, www.jstor.org/stable/40970650.

18. Robert J. Priest, "Missionary Positions: Christian, Modernist, Postmodernist," *Current Anthropology* 42, no. 1 (2001): 29–68, accessed April 25, 2018, doi:10.1086/318433; Vilaça, "Reconfiguring Humanity in Amazonia: Christianity and Change," 365.

19. Tanya Luhrmann, "Comment on 'Missionary Positions: Christian, Modernist, Postmodernist,'" *Current Anthropology* 42, no. 1 (2001): 55, accessed April 26, 2018, http://www.jstor.org/stable/10.1086/318433.

20. Lassiter, *The Chicago Guide to Collaborative Ethnography*, 56.

21. Joey Sprague, *Feminist Methodologies for Critical Researchers: Bridging Differences* (Walnut Creek, CA: AltaMira Press, 2005), 41; Judith Stacey, "Can There Be a Feminist Ethnography?" *Women's Studies International Forum* 11, no. 1 (1988): 22, accessed April 20, 2020, https://doi.org/10.1016/0277-5395(88)90004-0.

22. Brian Howell, "The Repugnant Cultural Other Speaks Back: Christian Identity as Ethnographic Standpoint," *Anthropological Theory* 17, no. 4 (2007): 376, accessed November 23, 2016, doi:10.1177/1463499607083426.

23. Howell, "The Repugnant Cultural Other Speaks Back," 372.

24. Martin Holbraad, Bruce Kapferer, and Julia F. Sauma, "Introduction: Critical Ruptures," in *Ruptures: Anthropologies of Discontinuity in Times of Turmoil* (London: UCL Press, 2019), 1, accessed March 6, 2020, DOI: https://doi.org/10.14324/1 11.9781787356184.

25. Bessire, *Behold the Black Caiman*, 127.

26. Robbins, "What is a Christian?, 192.

27. Vilaça, *Reconfiguring Humanity in Amazonia*, 365.

28. See also Eduardo Viveiros de Castro, "Who Are They?" Povos Indígenas no Brasil, accessed March 10, 2020, https://pib.socioambiental.org/en/Who_are_they%3F#Indians.2C_Amerindians; United National Permanent Forum on Indigenous Issues, "Who Are Indigenous Peoples?" accessed March 11, 2020, https://www.un.org/esa/socdev/unpfii/documents/5session_factsheet1.pdf.

29. Eduardo Viveiros de Castro, *Cosmological Perspectivism in Amazonia and Elsewhere* (Manchester, UK: HAU Network of Ethnographic Theory, 2012), accessed March 12, 2020, https://haubooks.org/cosmological-perspectivism-in-amazonia/.

30. For a discussion on this wide-ranging subject, see Martin Holbraad and Morten Axel Pedersen, *The Ontological Turn: An Anthropological Exposition* (Cambridge: Cambridge University Press, 2017); Paolo Heywood, "The Ontological Turn," in *The Cambridge Encyclopedia of Anthropology*, ed. F. Stein, S. Lazar, M. Candea, H. Diemberger, J. Robbins, A. Sanchez, and R. Stasch, 2017, accessed March 9, 2020, http://doi.org/10.29164/17ontology.

31. David Bond and Lucas Bessire, "The Ontological Spin," in Dispatches, *Cultural Anthropology*, accessed February 28, 2014, https://culanth.org/fieldsights/494-the- ontological-spin; Bessire, *Behold the Black Caiman*, 19; Alcida Rita Ramos, "Disengaging Anthropology," in *A Companion to Latin American Anthropology*, ed. by Deborah Poole, Blackwell Companions to Anthropology Series (Malden, MA: Blackwell Publishing, 2008), 469; Anthony Seeger, "Focusing Perspectives and Establishing Boundaries and Power: Why the Suyá/Kisedje Sing for the Whites in the Twenty-First Century," *Ethnomusicology Forum* 22, no. 3 (2013): 362–76; Terry S. Turner, "The Crisis of Late Structuralism, Perspectivism and Animism: Rethinking Culture, Nature, Spirit, and Bodiliness," *Tipití: Journal of the Society for the Anthropology of Lowland South America* 7, no 1 (2009), accessed March 12, 2020, http://digitalcommons.trinity.edu/tipiti/vol7/iss1/1.

32. Bessire, *Behold the Black Caiman*, 15.

33. Ibid., 2, 18.

34. John Burdick, *The Color of Sound: Race, Religion, and Music in Brazil* (New York: New York University Press, 2013).

35. Timothy Rommen, "Sounds Transcendent: Gospel Music and the Negotiation of Proximity in Trinidad," in *Resounding Transcendence: Transitions in Music, Religion, and Ritual*, ed. Philip V. Bohlman and Jeffers Engelhardt (New York: Oxford University Press, 2016), 97–110.

36. For a recent example, see Thérese Smith, "Music and Religiosity among African American Fundamentalist Christians," in *The Oxford Handbook of Music and World Christianities*, ed. Suzel Anna Reily and Jonathan M. Dueck (New York: Oxford University Press, 2016), 248–68.

37. Alan P. Merriam, "The Importance of Song in the Flathead Indian Vision Quest," *Ethnomusicology* 9, no. 2 (1965): 91–99, accessed April 13, 2020, doi:10.2307/850314; Chad Hamill, *Songs of Power and Prayer in the Columbia Plateau: The Jesuit, the Medicine Man, and the Indian Hymn Singer* (Corvallis, OR: Oregon State University Press, 2012), 1.

38. Clatterbuck, *Crow Jesus*, 207.

39. Lassiter, *The Jesus Road*, 82; David Graber, "The Cheyenne Hymns, the Hymnbook, and Plains Indian Culture," *Mennonite Life* 61, no. 2 (June 2006), accessed April 12, 2017, http://ml.bethelks.edu/issue/ vol-61-no-2/article/the-cheyenne-hymns-the-hymnbook-and-plains-indian/.

40. Lassiter, *The Jesus Road*, 88.

41. Ibid., 82.

42. Edir Pina de Barros, "Bakairi," Povos Indígenas no Brasil, accessed March 10, 2020, https://pib.socioambiental.org/en/Povo:Bakairi.

43. "Who Are They?" Povos Indígenas no Brasil, accessed March 10, 2020, https://pib.socioambiental.org/en/Who_are_they%3F#Indians.2C_Amerindians.

44. Anthony Seeger, "The Tropical Forest Region," in *South America, Mexico, Central America, and the Caribbean*, ed. Dale A. Olsen and Daniel E. Sheehy, vol. 2, *The Garland Encyclopedia of World Music*, advisory editors Bruno Nettl and Ruth M. Stone, founding editors James Porter and Timothy Rice (New York: Garland Publishing, 1998), 126.

45. For a detailed survey of terms, see Monique Ingalls, Muriel Swijghuisen Reigersberg, and Zoe C. Sherinian, "Introduction: Music as Local and Global Positioning: How Congregational Music-making Produces the Local in Christian Communities Worldwide," in *Making Congregational Music Local in Christian Communities Worldwide*, ed, Monique Ingalls, Muriel Swijghuisen Reigersberg, and Zoe C. Sherinian, Congregational Music Studies (New York: Routledge, 2018), 1–32.

46. Among various other taxonomies proposed, Krabill details "Six Stages of Music Development in Many African Faith Communities," while Sherinian notes five categories in an "Indigenization Taxonomy" of Tamil music. James R. Krabill, "Encounters: What Happens to Music When People Meet," in *Music in the Life of the African Church*, ed. Roberta King (Waco: Baylor University Press, 2008), 70; Zoe Sherinian, *Tamil Folk Music as Dalit Liberation Theology* (Bloomington: Indiana University Press, 2014), 36.

47. Swee Hong Lim, "*Forming Christians through Musicking in China*," *Religions* 8, no. 50 (2017): 1–10, accessed February 15, 2018, http://dx.doi:10.3390/rel8040050; Swee Hong Lim, "Sacred Song for All God's Children: A Perspective on

Post-Colonial Asian Congregation Song," in *Complex Identities in a Shifting World: One God, Many Stories*, ed. Pamela Couture, Robert Mager, Pamela McCarroll, and Natalie Wigg-Stevenson, International Practical Theology series, vol. 17 (Zurich: Lit Verlag GmbH & Co. KG Wien, 2015), 138–54.

48. Lim, *Forming Christians through Musicking in China*, 4.

49. Ibid., 5.

50. See track 14, *Wui Tcümü duügüü* (Conjunto do Povo), and track 16 *Weri Aru Cau* (Canto do Uirapuru), in "Cantos Indígenas," Various Artists, Prefeitura de Manaus—Cultura. PRC-021, no date, Compact Disc.

51. Other possible examples could include new compositions by Waiwai Christians, where according to Seeger, "communities compete in composing hymns." Seeger, "The Tropical Forest Region," 131.

52. Lim, *Forming Christians through Musicking in China*, 6.

53. Ibid.

54. "Ritmos Indígenas no Ami," Self-Published, 2009, Compact Disc.

55. Mark Clatterbuck, "Singer, Healer, and Powwow Dancer," 201.

56. Virginia Giglio, *Southern Cheyenne Women's Songs* (Norman: University of Oklahoma Press, 1994), 163. In one similar example, Giglio discusses her unexpected discovery of women singing Christian Cheyenne Hymns as part of their everyday lives while doing chores or driving.

57. Clatterbuck, *Crow Jesus*, 206.

58. Ibid., 204.

59. Ibid., 205.

60. Ibid., 206.

61. "Ritmos Indígenas no Ami."

62. Ephesians 6:10–18 and Isaiah 61:10 refer to "dressing with righteousness." Isaiah 6:10–18: "I delight greatly in the LORD; my soul rejoices in my God. For he has clothed me with garments of salvation and arrayed me in a robe of righteousness" (New International Version).

63. Oiara Bonilla, "The Skin of History: Paumari Perspectives on Conversion and Transformation," in *Native Christians: Modes and Effects of Christianity among Indigenous Peoples of the Americas*, ed. Aparecida Vilaça and Robin M. Wright (Burlington, VT: Ashgate Publishing Company, 2009), 127–46.

64. Psalm 32:1: "Blessed is he whose transgressions are forgiven, whose sins are covered" (New International Version); Hebrews 9:11–15 and 1 Peter 1:1–2 refer to the sprinkling with the blood.

65. Clatterbuck, *Crow Jesus*, 201.

66. My special thanks to those who gave feedback on earlier drafts, including my professors and fellow students at the University of Toronto, and especially to my wife Aimée who collaborated at each step. I am grateful for your help in thinking through the analysis of song types utilized in Brazilian Indigenous churches. In many ways, you are the third author of this essay and the story of Meiry's song is also your story. As both you and Yakawa have reflected many times, your collaboration greatly enriched and is essential to your applied ethnomusicology work.

FURTHER READING

Aplin, T. Christopher. "Expectation, Christianity, and Ownership in Indigenous Hip-Hop: Religion in Rhyme with Emcee One, RedCloud, and Quese, Imc." *MUSICultures* 39, no. 1 (2012): 42–69. Accessed April 24, 2020. https://journals.lib.unb.ca/index.php/MC/article/view/24616.

Barz, Gregory, and Timothy J. Cooley, eds. *Shadows in the Field: New Perspectives for Fieldwork in Ethnomusicology.* Second edition. New York: Oxford University Press, 2008.

Bass, Howard. *Beautiful Beyond: Christian Songs in Native Languages.* Washington, DC: Smithsonian Folkways Recordings, 2004. Accessed March 14, 2017. http://go.utlib.ca/cat/9851648.

Cadena, Marisol de la, and Orin Starn. "Introduction." In *Indigenous Experience Today*, edited by Marisol de la Cadena and Orin Starn, 1–30. New York: Berg, 2007.

Clifford, James. *Returns: Becoming Indigenous in the Twenty-first Century.* Cambridge, MA: Harvard University Press, 2013.

Dueck, Byron. *Musical Intimacies & Indigenous Imaginaries: Aboriginal Music and Dance in Public Performance.* New York: Oxford University Press, 2013.

Hinson, Glenn. *Fire in My Bones: Transcendence and the Holy Spirit in African American Gospel.* Philadelphia: University of Pennsylvania Press, 2000.

Magowan, Fiona. "Song as Gift and Capital: Intercultural Processes of Indigenisation and Spiritual Transvaluation in Yolngu Christian Music." In *Making Congregational Music Local in Christian Communities Worldwide*, edited by Monique M. Ingalls, Muriel Swijghuisen Reigersberg, and Zoe C. Sherinian, 97–116. Congregational Music Studies. New York: Routledge, 2018.

McNally, Michael David. *Ojibwe Singers: Hymns, Grief, and a Native Culture in Motion.* Oxford: Oxford University Press, 2000.

Wade, Peter. "Race in Latin America." In *A Companion to Latin American Anthropology*, edited by Deborah Poole, 177–92. Blackwell Companions to Anthropology Series. Malden, MA: Blackwell Publishing, 2008.

Chapter Thirteen

"Lift Every Voice and Sing"
Embodying Black Theology in Song
Stephen Michael Newby and Chelle Stearns

In 1899, James Weldon Johnson was asked to address a gathering honoring the birthday of Abraham Lincoln. He wanted to include a poem about Lincoln but did not find the appropriate inspiration for the task. Instead his mind turned toward writing an epic poem about African American life, inspired by Frederick Douglass.[1] After talking with his brother John Rosamond, a song arose. Five hundred children from the Stanton School, at which James was the principal, premiered "Lift Every Voice and Sing" at the Lincoln celebration on February 12, 1900. What started as a humble song for a community gathering in Jacksonville, Florida, soon turned into an anthem capable of sounding out the complex pains, sorrows, and hopes for the entire African American community. Its communal qualities guaranteed it was soon sung all over the South and beyond: in school assemblies, churches, and political rallies. In 1920, the NAACP declared "Lift Every Voice and Sing" the Negro National Anthem (now commonly referred to as the Black National Anthem), thus establishing its place and prominence within African American church and civic life.[2] Singing this hymn acted as the spiritual vertebrae, realigning the communal spine.

This restorative quality arises from the embodied theology of the music and the lyrics. James Cone, the father of Black Liberation Theology, argues Black theology cannot be separated from social contexts, for its perspective is embedded in Black narratives.[3] Music scholar William Banfield signifies, if one does not recognize particular "black cultural codes" and nuances within the culture, these Black narratives might be misconstrued and misunderstood.[4] Merging these two theses gives us a particular musical and philosophical angle from which to discuss the theology of Black sacred song because, to truly understand Black sacred song, one must be willing to embrace the development of a theology of Black liberation and Black cultural context.

Banfield's work argues there are cultural codes in Black song, immersing the community of singers into the mind of Black life, struggle, aesthetic, and ethos. "Lift Every Voice and Sing" is an African American sacred hymn espousing a treasury of theological motifs, tropes, cultural codes, and narratives. This essay expounds upon the Black cultural codes embedded in the song and the theological content of each verse as it poetically weaves a musical tapestry of Black lament, power, trauma, humility, admonition, victory, prayer, and agency. To discuss this hymn is, in many ways, to explore the contours of Black American culture, thus "Lift Every Voice and Sing" serves as a historic reflective missional litany of Black life.

This essay pays homage to this singing community by echoing a call-and-response artistic rendering. Within the Black community, meaning often emerges from the midst of gathering and discourse, embodied in the formation of the communal voice. This is shaped by a choral tradition that summons the many to sing with boldness and enthusiasm. Thus to make sense of the communal import and mutuality of this hymn, we explore through a call and response ethic. This allows a chorus of voices to articulate the wealth of wisdom that arises from this rich, diverse, and theologically infused musical tradition. As we demonstrate, voices that were once silenced and demeaned rise up with dignity and purpose through this anthem and establish a prophetic public theology unafraid to uphold Blackness and claim the goodness of God's promises for the African American community.

We decided to write this essay together (a white musical theologian and a black theological musician/composer) to model and engender collaboration and conversation and to commit to a different form of scholarship that values diverse antiphonal voices coming together with interdisciplinary intent. Incarnational theology and a theology of worship interacts with explorations of cultural codes, American history, and musical context. We have allowed the rhythm and the cadence of our voices to intermingle, diverge, and sometimes sound contrapuntal. We invite the reader to hear the lyricism of the lines and the dissimilarity of our writing styles, which requires a different lens to read and a different ear to hear the call and response of our cultural contexts, our scholarship, and our friendship. In this, we hope ethics and scholarship honor one another. Throughout, we have written with Bonhoeffer's admonition in mind: "the Christ in you is greater than the Christ in me."

THE VERSES

In order to illuminate the cultural, musical, and theological themes of "Lift Every Voice and Sing," we reflect on each of the three verses. In the first verse, *Lift*, we interrogate the impact of the paradoxical African American experience of accomplishment and oppression found at the beginning of the twentieth century and beyond. This verse both foresees and bears witness to a very particular rise in Black culture, as generativity and new cultural forms emerge in a racially fraught America. In the second verse, *Stony*, we turn to the past toward the practice and tradition of lament. This section expounds on the importance of taking time to lament, grieve, and weep over the stony road of history and oppression. In the final verse, *God*, we focus on how the community prays for hope and a renewed future, following the dark wisdom of the weary feet who have walked the path before. This verse calls for a prophetic and lived-out public theology to inspire the agency of the Black community today. To help adumbrate the theological resonance in each verse, we look to the work of theologians James Cone, Cheryl Kirk-Duggan, and M. Shawn Copeland. Each theologian, in his or her own way, resources the spirituals as rich theological material to unpack and rearticulate the formation and emergence of Black American theology and life. They recover the theological work of those denied a voice in formal Western theology, believing that God is revealed where the community of the oppressed bears witness to the movement of the Spirit.

Lift
Lift ev'ry voice and sing
'Til earth and heaven ring
Ring with the harmonies of Liberty
Let our rejoicing rise
High as the list'ning skies
Let it resound loud as the rolling sea
Sing a song full of the faith that the dark past has taught us
Sing a song full of the hope that the present has brought us
Facing the rising sun of our new day begun
Let us march on 'til victory is won

The first verse of this hymn captures the spirit of the age for Black Americans. At the turn of the twentieth century, there was a purposeful and concerted effort to lift up the entire community from the ashes of history. The Reconstruction era's broken promise of "forty acres and a mule" for almost four million formerly enslaved persons turned into a generative period born out of self-reliance and communal determination.[5] This determination was often spurred on through singing because the power of the voice was all the community had, a sung truth from deep in the heart, not the head. In the singing of this verse, a hope was embodied and sounded forth so that no one would forget, entreating the community toward agency. This hope was informed by "the dark past" yet declared that the sun that rises on this day will spur the community on "'til victory is won."

In *May We Forever Stand: A History of the Black National Anthem*, Imani Perry argues that this hymn was written at the "nadir" of African American life. A burgeoning of creativity and civic life in Black American communities was met by distrust and hostilities from white American communities, especially in the South. In Jacksonville, Florida, where the Johnson brothers were born and lived, success and accomplishment resulted not in accolades and status but in unwarranted violence and oppression. In the years following the writing of "Lift Every Voice," living in the South with dark skin became complex and dangerous, and authorities often turned a "blind eye" to overt racial attacks and property damage. A new form of "racial terrorism"[6] (which included lynching, riots, and neighborhood violence) and the assumptive rule of law known as Jim Crow were key factors in Southern African Americans migrating to the urban North.[7] As Perry describes this time, "The Johnson brothers and their contemporaries experienced this transition from the hope of Reconstruction to the devastation of the nadir as they came of age. They were called to both mourn dashed dreams and dream anew in their adulthoods as a pigmentocracy took hold where citizenship had been promised."[8] The combined reality that the color of one's skin determined one's ability to participate and thrive in American democracy and James's experience of an attempted lynching in a park were a signal that the future for the brothers may have to be nurtured and cultivated further north.[9] As Perry argues, Black intellectuals, artists, and politicians were not discouraged but became organized politically, created new artistic forms, and generally worked for "racial uplift." Thus "the nadir [in which this hymn was written] can be remembered as a time not simply of exclusion and racist violence but also of blossoming."[10] The dehumanization of Jim Crow could not stop the determination of artists like James and Rosamond Johnson.

Sociologist Ron Eyerman maintains that this paradox of possibility and repression created "the cultural politics of racial uplift and collective identity-formation" within the African American community.[11] Churches were the epicenter of Black life after the Civil War, but as it became clear that the promise of full citizenship was not forthcoming, the Black community turned to intellectuals, businessmen, and community organizers such as W. E. B. Du Bois and Booker T. Washington to gather folks to discuss political and civic action. One could refer to this as a political theology with an urgency toward justice and equity for today rather than a promised future that may never come. In these meetings, rules, codes, and rituals (such as the singing of "Lift Every Voice") were established, creating a culture of empowerment and inspiration. Perry refers to this as the rise of "black formalism."[12] She argues that "Lift Every Voice and Sing" became integral to Black ritual life, transcending the divides between sacred and secular, poor and rich, high and low. It was sung at political meetings, at graduations, in churches, at the end of variety shows, and in essence wherever the Black community gathered purposely and proudly. "The song proved to be, both then and soon thereafter, much bigger than an ode to any one leader or icon. It was a lament and encomium to the story and struggle of black people. The Johnsons at once wrote black history and wrote black people into the traditions of formal Western music with their noble song."[13] The hymn became a call to lift and to rise in unison, together.

The turn to singing in Black formalism acknowledged a deeply rooted practical truth in the Black community: singing calls forth one's humanity. In *The Spirituals and the Blues*, James Cone argues that Black music is "essential for identity and survival."[14] Through the writing and singing of the spirituals, enslaved people proclaimed their enduring humanity and their identity as God's children. Cone continues his argument, suggesting, "Black music is unity music. It unites the joy and the sorrow, the love and the hate, the hope and the despair of black people; and it moves the people toward the direction of total liberation. It shapes and defines black existence and creates cultural structures for black expression. Black music is unifying because it confronts the individual with the truth of black existence and affirms that black being is possible only in a communal context."[15] Formalized singing recognized the collective breath and purpose of those gathered. To sing was to call forth God's presence. In the spirituals the presence of the Spirit of God was bidden and celebrated in the full humanity of those who sang. Because the Spirit of God was with them, they were provided with what Cone describes as "the courage and the strength to make it through."[16]

For Cone, music is the birthplace of Black Liberation Theology. It ties the body and the soul together with the promises of God. He contends, "To interpret the theological significance of the spirituals for the black community, 'academic' tools are not enough. The interpreter must *feel* the Spirit; that is, he must feel his way into the power of black music, responding both to its rhythm and the faith in experience it affirms."[17] Music is a place of reclamation and proclamation, naming all of the contradictions in life with the greater reality of God's liberation. In song, the Bible comes alive with promise. As Cone maintains, "For black slaves, Jesus is God breaking into their historical present and transforming it according to divine expectations. Because of the revelation of Christ, there is no need to worry about the reality of liberation. It is already at hand in Jesus' own person and work, and it will be fully consummated in God's own ordained future."[18] Thus, Cone argues,

Jesus is in solidarity with the Black community as they sing their way into their promised future.[19]

By turning to the spirituals as theological texts, theologians such as Cone lift up the voices of the past. They give honor to the composers and poets who yearned for God's solidarity with their suffering and called forth God's Spirit to dwell within their daily experiences. From this theological conviction, African American Christians across the ages have leaned into the promise of liberation through song because God is a God who lifts up the oppressed—the One who is making all things right lifts all people heavenward.

Stony
Stony the road we trod
Bitter the chastening rod
Felt in the days when hope unborn had died
Yet with a steady beat
Have not our weary feet
Come to the place for which our fathers sighed?
We have come over a way that with tears has been watered
We have come, treading our path through the blood of the slaughtered
Out from the gloomy past
'Til now we stand at last
Where the white gleam of our bright star is cast

The second verse turns to lament to attend to past and enduring sorrows. The road to today has been stony, and the chastening rod all too real. Truth telling, grief, and lament are all necessary. The communal character of African American ritual and worship contextualizes and theologizes lament. The lament of the second verse gives folks permission to cry. Lament becomes a value. Lament unveils transparency. Lamenting together signifies that we are not alone. Walking stony roads is hard on the body. We walk stony roads with others. One road at a time. We will not be alone in our lament. The spirituals of lament demand God's presence on this stony road.

Theological ethicist M. Shawn Copeland argues for a visceral and embodied theology through sung lament: "This Jesus walks out of the pages of the Bible and makes himself 'available for services of every kind, on earth and in heaven, in life and death.' From the vantage of the spirituals, Jesus could do anything, and the enslaved people were not hesitant 'to make very unusual demands of [their] friend Jesus.'"[20] To understand this form of embodied and redemptive presence of God, one must feel the power of spirituals sung in the moment of sorrow. The Equal Justice Initiative's "Legacy Museum" in Montgomery, Alabama, attempts to replicate this form of anguished prayer. On the first turn into the museum, visitors walk past a row of jail cells filled with videos representing men, women, and children waiting to be sold at the slave market just a few steps away from the museum.²¹ At the far end of the row is a video of a woman singing, "I want Jesus to walk with me." With her entire person, she calls forth God's presence, verse after verse: "In my troubles, Lord walk with me / In my troubles, Lord walk with me / When my life becomes a burden, / Lord, I want Jesus to walk with me." We can hear in such spirituals the origins of "We have come over a way that with tears has been watered / We have come, treading our path through the blood of the slaughtered." To remember is to honor the feet and the bodies of those who had trod the stony paths. This remembrance is imperative for the formation of community, as theologian J. Kameron Carter claims, when there are so many broken and lost bodies from the past, "we can't be *us* without caring for the dead."²² As Copeland maintains,

> In anamnetic language or the language of memory, the spirituals venerate and honor the ancestors, the more than twenty million African women and men who disappeared in the Middle Passage, whose bones litter the floor of the Atlantic. Surely, they shall rise on the last day to meet Jesus face to face; the mother or father, wife or husband, brother or sister sold away at whim.²³

This form of lament, then, is a communal caring for the dead.

In this way, the practice of singing becomes a form of social ritual. Jeremy Begbie argues that this form of musical practice connects us to culture, to the world around us, to our bodies, and to the formation of our emotional life.²⁴ Begbie points out the power of music to form and guide our emotional lives, creating a kind of "countersentimentality" to the "pathology of sentimentality."²⁵ This pathology indulges emotional excess by trivializing evil through an inappropriate lack of response to suffering.²⁶ To participate in lament, in contrast, requires response, demands the revealing of truth, and does not look away from the "steady beat" of the "weary feet" of those who have come before.

To lament with courage and boldness, then, is to re-member the community of the saints, to re-member the community of today, to re-member the community of the future. In these spirituals, we find survival language and codes, invoking Black folks to cope with death, to cope with their trauma. Lament is an affirmation that language must be found in these places of lost and silenced bodily memory in order for healing to begin, as art therapist Stephen Levine insists, "Encouraging the soul to speak in its own way transforms darkness into light, the hidden and concealed into the open, and thus provides insight and release."²⁷ In this mode of encouraging the soul to speak, we might hear the preacher shout, "Lamenting is truth telling. Lament invites others to lament. Lifting. Singing. Burdened by stones under foot. Walking. Whipped with the chastening rod. Aborted hope. Keeping the music alive.

Working on your weary feet all day cleaning White folks' houses. Walking down dark streets finding your father hanging on a tree. Strange fruit.[28] Tears watering lament. Treading water. Water turning to blood. Slaughtered. Gloomy past. Will we stand free at last?" Lament, then, creates expression and identity where sorrow, terror, and trauma have dehumanized and depleted linguistic capacity and meaning.[29]

In this light, we observe how this verse creates new language for everyday ritual and worship. Work becomes a holy task and the weight of that work is Black theology expressed. Doctrines of Jesus Christ (Christology), Holy Spirit (pneumatology), redemption (soteriology), the church (ecclesiology), and the future (eschatology) reflect love, hope, faith, lament, and joy, encouraging voices to sing justice and the pursuit of Christ's reign to come. The bright stars from the hymn are Black folk. Words and their meaning are ideas that serve an orthopraxy. A prevalent theological trope in Black music is theology practiced. An ideology of Black thought—what to sing, when to sing it, and with whom should we sing it. A theology of Black sacred song is always tied to the intentions of its contributors. The very nature of musical mechanics serves to articulate Black thought. The belief that God is Trinity, God represents community. As the Holy Trinity is one. God is not alone. Three in one. We too are called into communal ways of being for the sake of one another.

God desires holiness for Black folk too. How do we sing a song in a strange land? How are we to lift our voices to sing when others do not want to hear what we have to say? We think about being human. We sing about being human. We sing lament. Theologizing our lament and existence together through the music is holy work. Practicing music, believing in God, is worship. Black sacred song exists to practice the art of becoming liberated and living in community with a purpose. In more contemporary life, hip-hop culture and rap music empower its participants to be fully present in community. Is this anger in some rap actually lament? Hip-hop and rap are more than musical genres. They are a way of living life. In her treatise on "The (Un)Intelligibility and Promiscuity of Rap's Religious Expressions: Three Examples," Monica Miller observes hip-hop's future engagement in the community. She writes, "The cultural productions of hip hop cannot be perceived as solely passive products waiting to be co-opted in the service of religious and institutional market maintenance, rather, they call us to listen, to begin the story again as they invite us into the messy, creative, and chaotic reality of every (black) life."[30] This method of story-telling is similar to the first-century church of appropriating the gospel. They practiced, in community, an apostolic way of being together in fellowship, breaking bread, and praising God. They lamented in their persecution and were moved to action, preaching (testifying), and praise. And thus it was possible to continue on the road to "Where the white gleam of our bright star is cast."

God
God of our weary years
God of our silent tears
Thou who has brought us thus far on the way
Thou who has by Thy might
Led us into the light
Keep us forever in the path, we pray
Lest our feet stray from the places, our God, where we met Thee
Lest, our hearts drunk with the wine of the world, we forget Thee
Shadowed beneath Thy hand
May we forever stand
True to our God
True to our native land

Traditionally, the final verse is filled with musical embellishments. The tempo evolves. Within Black performance practice, it is customary to execute the final verse of "Lift Every Voice and Sing" with the highest musical ornamentation possible. The pianist slows the tempo, improvises with melismatic text painting, interval stacking of thirds, and stretching the fermatas (seventh, ninth, and eleventh chords used to dramatic extreme, pausing at particular cadences). This musical expansion lifts the praises and prayers in the community of worshippers and invites us to engage in community.

Through this slower, regal pace, the congregation leans into the commanded purposefulness of a life of prayer. The lingering impact of trauma is acknowledged through the silent tears streaming, beseeching God to remain and bolster those who sing. We hear in this verse an enduring wisdom of how to live in the shadow of God's hand rather than live according to the oppression of the surrounding culture. In this, they follow the example of those who came before, singing justice and liberty into being. In this sung world, God shows up and the promises of God provide encouragement, edification, and endurance. God bears witness to the tears and walks alongside the community on the long path to liberty. As they sing, the community insists, "We don't want to stray, we want to get to our native land. And we don't want to become like the oppressor along the way." This is a weary wisdom admonishing the Black community to stand tall and to stay on the path.

The spiritual significance of walking feet is a potent symbol throughout the hymn. In the previous verses the feet represent those in the past who spent hours laboring in fields, caring for the household of plantation owners, trudging many miles to be sold at the slave markets, or, for the fortunate few, escaping to freedom and safety in the North. Cheryl Kirk-Duggan connects how work, worship, feet, and singing were intertwined. She argues that "ring shout" singing and dancing generated many ways of connecting foot work ("heel-toe movement, advance, and retreat") with singing and moving as a community.[31] This collective creativity "calmed and encouraged boatmen rowing, broke the monotony of the repetitive physical activity of laboring the fields and doing household tasks, and accompanied dancing."[32] Ultimately, she maintains the work of the feet that accompanied singing spirituals in community was a chance "to exorcize the collective racist evil" of American society.[33] The purpose of these practices was "to stop evil and to replace evil with something good."[34] This call to the stopping of evil and the nurturing of the good within the community is the message of the weary feet of the past. Women in particular took up this call throughout the twentieth century. From the women who walked to work during the Montgomery bus boycott to those who brought their families and baskets full of food to the March on Washington, the summons of this verse has inspired the feet of those who continue to sing hope and justice today. "How beautiful upon the mountain are the feet of those who bring good news, who proclaim peace!" (Isaiah 52:7). The feet of today are moving toward, moving from, and finally standing tall and firm.

In this verse, there is a directive to inhabit the "dark and hidden wisdom" of the weary feet of those in the past. Copeland argues that this wisdom is found in the crucified and resurrected Jesus. As a young child, she remembers asking her great-grandmother, "who is that man hanging on the cross?" when she saw her crucifix.[35] For her, this is the question that can lead the Black community into faith, hope, and love through the darkness of suffering and trauma and perhaps change the hearts of those who perpetuate hate and injustice. This was the core of her calling to become a theologian so that she might tend to this dark and hidden wisdom for the sake of others. As she asserts,

> Here is some of their dark and hidden wisdom: The power of God in the cross is its paradox—the unexpected, unimagined resurrection. God's logic interrupts, reveals, and projects justice, mercy, and love into the bleakest circumstances. The dark wisdom of the enslaved people shows us that "being human is a praxis." This wisdom teaches us what it means to live authentically, with integrity; to live mindfully and thus embody the seed of history, linking past-present-future, the ancestors and those yet to be born. The dark wisdom of the enslaved people teaches us all a love ethic that nurtures proper self-love (a love of blackness, a love that refuses cultural or racial-ethnic or class privilege). The dark wisdom of the enslaved people teaches a love ethic that demands that none of us are to love others uncritically.[36]

Copeland believes the presence and love of this embodied Jesus was sung into the present day through the spirituals; as she argues, "The enslaved people sung themselves a world, a *topos* far from the capricious brutality of slavery, and in that world they met and saw Jesus."[37] Thus the unexpectedness and the interruption of God's love and kindness was not just an abstract notion but one that demanded love for the Black body, for Black voices raised in song, and for Black lives who refuse to tolerate injustice and inequity. Love in this theological model is a powerful force, which establishes an ethic of uncompromising and prophetic truth telling, especially to those who have and maintain power.

This "love ethic" calls everyone in the Black community into an identity found in Jesus, an identity formed by God's particular love and presence in this community, regardless of suffering. In Copeland's ethic, "The dark wisdom of the enslaved people teaches us that none of us is to be defined by victimization, but, like Jesus, by a commitment in the here and now to the realization of the reign of God. The dark wisdom of the enslaved people teaches us not how to avoid or deny suffering but how to suffer suffering."[38] This focus on Blackness and identity through love creates a standard of living for Copeland, in that oppression ultimately has no place in the reign of Jesus. The Kingdom of God creates a new reality. As the hymn proclaims, "Shadowed beneath Thy hand / May we forever stand." This resurrection life is what the hymn espouses. Resurrection life has no place for those who perpetuate evil and oppression, therefore resistance and protest are inherent on the road to "our native land." Learning to "suffer suffering," for Copeland, then becomes not victimization but empowerment and agency.

Cone similarly argues that immersing his theology in the history of God and oppressed persons is the only legitimate location and framework for doing theology.[39] Much like Copeland, his language refers to the generativity of the community amid the ongoing activity of God's justice. As Cone claims, "to ask, 'Who is God?' is to focus on what God is doing; and to look at what God is doing is to center on human events as they pertain to the liberation of suffering humanity."[40] The arch of Cone's theology is to reclaim theological language from a theology shaped and formed by "whiteness . . . so that blacks can be liberated from alien gods."[41] He defines whiteness not simply as a racial category but as the construct of those persons and systems that historically and persistently demean and subjugate others for their own gain and advantage. Cone believes that to live into oppression rather than liberation is to live counter to the gospel and the ongoing historical work of God in the world.[42] His bold claim is that we know that we have witnessed the self-revelation of God in history when we witness liberation from this form of persistent and endemic oppression.[43] Thus, Cone argues, it is the task of all theological work to bear witness to this revelation of God's liberative work.

The hymn's petition for God to "Keep us forever in the path" can be understood through this theological frame of liberation. To stay on the path was not to simply live a quiet and pious life. To stay on the path was to resist and remain true to this gospel. The world might offer other ways to glory or success, but the way "into the light" is where the community has been led by God. Those who will be known as *blessed* do not "walk in step with the wicked" or stand with the "sinners" or sit with those who "mock." Instead the one who stands in the light of God takes "delight" in the gospel and law that establishes justice. To stand in God's light is to be like a "tree planted by streams of water" and generate life and liberation (Psalm 1). To "drink the wine of the world" would be to become like those who held the chastening rod to the backs of the ancestors, to become like those who deceive and impoverish others for their own gain. Success and riches that cost the freedom of one's brothers and sisters cannot, in this theological vein, be found righteous or worthy of the path.

Even from a more secular or civic stance, the lives of James and Rosamond Johnson mirror this love ethic. When the brothers moved north to Harlem, they devoted themselves to creative endeavors, to the expansion and performance of Black story and song, and to the task of creating civic order and influence.[44] James in particular is considered one of the great poets and civic leaders of the Harlem Renaissance. Throughout his life he met, was inspired by, and worked alongside some of the great Black civic leaders, such as Fredrick Douglass and W. E. B. Du Bois. Along the way, he started a newspaper; wrote music for the likes of Theodore Roosevelt; was appointed the US consul to Venezuela; helped found the American Society of Composers, Authors, and Publishers (ASCAP); worked at the Metropolitan Opera; gathered and edited with his brother multiple volumes of African American spirituals and poetry; and became a key member of the NAACP.[45] A path of civic duty and devotion to the uplifting and expansion of African American life and accomplishment. James not only wrote an inspiring anthem, he also walked its proposed long road, "True to our native land."

"Lift Every Voice and Sing" exemplifies an embodied theology of presence and communal agency. The performance practice of this hymn parallels much of what has been explored in this essay. It exemplifies the cultural value of the communal in African American life. Soloist or small ensemble renditions of this hymn are atypical and make little sense of the core meaning of the hymn. This is a song for gatherings and for significant communal events.

The invitation in the Black National Anthem is for all to lift up all the voices and stand together.

The performance practice of the African American community is mirrored in "Lift Every Voice and Sing." Not much Black music is transcribed on paper; this is an oral and aural musical tradition. When one is called on by God's Spirit to receive the gift of music, there is this sense of humble openness and God's music is transcribed in the soul. Most musicians from the Black sacred music tradition learn to play music by what they hear first, then second by what they see on the page. Even in such a well-composed work as "Lift Every Voice," the piano player must feel and improvise in the moment the appropriate chordal substitutions, extensions, ornamentations, etc. In this tradition, one never just reads what is on the page; one must learn to read the atmosphere and presence in the room.

The key signature, A-flat major, of "Lift Every Voice and Sing" is a template for the hands of those who play. The Johnson brothers knew hymn-singing with Black cultural codes on black piano keys of B-flat, E-flat, A-flat, and D-flat major were critical musical colors in the community.[46] Hundreds of church stories exist about Black folk receiving the gift to play the piano. Black folk received their musical gifts by laying their hands on the black keys. Approaching the piano for the first time, allowing the hands to rest on those black elevated keyboard keys—a natural means for resting hands, waiting for God to summon down the gift. The lifting of heads to receive the gift to play piano when one has never played that instrument before. The anointing from heaven comes down, folk in the midst of a miracle lifting up their voices, singing praises and hallelujahs and thank you Jesus, and perhaps speaking in the improvised language of the Spirit. For the church was not only a treasure trove of talent, but it was also the place you received your gift from God in the Spirit. The community affirms you and your gift. Then you are sent out with that gift to serve God.

The embodied theology of "Lift Every Voice and Sing" is an admonition to receive the gift of music and especially singing from God. To sing is to summon God's presence and to petition God to call forth liberation. Every time we sing "Lift Every Voice and Sing," we are invited to experience a fresh sense of being lifted up through the weary years of sojourning. Each generation of participants will hold the Black cultural codes with care, humility, and dignity. Knowing the generation before them made it through with silent tears, true to their God and true to their native land. Through the singing of "Lift Every Voice and Sing," the spiritual vertebrae are once more realigned as God pours out the Spirit on all who lift up their voices and sing.

NOTES

1. "Frederick Douglass's narratives told the story of his journey from slavery to freedom with drama, passion, breathtaking emotion, and stunning brilliance. James's poem did something quite similar: he told the story of black life in terms that were epic, wrenching, and thunderous." Imani Perry, *May We Forever Stand: A History of the Black National Anthem* (Chapel Hill: University of North Carolina Press, 2018), 6; see also 45, 138.

2. Ron Eyerman, *Cultural Trauma: Slavery and the Formation of African American Identity*, Cambridge Cultural Social Studies (Cambridge: Cambridge University Press, 2001), Kindle Edition, loc. 1273. In contrast, a competing movement, the United Negro Improvement Association (UNIA), chose "Ethiopia, Land of Our Fathers" instead of "Lift Every Voice and Sing." Eyerman, *Cultural Trauma*, loc. 1603–4. See also Perry, *May We Forever Stand*, 32–34.

3. All theology is contextual, but Cone's intention here is to acknowledge the value and importance of establishing a distinctively Black and liberative theology that is not beholden to the contextual theology of the white dominant culture in America.

4. William C. Banfield, *Cultural Codes: Makings of a Black Music Philosophy* (Lanham, MD: Scarecrow Press, 2010), 4.

5. Eyerman, *Cultural Trauma*, loc. 381–82 and 395–401.

6. Ibid., loc. 553.

7. For more on America's Great Migration, see Isabel Wilkerson, *The Warmth of Other Suns: The Epic Story of America's Great Migration* (New York: Vintage Books, 2010).

8. Perry, *May We Forever Stand*, 5.

9. For example, see ibid., 7–10, 47–48, and 80–81. See also Rudolph P. Byrd, ed., *The Essential Writings of James Weldon Johnson* (New York: The Modern Library, 2008), Kindle Edition, loc. 401.

10. Perry, *May We Forever Stand*, 5.

11. Eyerman, *Cultural Trauma*, loc. 1285.

12. "Black formalism doesn't follow the schema of what critics in the West conventionally describe as high- or low-status identities, nor does it adhere to the traditional Western rules of high and low culture. . . . The formalism in black formalism came from the structure of the rituals and the regard for their seriousness, and not whether the work of a classical European composer or a vernacular poet . . . was part of a given program or event." Perry, *May We Forever Stand*, 10.

13. Ibid., 7.

14. James Cone, *The Spirituals and the Blues* (Maryknoll, NY: Orbis, 1992), 1.

15. Ibid.

16. Ibid., 2.

17. Ibid., 5.

18. Ibid., 52.

19. "Christian eschatology is bound up with the resurrection of Christ. He is the eschatological hope. He is the future of God who stands in judgment upon the world and forces us to give an account of the present. . . . It is this eschatological emphasis

that black theology affirms." James Cone, *A Black Theology of Liberation: Fortieth Anniversary Edition* (Maryknoll, NY: Orbis Press, 2010), 140.

20. M. Shawn Copeland, *Knowing Christ Crucified: The Witness of African American Religious Experience* (Maryknoll, NY: Orbis Books, 2018), Kindle Edition, loc. 693; quoting John Lovell Jr., *Black Song: The Forge and the Flame; The Story of How the Afro-American Spiritual Was Hammered Out* (New York: Macmillan, 1972), 301, 302.

21. For more information, see Equal Justice Initiative, "The Legacy Museum: From Enslavement to Mass Incarceration," EJI website, accessed on April 28, 2020, https://museumandmemorial.eji.org/museum.

22. J. Kameron Carter, "Liturgical S/Zong: A Ceremony of Black Radical Care(ss)," Society of Christian Philosophers Section, American Academy of Religion Conference, November 24, 2019, San Diego, California.

23. Copeland, *Knowing Christ Crucified*, loc. 1127.

24. Jeremy S. Begbie, *Theology, Music, and Time* (Cambridge: Cambridge University Press, 2000), 13–15.

25. Jeremy S. Begbie, "Beauty, Sentimentality, and the Arts," in *Beholding the Glory: Theology and the Arts*, ed. D. J. Treier, M. Husbands, and R. Lundin (Downers Grove, IL: IVP Academic, 2007), 45, 61, 65, and 46.

26. Ibid., 46–55. See also Jeremy S. Begbie, "Faithful Feelings: Music and Emotions in Worship," in *A Peculiar Orthodoxy: Reflections on Theology and the Arts* (Grand Rapids, MI: Baker Books, 2018), 49–77.

27. Stephen Levine, *Poiesis: The Language of Psychology and the Speech of the Soul* (London: Jessica Kingsley Publishers, 1997), 96.

28. This refers to the song written by Abel Meropol and recorded by Billie Holiday, "Strange Fruit," Jazz at the Philharmonic, Commodore, 1954, LP.

29. In trauma theory, this is often referred to as "alexithymia," which is not only a loss of language but also a loss of emotional awareness and embodied knowing. As Bessel van der Kolk argues, "People with alexithymia can get better only by learning to recognize the relationship between their physical sensation and their emotions, much as colorblind people can only enter the world of color by learning to distinguish and appreciate shades of gray." He also maintains, "People can never get better without knowing what they know and feeling what they feel." Bessel van der Kolk, *The Body Keeps the Score: Brain, Mind, and Body in the Healing of Trauma* (London: Penguin, 2014), 101 and 17.

30. Monica Miller, "The (Un)Intelligibility and Promiscuity of Rap's Religious Expressions: Three Examples," in *Readings in African American Church Music and Worship*, vol. 2, ed. James Abbington (Chicago: GIA Publications, 2014), 629.

31. Cheryl A. Kirk-Duggan, *Exorcizing Evil: A Womanist Perspective on the Spirituals* (Maryknoll, NY: Orbis Books, 1997), 5.

32. Ibid.

33. Ibid., 4.

34. Ibid., 48. In this section, she expounds on Howard Thurman's theology of theodicy.

35. Copeland, *Knowing Christ Crucified*, loc. 58–67.

36. Ibid., loc. 837–47; quoting Katherine McKittrick, ed., *Sylvia Wynter: On Being Human as Praxis* (Durham: Duke University Press, 2015), 3–4.
37. Copeland, *Knowing Christ Crucified*, loc. 1059.
38. Ibid., loc. 847.
39. Cone, *A Black Theology of Liberation*, 1.
40. Ibid., 81.
41. Ibid., 65.
42. Ibid., 1.
43. Ibid., 49.
44. "The Johnson brothers were 'race men.' This meant the work they did was not pursued for mere personal achievement or acclaim. Race men and women understood that each accomplishment was meaningful for the aspirations of the race as a whole." Perry, *May We Forever Stand*, 6.
45. Byrd, *The Essential Writings of James Weldon Johnson*, loc. 401.
46. In 1983, music historian Dr. Eileen Southern published an excerpt from W. E. B. Du Bois's *The Souls of Black Folks*. In this chapter Du Bois discusses general characteristics of *enslaved* music, and he includes an excerpt of a song that appears to be some form of rhythmic genesis for the hymn "Lift Every Voice and Sing." Du Bois and others transcribed melodies to document the experience and cultural coding. This particular musical excerpt is in 6/8 meter and in the key of A-flat major. It is interesting to note that the Black National Anthem is published in the same meter and key as well. These rhythmic nuances, motivic gestures, and rising melodic lines serve as a cultural code pointing to hope and despair, and the Johnson Brothers seemed aware of these popular melodies sung by those enslaved. Eileen Southern, *Readings in Black American Music* (New York: W. W. Norton & Company, 1983), 208.

FURTHER READING

Banfield, William C. *Cultural Codes: Makings of a Black Music Philosophy*. Lanham, MD: The Scarecrow Press, 2010.

Cone, James. *The Spirituals and The Blues: An Interpretation*. Maryknoll, NY: Orbis, 1992.

Copeland, M. Shawn. *Enfleshing Freedom: Body, Race, and Being*. Minneapolis, MN: Fortress Press, 2010.

Floyd, Jr., Samuel A. *The Power of Black Music: Interpreting its History from Africa to the United States*. Oxford, UK: Oxford University Press, 1995.

Guenther, Eileen Morris. *In Their Own Words: Slave Life and the Power of Spirituals*. St. Louis, MI: MorningStar Music Publishers, 2016.

Johnson, James Weldon, and J. Rosamond Johnson, eds. *The Books of the American Negro Spirituals*. Boston, MA: Da Capo Press, 2002.

Jones, LeRoi. *Blues People: The Negro Experience in White America and the Music That Developed from It*. New York, NY: William Morrow, 1963.

Peretti, Burton W. *Lift Every Voice: The History of African American Music*. Lanham, MD: Rowman & Littlefield, 2009.

Perry, Imani. *May We Forever Stand: A History of the Black National Anthem*. Chapel Hill, NC: The University of North Carolina Press, 2018.

Thurman, Howard. *Deep River and the Negro Spiritual Speaks of Life and Death.* Richmond, IN: Friends United Press, 1975.

Chapter Fourteen

From the Sun to the Son

How Choctaw Spiritual Practices Expressed Through Music Changed in Response to Christian and Anglo-American Contact

Emma Wimberg

At the turn of the twentieth century there was some academic interest in Choctaw culture, but this research faded in the 1930s and left many Choctaw spiritual practices unidentified by outside researchers. The Choctaw Nation of Oklahoma is the third largest Native American nation in the United States with nearly two hundred thousand tribal members and was formally recognized in 1786 by treaty with the US government. The Choctaw were the first to traverse the Trail of Tears and currently reside in southeast Oklahoma.[1]

In this essay I assess the ways Christianity has been adopted and adapted by the Choctaw, first through looking at the social changes of Choctaw practices after contact with missionaries and then through a review of reports about their 1829 hymnal and a close examination of the most recent 2017 edition. For this assessment I look specifically at five types of Choctaw hymns. The original hymnal and its later versions are important documents that indicate the state of Christian practices in the tribe, which I supplement with firsthand oral reports from senior tribal members. These editions contain hymns of biblical passages translated by Anglo-American missionaries, original compositions by Choctaw ministers using Anglo-American tunes, translations by Choctaw ministers that incorporated key elements of prior Choctaw spiritual beliefs, traditional Choctaw tunes, and those that are direct translations of Anglo-American hymns written either by the original missionaries to the Choctaw people or have been incorporated into Choctaw worship in recent years by contemporary communities. This is part of a larger research project, so here I present some initial findings as I begin to explore these hymns written by and for the Choctaw people. There are many aspects of Choctaw hymns and worship, and this is just a small portion of the overall picture.

As a member of the Choctaw tribe, I have grown up with the stories and culture of the Choctaw people. Our culture is deeply rooted in the passing down of history via oral tradition, with much of my own information coming from my great-grandaunt who spent her childhood at one of the mission boarding schools after her family made the journey from Mississippi to Oklahoma. Through her stories, and those from other family members, I have grown up knowing and appreciating my Choctaw heritage. This inherited insider position has given me foundational knowledge that I have broadened through in-depth research, including communication with the tribe's historic preservation office.

INTRODUCTION TO CHOCTAW PRACTICES

Most written history of Choctaw musical culture begins after the introduction of Christian practices and was passed down by oral tradition before the missionary establishment of the written Choctaw language and alphabet. Because there was no written language before the arrival of the missionaries, members of the tribe worked closely with Anglo-American missionaries to translate the Christian message into Choctaw. This led to the creation of new hymns, a number of which were composed and sung on the Trail of Tears, the forced relocation of many Native American tribes, and are treasured by Choctaw communities today. My research seeks to understand sacred music practices before and after Christianity came to the tribe, with special attention to post-Christian assimilation of spiritual practices.

It is important to distinguish the missionaries from the overall white colonizing forces that invaded the traditional Choctaw way of life before further discussing the effects of their presence. While the displacing hegemony of the white colonizers as a whole was met with much justified resentment, the missionaries who came to the Choctaw were a welcome force seen as able to help with this unforeseen transition into the white culture now surrounding the people and into which they had to assimilate. Thus Christianity itself is not currently seen by the Choctaw as a part of the oppressive white hegemony but rather as the assistance the tribe desperately needed while undergoing forced cultural change. Aside from the religious message they wished to spread, the missionaries also brought much-needed education of Anglo-American ways to the Choctaw people. From the development of their own written language to the teaching of English, the missionaries were key to the tribe's survival during this tumultuous period of forced exodus and cultural reconstruction. In Louis Coleman's biography about the influential missionary and linguist Cyrus Byington composed from original Choctaw documents, he writes,

"Choctaw leaders soon petitioned the board to send missionaries to educate the Choctaw children in what they referred to as a better way of life."[2] While Christian influence ultimately meant either the adaptation or the disappearance of many traditional elements of Choctaw life, these effects would have been much more severe due to the new oppressive forces as a whole, without the mediation of the missionaries in this transition. Because of this aid, the missionaries are still viewed today as a benevolent force. Coleman documents in his Cyrus Byington biography the eventual deaths of the last original missionaries and the great loss felt by all. He writes,

> Thus ended an era of missionary activity by these dedicated men, their wives and others, who bravely went forth to spread the Gospel and to suffer alongside the Choctaw people during some of the worst of their times. The Choctaws mourned the loss of these men.[3]

The Choctaw tribe had settled in Mississippi by the sixteenth century, before the forced removal, and many Choctaw remain there today.[4] The tribe now extends throughout the southeastern United States. Before looking at the hymnal and its role in the introduction of Christianity to the Choctaw people, it is vital to acknowledge that Christian missionaries did not provide a new spiritual element to an otherwise untethered people. As noted in an article in the tribe's newsletter titled "Iti Fabvssa" (meaning "long, slender piece of wood"),[5]

> Long before Europeans arrived on this continent, Choctaw people had a deep spirituality and an ancient singing tradition. There were specific songs for hunting, for stickball, for playing hand games, for going to war, songs sung for the safety of loved ones away at war, songs a person sung when facing death, and songs sung during sacred dances at the Green Corn Ceremony.[6]

I will address some of these specific aspects later in this essay, but from this passage it is clear that spirituality, and more importantly spirituality expressed through music, was always an integral part of Choctaw life and traditions. Not much is known about these specific religious practices and beliefs. During his time with the Choctaw people, the Anglo-American missionary Reverend Alfred Wright (who would later be an important figure in the establishment of the hymnal) commented on the protected nature of this spirituality. He noted, "it [was] extremely difficult to ascertain what the tradition of the Choctaws were as a difficulty in ascertaining their ancient traditions arises from their unwillingness to divulge them, especially to foreigners."[7] After contact with Anglo-Americans, very few of the elders who retained this knowledge passed it on to the youth, due in part to cultural practices that did not allow outsiders to observe their dances and traditions. If they suspected an outsider was watching one of these ceremonies, they would immediately stop. While this level of protection of information is no longer as great, it was very extreme in some members of the older generations. Even my great-grandmother refused to sing in front of anyone outside of the tribe in Choctaw, making a special exception only for my father. The secrecy of these practices serves to show how important and sacred they were to the spiritual Choctaw people.

As many of these practices were, and remain, personal and sacred in nature, I will only give a very brief discussion of those that have been published for public knowledge with permission and are relevant to this essay. Choctaw practices have varied between communities and therefore there is no singular practice from which to draw; however, there are similarities because of the shared foundational history of these communities. For example, a common creation story of the tribe has two distinct histories centered on the Nanih Waiya earth mound in Mississippi. One version speaks of the first people emerging from the mound after being formed by the Creator, while another version speaks of people traveling from a far west land by use of a pole or staff that guided them by falling at night in the direction they were meant to travel until it finally stood still at the mound where half of the group remained and became the first Choctaw. Almost all of these communities reference the belief in one Superior Being, known by different names in the different communities, who watched over the people through the sun.[8] It is important to emphasize that this was not worship of the sun itself. Traditional Choctaw cosmology divides life into the Below World where death, fertility, and other powerful spirits resided; the Above World where the Superior Being lived along with the other cosmic entities; and This World where humans reside. The recognition of this cosmology is found most prominently in the traditional Green Corn Ceremony.

THE GREEN CORN CEREMONY

As stated in the tribe newsletter, "today, just as in the past, some of the parts of the Choctaw Green Corn Ceremony are private in nature and not intended for publication"; however, I will present as full a picture as possible of these practices while respecting their sacred nature, only drawing from existing published passages or knowledge allowed to be public.[9] The Green Corn Ceremony was an important socioreligious practice in the Choctaw community. It represented a time to come together to celebrate a successful harvest season and emphasized "balance, restitution, reciprocity, and consensus, all beloved values" to the Choctaw people.[10] The ceremony itself traces back to the original Choctaw beliefs surrounding the original giving of corn to the Unknown Woman. Corn itself also holds a special significance because of its ability to cross the Below World (via its roots into the ground deep below), the Above World (via its tall stalk that reaches above the heads of the people), and This World. All parts of the ceremony have special significance to the Choctaw, including the ground on which the ceremony took place, with the fire at the ceremonies representing a friend of God.[11] Corn was likely sacrificed to the fire to show thankfulness and gratitude for the harvest. In Christian terms, according to insiders writing in the newsletter, "Southeastern People believe that the Stomp Dance grounds is analogous to a church, the songs being prayers, and that those prayers travel with the smoke up to the Creator."[12]

The Green Corn Ceremony was a vital part of Choctaw social and spiritual life. However, as Michelene E. Pesantubbee notes, "by the 1820s it was in such a state of decline that it may be that some Choctaw did not know of the ceremony while others chose not to mention it" in an attempt to preserve it from outsiders who had already forced so much upheaval in the lives of the people.[13] Even into the late 1800s "traditional Choctaw people were facing increasingly forceful pressure to assimilate into surrounding Euro-American society," and as such these ceremonies fell out of practice for quite some time.[14] It is unclear from the available records and reports if there were specific texted songs sung at these ceremonies, with many publications saying that some of the songs in today's social dances were likely sung, but "if you go to the green corn ceremony today most of what they have are vocables not recognizable words."[15] These vocables are syllables and sound that do not hold specific meaning but are used "to express emotion within a song [and] accentuate the mood of the piece."[16]

While today there are no specific songs and dances performed during these ceremonies that can be traced back to their original inception, we can draw educated conclusions about some of these performances from the reports by various fieldworkers and by the songs and traditions that exist today. As Michelene E. Pesantubbee writes of these field reports,

> According to Chahta immatahah, whom Gideon Lincecum interviewed from 1823 to 1825, he learned from his elders that the Choctaw were already holding annual new fruits ceremonies when they received the gift of corn. When the first crop of corn matured they held a five-day dance and feast called *Tanchi Okchamali Hihla*, Green Corn Dance. They held the dance annually in early summer until the Europeans brought them alcohol and people began to get drunk instead of dancing.[17]

An interesting connection between this practice and those that exist today is the Drunken-Man Dance, also known by some as the Corn Dance, which is still practiced by Choctaw communities and dance troupes.[18] The dual name of this dance is intriguing when pieced together with this history of the decline of the Green Corn Dance, which came about due to the overwhelming turn to drunkenness during the ceremony in which it was practiced. This report shows another side of the impact of European contact with the tribe that caused a change in their traditions. The introduction of alcohol into the community changed the way this important socioreligious ceremony was practiced and played a part in its decline and temporary absence from its yearly celebration.

CONTEMPORARY CEREMONIAL PRACTICES

Possibly, we will never know the original history of these ceremonies because, as the tribe's newsletter notes, "traditional Choctaw dances were taken out their original contexts of the Green Corn Ceremony, or the stickball game, or the celebration at the return of a war party, and transformed into social dances that publicly express Choctaw identity in an ethnically mixed society."[19] Today these are still celebrated in the form of Choctaw social dances, which occur at Tribal festivals and events throughout the year. The importance of these social dance events is best stated by historians James H. Howard and Victoria Lindsay Levine, who say,

> The dances that survive are emblematic of a life that ceased to exist, for the most part, in the early twentieth century. Yet the values and cosmology integral to that existence still guide those contemporary Choctaws who are concerned with the preservation and revitalization of tribal traditions. For these people, the dances powerfully express social mores and reaffirm group cohesion; for outsiders, the dances open a portal on Choctaw culture and demonstrate its ability to endure.[20]

Throughout the changes of the nineteenth and twentieth centuries experienced by the Oklahoma Choctaws who were forced to leave their homes in Mississippi, there was an inescapable pressure to change their culture to better fit the Anglo-American culture in which they were now expected to live. This meant that the traditional ways of life and celebration for the people needed to change, or disappear altogether, in order for people to fit into this new world.

We can see that such changes are also present through an examination of the past and present funeral practices of the Choctaw people. These past practices involved a very intense and specific mourning process that originally lasted several months. During the forced removal of the tribe in the late eighteenth and early nineteenth centuries, this mourning process had to be changed to last only days for those who died on the journey. Today they appear as other Christian funerals. In some communities the practice of burning a fire for a few days after the death of a loved one is still practiced, although the meaning of the fire to comfort the deceased spirit does not seem to make an explicit appearance in these practices anymore and they are more for the continuation of spiritual tradition. The days of the Great Cry, a specific time in which family members and friends of the deceased would come together to give one last mourning wail, have been replaced by the traditional singing of Choctaw hymns. These traditional hymns are treasured by many of the Choctaw people, as they were born out of a time of great strife and represent an important part of Choctaw history.[21]

INTRODUCTION TO CHOCTAW HYMNODY

The construction of these hymns is the subject of the rest of this essay. When the missionaries came to the Choctaw people they brought with them their style(s) of worship, including their hymnals. The missionaries did not force themselves into the lives of the Choctaw but were invited by two chiefs, Chiefs Mushulatubbee and David Folsom. They arrived in 1819 prior to the removal of the Choctaw people to Oklahoma on the Trail of Tears. There had been previous contact with Europeans, mostly the French explorers, but prior to their invitation there was a strong resistance to the presence of missionaries due to their perceived association with the removal of the Indigenous people from their land. Once this association was deemed to be untrue, the missionaries were welcomed as they helped the tribe with the difficult journey they were about to take and provided vital education to the Choctaw. According to historian Dr. Ian Thompson, one of the Choctaw Tribe of Oklahoma's Historic Preservation staff, the Choctaws embraced the hymns translated and composed by the missionaries because the Choctaw people respected the missionaries. This was because many of them spent their entire lives serving the community after having been invited by these Choctaw chiefs. These missionaries later traveled the Trail of Tears with the Choctaw people. They endured the same hardships and some also experienced the same loss of family members as the Choctaw during the journey. The newly embraced Christian religion was a source of hope and strength for many members of the tribe who remained in their homeland as well as those who traveled the Trail of Tears, as a majority of them converted to Christianity.[22] The missionaries also worked to create the Choctaw written language and alphabet to help spread the gospel message to the people via translations of the Bible and hymns into Choctaw, as it would have been difficult for elder members of the tribe to learn English in order to have access to these materials.

The Choctaw Nation of Oklahoma's newsletter states that a few years after their arrival, "Alfred Wright and Cyrus Byington began to compile a formal Choctaw hymnal. First published in 1829, it contained Choctaw fifty-five hymns and five doxologies."[23] As this first 1829 edition came out right before the first wave of the Trail of Tears (which occurred in 1830–1833 for the Choctaw people), it is very probable that the hymns in the first edition of the hymnal were sung on the Trail of Tears. Some of the other most beloved hymns are listed as "Removal Songs," but with date of authorship indeterminable, it is not possible to know whether these songs would have been written or sung during or after the removal. Regardless, many of these hymns were inspired by the hardships faced during this time and reflect a different attitude than those written by the Anglo-American missionaries, many of whom did make the journey with the Choctaw.

The 2017 edition of the hymnal is important because of the different format through which it presents material. The first half maintains the original text-only format most familiar to those practicing Choctaws who have been able to continue their traditions over time, while the second half explains these traditions in a way that is more accessible to those engaging in the revival of the Choctaw culture by incorporating new musical notation and pieces of Choctaw history throughout. It is important to note that these hymns are not titled as we have come to expect from traditional hymnals. Instead of referring to hymns by name (commonly the first line of text), they are traditionally known by their numbers and do not have titles in their own right. Some list the topic that is covered, but titles are sparsely found throughout the hymnal and are usually only present in hymns by missionaries, most commonly those hymns that are direct English-to-Choctaw translations of English hymns that are often the rare exceptions to the title rule. The hymns are numbered by topic and not in the order written, which is why we do not know the order in which they were added into the hymnal, despite the numbering system. The most recent hymnal also now contains 168 hymns, as more have been added or translated over the years. The hymns are arranged by topic, and the numbers attributed to specific hymns would change throughout earlier editions to reflect this organizational system, making it difficult to determine which ones comprised the first original little hymn book. This new hymnal holds its identity as belonging to the Choctaw people rather than to any specific denomination, so it has become the common hymnbook to all Choctaw people in Oklahoma, Mississippi, Tennessee, Alabama, and Louisiana regardless of affiliation with a specific denomination. Most of the hymns have been learned orally and committed to memory. They are generally sung a cappella and therefore vary from community to community. This hymnal was compiled by members of many of these different Choctaw church communities, with the help of volunteers from these communities including those fluent in the language. This has created the most representative Choctaw hymnal that also facilitates learning of these hymns to those unfamiliar with them.

The key purpose of the newly translated hymns was the religious education of the Choctaw children, and mission schools also played a vital part in this religious conversion. These schools did not allow the children to speak Choctaw while they learned English, and as a consequence many forgot what they knew of the Choctaw language before entering the school. The forbiddance of speaking Choctaw was so widespread that my great-great-grandfather would not speak Choctaw in a mixed group of English-speaking and Choctaw people and would only worship in Choctaw in private or in a Choctaw church. As scholars James Howard and Victoria Levine note, "This was such an all-encompassing edict that in a speech at the National Conference for Teachers of Indian Students held in Lawton, Oklahoma, in July 1972, James Belvin, principal chief of the Oklahoma Choctaws, stated that his father had instructed him when he was a very small boy never to learn the Choctaw language, since it would only handicap him in later life. He followed his father's advice and refused to learn his native tongue."[24]

The fading of knowledge of the original Choctaw language caused a gap in the passage of oral traditions. The tribe has worked to promote a revival of the language over the past few decades, as evidenced by the renewal of Choctaw language education. The Choctaw have, however, always continued to sing their hymns in their own language during Choctaw services. There was a time during the history of one of the mission schools, Wheelock Academy in southeast Oklahoma near Millerton (which my great-grandmother and her sister attended), when children were not permitted to speak in their own language during school but were allowed to sing the hymns in Choctaw at the Wheelock Church located just off the grounds. Despite being forbidden to speak the language in schools, which disrupted the passing down of oral tradition and culture, Choctaw hymns have endured and served as a link to the old culture and traditions.

HYMN TYPES

Choctaw hymns comprise a variety of compositional histories due to the blending of two cultures. I have ordered these hymn types in a way that reflects a progressive timeline of how they would have likely been introduced by missionaries and subsequently incorporated into the hymnal. First are hymns that teach biblical passages and the Christian message. After this category are hymns that use Anglo-American tunes with different lyrical texts (which begin to incorporate elements of Choctaw spirituality), followed by hymns that use traditional Choctaw tunes. Last are translated hymns that the Choctaw people would have first heard in English, as they transitioned into services that were mixed Choctaw-language and English-language congregations.

HYMN TYPES: BIBLICAL PASSAGES

When speaking of the hymns translated by missionaries, we are not always referencing direct hymn-to-hymn translations. The first type of hymn to examine are hymns based on biblical passages translated by Anglo-American missionaries. For example, we will now take a closer look at Choctaw Hymn 11 (see figure 14.1), sung to the tune "Happy Land." Hymn 11 was translated by Cyrus Byington, who was one of the most beloved of the missionaries and played a key role in the development of the Choctaw alphabet. He was a Presbyterian missionary credited for the translation of twenty-one hymns, did

Ʋba Isht Taloa 11. P. M.
Auahachʋfa
(See Paraphrase Section)

1 Hatak hʋsh puta ma!
      Ho minti;
   Hatak hʋsh puta ma!
   Yakni achukma kʋt
   Ʋba talaiʋshke;
      Ho minti.

2 Hatak hʋsh moma ma
      Ho yimmi;
   Hatak hʋsh moma ma!
   Chisʋs im anumpa
   Hʋsh yimmi pullashke;
      Ho yimmi.

3 Okla e moma kʋt,
      Kil ia:
   Chisʋs pi hullo hosh
   Pi ʋlhtobʋt illit,
   Falamʋt tani tok;
      Kil ia.

4 Chisʋs im anumpa
      Ke yimmi
   Chisʋs im anumpa
   Achukma fehna ka
   Chukʋsh isht ahli hosh
      Ke yimmi.

5 Ʋba ayukpa yʋt
      Pimma chi;
   Chisʋs ai ahanta
   Yʋmma il onakmʋt
   Ʋba ayukpa yʋt
      Pimma chi.

6 Ʋba il onakmʋt,
      Pilla wa;
   Yakni achukma ya
   Yʋmma il onakmʋt,
   Antʋt e bilia;
      Pilla wa.   C. B.

Figure 14.1. Hymn 11 from the 2017 Choctaw hymnal.

the editing for the Choctaw Hymn Book, established schools, and was also a physician.[25] This hymn was published in the original hymnal and was likely sung on the Trail of Tears.

This example is taken directly from the first half of the most recent edition of the hymnal and appears as it does in the original iterations of the hymnal without musical notation. The initials at the bottom are an indicator of the author of the hymn, which for this hymn is Cyrus Byington. The P.M. stands for Particular Meter and denotes that the hymn requires a special tune to match the poetic meter of the text, as it does not fit any of the standard meters. The words "Vba Isht Taloa" simply mean "hymn" and are not a title but rather are present before a hymn number to indicate its full name as "Hymn 11."

The English translation that is present in the most recent edition of the hymnal under the "Hymn Paraphrases" section is noted here. It is a paraphrase translation by the publishers of the Choctaw hymnal. It is clearly stated that this English version is not to be taken as a literal translation but is to be used to aid in the study and singing of the hymns for the non-Choctaw speaker:

1. All mankind come, all mankind! The good land sets on high, all come. (Matthew 11:28)
2. All mankind, let us all believe! All mankind, Jesus's Word you must believe. Let us all believe! (Romans 10:17)
3. All of us people, let us go. Jesus loves us and died in our place. He rose from the dead, let us go. (Acts 10:38–41)
4. Let us believe Jesus's Word; His Word is very good. Let us believe with a sincere heart. (II Timothy 3:16–17)
5. Give us heaven, a happy place; Jesus is there. When we get there, give us heaven, a happy place. (Ephesians 1:20–21)
6. When we get to heaven, we will not die in that good land. We will live forever. (I Thessalonians 4:13–18; II Peter 1:11)

This is not the text of any existing English-language hymn. Rather, the missionaries found it more important to translate key verses of the gospel message they wished to impress upon the Choctaw during their Christian education. These translated verses are also not word-for-word literal translations from the Bible, as one might expect from a traditional Anglo-American hymn such as "Seek Ye First." Instead the key elements of the message that the missionaries wanted to impress upon the people (the love of Jesus, His death and resurrection on the cross, and the need for us to follow Him) are the parts emphasized in the verse.

HYMN TYPES: ANGLO-AMERICAN TUNES

The hymns translated by missionaries were key to the education of the Choctaw, but the skill of hymn writing was not unique to the missionaries. The second type of hymn we are going to look at is those written by Choctaws using Anglo-American tunes. As Christianity grew among the tribe, more and more Choctaws sought to become ministers to their own people. There are many Choctaw authors credited in the hymnal, but unfortunately there are also dozens of unattributed hymns that were reportedly composed, text and tune, by Choctaw authors that went unaccredited. This is due in part to the fact that some of the authors likely did not speak English or have any knowledge of the notation style of Western music traditions. Despite the challenges of this language barrier, it did not detract from their ability to create beautiful hymns from the Choctaw perspective using Choctaw tune melodies. Thankfully, missionaries and tribe members who had learned the English language and notation were able to transcribe and preserve these hymns. To emphasize this point, the next hymn we are going to look at is Hymn 121 (figure 14.2), written by Pliney Fisk, who was the first Choctaw Presbyterian minister and whose name is indicated by a small F at the top of the page.[26] Interestingly, this hymn is labeled with the tune "Watchman Tell Us" composed by Lowell Mason, as the music portion of the hymnal points out, however, it differs greatly from the actual tune, presented in figure 14.3.

Through a close examination of these examples we can see similarities between the two, but although they follow a similar melodic contour, no one would say they are the same. These differences are likely due to the role of oral tradition in the shaping of Choctaw hymnody, which meant that the music was rarely transcribed. It is currently unclear whether the tune was adapted to fit the composer's text or if the two fit together as the tune is originally written. Either way, the attribution of this Anglo-American tune with text by a Choctaw minister and composer shows the adoption of the missionary's Christianity into the practices of the Choctaw. The English translation of this text is:

1. The Son of God in His glory is coming from heaven. He is holy and He is surely coming from heaven. Are you all ready?
2. Are you ready to meet Jesus? The Son of God is coming from heaven. The Son of God, from heaven will appear to all mankind; watch and see, you will meet Him.[27]

After reviewing this translation, it is clear that this is not simply a hymn translated into the Choctaw language. What we can identify here is an

Figure 14.2. Hymn 121 from the 2017 Choctaw hymnal.

Hymn 121, Cont'd.

Figure 14.2. *(Continued)*

Figure 14.3. "Watchman Tell Us" from the 1985 Rejoice in the Lord hymnal.

example of a hymn written by a Choctaw who had converted to Christianity rather than an Anglo-American missionary. It therefore embodies a different worldview. This hymn has a more encouraging and hopeful tone, promising that Jesus will come to His followers to take them to Heaven and that His followers must be ready. Messages of hope and promise are common among those hymns written by Choctaw composers because the Choctaw were a newly displaced people trying to maintain their identity as they adapted to life in a foreign land. The translation is more fluid than of those written by the missionaries who worked hard to grasp the Choctaw language but did not have a mastery of it in the same way as those who were raised in it as a native tongue.

HYMN TYPES: INCORPORATION OF CHOCTAW SPIRITUALITY

Some of these hymns written by Choctaw authors incorporate existing Choctaw spiritual beliefs that were adapted to fit their new Christian beliefs. For example, some hymns talk about "Hina Hanta," which means the bright path to victory that is illuminated by the sun. The bright path was the way Choctaw warriors followed to be successful on the battlefield. Choctaw spirituality before the arrival of missionaries taught that the sun was God's eye watching people. If the sun was shining on an individual, he or she would prosper. This is why Choctaw diplomatic meetings with entities such as the US government were always done in broad daylight. During traditional stickball games (competitive athletic events that would last for days and are often still practiced today), the medicine people would take a mirror and direct the sunlight onto the players on their team to help them prosper. This sun imagery was incorporated into Christianity as the concept came to be understood in the tribe's new Christian terms as the gospel message of belief in Jesus coming to earth from heaven to die for sinners, this message being the only narrow path to heaven. The hymns that utilize this adapted meaning still retain the exact original Choctaw wording from their previous spiritual understandings despite the new interpretation.[28]

This sun imagery is very prominent in Hymn 46, which was translated and adapted by Peter P. Pitchlynn, described in the 2017 hymnal as "a former Principal Chief of the Choctaw Nation who encouraged missionaries to establish churches and schools in the Choctaw Nation."[29] This hymn is a translated adaption of the hymn "Jesus, My All, to Heaven Is Gone," originally penned by John Cennick. The chorus in Cennick's original chorus reads, "I'm on my journey home to the new Jerusalem, I'm on my journey home to the new

Jerusalem, So fare you well, So fare you well, So fare you well, I am going home."[30] Pitchlynn's translated version, which appears as the second verse but is also labeled as the chorus, instead translates into English as "I'm going to follow the white road to victory." In Choctaw, this meaning is similar to when a wagon wheel gets stuck in a rut and cannot move to the right or the left. This translation is readily transferred to the gospel message. In fact, in the Choctaw dictionary the phrase "Hina Hanta," which features prominently in the chorus, directly translates into English as "a bright path; the way of peace; the gospel path; the narrow way of life."[31] This translation correlates the existing imagery in Choctaw spirituality of a bright path and the new-found Christian identity of the Choctaw people that was entwined with their written language and English education. This exemplifies the impact of, and adaptions for, Christianity that occurred within the tribe. The following is the official hymnal paraphrase of the verses into English:

1. My Jesus went to heaven. I shall trust Him always.
2. I will continue to follow Jesus in the right way. When I reach heaven, I will meet Jesus face to face.
3. All the prophets have continued to travel this road; they turn away from being lost and stand in the truth.
4. The way of the Lord is holy. So I must walk diligently in the pathway of love.
5. My true Saviour! I will continue to follow You, until I reach to where You are.[32]

This hymn punctuates biblical themes appearing in many traditional Anglo-American hymns with the Choctaw-inspired chorus about following the bright path to victory, which translates into Christianity as following the gospel message to heaven. This demonstrates an important way in which the two practices were able to come together cohesively to preach the gospel to the Choctaw people. These verses reflect the Choctaw concept of the wagon wheel staying the narrow road as they speak of following Jesus in the "right way" on the "pathway of love" to reach "where [He] is."

Another part of Choctaw culture reflected in this hymn is its use of a chorus or refrain, as a number of hymns written by and translated for the Choctaw have this element. While many American nineteenth- and twentieth-century revivalist hymns also contain a chorus or refrain, it appears this trend might be derived from the tribe's musical practices that predate missionary contact. In her study of Choctaw music, Victoria Lindsay Levine identifies four types of musical form in Choctaw songs that she categorizes as Jump Dance, chant, refrain, and strophic form.[33] Each of these forms relies heavily on repetition, often in the form of call and response. The lack of traditional Anglo-American hymns that employ repetition within this particular hymnal demonstrates that the injection of a chorus into these Choctaw hymns could be a reflective characteristic of existing Choctaw song culture. Specifically, in reference to Hymn 46, the chorus is the part of the hymn that would have held the most significance for the Choctaw people as it contains the adapted reference from Choctaw spirituality.

Here it is important to note that in the creation of this hymnal, the most used tune found among the many surveyed Choctaw church communities was the one published for each hymn. Hymn 46, for example, is sung to many different tunes. The tune included was deemed to be the most popular but is not necessarily the one that will be sung by any given Choctaw congregation.

HYMN TYPES: TRADITIONAL CHOCTAW TUNES

There are also hymns that incorporated traditional Choctaw tunes, such as Hymn 9. Unfortunately, there are no initials listed for author, meaning it was most likely of Choctaw origin, although this cannot be confirmed. This hymn paraphrase translates as:

1. When the dawn breaks every day, God's abundant mercy continues forever.
2. Every morning He shows us mercy. It is like the morning dew.
3. He made the night so that we could rest. And He diligently watches over us while we are asleep.
4. His mercy is good, His love is forever. God is good, let us worship Him. (Psalm 36:5, 86:15, 100:5)
5. We all should loudly praise Him; do not be ashamed. God is good; let us worship Him. (Psalm 29:2, 95:6–7, 96:9; John 4:23)[34]

By using a traditional tune that the Choctaw already knew and attributing the Christian message to it, this hymn author demonstrates the full acceptance and embracing of Christianity into the Choctaw culture. This message is no longer only carried by the tunes of the Anglo-American missionaries but has now been integrated into the music of the tribe as well. Had one of the missionaries taken this tune out of context and put the Christianizing words to it in an attempt to connect with the people, the significance behind the marriage of the two cultures would have less meaning. If indeed written by a Choctaw, this melodic move is much more significant. The origin of this tune is currently unclear, as we have come to find with much of the surviving Choctaw music of today, but its designation as a traditional tune demonstrates that it was not extemporaneously composed but was rather an existing tune that this author used for this new purpose.

HYMN TYPES: TRANSLATIONS OF EXISTING ANGLO-AMERICAN HYMNS

In addition to these types of hymns that were compiled for the Choctaw people are hymns that are direct translations of common Anglo-American hymns. Such an example is found in Hymn 24, "There Is a Fountain," translated by Loring S. Williams, a Presbyterian missionary who is credited for the translation of thirty-one hymns found in the Choctaw Hymn book.[35] While it cannot be directly determined if this hymn was in the original hymnal, its credited composition by one of the original missionaries who authored a great number of the hymn texts suggests that it was at least found in one of the early editions.

HYMN TYPES: CONTEMPORARY/SEASONAL

The most recent edition of the Choctaw hymnal contains a section of recently added hymns (numbers 169–184), many of which are direct translations of existing hymns in English that congregations wished to have incorporated as a part of their Choctaw worship experience. These include several popular Christmas hymns—Away in a Manger (177), Joy to the World (178), O Come, All Ye Faithful (179), Silent Night (180), We Three Kings (181)—and songs that are synonymous with the contemporary Christian worship experience—Jesus Loves Me (182) and Amazing Grace (183). These hymns are different from the other ones in the hymnal because they are included for a different reason. In choosing hymns for this hymnal, the editors did not have the same evangelizing mission in mind because they were written for an already converted Choctaw Christian audience.

A SYMBOLIC AND UTILITARIAN HYMNAL

All of these hymns were specifically composed to reach the Choctaw people with the Christian message, which they successfully did by collaborating with the Choctaw to incorporate their compositional talents and beliefs. As Janet R. Walton writes concerning the use of cultural representation in sacred music, "Such diversity is critical because music interprets our faith through culturally conditioned symbols. To sing or hear music that reflects the reality of a particular culture acknowledges the theological claim that God's activity is known more accurately through many voices and symbols, rather than through one or only a few."[36] By fully collaborating with the Choctaws in the process of creating a set of sacred music texts for use within their community, the missionaries were better able to connect with the people. Using music to facilitate these connections speaks to the power of music to reach across language barriers, and how musically collaborating between cultural differences can be the key component in forming new relationships. The missionaries were successful in helping the Choctaw because of the mutual respect the two parties had for one another. This relationship was instrumental in helping the Choctaw adapt to life in the new Anglo-American culture by which they were surrounded.

Choctaw hymns are a key part of modern Choctaw identity. The hymns are an embodiment of a universal Choctaw heritage, regardless of denominational creed. In their mini-diaspora, the Choctaw people first learned how to successfully adapt to this new world through religion and music, as some of the first Choctaw-language texts were chapters of the Bible and the hymnal. While some Choctaw practices have been lost or discarded due to colonization, the hymnody brought by the missionaries created a way for Choctaw people to continue their musical traditions. Hymns were one of the few refuges where Choctaw identity could be retained as they assimilated into the Anglo-American world of the missionaries, in order to thrive in the changing country that had already forced many of them from their homes. By using the emerging hymns to express the hurt, longing, and hope of these experiences, Christianity became an enduring part of Choctaw culture, with hymns enduring at the center of this worship even now.

NOTES

1. Choctaw Nation of Oklahoma, "Choctaw Nation Fact Sheet," choctawnation.com, accessed May 30, 2020, https://www.choctawnation.com/sites/default/files/choctaw-nation-fact-sheet.pdf.

2. Louis Coleman, *Cyrus Byington: Missionary and Choctaw Linguist* (Durant, OK: Choctaw Print Services, 2018), 12.

3. Ibid., 137.

4. "History," Mississippi Band of Choctaw Indians, accessed June 12, 2020, https://www.choctaw.org/aboutMBCI/history/index.html.

5. "Iti Fabvssa-Iti Fabvssa," *Biskinik*, July 2009.

6. "Iti Fabvssa-Chahta Vba Ish Taloa: The Choctaw Hymns," *Biskinik*, February 2014, 1.

7. Michelene E. Pesantubbee, *Choctaw Women in a Chaotic World: the Clash of Cultures in the Colonial Southeast* (Albuquerque: University of New Mexico Press, 2005), 127.

8. "Iti Fabvssa-Spiritual Beliefs and Rituals," *Biskinik*, December 2009.

9. "Iti Fabvssa-Green Corn Ceremony," *Biskinik*, March 2010, 1.

10. Pesantubbee, *Choctaw Women*, 118.

11. "Iti Fabvssa-Spiritual Beliefs and Rituals."

12. "Iti Fabvssa-Green Corn Ceremony," 2.

13. Pesantubbee, *Choctaw Women*, 128.

14. "Iti Fabvssa-Green Corn Ceremony," 2.

15. Dr. Ian Thompson, telephone conversation with author, September 20, 2019.

16. J. Nathan Corbitt, *The Sound of the Harvest: Music's Mission in Church and Culture* (Grand Rapids: Baker, 1998), 237.

17. Pesantubbee, *Choctaw Women*, 129.

18. James H. Howard and Victoria Lindsay Levine, *Choctaw Music and Dance* (Norman: University of Oklahoma Press, 1997), 47.

19. "Iti Fabvssa-Green Corn Ceremony," 2.

20. Howard and Levine, *Choctaw Music and Dance*, 66.

21. "Iti Fabvssa-Ancient Choctaw Burial Practice," *Biskinik,* February 2012, 1–2.

22. Dr. Ian Thompson, telephone conversation with author, September 20, 2019.

23. "Iti Fabvssa-Chahta Vba Ish Taloa: The Choctaw Hymns," 1.

24. Howard and Levine, *Choctaw Music and Dance*, 13.

25. *Chahta Vba Isht Taloa Micha Taloa Ikbi Holisso Hoke: Choctaw Hymn and Tune Book* (Asheville, NC: Global Bible Society, 2017), 311.

26. Ibid., 312.

27. Ibid., 305.

28. Dr. Ian Thompson, telephone conversation with author, September 20, 2019.

29. *Chahta Vba Isht Taloa Micha Taloa Ikbi Holisso Hoke*, 313.

30. "The Way to Canaan," Hymnary.org, accessed March 12, 2020, https://hymnary.org/text/jesus_my_all_to_heaven_is_gone.

31. Cyrus Byington, John Reed Swanton, and Henry S. Halbert, *A Dictionary of the Choctaw Language* (Asheville, NC: Global Bible Society, 2017), 153.

32. *Chahta Vba Isht Taloa Micha Taloa Ikbi Holisso Hoke*, 294.

33. Howard and Levine, *Choctaw Music and Dance*, 73.

34. *Chahta Vba Isht Taloa Micha Taloa Ikbi Holisso Hoke*, 287–88.

35. Ibid., 312.

36. Janet R. Walton, "North American Culture and Its Challenges to Sacred Sound," in *Sacred Sound and Social Change: Liturgical Music in Jewish and Christian Experience*, ed. Lawrence A. Hoffman and Janet R. Walton (Notre Dame, IN: University of Notre Dame Press, 1992), 1–8, 4.</notes>

FURTHER READING

Baird, W. David. *The Choctaw People*. Phoenix: Indian Tribal Series, 1973.
Debo, Angie. *The Rise and Fall of the Choctaw Republic*. Norman: University of Oklahoma Press, 2001.
Morrison, James D., James C. Milligan, and L. David Norris. *The Social History of the Choctaw Nation, 1865–1907*. Durant, OK: Creative Informatics, 1987.
Reeves, Carolyn. *Choctaw before Removal*. Jackson: University Press of Mississippi, 2012.
Swanton, John. *Source Material for the Social and Ceremonial Life of the Choctaw Indians*. Alabama: University of Alabama Press, 2010.

Epilogue
Singing Worlds in the Americas
Michael O'Connor

The practice of Christian sacred music, like all musicking, is not simply a detached response to the world we inhabit, somehow floating above the fray.[1] It is a way of actively being in the world, a way of engaging with our personal, physical, and spiritual environment. Music can teach us how to live in and with time; not only with this passing moment, but with the very time-boundedness of God's creation.[2] Music also has a mysterious but well-recognized power to stimulate and educate our emotional life, desires, hopes, and dreams.[3] Whether using local instruments in the celebration of mass (Elias), or the rhetoric of country music (Case), or historic polyphony in Guatemala (Thomae), music reinforces identity and builds worldviews. Thus when we make music, music makes us, in time and space, in our bodies and our imagination. Each essay in this book, in some measure, describes how Christian music aims to give shape to a world before God, how it strives to "explore, affirm, and celebrate" a vision of ideal relationships; in other words, to sing into being, even if only for a fleeting moment, a world of peace, justice, and communion.[4] For Awet Andemicael, sacred music provides "opportunities for a singing individual or congregation to sing themselves into profound spiritual encounters."[5] Such is the ideal. Despite its great capacity for good, however, musicking is not always a benign practice, and it is never ethically neutral (Warren, Newby and Stearns). There is no guarantee that our music will not be a performance of our fears and a signal of our hardness of heart. I discern examples of this too in the preceding pages, though our authors are often so generous and discreet that we must read between the lines.

Over a billion people live in the Americas today, in thirty-five countries and dozens of dependent territories. Christianity is by far the majority religion in the Americas, so a volume on Christian sacred music in the Americas should come as no surprise. A book of this size can only hint at the breadth and variety of musics, languages, and cultures. Inevitably, the United States dominates (with the largest clutch on shape-note singing), while other essays take the reader to Brazil (Elias, Steuernagel, and Janzen and Yakawa), Guatemala (Thomae), and beyond. As a collection, these essays encourage the reader to reconsider several important questions: Why do we speak of "the Americas"? What has the role of Christianity been and what can it be? And what do we mean by "sacred music" in this context? In this epilogue, I will take those questions in turn, to reflect on the worlds built by Christian sacred musicking.

THE AMERICAS

An early modern Florentine merchant haunts this collection: working first for Spanish and then Portuguese patrons, Amerigo Vespucci (*Americus Vespucius* in Latin, 1454–1512) published accounts of his travels in the first years of the sixteenth century. On this basis, European cartographers attached his name to the whole of the "New World," a land inhabited already for many thousands of years and given many different names by its earliest inhabitants. With the stroke of a pen, the geographical and cultural diversity of this extended continent was overwritten as "The Americas" for the next five hundred years. Parents name their children, authors name their books, Europeans named the Americas.

Europeans came to America for a variety of reasons: fleeing from persecution, poverty, or hunger; searching for food, shelter, self-determination, or riches. Their longing for freedom and a fresh start was utopian; nowadays, "Americanization" can mean being open, welcoming, multicultural, and ecumenical (Hoch). But this is at odds with another type of "Americanization": having thrown off the shackles of empire in 1776, the former British colonies immediately began a march of imperial expansion and colonial absorption, revealing and revelling in a manifest destiny to greatness.[6] This territorial expansion is echoed by a cultural imperialism that does not pass undetected in some Christian worship music (Steuernagel, Warren). All across the Americas, European settlers found no blank canvas on which to paint their dream of a new world. Finding other people with their own societies and cultures, the process of painting required displacement and erasure. This was justified by racist ideas.[7] Some Indigenous peoples were wiped out completely; and those who were not saw their way of life shattered. The Canadian Truth and Reconciliation Commission of 2015 gives the following description of "cultural genocide," with particular reference to the church-run Residential

School system that separated children from their families to assimilate them into colonial society:

> Land is seized, and populations are forcibly transferred and their movement is restricted. Languages are banned. Spiritual leaders are persecuted, spiritual practices are forbidden, and objects of spiritual value are confiscated and destroyed. And, most significantly to the issue at hand, families are disrupted to prevent the transmission of cultural values and identity from one generation to the next.[8]

Strategies of invasion and conquest were abetted by outbreaks of infectious disease. It is estimated that, within two hundred years of Columbus's arrival in the New World, the Indigenous population may have declined by as much as 95 percent. "The main killers were Old World germs to which the Indians had never been exposed, and against which they therefore had neither immune nor genetic resistance. Smallpox, measles, influenza, and typhus competed for the top rank among the killers."[9]

Having run the native populations into the ground, colonial powers started looking elsewhere for a cheap labor force. The enslavement of African people, begun by the Portuguese in the 1440s, offered the solution; between 1500 and 1900, tens of millions of men, women, and children were trafficked across the Atlantic in cruel conditions. They included "farmers, merchants, priests, soldiers, goldsmiths and musicians" who identified themselves as "Yoruba, Igbo, Akan or Kongolese."[10] Millions did not survive the crossing. This was the "Middle Passage," the second leg in an entrepreneurial triangle that traded goods, human beings, and raw materials between Europe, Africa, and the Americas. It was a racist and racializing endeavor, founded on the commodification of human beings by human beings. And the Europeans who colonized the Americas and orchestrated the Middle Passage were Christians.

CHRISTIANITY IN THE AMERICAS

In origin, Christianity is not a European religion. It arose in Asia, between Galilee and Jerusalem. In its first millennium, Christianity flourished in Asia, spreading to southern India, to China and perhaps Vietnam, Indonesia, Japan, the Philippines, and Korea.[11] There were also substantial early communities of Christians in Ethiopia and North Africa. But Christianity is remembered chiefly as arising within the Roman empire, at first hated and persecuted, then reprieved and empowered under Constantine (272–337). By the sixteenth century, Christianity was seen as a European religion, rooted in European language, empire, and culture, at odds with Islam in the East and too easily forgetful of its own Asian and Semitic roots. The Europeans who brought Christianity to the Americas brought with it their own vision of a Christian society: "Christendom," a unified cultural, economic, and political way of life thoroughly infused with religion. Christendom had been weakened by centuries of dispute between spiritual and temporal authorities and dealt a fierce blow by the sixteenth-century Reformations, but it was still intact. Christianity was supposed to be good news, a song of joy, and the beginning here and now of eternal life. But this treasure was carried across the Atlantic in earthly vessels flying the flags of Spain, Portugal, Britain, the Netherlands, and France (see 2 Corinthians 4:7). There were missionaries on board these ships, but they served alongside government officials, merchants, and soldiers. David Tombs summarizes the deep structural entanglement:

> Cross and sword arrived together, and the church offered divine sanction for colonial society. The colonial church was a highly conservative force, which stood firmly on the side of the powerful. Despite the celebrated prophetic exceptions, such as Montesinos and Las Casas, the church usually served as an uncritical chaplain to colonial power and encouraged its exploitative practices.[12]

This book includes examples of other "prophetic exceptions," notably the liberation theologian, bishop, poet, and advocate for Indigenous peoples in Brazil, Dom Pedro Casaldàliga (Elias), and the Presbyterian missionaries who traveled with the Choctaw people on the Trail of Tears (the forced relocation from the Deep South to lands west of the Mississippi), sharing the same hardships and enduring similar bereavements during the journey (Wimberg). Nevertheless, from its arrival, Christianity in the Americas was compromised by systemic racism and structural oppression. One of the most striking images in this book is the juxtaposition of published advertisements selling shape-note hymnals with advertisements selling enslaved people (Smolko). The ministers of the good news offered little resistance to the bad news of colonial exploitation. As a result, "ordinary people were left to find solace in their prayers for charity and their hopes for a better life in another world."[13] Many also found solace in music that helped shape their faith and hope, as well as their anger, grief, and prophetic indignation.

CHRISTIAN SACRED MUSIC IN THE AMERICAS

The essays in this book offer many examples of the world-building potential of sacred music. I will consider three cases within or across the boundaries of Indigenous, African American, and settler communities.

The moving testimony of Meiry Yakawa (Janzen and Yakawa) shows how sacred music can be a source of more than solace. Her song includes the couplet "With my blood I will paint you, / With my clothes I will dress you." These words evoke the widespread Indigenous practice of body painting, without which traditional ceremonies are not complete, and the biblical notion of being washed in the blood of Christ, as well as the gospel parable of the wedding garment; through the layers of imagery, the song subtly explores the nature of initiation into the worship and service of God. Meiry's experience of music is not peripheral to her identity: it not only witnesses to but also embodies her own sense of prophetic calling ("Woman arise and go speak") and it contributes to her sense of ease with herself as both Indigenous and Christian. The experience of being gifted a song from God, including the *ritmo* (rhythm, melody, and dance) distantly remembered from childhood, brings her courage and quickens in her a mission of healing among others, as she carries her songs like bundles of medicine to those in need. Meiry's song flowed from the meeting of her Indigenous culture with a Christian community, a borderland experience that brought both trepidation and excitement. It demonstrates the absorption and adaptation of new materials (in this case biblical imagery) in dialogue with her own native spirituality; the outcome is something never heard before, music that embodies her distinctive experience of Christianity (for some other examples, see Marlui Miranda, Milton Nascimento, and others in Elias; Pliney Fisk, Peter P. Pitchlynn, and anonymous Choctaw hymn writers in Wimberg; and the ensembles Golgotha and Sal da Terra and other musicians associated with "Brazilian Christian Music" in Steuernagel).

For those whose life was a daily experience of violence, music became a way of imagining a different world altogether. Newby and Stearns quote M. Shawn Copeland's description of the creative power of Black spirituals: "The enslaved people sung themselves a world, a *topos* far from the capricious brutality of slavery, and in that world they met and saw Jesus."[14] She cites testimony of the creative process: the building blocks of these songs were real experiences of pain, grief, or joy. These concrete and individual experiences were also universal and emblematic; the songs built a world inhabitable by all: "In and through song, one man's or one woman's experience of sorrow or shout of jubilation became that of a people."[15] The world-building was acknowledged as the gift of the Spirit; in these songs, Jesus was encountered. We can see an important pattern here: the cry arises out of the people and is brought to the Lord; receiving the cry in prayer, the Lord then gifts back a song to the singers. By a kind of marvelous transubstantiation, the cry of the poor has become the revelation of God.

The spirituals acknowledged that the world was not made as slaveholders had made it and that God's kingdom would come on earth as in heaven (Matthew 6:10). At the same time, the thirst for justice was not deferred beyond the grave; the spirituals are full of the reassurance that, in the present, God walks with the downtrodden. The spiritual was an act of resistance, a sung refusal to allow the world to be defined by racists that went hand in hand with other practices of resistance and defiance.[16]

The world-building capacity of shape-note hymnody has been dealt with explicitly in several essays in this book, including revival stories that demonstrate the resilience of the practice (Granade, Smolko, and Karlsberg). Among the reasons for this success is an appeal to history and to roots, perhaps evoking a connection to land and to a simpler time. While practitioners acknowledge that the tradition has not been entirely static (that seven-note notation demonstrates the "survival of the fittest" of multiple possibilities), there is clearly a sense that the tradition is organic and authentic; and where earlier reformers of hymnody such as Thomas Hastings might have sought to "correct" the harmonies and temper the vocal timbre to meet updated norms (see the essay by David Music), today's practitioners treasure the distinctive voice leading and full-bodied vocal technique. Alongside the singing revivals, shape-note melodies have been incorporated into "classical" compositions by the likes of Virgil Thomson, Randall Thompson, and Aaron Copland, where they stand for an idealized "Americana," the sound of the people, the hard-working, plain-talking Christian folk who made the country what it is (Kuriyama).

It is instructive to compare shape-note singing with Black spirituals. On the one hand, spirituals look to the *future* to see God's coming kingdom take shape; the present is no abiding city (Hebrews 13:14). This is a music deeply marked by the experience and traumatic memory of injustice. On the other hand, shape-note singing looks back to the *past*, to a blessed prehistory capable of anchoring a nation in a storm-tossed world. This vision has shown both durability and plasticity, not only within the United States (especially in the South) but also in communities around the world where shape-note singing represents an appealing vision of the United States that is consonant with local cultural and political ambitions (for example, Poland; see Karlsberg). But this vision contains a risk: to confuse an earthly nation with the Kingdom of God; to tell a story of divine favor as a story of superiority and supremacy can easily fuel a vision of a (now-debunked) historical narrative that frames shape-note hymns as "White Spirituals," as the original wellspring of much American music (including Black spirituals), and as the fruit of a mythological "lost tonal tribe" in the Southern states.[17]

DIRECTION FROM PALESTINE

According to Charles Taylor, "Our past is sedimented in our present, and we are doomed to misidentify ourselves as long as we can't do justice to where we come from."[18] For Christians in the Americas, there are many different pasts: the pasts of Scottish, Catalan, Breton, and other settlers; the pasts of Inca, Aztec, Inuit, Choctaw, Cherokee, Wendat, and other Indigenous peoples; the pasts of Yoruba, Igbo, Akan, or Kongolese men, women, and children transported across the Atlantic into slavery. Telling the truth about these pasts is an essential task in the quest for reconciliation. Without this honesty, disharmony will not give way to a brave polyphony. Theologically, reconciliation is to be found in Jesus Christ (Ephesians 2:14–16), who is claimed as Lord by every Christian who sings in his memory. And his memory is a potent force capable of relativizing patriotism, nationalism, and xenophobia.

Jesus was a first-century Palestinian. There is no physical description of him in the Bible but, by studying archaeological remains, some things can be established with a degree of confidence: the average height for a first-century Palestinian male was about five feet, five inches (1.65 meters). Jesus likely had brown eyes and dark hair. In today's terms, he was a person of color (as was his mother, Mary, and also Joseph, and all the apostles). He was a Jew. He sang the psalms at Passover (Mark 14:26) and chanted the scriptures in the synagogue (Luke 4:17–20). His ancestors had known slavery in Egypt; his infancy is remembered as a story of homelessness and flight from persecution. He was educated in a manual trade. His own life was spent entirely under the colonial rule of the Roman empire; he was executed in his mid-thirties by the Roman security forces. This same Jesus of Nazareth rose from the dead and ascended into heaven; he is one of the Trinity.

The vast majority of Christians in the Americas (and worldwide) do not share Jesus's Jewishness. I am a Gentile and, as such, bound to receive the good news humbly as an astounding and undeserved gift. Paul describes the Gentile Christian as a branch of wild olive graciously grafted into the cultivated olive tree (Romans 11:11–31). As Willie Jennings has emphasized, a Gentile identity, a sense of having been *outside*, should be a profound disrupter of colonialism and racism.[19]

Perhaps Jesus sings the songs of the new creation in a Galilean accent, but his eschatological musicking makes room for many accents, for Gentile as well as Jew, for the outsider and the outcast, the prisoner and the refugee, the hungry and the homeless (Matthew 25:31–46). That as yet unheard symphony is faintly echoed here and now in the music of his people; it may be experienced in forms of music that have been created specifically for worship (hymns, songs, polyphony, chant) or in other forms of music (pop, jazz, hip-hop), as these are encountered at large in the culture (Case) or as incorporated deliberately into Christian worship (Hoch). "Sacred music" is music that allows itself to be led by the crucified prophet of Nazareth whose throne is a cross and who has cast down every monarch and emperor (Luke 1:52). Breathing with the Spirit of Christ, sacred music affirms the sacredness of God's handiwork in creation and the inviolability of every human life. It is music that looks forward to the end but also provides direction, focus, and strength for the journey; "the act of musically praising God brings coherence to the singing self"[20] and equips Christians to "imagine, through poetry and song, new pathways forward toward God's Reign."[21]

NOTES

1. I was sent the essays of this volume in spring 2020, during the COVID-19 pandemic lockdown; I began writing as the Black Lives Matter protests, sparked by the killing of George Floyd in Minneapolis, were multiplying throughout and beyond the United States. This context influenced these reflections.

2. Rowan Williams, "Keeping Time," in *A Ray of Darkness: Sermons and Reflections* (Lanham, MD: Cowley, 1995), 214–17.

3. Jeremy Begbie, *Resounding Truth: Christian Wisdom in the World of Music* (Grand Rapids, MI: Baker Academic, 2007), 301–2.

4. Christopher Small, *Musicking: The Meanings of Performing and Listening* (Middletown, CT: Wesleyan University Press, 1998), 49.

5. Awet Andemicael, "The Theology of Richard Allen's Musical Worship," in *Theology, Music, and Modernity: Struggles for Freedom*, ed. Jeremy Begbie, Daniel K. L. Chua, and Markus Rathey (Oxford: Oxford University Press, forthcoming 2021). This is the deep and inclusive musical theology that informs "Music That Makes Community," an initiative arising out of Saint Gregory of Nyssa Episcopal Church in San Francisco, California (Hoch).

6. Rosemary Radford Ruether, *America, Amerikkka: Elect Nation and Imperial Violence* (New York: Routledge, 2014).

7. Ibram X. Kendi, *Stamped from the Beginning: The Definitive History of Racist Ideas in America* (New York: Nation Books, 2016).

8. Truth and Reconciliation Commission of Canada, *Honouring the Truth: Reconciling for the Future. Summary of the Final Report* (Winnipeg: Truth and Reconciliation Commission of Canada, 2015), 1.

9. Jared Diamond, *Guns, Germs, and Steel: The Fates of Human Societies* (New York: Norton, 1999), 211–12.

10. The International Museum of Slavery in Liverpool, UK, "The Translatlantic Slave Trade," https://www.liverpoolmuseums.org.uk/history-of-slavery/transatlantic-slave-trade. This pioneering museum offers a growing body of educational resources: https://www.liverpoolmuseums.org.uk/schools-and-groups-resources-transatlantic-slavery.

11. Philip Jenkins, *The Thousand-Year Golden Age of the Church in the Middle East, Africa, and Asia—and How It Died* (New York: HarperOne, 2008).

12. David Tombs, *Latin American Liberation Theology* (Boston: Brill, 2002), 25.

13. Ibid.

14. M. Shawn Copeland, *Knowing Christ Crucified: The Witness of African American Religious Experience* (Maryknoll, NY: Orbis, 2018), 41.

15. Ibid., 44.

16. Ibid., 14.

17. George Pullen Jackson, *White Spirituals in the Southern Uplands: The Story of the Fasola Folk, Their Songs, Singings, and "Buckwheat Notes"* (Chapel Hill: University of North Carolina Press, 1933). On the shortcomings of Jackson's methodological assumptions, see Dena J. Epstein, "A White Origin for the Black Spiritual? An Invalid Theory and How It Grew," *American Music* 1, no. 2 (1983): 53–59.

18. Charles Taylor, *A Secular Age* (Cambridge, MA: Harvard University Press, 2007), 29.

19. Willie James Jennings, *The Christian Imagination: Theology and the Origins of Race* (New Haven, CT: Yale University Press, 2010).

20. Andemicael, "The Theology of Richard Allen's Musical Worship."

21. The Catholic Committee of Appalachia, *The Telling Takes Us Home: Taking Our Place in the Stories that Shape Us. A People's Pastoral* (Spencer, WV: Catholic Committee of Appalachia, 2015), 7.

Index

2 IHU Kewere, Rezar, xiii, 3, 4, 16, 17, 19

access, xiii–xiv, 23, 29, 32, 38–39, 42–43
accessibility, 189, 191
aesthetic, 178–79, 181, 187, 189, 192
affect (musical), 177, 179, 181–82, 184, 186–88, 192
Afro-centric liturgical music, 249–51
AHAG. *See* Archdiocesan Historical Archive of Guatemala
Aikin, Jesse, 63
Aliança Bíblica Universitária do Brasil (ABU/ABUB), 135–37, 140, 149n16
Allen, James, 113, 127n15
Alpine, Arkansas, 61–62, 65, 69, 76
alternative rock, 204
American classical music, 177, 179, 181, 189, 192
American sound, 179–80, 189
Americana, 190
Amerindian, xii, 3, 4, 5, 7, 8, 9, 11, 16, 17
Anglican chant, 242, 248
anthropology of Christianity, 266–69
Archdiocesan Historical Archive of Guatemala (AHAG), 23, 25, 29, 32, 33, 43, 52n3
Athens, Georgia, xiv–xv, 81–101, 101n1, 102n3, 106n80
Atlanta, Georgia, 81, 82, 97, 98, 100
authentic worship, 178

Bakairi, 265–66, 273–75, 278–79
Banfield, William C., 289, 290, 302n4, 304
Baptist, 179, 187, 191
Beecher, Charles, 116, 128n21
Beecher, Henry Ward, 116
Beecher, Lyman, 113, 128n21
Bermúdez, Pedro, 25, *28*, 29, *30–31*
Bethel Church, 155, 157, 159–61, 163–67
Billings, William, 107–8, 113; CHESTER (tune) 113
Bithell, Caroline and Juniper Hill, 67
Black (Liberation) Theology, viii, xx, 289, 293, 296, 302n3, 303n19, 304nn39–43
Black community, xx, 290, 211, 226, 289, 290, 291, 292, 293, 294, 297, 298, 299
Black cultural codes, 289, 290, 301, 302n4, 304
Black formalism, 293, 302n12
Black National Anthem, xix, 289, 292, 301, 302n1, 304n46, 305
Black sacred song, 289, 296, 301
Blevins, Brooks, 74
Bompastor (record label), 134
Book of Common Prayer, 241–43, 247, 258
book scanner, 32–33, 54n22

Bradbury, William B., 109
Brazil:
　Bahia, 21n27, 136
　black history and culture in, 11–16, 21n18, 21n25, 286n63
　indigenous, viii, xiii, xiv, xix, 3, 5–11, 16n20, 265–79, 282n3, 282n4, 283n16, 284n28
　Mato Grosso, 371, 373
　military regime in, xiii, 3, 4, 12, 20n2, 136, 149n26
　Minas Gerais, 11, 12, 14, 136
　Palmares, 12, 13, 21n18
　Pernambuco, 21n18
　São Paulo, 5, 6, 19, 21n24, 22n30, 134, 139–142
Brazilian church music, 144;
　female perspectives on, 146–47
　influence of Latin American music on, 137–38, 146
　influence of MPB on, 136–38, 142, 149n26
　influence of North American music on, 134–35, 138–39, 141, 143, 147
　influence of Transnational worship music on, 143, 147
　Pentecostal, 134–35
Brazilian theology:
　influence of Liberation Theology on, 137, 146
　influence of *Missão integral on*, 146
　influence of North American theology on, 148n8
Bruce, Neely, 227, 229, 231
Bruner, Jerome, 70
Byington, Cyrus, 308–309, 314, 316–17

Câmera, Dom Hélder, 12, 14
Canção de Protesto movements in Brazil and Latin America, 137, 146, 152
　See also Brazilian theology, influence of Liberation
　Theology on
Casaldáliga, Pedro, xii, 3, 5, 6, 10, 12, 13, 14, 22n35
Cayce Publishing, 63–64, 69

Celtic identity, 224–25, 229–30
Celtic music, 247–48, 252–53
chant, xiii, 11, 17, 19
Chase, Albon, 84, 85
Chase, Gilbert, 97–98
Choctaw, xx, 307–328, 332, 333, 335, 349
choirbook format / layout, 24–25, 29, 39
Christerson, Brad, 158–64, 166
The Christian Harmony, xv, 82, 85, 86, 99, 100, 232
Christian Minstrel, 63
Christian record labels, Brazilian, 138–40, 142, 150n40
Christian worship, 179
Church, Eric, 199
collaborative methodology, 267, 283n9
commercial considerations, 134–145, 147
Cone, James, xx, 289, 216, 289, 291, 293, 294, 299, 300, 302nn14–19, 303n19, 304nn39–43
contemporary worship music (CWM), 155–69
contextualization, 273
Copeland, M. Shawn, xx, 291, 294, 295, 298, 299, 303n20, 303n23, 303n35, 304n36–38, 333, 337
Copland, Aaron, 177, 179, 189
country music, 197, 199, 200, 203, 205
cover masses, 255–56
Crow Nation, 272, 276–77

declamation, 177, 185, 187
digital image(s), 23, 29, 32, 33, 39, 42
digitization, xiii–xiv, 23, 29, 32, 33, 38, 42. *See also* imaging
Docetism, 201

ecumenical traditions. *See* emergent music
embodied theology, xx, 289, 294, 300, 301
emergent music, 256
emerging church, 256
encoding, xiv, 23, 29, 32, 33, 37, 38, 39, 41, 42, 43, 52n6, 55n37

enslaved people, 4, 12 ,13, 16, 82–83, 87–88
Episcopal Church (USA), 241–50, 252–53, 255, 257–58, 261n43
ethics, 162, 167–69
ethnomusicology, 179, 272;
  of Indigenous Christianity, 269, 277, 283n16
Eucharist, 242, 250, 255, 257
Evening Prayer, 242, 246–50, 252–53, 255, 257, 260n27
expression, 180, 188

faith, rejection of, 201, 206–207
Fernández, Gaspar, 25, *26–27*, *28*, 53n14
Flory, Richard, 155, 158–64, 166
folk music, 210, 211
folklore, 224–27, 231
Franco, Hernando, 25, *28*, *30–31*

Garst, John, xv, 82, 86–87, 97–98, 100
Germany, 230–31
Gordon, Larry, 227, 228
Gospel FM (radio station), 140
gospel music, 81–82, 85, 90, 91, 96, 209
gospel music in Brazil
  commercial considerations, 134–145, 147
  history and style, 138–145, 147
Gospel Records (record label), 138–39, 142, 143
Green Corn Ceremony, 309–12
GuatC:
  choirbooks, 25, *28*, 54n19
  collection, 32, 34
  GuatC 1–6, *26–27*, 29
  GuatC 1, xiv, 23–25, 29, *30–31*, 33, 38–43, *44–47*, *48*, *49–51*
Guatemala, 23–29, 32, 42–43, 52n1
Guatemalan Cathedral choirbooks, xiii–xiv, 23–24, 29, 33, 42–43, 52n2. *See also* GuatC

Hamrick, Raymond, 82, 99
Hastings, Thomas, 107–130;
  biography, 108

  hymn texts by, 107, 112, 127n18. *See also* hymn tunes
  legacy, 123–25
  philosophy of sacred music and church music reform, 107–9, 111, 120, 122, 124–25
  pseudonyms, 110, 127n11
heavy metal, 205, 206
Hemans, Felicia, 112–3
Herman, Janet, 74
The Hesperian Harp, 84, 89
hip–hop/rap, 202–203, 206, 211, 212, 257–58
HipHopEMass, 257
Historic Protestantism, Brazilian 134, 135–137, 142, 146, 148n8
Holden, Oliver, 108
Hollingsworth, John, 82, 98–99, 101
Huckabee, J. J., 65, 67, 69
hymnbooks/hymnals/tunebooks:
  advertisements, xv, 81–91, 96
  Baptist Hymnal (Southern Baptist), 123
  Celebrating Grace (Baptist), 123
  Congregational Harmony (Hastings), 110, 126n10
  Crystal Fount (Hastings), 122
  Evangelical Lutheran Worship (ELCA), 123
  The Georgian Harmony, xv, 99, 100
  Glory to God (PCUSA), 123
  The Good Old Songs, 64, 71
  Good Tidings, 90, 103fn35
  The Hymnal 1982, 243–45, 247, 249–50
  The Hymnbook (Presbyterian/ Reformed), 123
  Hymns for the Living Church (nondenominational), 123
  Hymns from the Old South, 177, 179, 182, 188
  Juvenile Songs (Hastings), 112, 116
  Lift Up Your Hearts (Reformed), 123
  Lutheran Service Book (LCMS), 123
  Manhattan Collection (Hastings), 112, 127n11
  Mendelssohn Collection (Hastings), 110, 116, 126n10, 127n11

Musica Sacra (Hastings), 109–110, 112, 116, 126n9, 127n14
New Hymns for Youth (Presbyterian), 128n32
Plymouth Collection (Beechers, Zundel), 116
Presbyterian Psalmodist, 116, 122, 128n32
The Psalmodist (Hastings), 112, 116
Psalms and Hymns Adapted to Public Worship (Presbyterian), 122, 128n32
Resurrected Songs, 82, 90, 93, 94
The Sacred Harp, xv, xviii, 62, 63, 64, 74, 82, 85, 86, 89, 96–101, 178–80, 186–87, 192, 221–34, 249. *See also* Sacred Harp singing, shape-note singing
Sacred Songs (Hastings), 116, 128n32
Selection of Psalms and Hymns (Stowell), 127n16
Service Book and Hymnal (Lutheran), 123
The Social Harp, xv, 81, 82, 85–86, 88–91, 97–100
Southern Harmony (Walker), xvii, 84, 92, 93, 107, 177, 180, 180, 185, 247
Springfield Collection (Warriner), 110
Temple Melodies (Jones), 116
Worship and Rejoice (nondenominational), 123
publication, xv, 81–92, 96–101
hymnody, 243–53, 258, 259n6,
  indigenous hymnody, 273–74, 278
See also sacred songs, song types

Igreja Renascer em Cristo (IRC/Renascer), 138–40, 142–43, 145
Igreja Universal do Reino de Deus (IURD), 138, 145
imaging, 32–33
inculturation, 5, 7, 19, 273
Independent Network Charismatic Christianity (INC), 158–65
indigenous Christian music, barriers to the study of, 268–72
indigenous songs, 273, 278; definition of, 267
Ingalls, Monique, 164
inspiration, 177, 180, 188
Iona Community, 252–54
Ireland, 229–30
Ivey, David, 231, 233

Jackson, George Pullen, 77, 86, 90, 97, 98, 126n2, 221, 224–27, 229–31, 236nn14–16, 238n47
jazz, 247–49
Johnson, James Weldon, 289, 292, 293, 300, 301, 302n9, 304n44
Johnson, John Rosamond, 289, 292, 293, 300, 301, 304n44
Jones, Darius E., 115
Jovens da Verdade (JV), 135, 136
justice, 161–64, 166–69

Kieffer, Aldine 86, 89–90
Kiowa, 266, 272
Kirk-Duggan, Cheryl, xx, 291, 297, 303nn31–34

lament, 146, 270, 276, 278, 290, 291, 293, 294, 295, 296
Levinas, Emmanuel, 168–69
Liberation Theology, xiii, 4, 5, 10, 20n3, 20n5, 22
Line Records (record label), 138
liturgical, 177–78, 188, 189, 191, 194
liturgy, 3, 4, 7, 15, 17, 19, 179, 190, 194
Livingston, Tamara, 62, 66, 67
love ethic, 298, 299, 300

machine-readable, 32, 42;
  files, 33, 39
  See also symbolic
martyr, 3, 5, 6, 13
Mason, Lowell, 107, 109, 113, 125, 126n2, 129n37
McCurry, John G., 81, 82, 86, 88–91, 95, 98
McGraw, Hugh, 221, 226
MEI. *See* Music Encoding Initiative

mensural:
    notation, 23, 29, 32, 34, 36, 37, 55n35
    score, 37–39, 48
Miller, Kiri, 74, 82
Miranda, Marlui, xiii, 3, 16, 21, 22n30, 22n31
Missa da Terra Sem Males, xiii, 3, 4, 5, 6, 11, 12, 14, 15
Missa dos Quilombos, xiii, 3, 4, 11, 12, 13, 14, 15, 16, 21n17, 21n19, 21n23, 21n24
missionaries, 307–328
MK Music (record label), 138–39
Mocidade Para Cristo (MPC), 135–37, 141
Montgomery, Tim, 61–62, 66, 70, 74
Music Encoding Initiative (MEI), 32;
    CMN MEI file, 38–41, 49
    Mensural MEI file, 37–39, 48
Music That Makes Community, 254–55
The Musical Million, 89–90

Nascimento, Milton, xiii, 3, 11, 12, 13, 14, 16, 21n17, 21n19, 21n21
Native American, 307–8
Neopentecostalism, Brazilian, 138, 143, 145–46, 148n8, 150n40
New England Protestant, 191
The 1975 (musical group), 205, 208–10

OMR. *See* optical music recognition
oppression, 3, 11, 12, 13, 136, 181, 202, 291, 292, 297, 299, 300, 332
optical music recognition (OMR), xiv, 23, 32–35, 38, 41–43, 48, 54n27
oral tradition, 308, 315, 318
Organização Palavra da Vida (OPV), 135–37, 148n16

paperless music, 254–55
para-ecclesiastical organizations (PEOs), 135–38, 142, 146
Patterson, Daniel, 82, 86, 98
Pentecostalism, Brazilian, 134–35, 148n8, 150n40
personal song, 276–79. *See also* "one song", women's songs (music making)

Perry, Imani, 292, 293, 302n1, 302n8, 302n10, 302n12, 304n44, 305
perspectivism, 270–71
Pittman, Orene, 61, 63–69, 75–76
Poland, 231;
    politics of, 233
postmillennialism, 162
Primitive Baptist, 63–64, 68, 72, 75;
    musical practices of, 68–69, 71, 73, 75
Primm, Shannon, 82, 99–100
Protestant Episcopal Church in America. *See* Episcopal Church (USA)
Psalm 23, 182, 188–90
punk, 201, 204–207

Quirós, Manuel José de, 25, *26–27, 28,* 53n14

Read, Daniel, 107–8
reception, 177, 188
regular sing, 178, 187, 191, 193
religious education, 315
renewal (music), 67–68, 75–76
RESIGNATION (hymn tune), 177, 181–82, 192
Revival:
    definitions of, 66
    elements of, 67, 74
    expansions to definition of, 68, 76
The River (movie), 177, 179–81, 183, 192
Robbins, Joel, 268–69
Roman Rite, 3, 7, 11, 16, 17
ruptures, anthropological concept of, 268, 270

The Sacred Harp, see hymnbooks/hymnals/tunebooks; *see also* Sacred Harp singing, shape-note singing, shape-note hymns
Sacred Harp singing, 221–40;
    Camp Fasola singing school, 231, 232, 233, 239n54
    community in, 228, 237n32
    history of, 222–24
    hollow square in, 228

score format, 29, 32
scoring up, 32, 36–38, 43, 48
separate-parts layout, 29, 32
shape-note hymns xiv–xv, 81–101, 177–78, 181, 191;
  four-shape, 81, 95, 96
  seven-note, 62, 63, 64, 70, 81, 82, 85, 86, 90, 91, 99
shape-note singing, xv, 62, 73–74, 81–82, 85–86, 89–91, 95–101, 107, 178–79, 221–34, 249–50; *see also* Sacred Harp singing, hymnbooks/hymnals/tunebooks
Showalter, A. J., 89–90
singing schools, 63, 64, 67, 69, 73; *see also* hymnbooks/hymnals/tunebooks, Sacred Harp singing
  structure of, 69–71
The Social Harp, see hymnbooks/hymnals/tunebooks
solfège, 63, 70
song types:
  song types in use in Indigenous churches, 273–74
  taxonomies used in description of, 273
The Southern Harmony, see hymnbooks/hymnals/tunebooks
spirituals, xx, 77n3, 105n68, 106, 126n2, 181, 216, 225, 227, 234n1, 236n15, 238n39, 243, 245, 248–50, 291, 293, 294, 295, 298, 299, 300, 333, 334, 337
Stowell, Hugh, 124
subject position, of Christian scholars, 268–70
Sutton, Brett, 68
Sweet Home Primitive Baptist Church, 61–62, 67, 69–71
Symbolic (computer program), 24;
  file, 32, 39, 40, 43, 48
  music, 39, 40
  score, 32, 38
  See also machine-readable
synthesis, 177, 179, 181–82, 185–86, 188, 194

Taizé, 246, 248, 251–54
The Temple Star, 86
Thompson, Randall, 177
Thomson, Virgil, 177–83, 185–92
Tierra, Pedro, xiii, 3, 5, 12, 13
Titon, Jeff Todd, 75–76
Toplady, Augustus, 122, 126n3, 127n15
Trail of Tears, 307–8, 313–14, 317, 332
trope, 3, 4, 6, 15, 16 19
Trump, Donald, 155–57, 166–67
Tupí, 3, 5, 17, 18, 19, 20n5, 22n34
tunebooks, see hymnals

United Kingdom, 228–29, 232–33
United States:
  Midwest, 227
  New England, 227, 229, 232–33, 238n46
  politics of the, 232–34
  South, 223–27, 231
University of Georgia, 81, 82, 95, 97, 98, 101

Vatican, xiii, 3, 4, 6, 14, 16, 19, 22
Vaughan, J. B. 81, 82, 90–96, 101
Vencedores Por Cristo (VPC), 135–137, 141, 143, 146, 148n16
Verovio, 38–39, 55n39
Viceroyalty of New Spain, 25, *28*
Vieira, Padre Antonio, 13, 21n20, 21n21
Vilaça, Aparecida, 268, 270
Vineyard Church, 158–61, 163–65

Walker, William, 177, 180, 182
Warriner, Solomon, 110
Watts, Isaac, 182–83, 187, 188
weary feet, 291, 294, 295, 296, 298
West, Kanye, 202, 204, 212
Wimber, John, 159
women's songs (music making), 265, 286n56
Work III, John W., 225–26
work songs, 243–44, 248

Yoruba Gods, 14, 15, 21n25, 21n26

Zundel, John, 116

About the Contributors

Delvyn Case is a composer, conductor, scholar, and educator based in Boston. His music has been performed by over eighty orchestras across the world, as well as by Grammy-winning artists Richard Stoltzman and the Chestnut Brass Company. As a writer, speaker, and scholar, his work has covered topics from hip-hop to music pedagogy to theology. He is the founder of Deus Ex Musica, an international organization that brings together musicians, scholars, clergy, and laypeople to promote sacred music as a resource for learning and spiritual growth. He is currently associate professor of music at Wheaton College Massachusetts, a secular liberal college, where he conducts the Great Woods Symphony.

Cathy Ann Elias is a professor in the School of Music, a distinguished professor in the Honors Program, and a fellow in the Catholic Studies Department at DePaul University. She was honored by the Associazione Internazionale delle Città Murate (Lions Club, Lucca) for her work on Claudio Baglioni (1951–) and Giovanni Sercambi (1348–1424). Recent articles include "More on Imitatio and Mid-16th-Century Chanson Masses: Erasmus on Christian Reflections and Lying Mirrors" and "Pietro Aretino and His Musical World" (forthcoming, Brill Companion to Pietro Aretino). Her edition of madrigals by Antonio Buonavita (1548–1618) for the American Institute of Musicology is forthcoming.

S. Andrew Granade is professor of musicology at the University of Missouri–Kansas City Conservatory. His research into the American Experimental Tradition has resulted in the book *Harry Partch: Hobo Composer*, and he is widely published on music for science fiction film and television. In addition to his work on shape-note hymnody in the Primitive Baptist tradition, Granade has also published on Chinese hymnody, particularly through the creation and dissemination of the 1936 hymnbook *Hymns of Universal Praise*.

Matthew Hoch is professor of music at Auburn University and choirmaster and minister of music at Holy Trinity Episcopal Church in Auburn, Alabama. He is the author, first author, or principal editor of eight books and many peer-reviewed articles in over a dozen academic and professional journals, including the *Choral Journal*, *The Hymn*, and the *American Organist*. Hoch has presented clinics and interest sessions at the national convention of the American Guild of Organists and the annual conference of the Hymn Society of the United States and Canada. In 2016, he was a fellow-in-residence with the School of Theology at Sewanee: The University of the South.

Andrew Janzen is a PhD student in Ethnomusicology (University of Toronto). He has worked in applied ethnomusicology in West-Central Brazil since 2006. Drawing on theology, anthropology, and critical Indigenous studies, he explores the unexpected articulations of Christian *and* Indigenous identities. His interests include collaborative ethnography and the ethnomusicology of Indigenous Christianity.

Jesse P. Karlsberg is senior digital scholarship strategist at Emory University's Center for Digital Scholarship (ECDS). Jesse's research examines race and place in vernacular American sacred music. Jesse is editor-in-chief of Sounding Spirit, an NEH-funded research lab and digital publishing initiative promoting engagement with American sacred songbooks copublished by ECDS and the University of North Carolina Press. Jesse is product owner of Readux, a digital platform for thematic collections and scholarly editions of digitized books. An internationally recognized singer, teacher, composer, and songbook editor in the Sacred Harp tradition, Jesse serves as vice president of the Sacred Harp Publishing Company.

Zen Kuriyama is a PhD student in musicology and a teaching fellow at Brandeis University. An emerging scholar in the field of sacred music, Zen currently provides the program booklet essays for Musica Sacra New York and holds a master of sacred music degree from the University of Notre Dame, where he was active as a conductor and in theological study. A lyric baritone, Zen holds a master of music degree in voice performance from Stony Brook University. Zen's work on the composer Gerald Finzi has been published in *The Finzi Journal*, and he recently gave an invited lecture on Finzi at the University of St. Andrews, Scotland.

David W. Music retired from the church music faculty of Baylor University in 2020, where he taught for eighteen years. He previous taught at Southwestern Baptist Theological Seminary and California Baptist University. His writings on American church music include *"I Will Sing the Wondrous Story": A History of Baptist Hymnody in North America* (with Paul A. Richardson, 2008), *Church Music in the United States 1760–1901* (with Paul Westermeyer, 2014), and an edition of anthems by Thomas Hastings for the series Recent Researches in American Music (A-R Editions, 2017).

Stephen Michael Newby is professor of music at Seattle Pacific University. He has research interests in the theology of Black sacred music. Dr. Newby is composer-in-residence with the Nathaniel Dett Chorale in Toronto, Ontario, where they recently premiered his oratorio HOSEA. His music is published by Fred Bock Publishing.

Michael O'Connor, STL (Gregorian), DPhil (Oxford), is associate professor, Teaching Stream, at the University of St. Michael's College in the University of Toronto, where he teaches in the Christianity and Culture Program. A former Warden of the Royal School of Church Music (RSCM), he is a board member of RSCM Canada. His scholarship concerns early modern Christian intellectual culture and contemporary debates on music, ritual, and liturgy. He is coeditor, with Hyun-Ah Kim and Christina Labriola, of *Music, Theology, and Justice* (Lexington, 2017). He is active as a choral conductor and occasional composer.

Andrew Shenton is a scholar, prize-winning author, performer, and educator based in Boston. Born in England, he holds bachelor, master, and doctoral degrees from London University, Yale, and Harvard respectively. He has been the recipient of numerous scholarships and awards including a Harvard Merit Fellowship, Harvard's Certificate of Distinction in Teaching, and a Junior Fellowship from the Humanities Center at Boston University. Dr. Shenton has given more than eighty premieres by composers such as John Tavener, Judith Weir, and Arvo Pärt. Moving freely between musicology and ethnomusicology, Shenton's work is best subsumed under the heading "music and transcendence" and includes several major publications on Messiaen, Pärt, and others. His most recent monograph, *Arvo Pärt's Resonant Texts*, was published by Cambridge University Press in 2018. Dr. Shenton is professor of music at Boston University and conductor of Vox Futura.

Joanna Smolko (University of Georgia) is a musicologist who teaches various music courses through the University System of Georgia. Her research areas include American popular music from the nineteenth and twentieth centuries, American sacred music, American folk music, and film music. She was a contributing editor for the second edition of *The Grove Dictionary of American Music* (Oxford University Press, 2013). Some of her publications include "Southern-Fried Foster: Representing Race and Place in Looney Tunes Cartoons" (*American Music* 30, no. 3 [2012]) and coediting *Stephen Collins Foster: 60 Favorite Songs* (Mel Bay, 2010) with Stephen Saunders. She coauthored with Tim Smolko the forthcoming book *Atomic Tunes: The Cold War in American and British Popular Music* (Indiana University Press, 2021).

Chelle Stearns is associate professor of theology at the Seattle School of Theology and Psychology. She has a broad interest in theological engagement with the arts, but her primary work is in music and theology. Dr. Stearns has published *Handling Dissonance: A Musical Theological Aesthetic of Unity* (Pickwick Press).

Marcell Silva Steuernagel is assistant professor of church music and director of the Master of Sacred Music Program at Southern Methodist University's Perkins School of Theology. Steuernagel writes at the intersection of church music, theology, musicology, and performance theory. He served as minister of worship, arts, and communication at Redeemer Lutheran Church in Curitiba, Brazil, for more than a decade and is an internationally active composer and performer. Some of his recent writings can be found in *Celebrating Lutheran Music* (Lundblad, Lundberg and Schildt, 2019) and *Linguagens Litúrgicas e Artísticas na América Latina: Memórias e Identidades* (Machado and Adam, 2019).

Martha E. Thomae is a PhD candidate in music technology at the Schulich School of Music, McGill University. She has a BSc in mathematics from Universidad del Valle de Guatemala and a MA in music technology from McGill. Her research focuses on the preservation and encoding of mensural music. She is a member of the Distributed Digital Music Archives and Libraries Lab led by Ichiro Fujinaga (2015–present) and a board member of the Music Encoding Initiative (2020–2022). Her dissertation is on the digitization and encoding of Guatemalan choirbooks from the colonial period using optical music recognition and computational error detection.

Jeff R. Warren is interim chief academic officer and professor of music and humanities at Quest University in Squamish, British Columbia. His book *Music and Ethical Responsibility* (Cambridge University Press) examines the ethical implications of everyday musical experiences. Current research projects include musical multimedia and mountain biking culture, Christian congregational music, and the relationship between music, politics, and phenomenology using post-1968 Paris as a case study. His creative work includes sound recording, sound installations, and performance on double and electric bass.

Emma Wimberg is currently working toward a PhD in musicology at the University of North Texas. She holds a master of sacred music degree from Boston University and a bachelor of music education degree with a double major in church music from Texas Christian University. She serves as a church organist, most recently as the Boston University scholar at Holy Name Parish in West Roxbury, Massachusetts. Her primary research interests include the role of paraliturgical organ music in worship, specifically in the contemporary worship setting. She also has a special interest in Choctaw hymnody as a member of the Choctaw Native American tribe.

Meiry Yakawa, of the Bakairi-Kurâ Nation in Mato Grosso, Brazil, is an educator, speaker, artist, and a founding member of the Teruwah Indigenous Musicians conference. In 2010 she completed a linguistics diploma specializing in intercultural education. She is currently the director of an Indigenous Bible college and actively encourages the use of Indigenous music and visual arts, as exemplified in her Indigenous graphic design paintings.

www.ingramcontent.com/pod-product-compliance
Lightning Source LLC
Chambersburg PA
CBHW070010010526
44117CB00011B/1495